A House Divided

Orthodoxy and Schism in Nineteenth-Century

Central European Jewry

Jacob Katz

Translated by Ziporah Brody

Brandeis University Press
Published by University Press of New England
Hanover and London

Brandeis University Press
Published by University Press of New England, Hanover, NH 03755
© 1998 by the Trustees of Brandeis University
All rights reserved
Printed in the United States of America
5 4 3 2 1
CIP data appear at the end of the book

This book was published with the help of the Lucius N. Littauer Foundation, Inc.

The publisher and author gratefully acknowledge the assistance received from the Fund for the Translation of Jewish Literature in support of this publication.

A House Divided

The Tauber Institute for the Study of European Jewry Series

Jehuda Reinharz, General Editor
Michael Brenner, Associate Editor

The Tauber Institute for the Study of European Jewry, established by a gift to Brandeis University from Dr. Laszlo N. Tauber, is dedicated to the memory of the victims of Nazi persecutions between 1933 and 1945. The Institute seeks to study the history and culture of European Jewry in the modern period. The Institute has a special interest in studying the causes, nature, and consequences of the European Jewish catastrophe within the contexts of modern European diplomatic, intellectual, political, and social history.

Gerhard L. Weinberg
World in the Balance: Behind the Scenes of World War II 1

Richard Cobb
French and Germans, Germans and French: A Personal Interpretation of France under Two Occupations, 1914–1918/1940–1944 2

Eberhard Jäckel
Hitler in History 3

Frances Malino and Bernard Wasserstein, editors
The Jews in Modern France 4

Jacob Katz
The Darker Side of Genius: Richard Wagner's Anti-Semitism 5

Jehuda Reinharz, editor
Living with Antisemitism: Modern Jewish Responses 6

Michael R. Marrus
The Holocaust in History 7

Paul Mendes-Flohr, editor
The Philosophy of Franz Rosenzweig 8

Joan G. Roland
Jews in British India: Identity in a Colonial Era 9

Yisrael Gutman, Ezra Mendelsohn, Jehuda Reinharz, and Chone Shmeruk, editors
The Jews of Poland Between Two World Wars 10

Avraham Barkai
From Boycott to Annihilation: The Economic Struggle of German Jews, 1933–1943 11

Alexander Altmann
The Meaning of Jewish Existence: Theological Essays 1930–1939 12

Magdalena Opalski and Israel Bartal
Poles and Jews: A Failed Brotherhood 13

Richard Breitman
The Architect of Genocide: Himmler and the Final Solution 14

Jehuda Reinharz and Walter Schatzberg, editors
The Jewish Response to German Culture: From the Enlightenment to the Second World War 15

George L. Mosse
Confronting the Nation: Jewish and Western Nationalism 16

Daniel Carpi
Between Mussolini and Hitler: The Jews and the Italian Authorities in France and Tunisia 17

Walter Laqueur and Richard Breitman
Breaking the Silence: The German Who Exposed the Final Solution 18

Ismar Schorsch
From Text to Context: The Turn to History in Modern Judaism 19

Jacob Katz
With My Own Eyes: The Autobiography of an Historian 20

Gideon Shimoni
The Zionist Ideology 21

Moshe Prywes and Haim Chertok
Prisoner of Hope 22

János Nyiri
Battlefields and Playgrounds 23

Alan Mintz, editor
The Boom in Contemporary Israeli Fiction 24

Samuel Bak, paintings
Lawrence L. Langer, essay and commentary
Landscapes of Jewish Experience 25

Simon Rawidowicz
*State of Israel, Diaspora, and Jewish Continuity:
Essays on the "Ever-Dying People"* 26

Jacob Katz
*A House Divided: Orthodoxy and Schism in Nineteenth-Century
Central European Jewry* 27

Jeffrey Shandler and Beth S. Wenger, editors
*Encounters with the "Holy Land": Place, Past and Future
in American Jewish Culture* 28

Elisheva Carlebach, John M. Efron, and David N. Myers, editors
Jewish History and Jewish Memory: Essays in Honor of Yosef Hayim Yerushalmi 29

Shmuel Almog, Jehuda Reinharz, and Anita Shapira, editors
Zionism and Religion 30

Contents

Introduction   1

I. The Beginning of Thought and Deed in Germany

1. The First Signs of Conflict within the Community   7
2. Breslau-Style Compromise, Frankfurt-Style Conflicts   20

II. The Hungarian Scene

3. Quiet Cultural Adaptation   31
4. The Emergence and Characteristics of the Neolog Movement   40
5. The Reaction of the Pious, "Oberland"-Style   48
6. Hassidim and the Zealous in the Unterland   56
7. Pressburg as the Target of Zealot Arrows   70
8. The Fruits of Zealousness: The Judicial Decision of Michalowitz in 1866   77

III. On the Eve of the Congress

9. Emancipation and the Idea of a Nationwide Jewish Organization   89
10. The *Shomrei Ha-Dat* Society and the Assembly of Notables   96
11. Tensions and Fluctuations in the Orthodox Camp   108
12. The Conference of Rabbis in Buda in Advance of the Congress   122

IV. The Congress

13. The Composition of the Congress and Its Chances of Success   137
14. The Inevitable Clash   149
15. A Rump Congress and a Divided Orthodoxy   159

V. In the Aftermath of the Congress

16. The Battle over Ratification of the Statutes — 169
17. The Parliamentary Decision: Orthodoxy's Purim Miracle — 183
18. The Orthodox Organization and Its Founders — 191
19. The Fate of the Uncommitted: The Status Quo Congregations and Their Ostracism — 204

VI. Looking Forward, Looking Back

20. Theoretical and Practical Limits of the Schism — 217
21. The Painful Process and Its Aftermath — 225

VII. The Schism, German Style

22. Eduard Lasker, the Prophet of Freedom of Conscience — 237
23. Hirsch's Failure in His Own Community and His Ideological Legacy — 257

Notes — 279

Index — 333

A House Divided

Introduction

The focal point of this book is the Hungarian Jewish Congress of 1868–1869, the occasion of the split between the Orthodox and their opponents. This schism led to the establishment of two separate Jewish national organizations, whose existence served to deepen the divisions between the two camps. The book depicts the history of the split, its causes, and its sad consequences.

An almost personal connection exists between the topic of this book and someone like myself, who in his youth heard the story directly from people personally acquainted with some of the major protagonists. My mother, of blessed memory, the daughter of R. Joseph Breznitz, a nephew of R. Moses Schick, grew up in her uncle's home in the city of Győr. Her uncle, R. Jacob Snyders, was a member of the Congress and one of the most zealous representatives of the Orthodox camp. He died in 1904, the year of my birth, and I was named after him.

The second arena of the events depicted in this work is Germany, and in particular the city of Frankfurt, where R. Samson Raphael Hirsch led the struggle for the independence of his community, the Orthodox *Adath Jeschurun*. I lived in this community for seven years, in the course of my studies at the *yeshivah* and the university in the city, and there too I heard reverberations of the battle, as recreated in the imaginations of the second and third generations after the events.

With the development of my critical sense as an historian, I understood that these oral traditions fell short of reflecting reality, and that the topic must be researched on the basis of contemporary sources. I used these from time to time in my lectures and seminars at the Hebrew University in Jerusalem and other institutions, when I had occasion to teach this topic, but did not set aside time for an exhaustive study. Like other teachers at universities, I hoped to find students whom I could guide to examine the topic in depth. This hope was partly fulfilled. Nathanel Katzburg published a comprehensive bibliographical article on the Congress at his own initiative in 1956, and also summarized its history upon various occasions, in the course of his research into the history of Hungarian Jewry. But Katzburg himself noted that his summary was but an initial attempt to exploit the sources noted in his bibliography, and left it to others to expand and complete the work. A condition for the fulfillment of this task was of course a mastery of Hungarian, and only towards the end of my active service at the Hebrew University, in the early 1970s, did I gain a student who was fluent in Hungarian, Michael Silber.

By virtue of his origin, education, and interests, Silber seemed the natural candidate for this task. And indeed, in his dissertation he set out to follow the struggle between the Orthodox and the Neologs in Hungary up to and including the split in the Congress. However, it was naïve of both the teacher and the student to assume that this program could be carried out within the confines of a doctoral dissertation. The candidate wrote an excellent dissertation, but the period surveyed ended an entire generation before the date at which Katzburg's bibliography begins. The reason Silber limited the period under consideration was his novel method of research, the comparative-statistical method, with which Silber succeeded in describing the social-cultural transformation of Hungarian Jewry up to the Revolution of 1848. The larger topic was once again set aside, although Silber continued to contribute to the study of the period in his own way. He is director of a Center for the History of Hungarian Jewry, which was established within the Hebrew University. My work has benefited from the valuable sources that have been collected at the center, and even more so from frequent contact with its director. Our relationship has been mutually enriching, and I do not ask who has gained more by this partnership. I at least can testify that it is doubtful whether I would have dared to begin work were it not for Katzburg's bibliography, and whether I would have been able to complete it were it not for Silber's support and encouragement.

I turned to a third former student, Mordechai Breuer, for clarification and assistance on points concerning the German-Jewish aspect of this work. Breuer himself wrote an important work on German Orthodoxy, but he did not include the so-called "political" aspect with which I am concerned, leaving it for another opportunity. Indeed, at times I asked myself if I was perhaps encroaching in some way on his and Silber's territory by starting work on this topic, parts of which were set aside for their future work. Their generosity with the material in their possession reassured me, and if I had hesitations, they did not share them.

I consider myself blessed by the good relationship between myself and my students. Most of them became colleagues and many close personal friends. God has granted me long years, but with old age comes loneliness, and several of my works in recent years have been dedicated to contemporaries who passed away. I dedicate this book to my students—long may they live—who fill the role of my contemporaries without allowing me to feel the generation gap that separates us.

Let me return to the conception and birth of this book. At the beginning of my work, I imagined that an article or several articles would exhaust the subject. As the accumulating material and its analysis demanded the addition of chapter after chapter, I was seized with the fear that I might not finish, and that the work of years would be lost. Therefore the day that I submit the manuscript to the publisher, having nothing further to add, is for me a day of thanksgiving and rejoicing, and I am grateful from the bottom of my heart.

The author of this type of book, the contents of which are based on tiny details from innumerable sources, requires many assistants, both on a regular basis and at specific times. Most of the sources cited in this book are found in the National and University Library of the Hebrew University in Jerusalem. I must thank the faithful staff of this wonderful institution and particularly those in charge of the Judaica Reading Room, whom I have troubled for many years on an almost daily basis, and who have always helped me cheerfully and politely. Unlike the younger generation, who use modern technology in their work, my tools remain pen and paper. Rachel Grossman transcribed my words into the computer, her generous assistance and sharp eyes catching many mistakes; and even then, further checking was needed. I was fortunate that the Zalman Shazar Center for Jewish History gave the job of preparing the book for publication to Yehezkel Hovav, whose corrections and improvements are evident throughout the book. And last but not least, my thanks to Zvi Yekutiel, the director of the Shazar Center, who made it his special concern to have the book appear in its finished form and on schedule.

Jerusalem, The Hebrew University

I

The Beginning of Thought and Deed in Germany

Chapter 1

The First Signs of Conflict within the Community

In a series of articles about various episodes in Jewish life in western Europe in the first years after the breakdown of traditional society, I demonstrated how the gap between two factions of this society widened.[1] One part continued to demand the observance of tradition in all its details, in private and public life, despite the changes in the status of the congregations (*kehillot*) and the abrogation by the secular authorities of their power of religious coercion. The other part shook off the burden of tradition, totally or partially, demanding moreover that the tradition be adapted to the needs of the time, and the changed conditions of life, and to the enlightened ideas held by contemporary society, which contradicted the basic assumptions of tradition in its old form.

This would seem to be a religious rift between two sectors of the community, destined to create two separate organizational frameworks—"churches" or congregations. And this indeed happened in those places where no external factors, legal, political or others, impinged. For example, in the United States, due to the separation of church and state, Jewish communities were permitted to organize around synagogues with different styles and prayer services, according to their individual choice. This idea was raised in Europe as well, when the plan to integrate Jews into the state as free citizens began to take shape. Moses Mendelssohn imagined the Jewish congregations as voluntary frameworks, within which those loyal to Judaism and its commandments could find their spiritual fulfillment.[2] However, this utopian vision was slow to materialize. The inclusion of Jews among the citizens of the state brought about the abrogation of many functions and powers of the *kehillah*, but not of the obligation of membership in it incumbent on all adherents to the Jewish religion. The requirement of membership in a congregation remained in force for most of the nineteenth century, and not only in lands that granted Jews citizenship gradually, but even in France, where the revolution won full citizenship for the Jews

8 · The Beginning of Thought and Deed in Germany

in 1790–1791. After less than one generation, in 1808, near the end of Napoleon's rule, all members of the Mosaic faith in France were once again required to join the Jewish congregation of the area in which they lived. Moreover, the individual congregation was not free to do as it wished. It was subject to the provincial organization, the *consistoire*, which in turn was subject to the central *consistoire* in the capital, Paris. This central *consistoire* issued guidelines for the religious life of all the congregations of the state. In a paradoxical way, the congregations and the supra-communal organizations, which were defined as religious institutions, were also assigned civil administrative functions, such as supervising the enforcement of the draft.[3]

National organizations such as the *consistoire* in France were also found in several of the Germanic states, for instance, in Würtemberg and Baden. These also performed some secular functions, such as drawing Jewish youth away from the traditional professions, which were thought to be detrimental, and attracting them to productive professions. Even in those states in which national organizations were not set up (in Prussia, the largest of the Germanic states, the authorities opposed this), the existence of individual congregations, which encompassed all the Jews of the area, was mandatory. The *kehillah* fulfilled those functions in which the secular authorities had an interest: It was assigned to register the Jewish population in the register of births and deaths, and was responsible for the establishment of schools and for enforcing the mandatory educational requirements. The activities and failures of the *kehillah*, not only in these areas, were under the continuous supervision of the state authorities.[4]

This situation stemmed only in part from the special status of the Jews vis-à-vis the other inhabitants. It was essentially a product of the complex attitude taken by the state to religion in this period of transition from the pre-modern to the modern. During the *ancien regime*, that is, until the French Revolution, the state took responsibility for the observance of the religion or religions that were permitted to exist within its borders. In reality, only the Christian churches— and indeed only one Christian church, the Catholic (in France and Austria) or the Protestant (in Prussia)—had full rights to exist. Other religions, if they were tolerated at all, had an inferior status. In any event, if a religious community was permitted to act within the state, it was also delegated the power to enforce religious discipline upon its believers, to wit, the religious commandments and ceremonies. The French Revolution and the shocks that reverberated in its wake throughout Europe weakened the link between religion and state, but did not completely sever them. The state ceased to view itself as responsible for the observance of religious directives, and even rejected the use of force by the agents of the church. Nonetheless, the state reserved for itself the right to permit or forbid the existence of a church, body, or religious institution within its borders; to demand information about the principles of those which were permitted; and to investigate their activities, behavior, and shortcomings.

Under the *ancien regime*, wherever the Jews were tolerated, it was because their religion was based on the same holy Scriptures that Christianity also revered. The New Testament overshadowed the Old Testament but did not nullify its value and validity. Jewish presence in a Christian country demanded religious justification, but Jews were separate from their Christian environment in many non-religious spheres. The *kehillah*, the social organization of the Jews, fulfilled many roles—political (in a limited sense), judicial, economic and social. The *kehillah* more closely resembled a corporation or guild, the mainstay of the state in the old regime, than one of the churches found within it.[5]

Traces of the many-faceted functions of the *kehillah* within the framework of the old regime seem to have remained even in the next period, at a time when it officially ceased to be a corporate body and became a religious organizational framework. As stated, the secular authorities themselves did not hesitate to assign the *kehillah* certain civil administrative functions, and it continued, on its own initiative, to maintain educational and social welfare institutions, and even mere social frameworks, which had no religious purpose in the narrow sense of the word. Moreover, the members of the *kehillah* were connected by way of familial relationships, by way of their concentration in the same types of employment, and in drawing on the same sources of culture. However, officially, most of these aspects were ignored, and the *kehillah* was treated as the organizational framework of a religious community, like one of the Christian churches. Because of this formal classification, the *kehillah* could, with the help of the authorities, obligate every Jew in its area of jurisdiction to be a member. Until the 1840s the requirement to belong was conditional upon every Jewish male child's being circumcised (in parallel to Christian baptism). When the authorities ceased to enforce this requirement, they nonetheless forbade anyone to leave the Jewish congregation without joining a Christian congregation. The state did not accept a person without a religion, just as it only accepted the recognized religions, of which Judaism was one.

The strict adherence to this last principle created a situation where, upon being confronted with the minority that instituted a Reform ritual, the authorities had to deal with the question: Can this form of ritual be considered a legitimate variation of the approved Jewish faith? This happened for the first time in 1818, with the foundation of the famous Hamburg Temple, and with the opening of a similar synagogue by Israel Jacobson in Berlin.[6] This was also the case when a strict Orthodox minority demanded organizational independence for itself in order to fulfill its special religious needs, and granting this request was the prerogative of the secular authorities. The idea of turning to the authorities was raised in the course of the controversies in Breslau in the 1840s, and in a more decisive fashion in Frankfurt at the end of the same decade; we shall read about these events in greater detail. In these cases the authorities debated whether the secession of part of the community was to be viewed as sectarianism, which they looked upon with disfavor in any church or religious entity.

In the course of the extended controversy surrounding Orthodox secession, Rabbi Samson Raphael Hirsch argued that the fate of an Orthodox individual or minority living in a Reform community is more difficult than that of someone of a Reform persuasion who lives together with the Orthodox. For the latter, such a situation demanded only a certain amount of compromise or adaptation: If he wished, he could use the communal institutions; if not, he need not. In contrast, the Orthodox individual or minority in a Reform environment was not only prevented from fulfilling the religious commandments, but also lacked the basic means for existence. He could not join the Reform prayers, rely on the opinions of their rabbi, eat their meat, and certainly not entrust his children to their teachers.[7] On the surface, this argument carries a whiff of Orthodox arrogance. It sounds narrow and superior, and makes no attempt to understand the Reform position; the latter is likely as repelled by Orthodox ritual and education as is the Orthodox by Reform ritual and education.

Nonetheless, Hirsch's description was not completely divorced from the reality of his time. It is true that in many Jewish circles, the process of abandoning tradition had a purely negative character. People who were no longer willing to maintain the severe restrictions that the Jewish religion placed upon them viewed Reform as an excuse to throw off the burden without a crisis of conscience. It was comfortable for them to hear the rulings of experts and authorities to the effect that the validity of the tradition in which they had been raised had been abrogated by the new circumstances that had arisen. Those who upheld this approach wished to detract from the old without replacing it with anything new. The novelty of Reform was that it founded a new religion which was anchored in Jewish tradition but was not identical to it, a religion which, like all religions, demanded constant dedication and even zealousness. While this aspect of Reform had its faithful adherents, they were few. Hirsch ignored this aspect, and contrasted the two camps by portraying their average representatives: the Reformer as one who is open to compromise in his opposition to Orthodoxy, the Orthodox as one for whom compromise with the opposition is a deadly sin. Regarding Orthodox Jews, Hirsch certainly had a basis for his description. Upon finding himself in an environment in which Reform prevailed, the Jew who adhered to tradition in all its details could not assimilate. He could react in either of two ways. He could attempt to avoid taking part in a ritual which he considered unacceptable, and to fulfill his other needs insofar as he could. Or, he could take the offensive and attempt to free himself from the domination of Reform. Both reactions may be documented in reality: the first, in the behavior of the Orthodox in France and some of the Germanic states; the second, in some German communities and, most of all, throughout Hungary.

In France only a few non-influential intellectuals supported the idea of religious reform.⁸ Nonetheless, the central *consistoire*, which was composed of the notables of the community and a number of rabbis, with a chief rabbi at their head, gave instructions for changes in the ritual. Most of these were structural changes, which were designed only to add an aesthetic dimension to the ceremonies—order, splendor, and reverence in the public prayer, restraint and decorum at funerals, and the like. One regulation concerned the ceremony of circumcision; it abrogated the *mezizah*, the third stage of the ceremony following the cutting of the foreskin and its removal. *Mezizah* was considered unaesthetic, in addition to being dangerous, according to the opinion of the physicians.⁹ The changes enacted fit the ideas and tastes of the leadership of the community, but offended the sensibilities of most of the common people, who adhered to the tradition in all its details, as they had from ancient times. They preferred prayer in small, intimate buildings to splendid ceremonial rituals. They similarly favored the sermons of popular preachers—at times given in the Yiddish of Alsace, which was the place of origin of most urban Jews, including those of the capital—over the speeches given by the rabbis in French, which were constructed upon rhetorical principles. Indeed, the common people did not hesitate to disobey the instructions of the *consistoire*, despite the fact that the *consistoire* was backed by the government, and more than once attempted to enforce its directives with the arm of the law. It was not always those with enforcement powers who emerged victorious in this struggle. The members of the rebellious minority found ways to trick those who wished to enforce the laws and even to embarrass their superiors, by presenting them as quixotic battlers.¹⁰

What the minority could not do, or even imagine doing, was secede from the general Jewish community and set up their own separate congregations. The authorities recognized the *consistoire* as the supreme organization of the Jewish community as a whole. This recognition was anchored in the laws of the state, until the lawmakers decided, at the end of a struggle which lasted for decades, to separate church and state. However, this separation was carried out only in the first decade of the twentieth century.

The consistorial system branched out as early as Napoleon's time—to Westphalia in Germany, which was ruled by Napoleon's brother Jerome. This *consistoire* functioned under the guiding spirit of one man, Israel Jacobson, whom we mentioned above.¹¹ He was on close terms with the ruling powers because of his tremendous financial success, and at the same time was dedicated to improving the lot of his fellow Jews, both materially and spiritually. In the material sphere, Jacobson succeeded in improving the civil status of the Jews, not only in Westphalia, but also in other states, where he had considerable influence upon the rulers due to his economic activities. In the spiritual realm, Jacobson wished to set an example for adapting educational institutions and Jewish ritual to the spirit of the times, using the reforms of the Westphalian *consistoire*. The schools were designed to teach good citizenship and useful employment, and the synagogues to conduct Jewish worship of God according to the tastes of the intellectuals, Jewish and non-Jewish. The regulations of the *consistoire* gave very detailed instructions for performing the religious ceremonies, and for shortening public prayer by eliminating the recitation of psalms and ritual poetry. On the other hand, it mandated the use of the vernacular in at least some of the prayers, and especially in the sermon. Moreover, Jacobson forced the local rabbis to permit the eating of *qitniyot* (rice and beans from which flour could be made) on Passover, a prohibition which has no source in talmudic law, but which had been accepted among the Ashkenazim since the Middle Ages. Jacobson based his directives on the opinion of a Jewish court which he had appointed, but the authority of this body was not great enough, and their rulings were not accepted without protest. Other rabbis differed with the opinions of their colleagues, the members of Jacobson's *beit din* (rabbinical court). Jacobson was a native of Halberstadt, whose Jewish community was one of the oldest and strictest in Germany. The members of the community were proud of Jacobson, who had become great but remained of their flesh, and who used his money and power to assist his brethren. But their admiration for him did not supersede their opposition to his regulations, which ran counter to tradition. The people of Halberstadt, together with all the conservative Jews of Westphalia, ignored his directives and prevented the new practices from becoming entrenched in the life of the community.[12] They thus preceded the conservative Jewish public in France in its attitude to the reforms of the *consistoire*.

With the fall of Napoleon and the beginning of the Restoration, the political underpinning of Reform activity disappeared. Jacobson learned this to his own cost after he moved to Berlin. Here his attempt to introduce a prayer service according to the Westphalian paradigm was frustrated by the conservatives in the congregation and the intervention of the Prussian king, the devout Christian Friedrich Wilhelm III.[13] The opportunities for the success of reformist ambitions were enhanced with the awakening of the spirit of Liberalism, in the 1830s and 1840s, but not in every state. Prussia's attitude continued to be one of reservation and hesitation, as we shall see. However, wherever the new spirit took hold in public opinion, it led to an intensive cooperation between the adherents of reform for religious or ideological reasons and those who saw it as a means to advance the acceptance of Jews among their neighbors, if not their actual assimilation into the general population. This is why conservatives who adhered to tradition encountered intense pressures, which were not easy to withstand. Dramatic examples of this situation are the events in the states of Würtemberg and Mecklenburg-Schwerin.

Würtemberg was the first German state to grant its Jews citizenship; in 1828 they numbered nine thousand legal citizens. In return, it demanded that the Jews take on the responsibilities of citizenship such as military service, and leave their traditional sources of employment, like peddling, dealing in animals, and usury.[14] The prevalent idea in governmental circles was that the goal of integration would not be reached unless the cultural barriers dividing the Jews from the general public were destroyed. The most formidable barrier was Jewish religious practices, which were considered strange and curious. The elimination of this strangeness was henceforth the declared policy of the government. Judaism was given equal footing with Christianity in its various forms; just as these were led and guided by a central institution, so a similar institution was established to oversee the Jewish congregations. This tendency to equate it with the Christian religions is reflected in the name of the institution: *Die israelitische Oberkirchenbehörde*, that is, the Supreme Authority of the Israelite Church.[15] Similarly, the rabbi who was the official representative of the Jewish religion on the council of the Authority held the title *Kirchenrat*, that is, church counsellor. This central Jewish institution, whose members were chosen from among Jewish notables, and which was headed by a non-Jewish representative of the government, was meant to direct the life of the congregations: their organization, their financing, their overtly religious functions, the choice of their leaders and service personnel—slaughterers, precentors, teachers, and rabbis—the form of service and ceremonies, and the like. In theory, the government did not intend to interfere in the religious life of the Jewish community. Therefore, one of the rules of the constitution of the Authority was that while the discussions of the council concerning religion should take place in the presence of the representative of the government, he should not have a vote in the decisions and if there was a tie, he should not cast the deciding vote between them (this was not the case regarding administrative affairs).[16] In actuality, the government had no need of direct influence in the area of religious ceremony and ritual; this was achieved indirectly by its choice of the rabbi who sat on the council of the Authority and was endowed with religious authority. The choice was Joseph Maier, the rabbi of Stuttgart, the capital of Würtemberg, who was known to be a fervent supporter of the reformist tendency of the government.[17] Under Rabbi Maier's influence, a system of reforms of Jewish religious ceremonies was enacted; this was published in 1838 by the Authority, thus granting it legal and royal sanction.[18]

The general objective of the reforms was to eliminate those characteristics of the Jewish ceremonies that could startle the stranger who chanced to see them. And indeed, Jewish synagogues were notorious among their neighbors for their lack of decorum and discipline, and the general pandemonium that prevailed. From now on, order, pomp, and circumstance would be the rule of the day, and any custom that could adversely affect these was to stop. The worshipers were required to appear for prayer in appropriate clothes, to stand in their places and refrain from going to greet and kiss the Torah scroll as it was taken out of the Ark, and to refrain from any loud comments. "Striking" Haman during the reading of the Scroll of Esther was forbidden, as was circling the pulpit with *lulavim* and *etrogim* (willow branches and citrons) on Sukkot and with the Torah scroll on Simhat Torah. Some of these orders uprooted customs that were already anchored in talmudic law, such as the prohibition against wearing leather shoes on the Ninth of Av, or the custom of striking the willow branches on Hoshanah Rabbah. In any case, it is doubtful whether those Jews who were called upon to follow these regulations made distinctions between them, according to the extent to which they impinged on the *halakhah* (Jewish law). The Jews of Würtemberg, who were scattered in about fifty congregations, most of them small, were not experts in Jewish learning, but were steeped in tradition. For them any deviation from the accepted was likely to be interpreted as a religious transgression.

Since the reforms had royal approval, the congregations were afraid to protest against them. However, the local authorities lacked any motivation to enforce them, unless ordered to do so by the representatives of the central Authority. In the absence of a supervisory mechanism, those congregations that resented the innovations could ignore all or part of them. A devout adherent to Reform ideas who travelled through several congregations seven years after the reforms were issued, saw to his dismay that they were almost completely ignored. For the most part, the old order remained: Synagogue worshipers would enter and leave during the prayer; the householders would lead the prayers, rather than the precentor, as the rules demanded; and in one of the relatively large congregations a private prayer service was held in the home of a retired rabbi, which the rules were careful to prohibit.[19] Twenty years later, one of the sharpest critics of the system, Ludwig Stern, summed up the results of the effort in Würtemberg. According to him, unruly behavior in the synagogues of Würtemberg, the heritage of the premodern generations, persisted, and was even more noticeable than in those of the two neighboring states, Bavaria and Baden.[20] Stern even proposed a reasonable explanation for this situation. There was a sense of the need to change things everywhere. In those places where this demand was made in the name of religion itself, it was heeded. In Würtemberg no one turned to the public to change its ways in the name of religion, and R. Joseph Maier's regulations ignored the public at large. Appointees presided over the ceremonies, and the public was sentenced not only to silence, but to muteness and total passivity. The result was that the public ignored the rules and continued to cling to the state of affairs the rules were designed to improve.

Mecklenburg-Schwerin lagged behind Würtemberg by only one year in enacting a constitution for a national organization of its Jews. This was issued in 1839, and resembled the constitution of Würtemberg in its contents and goals.[21] The forty-two congregations in the state, which comprised more than three thousand people, were subjected to the authority of a council of five members, which they were to choose. At their side were two representatives of the government, non-Jews of course. These took part in all the discussions of the council, but had only the status of advisers, being unable to vote on religious matters. The chief rabbi ruled on religious issues. This rabbi had to present a certificate of ordination from a religious authority, which attested to his ability to pronounce on halakhic issues, and a certificate of study from an academic institution, which proved his readiness to lead his flock according to the spirit of the times.[22] Both of these criteria were met in the person of Samuel Holdheim, the rabbi of Frankfurt-an-der-Oder. He had gained his mastery of halakhic sources in his native province, Posen, and began his general education at the University of Prague.[23]

Holdheim was thirty-four upon reaching Mecklenburg-Schwerin; only at this stage of his career did he develop his extremist Reform views, for which he gained enthusiastic admirers and harsh critics among the public, in the rabbinical assemblies of the years 1844–1846 and elsewhere. His extremism is evident in his activities as chief rabbi, in his unbridled efforts to endow public prayer in the congregations with a modern character. Under his guiding spirit, the council of the national organization adopted the Württemberg constitution for its congregations.[24] Moreover, he added something which was not included in the Württemberg regulations, and which was not customary in any other place in Germany: reading the Torah in declamatory fashion, without the traditional tune guided by the cantillation signs.[25] With his deep knowledge of the halakhic sources, Holdheim had no trouble proving that reading the Torah according to the cantillation signs was not mandated by Sinaitic law.[26] However, proofs of this sort made no impression upon the general public, which adhered to the accepted practice. On the other hand, there were circles in Mecklenburg-Schwerin that were ready to deviate from tradition, and some that were completely estranged from it. In his report to the government following his tour of the congregations in 1843, Holdheim tells of rich people who do not avail themselves of the services of a ritual butcher, and therefore refuse to contribute to his salary. There were those who did not attend synagogue and come, at most, to hear the sermon of a rabbi or preacher whom they like, without participating in the public prayer taking place at the same time.[27] However, most of the public remained faithful to tradition, and the directives copied from the Württemberg example were galling to them. Indeed, a more overt opposition arose here than in Württemberg, and did have some success. Some of the wealthy and respected members of the congregation, who were influential with the government, were counted among the opposition in Mecklenburg-Schwerin.[28] Their protest bore fruit; approximately one year after the proclamation of the reforms, the first clause, which forbade private prayer groups, was abolished.[29] Those adhering to the traditional character of the prayer service thus found a way to evade the new rules. About two years later we hear of permission being granted to a group of traditionalists in the city of Schwerin to build a synagogue of their own. According to the notice in *Der treue Zions-Wächter*, this was given despite the opposition of Holdheim and his circle.[30] But there was a limit to the influence of the traditionalists; when Holdheim left Mecklenburg-Schwerin—he was called to preside over the radical reformist congregation in Berlin—the traditionalists attempted to prevent the appointment of a successor of his ilk. This is exactly what happened, however, with the appointment of David Einhorn, who was no less radical than Holdheim in his reformist tendencies. Einhorn followed the path of his predecessor, and the confrontations between him and the conservative public continued. A great scandal arose over an incident that occurred in one of the small congregations: a father refused to circumcise his son, and Einhorn ordered the local rabbi to declare the child a Jew in all respects, according to the father's request.[31]

The events in Würtemberg and Mecklenburg-Schwerin were only examples of what could happen elsewhere. The institution of a chief rabbi, who decided religious issues for all the congregations in his jurisdiction, was prevalent in the many kingdoms and principates throughout Germany. If the faithful were unlucky, and the post was filled by a rabbi with reformist tendencies, he could force them to accept his directives. An anonymous writer described such an incident in the 1859 edition of the journal *Jeschurun*, whose editor was Samson Raphael Hirsch.[32] In a certain province, the post of rabbi became vacant with the demise of the old rabbi. The authorities ignored the natural right of the congregations to choose their religious leader themselves, nor did they take into consideration the congregations' request that the candidate for the post be chosen from among adherents to tradition like themselves. Instead, the authorities heeded the people of the capital city, "respected personalities, intellectuals, bankers, merchants and physicians," who claimed that only a rabbi who would guide his flock to follow the spirit of the times would fit the post and bring blessing to those he was to guide. And so a man to their liking was chosen, who, as expected, commenced his tenure by enforcing the new regulations, beginning with the erasure of parts of the prayer and their translation into German, and ending with the introduction of an organ into the synagogues, where the congregations were forced to pray.

What could the congregations do against the threats of the chief rabbi that refusal would bring about government intervention? They surrendered, except for one, a local teacher who demonstrated to the members of his congregation how to take a determined stand in defense of their rights. The teacher preferred to lose his job and to be exiled from the state than to surrender to the directives of the rabbi that went against his conscience. Now the other members of the congregation also dared to protest to the chief rabbi, and the rabbi retaliated by enlisting the aid of the authorities. One morning following the protest, at the end of the prayer service in the synagogue, two policemen appeared with an order to close the synagogue. The Torah scrolls were brought to the nearest major city and the worshipers were henceforth compelled to go to nearby towns.

At the end of his description of this event, the author, or perhaps the editor, added the words, *Ist historisch*, meaning that the reported event had actually occurred.[33] Indeed, we shall encounter further testimonies to the reliance of the Reform rabbis upon the governmental arm, and conversely, the protests of the faithful adherents, crying out in anger against the injustice done to them. The conservatives did not remember that the tradition to which they adhered permits and even mandates the use of force, in order to compel rebellious Jews to follow the beaten path. Moreover, some of the outstanding representatives of tradition at this very time were also ready to seek governmental assistance, if they saw any chance of being answered.[34] However, historical accounts of this sort, even if they were brought to mind, were irrelevant. At that time and place the conservatives were the ones who felt persecuted and who wished to escape their unhappy situation. We must ask: In what way did they feel injured, and what did they view as the remedy?

There is no doubt that given this state of affairs, the idea of separation from the communal organization already began to glimmer in the eyes of the faithful. In a news item in *Der treue Zions-Wächter* about the attempts of the conservatives in Mecklenburg-Schwerin to prevent the appointment of a Reform chief rabbi to replace Holdheim, the writer ends the item by expressing his confidence that the integrity of the authorities, and in particular the sense of justice of the prince of the state, will foil such an attempt. "We prefer complete separation to a second Holdheim. We can no longer sacrifice our conscience and convictions as has been done until now."[35] As we know, the founder of *Shomer Zion ha-Ne'eman*, both the Hebrew and German editions, was Rabbi Jacob Ettlinger of Altona; this is therefore a sign of the awakening of Orthodoxy to an active struggle with the phenomenon of Reform, in the wake of the Braunschweig Rabbinical Assembly. One of the declared goals of these journals was to encourage the Orthodox to demand their rights. There were those who also viewed this as the proper venue for a self-accounting by Orthodoxy itself.

Approximately half a year after the appearance of the first issue of the German edition, in an article in five installments (beginning January 27, 1846), an anonymous author described "The Role of Orthodox Jewry Today."[36] The author reviews the process of estrangement from tradition by a growing sector of the Jewish public, up to the time of the Reform rabbinical assemblies, which sought to give a theoretical justification for their actions. The author does not polemicize with the reformers about their doctrine. He complains that they did not stop at building a platform for themselves, but attempted to force their way on others. They compelled those faithful to tradition to participate in prayers that the faithful considered illegitimate, and brought them under the rod of rabbis upon whose rulings they could not rely. The major novelty of the article is its criticism of the rabbis who opposed Reform: They deluded themselves that their opposition was sufficient to stop it, when they should have declared that the reformers had gone too far in trying to shake off the burden of tradition, and that there was no common ground between them and the faithful. The author argued that a declaration such as this was called for as early as the foundation of the Hamburg Temple in 1818.[37] Why did the Orthodox rabbis not take this logical step? This is the question the author raises in his article. In his opinion, they were afraid of schism, internecine quarrels, and factionalism. There was a dual reason for their recoil from division, both economic and political. Indeed, it may be asked, would the authorities have allowed the division of the Jewish public into what they considered factions? And even if they were to agree, would not the division dissolve the economic basis of the congregations? The author is aware that in a case of division, the less affluent would be found in the Orthodox congregations, and it is not clear whether and how they could finance their institutions.[38] But practical difficulties of this sort are not to be weighed against fundamental principles. What right do the Orthodox have to demand the participation of those who abandon the tradition in financing ritual slaughterers, when they buy meat in the market? There is no recourse for the Orthodox but to finance their institutions themselves. Every Jew can lead the prayer, and the rabbis would have to make do with modest salaries, following the example of the talmudic scholar who made do with a bushel of carobs from one week to the next. As for the stumbling block presented by the authorities, the anonymous author relies on the spreading spirit of tolerance, and in a paradoxical way takes as an example the congregation of extreme reformers in Berlin—later to be led by Samuel Holdheim—which the Prussian authorities tolerated, at least tacitly. If the Prussian authorities, who are considered to be extremely conservative, do not enforce the unity of Jewish worship, other, more enlightened, governments would not either.[39]

This bold analysis, which constituted a challenge to the policy of the Orthodox leadership, evoked positive reactions in the pages of *Der treue Zions-Wächter*, but met with reservations. The anonymous author's prognosis, especially his estimate of the probable attitude of the governments, seemed wishful thinking.[40] However, no more than two years passed and it seemed that his utopian vision would be realized, following the Revolution of 1848. In December of that year, the National German Parliament in Frankfurt enacted the basic constitution for all the united German states. One of its clauses determined that every citizen is free to choose his religion, and that his choice would not affect his status and rights as a citizen. *Der treue Zions-Wächter* hailed this constitution enthusiastically, for it seemed to put an end to the subordination of the God-fearing in the various states to the Reform leaders of the congregations. The author of this laudatory article derided the chief rabbis. Has the news of the new law reached you? "You will no longer be able to force your modern form of worship on those for whom it is an abomination and to bring them by force to your temples. They are as free as you are."[41]

As we know, the hopes that were pinned upon the Frankfurt parliament were dashed, and, just as the other aspects of government were once again put into the hands of the old guard, so were the Jewish congregations subjected to those appointed by the old rule. The idea raised by the anonymous optimist two years earlier, of congregations organizing according to shared religious views, was out of the question. In truth, these wishes were divorced from reality, not only with regard to the state government. The Jewish community as well was unprepared for this leap, that is, removing the congregations from governmental auspices (which had clear advantages) and founding them upon a purely voluntary basis. Both parts of this thesis can be proved by following the history of the two major congregations, Breslau and Frankfurt, prior to the Revolution of 1848.

Chapter 2

Breslau-Style Compromise, Frankfurt-Style Conflicts

The contemporary historian, Marcus Jost, described the Jewish community of Breslau as one of the largest, most complex and dynamic in all of Germany:

> Its substantial membership (whose number reached five or six thousand) comprises all sorts of contrasts, from oppressive poverty to extreme affluence, from a distasteful Polish manner and lifestyle to the most refined culture, from total ignorance to the pinnacle of rabbinic learning, from rude zealousness to complete apathy.[1]

Breslau Jews, like all Prussian Jews at this period, were officially recognized as citizens, although this citizenship was restricted, primarily in the political sphere. These restrictions nonetheless left enough space for developing vigorous economic activity. Indeed, despite being a minority of no more than seven percent of the population, the Jews filled a decisive role in the development of trade and industry in the city, thanks to their widespread ties within Germany and outside it, and the spirit of enterprise characteristic of the first generations who emerged from the ghetto.[2]

The fate of the Breslau Jewish collective, which was organized within the framework of the congregation, was like that of other Prussian congregations. The governmental authorities had reservations about founding a national organization for the congregations in their jurisdiction. They awaited the degeneration of the Jewish congregations and the estrangement of their members from Judaism in favor of Christianity. In the meantime, they contented themselves with a superficial and inconsistent form of supervision. At the beginning of the period, any public prayer that deviated in content or form from that of the accepted norm was forbidden by order of King Friedrich Wilhelm III. In time, however, the authorities acquiesced to the variations in ideas and activities within Jewish society, and sometimes even supported them. This attitude reflected contemporary society at large. Nonetheless, in cases where conflicting ideas led to confrontations between parts of the Jewish public, the authorities remained the supreme arbiters of these conflicts, as the history of the Jewish community of Breslau clearly demonstrates.

Despite the emergence of divergent religious positions within the ranks of Breslau Jews since the Enlightenment, the rabbinic leadership of the congregation remained in the hands of R. Solomon Tiktin, an outstanding representative of tradition. R. Tiktin was a rabbi of the old school, neither desirous nor capable of fulfilling the demands that many insisted were a necessary response to the changing times. He continued to limit his sermons to specific occasions—the Sabbath before Passover, the Sabbath before the Day of Atonement, and the like. The language of the sermon remained Yiddish, at a time when most of the new generation spoke and thought in German. The contents of the sermons and their style were in keeping: the rabbi lectured rather than preached, although the modern sermon as a source of spiritual inspiration was an integral part of public prayer for those who saw themselves as progressive. When these people saw that R. Tiktin did not adjust himself to their demands, they sought a solution by choosing a second, junior rabbi, who would be capable of fulfilling those tasks that Tiktin could not. They chose Abraham Geiger, at the time rabbi of Wiesbaden. In addition to being a stirring speaker—he proved this in a sermon he gave in Breslau in the summer of 1838, prior to his appointment—Geiger was also known to have a historical-critical approach to the essentials of Jewish faith, from which derived certain conclusions regarding the shaping of its future. His sermon to the Breslau community contained hints at this side of his personality as well. It is no wonder that his appointment met the spirited opposition of the conservatives, with R. Tiktin at their head. The opposition sought to bar him from taking the post by means of governmental intervention—as a foreign citizen, Geiger needed a special license to hold office in Prussia—but this was only the first step in the attempt to prevent Geiger's holding office in Breslau.[3] There is no point in giving here the details of this famous controversy, which was a *cause célèbre* outside Breslau as well, for almost a whole generation, from 1838 to 1856. Let us just point out that in this case there was good reason for the division of the community, but the process was halted midway and did not reach its logical end.

The unique feature in the confrontation was that it did not concern practical religious reforms, such as changes in the synagogue service, but unfolded against the background of theoretical-dogmatic conflicts. R. Tiktin refused to recognize Geiger's authority to serve as rabbi, not because of any lack of knowledge or expertise in *halakhah*, but because he deviated from the basic principles of Orthodox faith, and its view of the Oral Law as the legitimate elaboration and interpretation of the Written Law. Tiktin not only refused to serve on the same court as Geiger, but he even rejected the proposal to set up two *batei din* in the congregation—one over which he would preside, which would serve his followers, and the second to serve those who recognized Geiger's authority. As the official rabbi, Tiktin felt himself to be responsible for the religious integrity of the members of his congregation, and this would be flawed by their obedience to a halakhic master unworthy of his robes. A number of well-known rabbis in the districts of Silesia and Posen supported this position.[4] He also sought the aid of the authorities, which had previously discouraged any attempt to deviate from traditional Jewish patterns of theory or practice, but found he had erred. Even the conservative rulers of Prussia could not ignore the change in public opinion, which no longer upheld absolute adherence to the accepted and traditional. Rabbis of major congregations throughout Germany sided with Geiger, stating that a historical understanding of the development of a religion does not disqualify its proponent from guiding the religious community that appoints him to do so.[5] Geiger was granted Prussian citizenship, and the state even acknowledged his qualifications for the post, but this did not bring to a halt the opposition of R. Tiktin's supporters. At a certain stage of the conflict, these were relegated to the ranks of the opposition within the congregation, which supported Geiger, and they went so far as to refuse to pay their congregational dues. There is reason to believe that the opposition camp was composed not only of isolationist Yiddish speakers, sunk in the world of tradition, like Tiktin himself, but also of those whose modern education gave them the tools to explain their position and their Orthodox faith.[6] The idea of a split in the congregation was in the air, and the historian Jost, who reported on the controversy while it was at its height, thought this to be unavoidable.[7] But his forecast did not come true.

R. Solomon Tiktin died in 1843, leaving a son, Gedaliah, who was considered by his supporters worthy of taking his father's place. Indeed, the son was appointed to his father's seat, and the controversy continued under his leadership. However, the son was found to be more moderate than the father; perhaps experience had taught him that the possibility of imposing the Orthodox view on the entire congregation was no longer realistic. He therefore agreed to the compromise his father had vehemently rejected: two committees would be established within the framework of the united congregation. Each would operate independently in religious matters, including the choice of a rabbi and the members of his *beit din*.[8] This relative independence of the Orthodox branch was also the maximum freedom to which the state authorities would agree. The establishment of two separate congregations would have been interpreted as a relinquishment of governmental opposition to the establishment of new religions, for the state law recognized only one Jewish religion. In any event, it seems that most of those involved wished to preserve a united framework. The mutual accusations that were heard in the heat of controversy, which gave the impression that the two camps could not live together, disappeared without a trace. The sense of a shared communal destiny had not yet dissolved, and it contributed to the preservation of a common organization, despite the religious conflicts.

Frankfurt was unique in its emergence from the traditional world, at least since the conquest of the city by the French in 1806. Nothing parallels the Frankfurtian process in terms of its pace or dimensions in the history of similar congregations, such as those of Prague or Hamburg. This uniqueness is exemplified by two initiatives taken by one man, Sigismund Geisenheimer: the establishment of a lodge of the Freemasons called "Morgenröthe" (Dawn), and the founding of a school, the "Philanthropin."[9] The lodge was designed for Jews whom the older lodges in the city refused to accept, while the school took in boys and girls whose parents wished to give them a general humanist education, and restrict the Jewish content to the barest minimum. These two institutions of Geisenheimer's had a certain shared motivation and atmosphere. While the Freemasons did not demand that their members deny their religion, their deistic principles—the belief in God, nurture of love of man, justice, and incorruptibility—and the symbols and Masonic ceremonies that expressed them, could serve as a substitute for the dogmas and commandments of the historical religions. As I have demonstrated elsewhere, the elected leaders of the congregation were, for the most part, members of this lodge, which contemporaries called the "Judenloge." The influence of the lodge on their *Weltanschauung* is discernible in their congregational activities.[10] They did not attempt to remove the traditional institutions, in order to put others in their place, but anticipated their slow decay. Official religious leadership remained in the hands of the *beit din*, at whose head stood R. Solomon Abraham Trier, one of the oldest rabbis in the German states. R. Trier continued to surround himself with students who were occupied in traditional study. But the rabbi's *beit midrash* (studyhouse) seemed a relic of the past, while the life of the congregation—both private and public—underwent change, at times to the extent of completely losing its traditional character. The *beit din* lacked influence on contemporary events and was incapable of using its authority even in questions that related to the fate of the religious institutions of the congregation.[11] The two major synagogues of the congregation, which were in close proximity to one another, needed repair, but the congregational administration would provide it only on the condition that the two buildings be consolidated, and that the new building would have a new, more modern character. Due to the lack of agreement between the two bodies, both synagogues remained in their state of disrepair and worshipers were forced to pray in private houses or in the localities of the many *hevrot* (societies) that operated in the city.[12] It should be noted that despite the fundamental changes that occurred within the congregation, many still attended synagogue regularly and there was still a demand for other religious services, such as observance of *kashrut* (dietary laws), and so on. The administration's attitude to this is evident from the wording of a memorandum to the Senate, dated January 1839. The administration praises itself in this memo for supplying the needs of the conservatives in the congregation: It employs ritual butchers, has built a slaughterhouse, and over ten years before even renovated the ovens for heating the Sabbath meal "for those members of the congregation who do not cook in their houses on the Sabbath, although the need for this has lessened."[13] The administration thus sees those who persist in following a Jewish lifestyle as a vanishing breed.

The members of the administration made the common mistake of those belonging to a certain social-historical camp, who assume that their trend will persist until it fully realizes its aims. In general, however, as a process progresses, it arouses a reaction, which arrests it before it completes its course. The reaction against the process of decay so close to the hearts of the Frankfurt communal administration was presented in a memorandum signed by ninety-nine people, submitted to the Senate in 1838, which protested against the authority of the congregational leadership in religious matters (the words quoted above are from the administration's defense, submitted a year later).[14] In the memorandum, the signatories demanded of the Senate that their religious affairs be taken out of the hands of the congregational administration and placed in the hands of a committee of five people, whose names were given. One of them was R. Aaron Fuld, and the inclusion of his name allows us to deduce the character of the group that pitted itself against the administration. Aaron Fuld was a wealthy householder and a learned man, who did not hold a rabbinic position, but was called to sit on the *beit din* of his teacher, R. Trier, when needed.[15] Nonetheless, signs of the influence of the times are discernible both in his method of study—interpretation of the sources in their plain sense and without *pilpul* (casuistry)—and in the positions he adopted regarding practical questions of education and religion. Fuld supported granting secular studies a place in children's education, and wished to ensure the preservation of tradition in public and private life by endowing the ceremonies and rituals with a character in keeping with contemporary tastes. He often gave public sermons on the Sabbath for various *hevrot*, and his sermons, like his Talmud lessons, were outstanding in their simplicity, bringing his listeners to an understanding of the sources upon which Judaism was based. His approach gives us a clue to the nature of the committee of which he was a member. Its goal was not only to ensure that the religious matters under the jurisdiction of the congregation be treated according to halakhic principles, but also that they be presented in a manner which would endear them to their adherents. The group represented by the committee grew to 212 people, almost one third of the members of the congregation at the time.

From this description of the religious situation in Frankfurt we can deduce that, while the decay of tradition was more widespread than in other comparable congregations, Frankfurt was also unusual in the vigorous reaction of the traditionalists to this phenomenon. Even the social composition of the traditionalists was unusual. As we heard above from contemporary sources, the adherents of tradition, the Orthodox, were usually of the lower economic classes. This was not the case in Frankfurt, where among those who struggled for the preservation of tradition in the city were great financiers, bankers who controlled the stock market, and at their head the representatives of the House of Rothschild.[16] One of the first generation of Rothschild brothers, Anschel Meyer, and Meyer Carl of the second generation, were strictly observant and supported the conservatives both personally and financially.

The greater economic power of the minority could not of course decide the struggle, which centered around differences in viewpoint and belief. But at the opportune time, the well-established minority could free itself of the guardianship of the majority and establish its own religious institutions. This opportunity came after the Revolution of 1848, in the wake of which a spirit of relative tolerance prevailed in the Germanic states. On January 28, 1850, a group of eleven men notified the Senate that their consciences forced them to secede from the congregation, which could not and did not wish to fulfill their religious needs. They formed a separate religious congregation, "without detracting from their rights and obligations as members of the political Jewish community." They wished to choose an Orthodox (*rechtgläubig*) rabbi, who would gather around him "the great number of believing Jews in this city."[17] They requested of the Senate that the rabbi whom they would choose should be permitted to fulfill all the tasks incumbent upon the holder of such an office, such as performing marriages. A sort of myth was later created, that these eleven were the only Jews within the large congregation who remained faithful to Judaism, a legend that R. Samson Raphael Hirsch fostered. This myth contradicts clear evidence, and was disproved once and for all by Robert Liberles in his fundamental work on the foundation of Hirsch's *Adath Jeschurun*. Eleven of the faithful signed the request to the Senate, but their request was submitted at the behest of a group of approximately one hundred people, who took part in the formation of the new congregation.[18]

The wording of the appeal submitted by the founders has a certain importance from our perspective. It reveals that their aim was the fulfillment of their religious needs, and in particular the appointment of a rabbi who would be attuned to their views. R. Trier had recently died (1846), and R. Leopold Stein, who was appointed during R. Trier's lifetime and over his protests, was considered a Reform rabbi, upon whose decisions the Orthodox could not rely.[19] The founders differentiated between the Jewish congregation as a general public body—"political" in their words—and the sub-units within it, which are distinguished from one another by their religious position. They did not even entertain the thought of releasing themselves from the payment of taxes to the congregation or of relinquishing the rights that derived from their membership in its framework. These aspirations were the development of later years.

After the fruitless attempt of the new congregation to engage R. Michael Sachs, who officiated in Berlin as a preacher and member of the *beit din*,[20] the choice fell upon Samson Raphael Hirsch, who lived in Nikolsburg and served as the state rabbi of Moravia. His relinquishing this respected office can be explained both by the difficulties he encountered in this foreign environment, and by the prospect of success in his native land. A childhood friend of Hirsch, Gershom Joschafat, who lived in Frankfurt at the time, described to him the nature of the emerging congregation: "You have probably heard that a new congregation has arisen here within the Jewish community, which despite this is old and pious [*fromme*]. The most respected and wealthiest people, with the Rothschild family at their head, belong to it." He praised the founders, whose entire goal is only to "restore the crown to its former glory." Were Hirsch to come, those who chose him would carry him on their shoulders: "And the most important thing is that here you can do much, perform great things; the foundations and the means for all this exist, the need is only for someone who knows how to combine them."[21] Later developments completely vindicated this assessment. While it is true that the conditions for this turning point in the history of Jewish Frankfurt had been created previously, the end result—the creation of a new religious stream within Judaism, the Neo-Orthodox—was the result of "happenstance," in that the man to whom the task of guiding this turning point fell was Samson Raphael Hirsch. Some have already posed the question of how things would have developed if Michael Sachs had remained firm in his initial agreement to serve as rabbi of *Adath Jeschurun*,[22] but of course, this question is unanswerable, except to say that things would have been different.

Joschafat's terminology in describing "a new congregation" that was coming into being in Frankfurt was not exact. *Adath Jeschurun* never achieved the status of an independent congregation, even after it succeeded, under the vigorous leadership of its rabbi, in setting up most of the institutions necessary for a traditional Jewish community: a synagogue, school, *mikvah* (ritual bath), and butcher shop (but not a cemetery). These were all considered, both by the officers of the mother congregation and by the members of *Adath Jeschurun*, including its new rabbi, to be no more than a minority effort at organization within the framework of the congregation, in order to provide for its special needs. There is no indication that Hirsch himself entertained at this time the idea that his community's adherence to the minutiae of the *halakhah* would move it to attempt to sever itself completely from the mother congregation. This emerges from the changes he wished to make. Unlike the founders of his congregation, who were ready to bear the double burden of paying taxes to the mother congregation and of providing for their special needs, their rabbi and teacher refused to accept this situation, not because of the financial burden it entailed, but on principle. The taxes paid to the mother congregation served to support its form of worship, the rabbinate, and study in the congregational school. The Orthodox taxpayers thereby assisted in their preservation and could be considered to be abetting sinners, in itself one of the greatest sins. Hirsch's demand was, therefore, that an amount equal to the money spent on these institutions be deducted from the taxes of the members of *Adath Jeschurun*. The leadership of *Adath Jeschurun* agreed in principle with the rabbi's demand,[23] but Hirsch himself waged the battle for its acceptance. Already in his first polemical pamphlet of 1854, defending the founding of *Adath Jeschurun*, he protested against the leadership of the congregation, for its desire to compel his flock to support financially the rituals they despised.[24] He also formulated the group's memorandum to the Senate, explaining their demand for a partial exemption from taxes, and refuting the arguments of the congregational leadership, which persisted in its refusal. The government upheld him on this issue, as he says later. Hirsch's authorship of the memorandum emerges from his son Mendel's testimony; after his father's death, he felt the need to defend his father's position, which seemed inconsistent. The appeal for a partial exemption from taxes was a minimal demand, in contrast to the bid for complete separation from the congregation, for which Hirsch strove in a later stage of his life.[25] Mendel attempted to reconcile the contradiction by claiming that his father upheld the principle of separation from the beginning of his activity, but that in the 1850s, political conditions were not ripe for complete achievement of this aim.[26] This however, is pure apologetics. For even the partial exemption from taxes did not gain the Senate's approval, and Hirsch nonetheless persisted in presenting it as an essential demand. Had he crystallized the principle of complete separation by this time, Hirsch would have pursued it without considering its chances of acceptance.

But we do not need indirect proofs. Hirsch's own statements show that in the 1850s the idea of separation from the congregation went no further than the demand for exemption from financial participation in Reform worship. In the first issue of the journal *Jeschurun*, of 1855, Hirsch describes the establishment of a parallel congregation in the nearby city of Mainz, which, according to his testimony, came about thanks to the financial support of his community. And he added that permission had still not been given to the members of this community to exempt themselves from participation in the forbidden worship practiced by the members of the mother congregation of Mainz. This demand, writes Hirsch, is no less justified than the permission given to the community to organize as a separate unit within the congregation.[27] This means that this sort of limited independence, so long as it also included the tax exemption, was the pinnacle of Hirsch's aspirations as well, at this stage of his life.

There is some basis to Mendel Hirsch's claims that it was still not possible in the 1850s to aspire to complete secession from the congregation. The leadership of the Frankfurt congregation maintained before the Senate that *Adath Jeschurun*'s demands stem from the principle of separation of religion and state,[28] while in his response Hirsch denied this "accusation."[29] The principle of separation of religion and state, which was part of the fundamental laws of the Revolution of 1848, was indeed put aside and not considered again until the 1860s. The difference in the spirit of the times is evident in Hirsch's position, but not as his son interpreted it, that he upheld the idea of complete secession, but was forced to deny it in the 1850s. The truth is that, at the beginning of his service in Frankfurt, he would have been content with an exemption from participation in the expenses of Reform worship. The idea of complete secession was born in the wake of the changing times, the practical effects of which are seen in the efforts of the Orthodox, not in Frankfurt but in Hungary, efforts shared by Hirsch to a greater extent than one generally thinks.

II

The Hungarian Scene

Chapter 3

Quiet Cultural Adaptation

The factors that caused tremors and transformations in Jewish life in western and central Europe, as part of the process of modernization, reached Hungary as well, although one or two generations later. But the results were different there, because of the special conditions prevailing in Hungary, in the non-Jewish environment as well as within Jewish society. Until the 1830s, the economy continued to be feudal, while the governmental system was somewhere between parliamentary and autocratic. The lands belonged to the higher nobility, the magnates, and the lesser nobility, the gentry. Exceptions to this were some lands belonging to cities, whose inhabitants were not dependent on the nobility. The peasants were serfs, subject to the landowners. Hungary was divided into relatively small counties, more than seventy in number, and the governmental and judicial bodies of each county were run by representatives elected by those with electoral power, the nobility. The country had one central legislative body, the Diet or the Estates, which was divided into two: the lower house, composed of the representatives of the counties, and the upper house, whose members were the magnates and the heads of the churches. These gathered in the main city, Pressburg, when convened by the Hapsburg emperor, who lived in Vienna, the capital city of the Austrian Empire.

The Kaiser's rule extended throughout the Austrian Empire, from Galicia to large areas of northern Italy. Hungary was exceptional in being the only part of the empire still to have its own legislative bodies; in all other territories, the emperor ruled absolutely via his army and his official representatives. In Hungary, he was also not called "emperor," but "king." Like other emperors, those of the House of Hapsburg wished to institute a uniform method of government throughout their realm, and from the time of Maria Theresa's reign (1740–1780)—and especially during that of Joseph II (1780–1790)—steps were taken to impose absolute rule upon Hungary as well, by almost totally ignoring the autonomous institutions of the state. The representative assembly was convened only rarely, and when it gathered, its authority was limited to deciding two questions alone: the number of soldiers that Hungary would place at the disposal of the kaiser's armies, and the yearly quota of taxes to be levied for the empire's coffers. A bureaucracy appointed by the rulers in Vienna operated in Hungary as well. At the head of this staff was the king's deputy, the *Paletine*, usually a member of the royal family. Second-in-command was the lieutenant governor, who lived in Buda (at the time still separate from Pest), and supervised affairs from there. The different counties in Hungary were run, as stated, by their own elected bodies, but the lieutenant governor's staff closely supervised their actions.[1]

The status and condition of the Jews of Hungary were affected by the nature of this complicated governmental system. In cities where the citizens ruled, Jews were generally not permitted to settle, since the merchant guilds and artisans viewed them as unwelcome competitors. In contrast, in cities under royal rule, where the army was stationed to protect the borders of the state, in the south, Jewish communities such as Arad or Temesvár developed. Other cities and market towns, which were located partly or entirely on the lands of magnates, like Pressburg, Eisenstadt, and Pápa, also opened their gates to Jews. But most of the Jews of Hungary, who at the end of the eighteenth century numbered approximately one hundred thousand, lived in villages and estates that belonged to the magnates. These required Jews as merchants, as consumers of surplus agricultural products, and as suppliers of goods from abroad. The royal treasury in Vienna claimed the right to tax all Hungarian Jews, no matter where and on whose territory they dwelled. This tax, levied on Jews during the reign of Maria Theresa, was called the Toleration Tax: the royal house was only prepared to tolerate the Jews upon its land in return for this payment. The representatives of the counties and the legislative assembly did not acknowledge the legality of this tax, but the treasury had at its disposal the lieutenant governor's staff in Buda to execute its orders. Indeed, the tax was paid without protest until the 1830s, when the confrontation between the two systems of government, the royal Austrian arm and the independent Hungarian government, began. This ongoing confrontation grew out of Hungarian nationalism, which arose together with economic modernization, and in the wake of which both the condition and status of the Jews changed thoroughly.

The 1830s and 1840s are called the "Reform Period" in Hungarian history, after the reforms that were enacted in all walks of life. During this period, economic life extricated itself from its feudal patterns. The partially closed economy revolving around the magnates' holdings was largely replaced by a market economy based on investment and capitalist enterprise. Laws that were appropriate for the former system, such as the exemption of the nobility from taxes, or the subjugation of serfs to landowners, were now seen to impede economic and social progress. Similarly, to liberals it seemed absurd to maintain the status of Jews as aliens at the fringes of society, given their visible contribution to the development of new branches of the economy, trade, finance, and the like. Indeed, the question of the Jews was discussed again and again in the Diet from the 1820s on, until a law was enacted in 1840 which changed their situation. Jews could now settle in most places in the state; they were still not on an equal footing with the citizens of the cities, but they were permitted to found new communities, and most of the impediments to their economic activity were removed. Below we shall examine the results of this turning point in the internal life of Hungarian Jewry. For the moment, let us follow the influence of these revolutionary changes on the two systems of government mentioned above, the autonomous counties, and the royal regime.

The process of economic modernization came, as stated, arm in arm with national awakening. This awakening expressed itself in the wealth of literature produced in Hungarian, which only at this period was transformed from the spoken tongue of the peasants to the means of expression of the intelligentsia. This national renaissance created areas of friction and confrontation on two fronts. The first front was that of the relationship between Hungarians (*Magyars*) and other ethnic minorities in the country, the Romanians, the Serbs, and the Slovaks. These comprised nearly one-half of the population of the state, but their status was lower than that of the Hungarians. Nonetheless, so long as the empire's administration had a firm rein on the entire nation, the inferior status of the ethnic minorities vis-à-vis the Hungarians was not apparent. The language of the royal staff was German, while local institutions used Latin. With the advent of the Hungarian national awakening, holders of public office were required to use the language of those who claimed for themselves the greater identification with the state. The minorities could be absorbed into the society of the privileged by adopting the Hungarian language. Some of them chose this path, while the great majority of the Romanians, Serbs, and Slovaks remained faithful to their language and culture and immersed in their original communities. A similar movement, parallel to the Hungarian national awakening, arose among the ethnic minorities, which led to tension and conflict between them and the Hungarians.

The second area of conflict created by the Hungarian national awakening was with the Austrian royal house. A tenet of the new nationalistic doctrine was the wide-ranging autonomy of governmental institutions as a precondition for the renaissance of the society. In practice, this meant loosening the bonds with Austria, or, in the extreme view, severing all ties. The issue of the link to Austria hung in the air throughout the entire reform period, until the outbreak of revolution in 1848, when the extremists gained the upper hand and declared the severance of ties with Austria and independence from the House of Hapsburg. This revolution was part of a phenomenon that originated in France and engulfed Germany and the entire Austrian Empire.

As we know, the pan-Europe revolution was suppressed. The Hungarians were the last to surrender, in the summer of 1849, and they paid the highest price for their daring. The Austrians took over the country, and for an entire decade suppressed any expression of political independence or of Hungarian nationalism. This changed only in the wake of the Austrian defeats on the battlefield against Italy in 1859, and against Prussia in 1866. The Hungarians then gained a limited measure of political independence, the result of a compromise with the Austrians, which was accepted by the moderates in the nation, who now had the upper hand.

The Jews of Hungary participated in all these events, at times actively and at times passively, but always with a significant effect upon their fate. It may be said that Hungarian Jewry as a whole, as it appears in the nineteenth century, is the product of the historical process undergone by society and government in Hungary in this period. The basic demographic statistics attest to this. The Jewish community grew from one hundred thousand people at the end of the eighteenth century, to about half a million by 1867, the year of the Austrian compromise and the emancipation of the Jews. This tremendous increase was due partly to the improvement in the national standard of living; to the move from villages and estates to cities and centers of trade and industry; and to increased immigration from neighboring lands, Galicia in the north and Bohemia and Moravia in the west. Many new communities arose in the wake of this dynamic process, and old ones changed their composition and character. A by-product of this process were the contrasts that arose between regions and communities, and even between different sectors within the same communities. These were caused by the differing backgrounds of the immigrants, and by differing positions concerning religious matters, for the days of religious unity and uniformity had passed from the world.[2] The first cracks in the walls of tradition were already apparent in the first third of the century. The struggle of the Hatam Sofer against the *maskilim* (enlighteners) and the first budding of Reform during his service in Pressburg (1806–1839), in particular his attack against Aaron Chorin in the latter's city of Arad, are well known. At that time, the Hatam Sofer still believed he could arrest the phenomenon by the force of his personality, and, in times of need, by turning to the government for assistance.[3] This aid was not available to the religious leaders who succeeded him. The process of modernization, by which the Jews gained the right of untrammeled activity in the economic field, included granting freedom to individuals to act as they wished in matters of religion. Their mobility, their abandonment of traditional places of habitation, and their shift to new forms of employment, which for the most part also enabled them to ascend the social ladder, served as a challenge and temptation to free themselves to some extent from the burden of religious tradition.

This new reality was the opportunity for Jewry as a whole to extricate itself from its inferior status. The permission given in 1840 to Jews to settle throughout the land was interpreted as the first step towards granting them citizenship and equal rights, as had been done in France and several of the German states. There were also those—not only Jews but patriotic Hungarians as well—who went farther and hoped that the process would end with the integration and absorption of the Jews into the Hungarian nation. These voiced the demand that the Jews adopt the national language, just as was demanded of the ethnic minorities. But this demand was greater for the Jews: The adoption of the Hungarian language by a Romanian or Serb paved the way for his cultural absorption by way of social ties and marriage. This was not the case for the Jews, whose customs and religious practices created a barrier between them and their neighbors. Thus, another condition was added: if the Jews wished to be absorbed into the Hungarian nation, they must enact basic reforms in their religious laws. This idea was publicly voiced by the person who became the national leader during the revolution, Lajos Kossuth, and it no doubt reflected the view of the radical revolutionary camp.[4] Just as these revolutionaries were extreme in their political demands, so were they in their expectations of change on the social level.

The spirit of revolution seized Jewish society as well, and some of its members responded to the demands of the radical revolutionaries. Societies were formed by young people who announced that they would no longer observe the ritual commandments, including the Sabbath and circumcision. Their members resigned from the general community and formed synagogues like those of the extreme Reform in Germany. Such a synagogue was established in the capital by Ignác Einhorn, at the outbreak of the revolution, and similar societies sprang up in Nagyvárad and Pécs and in some other communities.[5] This was the only period in which Reform, in the full meaning of the word, found a foothold among the Jews of Hungary. And, just as it arose on the waves of revolutionary enthusiasm, so it disappeared with the decline of this enthusiasm. Einhorn's synagogue in Budapest was closed by the order of the Austrian authorities who, not content with suppressing the revolution, wished to eradicate any of its remnants.[6] In other places, these societies dissolved by themselves, under pressure of the conservative atmosphere that prevailed in the wake of the failure of the revolution.

The government was now put in the hands of the army and the Austrian bureaucracy. They acted in the name of the young kaiser, Franz Joseph, who claimed absolute power over the nations of his kingdom, as heir to the House of Hapsburg. The kaiser's emissaries ruled with a heavy hand over the Hungarians, who had attempted to shake off their rule: The leaders of the revolution, who had surrendered, were executed; fines were imposed on parts of the population; and, most important, any vestige of political independence was removed. Most of the Jews were also found guilty of supporting the revolution, either physically or financially, and they were fined 2.3 million florins. Their institutions were put under strict supervision, and even the community officials were generally appointed by the emperor's representatives, rather than being chosen by the community.

Nonetheless, the absolute Austrian regime, which continued through the 1850s, was not solely detrimental to the Hungarians, and de facto it became a decisive stage in the emergence of Jewry from its restricted conditions—economically, socially, and culturally. The goal of the Austrians was to swallow up Hungary within the empire and to make it one of the many provinces of the realm. Therefore, they encouraged the modernization of the state, improved transportation, initiated new methods in agriculture and industry, and in particular, encouraged financial investments and enterprise.[7] The Jews who were involved in this process enjoyed the economic prosperity it brought. Indeed, we are witness in the 1850s to the unprecedented economic and social betterment of Jewish individuals, families, and an entire stratum.

And while the Jews benefited only indirectly from this economic policy in the spheres of education and culture, the authorities attempted to further their interests directly. The accelerated modernization of the state demanded an improvement in the level of the educational institutions, which for the most part were run separately by the members of the churches of each religious body. The educational institutions of the Jewish community were the *heder* and the *yeshivah*. The *heder*, or religious elementary school, was meant for the entire population, and the *yeshivah*, or rabbinical school, for the elite of Torah learning, from whose ranks came the religious leadership—the rabbis and the other religious functionaries. Alongside the *heder*, which concerned itself primarily with religious studies, there existed here and there schools which taught also—or primarily—general studies. These were few, about thirty throughout the entire country, and their quality was low.[8] Wealthy families could employ private tutors to provide their children with the knowledge needed for their advancement in life. The authorities, on the other hand, were anxious that the entire Jewish public be freed of the restrictions of an exclusively Jewish education. Immediately after the revolution, with the consolidation of Austrian rule, the leaders of the communities, rabbis, and functionaries, were called upon to produce a description of the educational institutions in their towns for the governmental representatives in the capital. This was one of several ways in which the government expressed its interest in the situation of the Jewish communities and the tendencies prevailing within them.[9] Let us note the report of R. Meir Eisenstädter (Maharam Ash), one of the Hatam Sofer's leading students (R. Meir had studied with the Hatam Sofer while the latter was still rabbi of Mattesdorf and was now the rabbi of Ungvár). He suggested leaving the educational institutions as they were, at most adding the necessary general studies to the religious curriculum, but employing only non-Jewish instructors for these. However, most of the reports to the authorities advocated the establishment of schools. This suggestion was in line with the government's policy and it acted accordingly. During that same year, 1850, an order was given to the Jewish communities throughout the land, to open schools which would replace the *hadarim*. The emperor's interest in and support of this plan is evident from his agreement to forgo the fine levied on the Jews if they would instead establish a fund of one million florins to be dedicated to the establishment of a rabbinical seminary, and for aid to schools in those communties that could not afford to support such institutions on their own.

The authorities had an additional interest in the existence of the schools, aside from preparing the Jewish public to take a more active part in the modernization of the society and economy. The hegemony of Austria over Hungary, as conceived by those in power, also meant the strengthening of the German elements of Hungarian culture. German culture was deeply rooted in Hungary, but it had been pushed aside by the tide of national awakening that preceded the revolution. Now the Austrian rulers wished to tip the scales in favor of their culture, and the natural choice for implementation of this policy was the Jews. Since the various ethnic groups were allowed to choose their own language as the language of their schools,[10] and the spoken language among the Jews, Yiddish or Yiddish-German, was considered a dialect of German, it was understood that the language of instruction in schools set up in place of the *hadarim* would be German. The teachers who received employment in the schools were usually immigrants who had recently arrived from the western districts of the empire, Bohemia and Moravia, the place of origin of many of the students' parents. At times it seemed as if the Jews were the only transmitters of German culture among a population that spoke Hungarian or Slovak.[11]

The educational program of the government was very successful. During the 1850s the number of Jewish schools rose rapidly, from thirty to three hundred.[12] These institutions brought about a gradual and quiet cultural revolution in the cities and districts in which they were established, and not only in the sphere of language. An entire generation arose that did not know the atmosphere of the *heder*, saturated as it was with the values of an intimate Jewish tradition. The three or four years of a child's education passed under the hand of an enlightened teacher. Although this new education introduced the child to basic Jewish sources, it did not do so in the special Jewish language, and these sources were not the only ones from which the child drew the elements of his identity and to which he related emotionally. Unlike the *heder*, the new school added general studies to the religious studies, in order to aid the child to find his place in the non-Jewish world, and in order to make him identify with the personalities and concerns of this foreign world.

Escape from the confines of the closed Jewish world was of course the purpose of the new education, and if those involved, the parents and the religious leaders, were aware of the danger it presented to adherence to Judaism, they were probably unable to oppose it. The hand of the authorities was heavy upon all during those years, not just on Jews. When the order was given to replace the *hadarim* with schools, the Jewish officials heeded it, even if it was not to their liking.

However, not all places were equally reluctant to give up the old system of education, or equally able to retain it despite the authorities. There were communities that established schools at their own initiative, before the intervention of the authorities, such as Arad in the south, Nagykanizsa in the southwest, and Liptószentmiklós in the northwest.[13] It is true that these also preceded most of the communities in introducing changes demanded by the times, primarily in the religious sphere, about which we shall hear shortly. However, even a conservative community such as that of Eisenstadt, when it invited Dr. Esriel Hildesheimer of Halberstadt, Germany, to fill the rabbinic post and improve the state of education, was no doubt aware that this reform involved establishing a school to replace the four *hadarim* of the community. Indeed, we later hear from the rabbi himself that he required only two weeks after reaching Eisenstadt to gather the financial backing to establish the community school, which means that people of means and standing in the community were ready and able to take this decisive step.[14]

It seems that the barriers that had previously insulated the communities in the northwestern counties of the state, generally called the Oberland, from contact with the surrounding culture, had long since begun to weaken. All branches of the community, including the conservative, accepted the situation, and attempted to use the new educational instrument, the school, for their respective purposes.

The situation was different in the northeastern part of the country, the Unterland. Most of its Jewish inhabitants came from Galicia and spoke Yiddish, and many of them practiced a Hassidic lifestyle, which involved unique cultural symbols of a special Jewish nature. On the one hand, the reluctance to give up the symbols of the Jewish experience, especially in the area of education, which had ensured the preservation of the community for generations, was much greater here than in the Oberland. This reluctance was shared by the lower levels of society and by the rabbinic leadership, and not by the wealthy and intellectuals, or would-be intellectuals, who were active in some of the cities, as we shall see. They did not use the communal educational institutions, but employed private teachers, or sent their children to non-Jewish high schools. On the other hand, those who hesitated to give up the traditional education had no trouble evading the directives of the authorities. The northeastern counties preserved their feudal nature to a greater extent than the other parts of the land, and one of the signs of this was the weaker enforcement of the directives of the central authority. Those appointed to supervise could overlook the failure to observe the law, either because of their own negligence or because they were bribed. In any event, the fact is that during the years when the school set its stamp upon an entire generation in most districts of the country, the character of the children of the Unterland was formed by the language and culture of the *heder*.[15]

Chapter 4

The Emergence and Characteristics of the Neolog Movement

The aforementioned governmental request to the representatives of the Jewish community to describe the state of their communities, and to express their wishes for the future concerned not only educational matters. The state of Judaism and its future prospects also interested the authorities. R. Meir Eisenstädter's response was unusual in this respect as well. The rabbi apparently believed that the Austrian suppression of the revolution would bring about the return of a pre-Reform state of affairs, and he therefore dared to request the authorities' assistance in compelling those who deviate from religious customs to mend their ways, as was customary at the time of the Hatam Sofer.[1] However, he was mistaken. The authorities were not interested in overt religious reforms and, as we saw, they acted to uproot these. But they had similar reservations concerning the conservative tendency to adhere to tradition in all its details. They viewed this as an obstacle to the integration of Jews into society and to their maximum contribution to economic development.

This governmental interest was directly expressed in the reaction of the authorities to the letters sent by the communal leaders. They decided to establish a committee to formulate a sort of constitution for administering the Jewish communities. This committee gathered in the capital in November 1851. It was comprised of four rabbis and three laymen, all known to favor, to differing extents, the modernization of Jewish communal life.[2] The authorities did not see fit to include a representative of the conservative wing, to wit, they did not wish to encourage the conservative tendency. Encouragement was instead given to the moderate wing, which hovered between the conservatives and reformers, represented by three rabbis on the committee, of whom we shall hear below: Loeb Schwab, rabbi of Pest, his son-in-law, Leopold Löw of Szeged, and Meir Zipser of Székesfehérvár. Leopold Löw in principle supported real reforms, but, as he himself later admitted, he took into consideration the constraints imposed by the times.³ He was the most learned among the rabbis on the committee, none of whom were to be taken lightly, and was appointed to formulate the proposal for the constitution that was meant to serve as the basis for Jewish communal life in the future. For some reason, the constitution was not ratified by the government, and its historical importance is the evidence it provides for the consolidation of the Neolog wing, both in theory and in practice.

Let us now describe the nature of this group, which its Orthodox opponents equated with Reform, but which viewed itself as different from Reform. The Neologs proposed opening the doors of the synagogue to the fresh winds that blew from the non-Jewish world, bringing the spirit both of civic freedom and of aesthetics. The response to these should be expressed in the physical structure of the synagogue and its internal structure, in the style of the sermons and the prayers of the precentor and choir, without affecting halakhic norms. The Neologs opposed any infringement on the fundamental religious laws—marital and ritual law, and especially the Jewish calendar, the Sabbath, and the holidays. The reforms that the committee proposed were, for the most part, already practiced in the communities over which the committee members presided, and they wished them to be accepted in other congregations as well, either voluntarily or by governmental decree. However, the members of the committee were well aware that government aid would be useless if the reforms did not receive the blessing of the local rabbis, which could not be taken for granted. Indeed, a complementary and crucial part of the program was gradually to oust the rabbis of the old type, whose world was limited to the knowledge and ideas gained in the *yeshivot*, and to replace them with others who, in addition to their knowledge of the Jewish sources, had earned a general education at a secondary or even at a university level. It was understood that no appropriate *yeshivot* existed for educating this new type of rabbi. The conclusion was therefore obvious, that the *yeshivot* must either add general studies to their curriculum or leave the ordination of rabbis to a new type of institution, a rabbinical seminary. The members of the committee could be sure that on this point their program agreed with the intention of the authorities, for the educational fund that was established in place of the tax after the revolution was primarily intended for the establishment of a rabbinical seminary.

The committee's proposal, the work of Leopold Löw, should be viewed as the practical program of the Neologs. Their reservations about Reform are expressed in the demand that the rabbi must receive testimonials from three known rabbis, which testify to his ability to render decisions on ritual law ("Die Fähigkeit kasuistische Fragen zu entscheiden").⁴ Löw himself was considered, and rightly so, a sharp critic of Orthodoxy, but nonetheless did not support Reform ideology and did not strive to find an alternative to *halakhah* as the basis of Judaism. He also did not distort the meaning of the halakhic sources in seeking a basis for every deviation from accepted norm, as did the first Reformers. If he was asked a halakhic question—and he became *the* authority on religious matters in the eyes of the government, as was the Hatam Sofer in his own time (this is the greatest sign of the changing times)—he answered from the great store of his knowledge, remaining loyal to the letter and spirit of the law.[5] Rather than initiate changes in the religious tradition, Löw apparently hoped that it would change of itself with the spread of higher education, and a more refined sensibility, and especially with the intensification of the scientific study of religion itself. Needless to say, however, that while he detailed the demands of the *halakhah* on any specific matter, he did not see its observance by any individual as a precondition for membership in the Jewish community. One of the basic principles of the Neologs was the abandonment of any attempt to enforce the observance of religious commandments, either by physical force, via the government, or by social coercion applied by the Jewish community itself. This guideline was the basis of Löw's proposals, which were accepted by the committee. We find a defense of this guideline, but also its limitations, spelled out by another member of the committee, Loeb Schwab, the father-in-law of the author of the proposals.[6]

In the throes of the revolution, in the summer of 1848, when Ignác Einhorn and his circle founded the Reform synagogue, Schwab was asked, as rabbi of Pest, how the community should react: Should the leadership acknowledge them as a minority, despite their deviation from the religious guidelines of the majority? Schwab rejected this vehemently. A circle that announced the abolition of circumcision and the transfer of the Sabbath to Sunday, thus renouncing two clear hallmarks of Judaism from antiquity, had removed itself from the Jewish community, and could not be considered part of it.[7] However, there were two arguments against this unequivocal decision, and Schwab saw the need to respond to them. The first, that certain hallmarks that had until recent generations been considered typical of Jewish ritual—the reference was to the location of the *bimah* in the center of the synagogue, and that of the marriage canopy outside the synagogue—had been changed in his community, as in other communities, with his consent and that of his progressive fellow rabbis. To this Schwab responded that these changes not only did not impinge on religious fundamentals, but actually removed some accretions and distortions that had become attached to them with the passing of time; now, with the growth of culture, and the increasingly refined sensibilities of our time, they must be removed. Schwab could not ignore the fact that deviations from basic Jewish customs, for which members of the Reform movement were criticized, were also found in his community, as in other similar ones. Many had cast off the burden of religion, profaning the Sabbath, and failing to abide by the laws of *kashrut* and the like. What, then, was the difference between them and the Reformers? This was the second argument to which Schwab referred. In his response,

Schwab relied on the difference between those who transgress under the influence of various temptations, and those who consciously and arrogantly reject the religious laws. These types differ from each other not only in their motives but also in their objective state. Those who are tempted as the result of weakness will likely repent; their deviations do not constitute a declaration of having left the community. Those who proclaim their abandonment of the religious laws with conscious forethought, however, are considered to be incorrigible.[8]

As an ideologue, Schwab wished to support the Neolog position from both ends: on the one hand asserting the necessity for aesthetic changes as a requirement of the time, and on the other hand opposing an ideological uprooting of the *halakhah*, while accepting its infringement by individuals. In retrospect, we must wonder at the historical background of this theory, which contains an inherent contradiction.

As stated, the modernization of Hungary, from the reform period onward, made new means of livelihood available for Jews. This change raised religious-halakhic problems which had no precedent under the former conditions. Some of these arose as early as the first decades of the century, but they became a widespread and daily phenomenon only in 1840, with the granting of permission to Jews to settle in the cities.

The difficulties confronting the urban merchant who wished to observe the religious laws were many times greater than those facing the villager, whether he was a tenant farmer or supplied the needs of the peasants as a storekeeper or innkeeper. The city dweller who changed his place of work from the Jewish quarter to the general market was also confronted by new difficulties. Previously, his customers had come to him, or he had set out to peddle his wares when he wished. Now he had to accustom himself to the hours of the market, which were determined by others. Those practicing the traditionally Jewish professions had the benefit of religious guidelines, established by custom. Only on rare occasions did they require guidance for problems that had no ready precedent. This was not the case in the new situation, which afforded the Jew sources of livelihood involving desecration of the Sabbath, or transgression of other religious boundaries. When approached for advice, the halakhist could not always find a modus vivendi for preserving the laws of the Sabbath, *kashrut*, and other laws, without damaging the chances for profit.[9] In truth, not all those who found themselves in such a dilemma turned to the halakhist for guidance. There was no objective need to do so, for the time had long passed when rabbis or community leaders had authority over the behavior of individuals. Someone whose personal commitment to the religious tradition was not strong enough to bear a clear financial loss could solve his problem by ignoring religious demands, at least in economic issues. Within a short time after the major transformation in the political status of the community, with the granting of permission to settle in the cities, this became a prevalent pattern of behavior among the public. Many testimonies by contemporaries attest to this.

The writer of the *Allgemeine Zeitung des Judenthums* reports with sorrow in 1862 on the desecration of the Sabbath, which had become a widespread phenomenon in the preceding decade, even in the villages. He mentions Szeged, Temesvár, Arad, and Nagyvárad among such cities. According to him, rich wholesalers and simple shopkeepers were equally guilty.[10] The cities mentioned are located in central Hungary, containing Jewish communities that had been founded before Jews were permitted to settle in all the cities. That this was not a factor is proved from what we hear about two widely separated cities, Dunaföldvár on the right bank of the Danube, and Szarvas in the center of the country. The Jewish communities in these cities were founded only in the 1840s, and here too the rabbis cried out in vain against widespread desecration of the Sabbath. From the continuation of the story, it emerges that the deciding factor was the economic one. In both places, the rabbis succeeded in persuading the authorities to change the weekly market day from Saturday to one of the weekdays, and thus rescued the Sabbath.[11] Some thought to prevail upon the central authorities to take the Jewish days of rest into consideration in setting the market days. At the inauguration of the Jewish Congress in 1868, one of the representatives proposed putting this topic on the agenda. From the heated discussion of this topic in the closed session of the Congress, we learn of the severity of the situation, but also of the leaders' inability to make a concerted effort to repair it.[12] Even Hildesheimer, who did not ignore the practical difficulties of Sabbath observance and wished to help those who desired to overcome these difficulties, by setting up a society that would support them, did not achieve any visible results.[13]

Although the breach in the walls of religion and tradition came about as the result of economic factors, once the breach occurred, it was destined to widen beyond what these factors required. Moreover, economics was not the only reason for the breach; social ambition often led to the same result. In many cities, social circles, called casinos, had already been founded in the reform period, as meeting places for members of different social strata, who had hitherto led totally separate social lives. As Michael Silber proved in an insightful article, these clubs were at times open to Jews as well, and it goes without saying that membership in them meant abandoning Jewish laws concerning food and drink, and the like.[14] This trend penetrated to the Jewish home as well. In Nagyvárad and some other communities, the congregation's main source of income was the tax it levied on kosher meat; this method was now found to be financially unviable, for some of the rich people had stopped buying their meat in Jewish butcher shops.[15]

A generation or two earlier, transgressors of such prohibitions would have been ejected from the congregation, with no choice but to convert. It happened, of course, in this period as well, that estrangement from the community of origin brought about conversion; the extent of this phenomenon is a subject worthy of study, but this is not the place for it.[16] It is certain that conversion did not come about under pressure from the community's refusal to tolerate sinners in its midst: those who were more or less nonobservant in their private lives remained members of the community. At times they even gained positions of leadership, especially under the neo-absolutist Austrian regime, for the governmental representatives supported the community leaders. The fact that transgressors of the religious laws remained in the community gave birth to social tension between them and those who continued to view observance of the commandments and of the Jewish customs as the precondition of membership in the Jewish community. Moreover, the situation created a psychological problem for the nonobservant. It is a tenet of social psychology that people aspire to maximum harmony between their personal ideas and behavior and the expectations of their environment. If this harmony is disrupted by a change in one of the factors of the situation, those involved will do their utmost to achieve a new balance.[17] And there is no greater disruption of harmony than the presence of nonobservers within a community of the faithful. Nonobservers could not leave the community without converting, because the law of the land obligated every person to belong to one of the recognized religions; the obvious solution therefore was to change the nature of the community to the extent that it cease to demand full adherence to the commandments as a condition of membership.

In my opinion, the aspiration to create harmony between public behavior and the injunctions of the *halakhah* also played a certain part in the creation of the Reform movement in Germany. It is true that the leaders of the movement, most of them rabbis with an academic education, took a critical approach to the tradition, distinguishing between the important and unimportant on the basis of various criteria—biblical versus talmudic, religious versus national, and the like. The rise of this type of rabbi was the culmination of a process lasting about three generations. Between the death of Mendelssohn in 1786, at which time the walls had already been breached, and the first Reform Rabbinical Assembly in Braunschweig in 1844, fifty-eight years had passed. During this time a stratum of intellectuals had arisen in the communities which was ready and willing to identify with the principles of Reform; some of these even took part in developing them.[18] However, most of the members of the Jewish communities, although they preferred Reform rabbis to the traditional ones, did not identify with all their tendencies. For most it was enough to institute changes like those adopted by the Neologs in Hungary, which symbolically demonstrated their release from subjection to the strictures of religion in their private lives.

In contrast, even during the revolution, only a few exceptional Hungarian rabbis supported Reform on an intellectual basis. After the revolution, conditions did not support the rise of this type of rabbi. Even the moderate reforms that were widespread in the communities were only rarely carried out at the initiative of these rabbis. They were usually introduced by the householders. And so we can arrive at a social characterization of the Neolog movement in Hungary. It differed from the Reform movement not only in the moderate nature of its demands, but also in its social representatives. While the intellectuals carried the Reform movement on their shoulders, the Neolog movement relied on the householders and was spurred on by them. They were not motivated by an intellectual critique of tradition. They were propelled to action by the force of their experiences on the social and economic level. They were moved to transgress religious laws and customs by economic needs and social temptations. If they wished to diffuse the social and psychic tension created by this, there was no easier way to do so than to demonstrate publicly that they were moving with the times, and moderating the demands of religion.

The initiative for change generally came from the leaders of the community. They had previously been the ones to ensure the observance of religious laws by the entire community. Now, even if they themselves were not among the nonobservant, they felt it necessary to wink at the religious deviations of their fellows. The institution of changes in the synagogue served as a notice to the rabbi of the city, be he an incumbent of long standing or one who was about to be chosen, that he must abandon his role as supervisor of the religious behavior of individuals, a role maintained by rabbis of the previous generations. Except for certain cases, where changes were initiated by the local rabbi, most communities introduced changes with traditional rabbis in office, sometimes even despite their express opposition. This was the case, for example, with R. Solomon Ullmann in Makó, and R. Isaac Moses Perls in Bonyhád.[19] Other rabbis acquiesced in the changes, while attempting to minimize them, so that they did not infringe upon the Shulhan Arukh (Jewish Code of Law). We shall read of the rabbi of Miskolc, R. Ezekiel Moses Fischman, who explained his agreement to the changes made by claiming that he had thereby succeeded in preventing more extensive reforms,[20] and he was not the only one to take such a position. R. Israel David Margoliot, author of *Meholat ha-Mahanayim*, who had no equal in his fight against aesthetic changes, as we shall see, testifies that: "Some great scholars who cried out against placing the marriage canopy in the synagogue [one of the changes which was the subject of controversy], later themselves put the canopy in the synagogue when their congregants gained the upper hand." The reason they gave: "In order that the marriage not be performed by one who does not know the laws."[21] A similar testimony was offered by R. Isaac Nathan Lipschitz, rabbi of Abaujszántó, to the effect that "some righteous and just men," who could not prevent the building of a synagogue in the new style, prayed in it after the fact.[22]

However, this readiness to compromise with reforms was a passing phenomenon. It disappeared with a crystallization of the reaction by the faithful to modernization. From then on they did not distinguish between an infringement upon the fundamental laws through reform and a deviation from the traditional patterns that were only a matter of custom.

Chapter 5

The Reaction of the Pious, "Oberland"-Style

This blurring of a rabbinic and a biblical injunction, or a talmudic prohibition and one rooted in custom alone, had a precedent in the doctrine of the Hatam Sofer, who viewed it as a method for shoring up the wall of tradition. So, for example, he transformed the second day of the festivals, celebrated in the Diaspora, whose post-biblical source is evident, into a biblical law. Similarly, the prohibition against eating *qitniyot* (beans, rice, and other starches from which flour could be made) on Passover, an Ashkenazic injunction, underwent a metamorphosis from a custom to a prohibition anchored in talmudic law.[1] In general, these customs belong phenomenologically to the religious sphere. At times, however, the Hatam Sofer went even farther, attempting to endow purely cultural phenomena with a halakhic basis. This is the case with the preference for Yiddish-German over standard German. In a responsum sent to Loeb Schwab and his *beit din* in Pest in 1839, the Hatam Sofer's last year, he remarks in an aside: "And in my opinion, the ancients were also versed in foreign languages, but deliberately distorted these languages because of the eighteen decrees [whose purpose was to distance Jews from their non-Jewish surroundings] in PT Sabbath, chapter 1 '... and concerning their language.'"[2] To wit, a special Jewish language was introduced deliberately, in accordance with a talmudic source. We shall see below how those who wished to preserve a special spoken Jewish language, used in their area of the Unterland, relied on their illustrious teacher's words. They considered this statement a halakhic judgment in the fullest sense. In reality, this is a typical case of giving halakhic weight to a precautionary measure, when considered necessary by the halakhist. The halakhic argument does not follow the accepted rules of adjudication, as the Hatam Sofer's major student, Maharam Schick, proved. We shall hear more of this.[3] The Hatam Sofer wished to circumscribe the use of German, especially in the rabbinic sermon, partly because of his general conservatism, but primarily because knowledge of German was gained through the study of secular and heretical literature. He had good reason for mentioning in one breath the two requirements for a rabbi in his testament to his community: "That he not study heretical literature, and that he not sermonize in the gentile tongue." He then goes on to describe the desirable kind of sermon: "But in the style that you have heard from me, sermons and homilies of the Sages."[4] The Hatam Sofer wished to prevent the spread of the new type of sermon, aimed at edification alone, which had become entrenched in his native land of Germany, and had spread near Pressburg as well, in places like Vienna, where Isaac Noah Mannheimer used it with great success from 1824, when he was appointed preacher.[5] Those who preached the new type of sermon were suspected, often with good reason, of Reform tendencies.

Even in the early 1850s conservative rabbis apparently attempted to prevent German-speaking rabbis with a background of general culture from entering their territory, even if they fulfilled all other criteria for the posts. From a reporter for the *Allgemeine Zeitung des Judenthums*, who was none other than Leopold Löw,[6] we learn that a group of traditionalist rabbis made a pact not to grant ordination to anyone who would preach in German. According to the same source, one of them, R. Judah Aszód, was sent to R. Samson Raphael Hirsch, while the latter was still in Nikolsburg, to request that he refrain from ordaining a specific candidate from Hungary, and the latter agreed. We do not know if this is literally true but it is not plucked from thin air. From another source, a letter sent by R. Meir Eisenstädter (Maharam Ash) of Ungvár to R. Judah Aszod, we know that both of them were afraid of Hirsch's possible influence on the situation in Hungary.[7] The former thought of writing to Hirsch when he came to Nikolsburg, but refrained from doing so.

The efforts of the traditionalist rabbis to place obstacles before the change in language was a sort of rearguard battle. In the generation following the Hatam Sofer, that is, in the 1840s–1850s, Yiddish-German was pushed aside, to some extent in favor of Hungarian and primarily—especially in the second decade, under Austrian rule—in favor of German. The similarity between "the western Yiddish dialect . . . and German" was great enough so that the introduction of German as the language of instruction in the schools, and the practical need for mastering the language of the rulers, were sufficient to turn German into both the spoken and the written language of the entire Jewish population. The conservatives still preferred to write in the Hebrew alphabet, but their vocabulary and grammar were really standard German.[8] Knowledge of German created a bridge to the Western intellectual currents, and as the regular readership of the *Allgemeine Zeitung des Judenthums* grew in progressive circles, so were there readers of *Der treue Zions-Wächter* (*Shomer Zion ha-Ne'eman*) in conservative circles.[9] This journal, inspired and directed by R. Jacob Ettlinger of Altona, was active from 1845 on. R. Samson Raphael Hirsch's monthly, *Jeschurun*, appeared in Frankfurt from 1855, and five years later was joined by the weekly, *Israelit*, edited by Markus Lehmann in Mainz. The two latter journals served as a vehicle for transmitting news from conservative circles in Hungary, and, because of the influence of their editors, especially Hirsch, on events in Hungary, we shall use them frequently.

Hirsch's geographical distance from Hungary did not prevent contact with him. On the contrary, his success in establishing an exemplary traditional community in Frankfurt while maintaining an openness to the surrounding culture, made him an ideal type, worthy of emulation. He became an authority for many in Hungary, and Leopold Löw attests that he saw a responsum by Hirsch to the community of Baja, regarding a certain candidate for the rabbinate.[10] In this chapter, and to a greater extent in the next chapter, we shall see the traces of Hirsch's contact with personalities and institutions in Hungary, and the deep impression made by his ideas. This affinity should not surprise us, for there was much similarity between the situation in western Hungary in this period and the background to Hirsch's thought development. The political, social, and cultural bonds that had previously tied the individual to his community were disintegrating. Willy nilly, the Jew became—via his profession, his mastery of the language of the surrounding culture, and his vulnerability to the problems of society, culture, and nation—a citizen, at least partly, of a world that was not his. As we have seen, those who deviated from the Jewish way of life under the pressure of these conditions solved their problem by limiting the demands of religion along Reform principles, or by reducing the authority of religion to uphold its demands, as in the Neolog method.

Orthodoxy reacted to the new reality in the opposite way. Because the Jew was now part of a world that was not his, it was incumbent upon him to observe all the religious safeguards if he wished to remain faithful to his destiny and faith. Involvement in the non-Jewish world meant relinquishing the external signs of Jewish appearance, language, clothing, and at times even physiognomy (shaving the beard). These external signs had formerly been considered tokens of the individual's membership in his community and testimony to his identification with his faith. Nonetheless, these were not actually anchored in halakhic sources, and they could be abandoned with the changing conditions. In contrast, everything, without distinction, that was considered a halakhic edict was made absolutely obligatory by the Orthodox. This is not surprising, for Orthodoxy sought a criterion by which the believer would be set apart from others, and his cultural assimilation to the environment made absolute subjection to *halakhah* the only remaining watchword. This position found its linguistic expression in the creation of the term *gesetzestreu*, that is, faithful to the law, which originated in Germany, but also became part of the vocabulary of Hungarian Orthodox spokesmen.[11]

Another consequence of Orthodox acculturation was expressed in the need and ability to endow the details of Jewish ritual with a symbolic significance in terms drawn from contemporary non-Jewish sources. This tendency also originated in Germany, and its most outstanding cultivator was once again Samson Raphael Hirsch.[12] But a representative of this tendency was found in Hungary as well. R. Margoliot, author of *Meholat ha-Mahanayim*, finds many spiritual allusions, borrowed from popular scientific literature, in the details of the customs and ceremonies that the Neologs wished to eradicate.[13] The paradox is that acculturation in the Reform and Neolog camp brought about the collapse of *halakhah*, while it served to strengthen and entrench the *halakhah* in the opposition camp. Glorification of the *halakhah* was not a literary phenomenon alone. It became a factor in historical terms as well, as emerges from the course of events in one of the communities of western Hungary, Székesfehérvár (in German, Stuhlweissenburg).

Székesfehérvár is one of the oldest cities in Hungary. It is located west of the Danube, not far from the capital. In the Middle Ages it was the city where the king was crowned. It contained a Jewish community during that period, but it had ceased to exist long before the modern period. The new community was created only after permission was granted to the Jews to settle in the cities in 1840, and it quickly grew. During the period of modernization, the city became a commercial center and drew Jews both from the surrounding villages, and from afar, from other communities in the country and outside it.[14] Since it had no local tradition, its rabbi, Meir Zipser, who was appointed in 1844 soon after the founding of the community, felt that he could act as he saw fit in the religious sphere.[15]

We have already encountered Zipser as one of the rabbis to whom the government turned for aid in encouraging the modernization of the Jewish community.[16] Indeed, he was one of those few rabbis, especially among the natives, who identified with moderate reform, better called Neologism. He had gained his Jewish knowledge in the *yeshivot* of Moravia (Prossnitz, Nikolsburg), where he also became acquainted with the Haskalah. Upon returning to his land, he served as a tutor in the houses of the wealthy in the capital. He enjoyed the friendship of the rabbi of the city, Loeb Schwab, and was greatly influenced by him. At the same time, he became acquainted with the scientific methods of *Wissenschaft des Judentums*, to the extent of being able to make an authentic contribution to its findings. Zipser enacted reforms in his community with the examples of the western communities in mind. He copied from them what he thought would guarantee order, dignity, and discipline, and enhance the prayer service and religious ceremonies.[17] The liturgical text was left unchanged, but the prayer for the king and government was now said in Hungarian, and the phrase, "May He avenge before our eyes the blood of your servants which has been spilt" (from the *Avinu Malkenu* prayer), was omitted. Both changes expressed the sense that a major turning point had been reached in the history of the Jewish community: It was moving towards integration into the Hungarian nation, and was shaking off the traditionally hostile attitude of its surroundings.

This was one of the few cases in Hungary where the initiative for reform came from the rabbi of the community and not from the householders. Zipser no doubt believed that although his reforms deviated from the accepted custom in traditional congregations, they adhered to halakhic norms. There is no evidence that his changes aroused opposition within the community. They were approved by the city officials, as was customary, and peace reigned between the rabbi and his congregation. However, in time, the congregation was joined by new members, among them conservatives for whom any deviation from the prevailing norm was tantamount to abandonment of the tradition. One of these was Gottlieb Fischer, a learned man who had studied at the school of the Hatam Sofer. Fischer's reservations about the rabbi's reforms were evidenced by his desire to hold a private service in his home, but such a service was forbidden by the communal regulations.[18] And so, a conservative faction coalesced around Fischer, composed of people who were unhappy with the rabbi's leadership, and watched his steps with critical eyes. A writ of divorce arranged by the rabbi gave his opponents an excuse to come out against him and undermine his position.[19]

Since the Székesfehérvár community was new, there was no clear tradition about the spelling of the name of the city in a writ of divorce. In such cases, scrupulous halakhists refrained from writing a writ of divorce in such a town, or first turned to one of the great rabbis for guidance. Zipser decided the issue without consulting anyone. Moreover, it was accepted throughout the Ashkenazic congregations that whoever arranges a divorce should attach two other rabbis to himself to form a *beit din*, in whose presence the divorce ceremony would take place. This custom had no roots in the Talmud, but it was endorsed by the greatest of the eighteenth-century halakhists, R. Ezekiel Landau of Prague, author of the *Noda' bi-Yehudah*. Zipser did not ignore this custom, but he was not scrupulous in honoring its details. One of the members of *beit din* was his brother; a court including two brothers is invalid, but Zipser thought that there was no need to concern himself over its validity, since the presence of a *beit din* at a divorce was not talmudically required. By this deviation from custom he called down upon himself the wrath of the conservatives in the community and, in their wake, of the rabbis of communities near and far.[20]

In his distress, Zipser composed a pamphlet defending his actions (1853),[21] but found no supporters aside from some of his colleagues of a similar modernist bent.[22] His rival and opponent, Gottlieb Fischer, published an entire book (1855) devoted to refuting his arguments, and the latter's publication received the approbation of the rabbis of important congregations, not only in Hungary but in Moravia as well.[23] One of those who supported him, R. Pinehas Loeb Frieden of Komárom, formulated the principle that became the slogan of Zipser's critics: Even if one thousand proofs can be brought from the Talmud that there is no need for a *beit din*, "since it is now a custom, we have no power to change it."[24]

This was the stance taken by Fischer as well. But Fischer did not stop at criticizing Zipser's decision in halakhic terms. He critiqued Zipser for his views on the past and present status of *halakhah*, which Fischer considered heretical, and not without reason. Zipser was one of those who in 1845 was asked by the officials of the Jewish congregation of Pápa, a city near Székesfehérvár, whether aesthetic reforms are permitted by law. He approved most of these, and in doing so, also expressed his views about the status of the prayer service. According to him, it took the place of the sacrifices when they ceased to arouse the religious sensibilities of the public, a view that was considered heretical by the faithful.[25] Fischer also attributed Zipser's leniencies to his unorthodox theories, and in essence disqualified him from serving as a halakhic authority to a congregation of believers. And so, three years after the episode, Zipser left his post in the controversy-ridden congregation. In 1858 he was appointed rabbi of nearby Rohonc (Rechnitz, in German), an old congregation which nevertheless promoted acculturation in keeping with the times; there Zipser could proceed without critics and impediments.

The course of events in Székesfehérvár after the departure of Zipser proves that the conservatives who ousted him were only a minority of the congregation, while the majority, including the elected officials of the congregation, upheld his views even after he departed. These wished to appease the conservative minority by choosing a rabbi considered to be absolutely Orthodox, although he had an academic background. This was R. Joseph Guggenheimer from Aussee, Moravia, the son-in-law of R. Samson Raphael Hirsch of Frankfurt. The connection to the Hirsch household had a decisive influence on his personality: he disappointed his sponsors by favoring the conservatives totally, instead of acting as conciliator between the progressives and the conservatives. He attempted to abolish his predecessor's reforms, to which most of the community had already become accustomed, and which the leadership of the congregation defended.[26] During the two years that Guggenheimer held his post, between 1859 and 1861, the controversy spread beyond the boundaries of the congregation. Both sides requested the opinions of rabbis whom they considered authorities.[27] The conservatives turned to R. Hirsch, and surprisingly enough, he did not disqualify himself from a case that involved his son-in-law. Hirsch upheld Guggenheimer's demands, which entailed eradicating any deviation from the accepted custom.[28]

More serious than the intervention of external Jewish experts, which was in any case futile, was the appeal of both sides, including R. Guggenheimer, to the secular authorities.[29] On the basis of its majority among the electorate (one hundred and fifty versus eighty-eight), the congregational leadership requested the aid of the authorities in forcing the minority to accept the changes approved by the majority.[30] These changes included the reforms initiated by Zipser, which the conservative minority had refused to accept. The conservatives requested of the government that they be permitted to secede from the congregation and to form a separate congregation. In their petition to the authorities, the conservatives listed their reasons. This was the earliest formulation of a separatist Orthodox ideology; let us therefore consider it in detail.[31]

The petitioners list the deviations in the prayer service and rituals which were at the heart of the controversy under the two rabbis, Zipser and Guggenheimer. These arrangements were forced upon them against their conscience. The nature of the deviations or their number are of no account, for "any shift from the letter of the law, be it seemingly insignificant, is to be viewed as apostasy, whose final outcome no one can know."[32] The religious law is formulated in the Torah, the Talmud, and the Shulhan Arukh. A Jewish congregation that wishes to make changes must make sure that they are in the spirit of these fundamental works. If our opponents wish us to remain together with them, the conservatives say, they should submit the controversial changes for approval to rabbis who are of our persuasion. As examples they mention the rabbi of Pressburg, Abraham Samuel Benjamin Sofer, the Ketav Sofer, and the rabbi of Eisenstadt, Esriel Hildesheimer.[33] They add that it is necessary to ensure that any future reforms be subject to similar tests, and no rabbi should be chosen who was not ordained by authoritative rabbis of the sort mentioned above.

Aside from listing the conditions for enacting reforms, the members of the minority expressed their desires concerning the educational system, and these clearly attest to their affinity to the new ideologue of Germany, R. Samson Raphael Hirsch. They tacitly assumed that their children's education would take place in a school (and not a *heder*), and that, aside from Jewish learning, this institution would give its members a general education suitable to the needs of the time and place. In this context, they used the term "social education," a phrase drawn from Hirsch's vocabulary.[34]

The contact between the minority group and Hirsch continued after his son-in-law left Székesfehérvár. The documents relating to their struggle were published in *Jeschurun*, which he edited, with accompanying expressions of sympathy and encouragement by the editor. In November 1862, when the controversy reached the capital, and the lieutenant governor decided in favor of the separatists, Hirsch celebrated their victory with them. They were permitted to establish, at their own expense, all the institutions necessary to provide for their religious needs, and were excused from the payment of parallel taxes to the community. Nonetheless, to the authorities, all the Jews of one place were considered members of one congregation, so one person alone could represent both factions, and he was responsible for registering births and deaths.[35] Upon publishing the decision of the lieutenant governor, Hirsch noted with satisfaction that only an administrative connection remained between the two parts of the congregation, and that the Orthodox had won their desired independence.[36] When the members of the congregation became aware of the difficulties involved in maintaining two systems of services, proposals were made to abolish the separation, with the majority expressing readiness to accommodate the minority. The latter requested Hirsch's guidance, and rejected the proposal at his urging.[37]

Internal and external factors governed the events in Székesfehérvár. They reflect the state of affairs that was created throughout the Oberland, as expressed in the coalescence of Orthodoxy, which upheld its dogmatic subjection to the *halakhah*, while giving up the popular cultural signs of Judaism. The singularity of this state of affairs is even more prominent when juxtaposed with developments in the Unterland, a contrast which brought about clashes between the representatives of the two areas.

Chapter 6

Hassidim and the Zealous in the Unterland

The character of Unterland Jewry was formed primarily by two external factors: its geographical proximity to Galicia, and its economic and political backwardness in relation to other parts of the country, even during the reform period. Because of this backwardness, most Jews remained tied to professions related to the sale of the agricultural produce of the estates, and to supplying the needs of the tenant farmers and their masters, whether they lived close by in the villages and estates, or dwelled in relatively established communities like Ungvár and Munkács.[1] The move to the towns was late in coming. However, the emigration from Galicia continued, and even increased, for despite the relative backwardness of the Unterland, it still provided better opportunities than Galicia, which had suffered severe economic deprivation since its annexation to Austria in the partition of Poland in the late eighteenth century.[2] The new streams of Galician immigrants continued to make their mark on the religious and cultural makeup of the Jewish settlement through the first decades of the nineteenth century.[3] Only towards the middle of the century did Unterland Jewry begin to exhibit a special character of its own, in contrast both to Galicia and to other parts of Hungary, although they were considered one unit in political terms.

The most outstanding expression of the relationship between the Unterland and Galicia was the influence of Hassidism. Large groups of Galician Jews were concentrated around the courts of the *Admorim* (the hassidic rabbis, or rebbes), each group around its spiritual leader. These hassidic centers served the Jews of Hungary as well, in the area close to its northern border. Some of the local people visited the hassidic courts on the other side of the border, either because they had emigrated from there, or because they had heard about this or that rebbe, and they wished to hear his wisdom or receive his blessing. At times, hassidic leaders from Galicia would come to the Hungarian communities and impress the public with their prayers and special customs.[4] In 1808, one of these, R. Moses Teitelbaum, settled permanently in Hungary, upon assuming the post of rabbi of Sátoraljaujhely (Ujhely for short). Although he was also a scholar, the impression he made in his generation, and his influence on later generations are due to his talents as a hassidic charismatic.[5] The city of Ujhely, which is located in the south of the Unterland, was one of the most developed and progressive of the area. It served as a center of trade and industry, largely thanks to the activity of the area's Jews, who had received permission to settle there as early as the beginning of the eighteenth century. During R. Teitelbaum's time, their number reached two thousand—approximately twenty percent of the population.[6] R. Teitelbaum found great support in the city. Many strangers came on business matters and became acquainted with the rabbi. He became famous for his hassidic-style prayer services, and especially for his willingness to distribute amulets, which according to popular belief, could work wonders and forestall harm.

However, the Jewish population, both in the city and in its environs, was not homogeneous, and some opposed the rabbi's ways. Evidence of this may be found in the fact that, after thirty-three years as the Ujhely rabbi—he died in 1841—R. Teitelbaum did not succeed in the final run in bequeathing his post to one of his descendants, and the dynasty he founded moved to Sziget, the main city of the Márámáros county, which borders Galicia and was under its direct influence.[7]

In 1852, after an entire decade of indecision and no small number of disagreements, R. Jeremiah Löw was appointed rabbi of Ujhely, the third generation of great rabbis of Polish and Bohemian origin. He was a complete contrast to his predecessor. First of all, he originated in the Oberland, and his character and horizons carried the imprint of that environment.[8] Second, he had had a certain amount of general education, even though his attention was directed exclusively towards rabbinic learning. He wished to shape private and public life according to the classic Ashkenazic tradition. We shall later find him leading the opponents of those who moved away from the tradition toward Reform, a campaign which took on a national dimension during the 1860s. R. Löw's adherence to classical Ashkenazic Judaism also brought him to reject publicly the hassidic way of life, which he encountered as soon as he arrived in Ujhely. Despite the fact that R. Teitelbaum's descendants had been rejected for the rabbinical post, certain groups within the community remained faithful to his way of life. Moreover, once Hassidism began to become entrenched in Hungary, some of the natives donned the mantle of the *Admor*, and were accepted as hassidic charismatic types by the lower classes. The best known of these after the death of R. Teitelbaum was his student R. Zvi Hirsch Friedman, who served as rabbi in the village of Liszka, near Ujhely.[9] Hordes of the simple folk visited him, as he was considered to be a miracle worker. This phenomenon was a strange one to someone with the background and personality of the new rabbi of Ujhely. It is not surprising that he and the rabbi of Liszka were soon at odds, and the disagreements between them became a byword among the local population.

Despite the gap between the worlds of the Oberland and Unterland, the choice of R. Jeremiah Löw as rabbi of Ujhely was not exceptional. As the Unterland communities grew in the wake of political and economic changes, in particular the Revolution of 1848, they required halakhic masters. These were to be found in great numbers among the graduates of the Oberland *yeshivot*, first and foremost among them the students of the Hatam Sofer.

A whole string of rabbis was called upon to serve in this strange environment. Their degree of acclimatization to their new environment, including their attitude to the hassidic way of life, differed from one to another. If the strangeness of the environment was oppressive to the Oberland natives, they could find compensation in the traditional way of life, which was preserved here, both in private and in public life, to a much greater extent than in the Oberland communities. For those who rejected the cultural accommodation of Oberland Jewry, the Unterland was a refuge. But this could not last forever, and slowly the waves of modernization also reached the shores of the Unterland. At least in some communities in the peripheries of its territory, which were not well established —Miskolc, Kassa, and Eperjes—the walls were breached, and in the early 1860s this was expressed in the desire for aesthetic changes in rituals and religious ceremonies. Controversy soon followed the appearance of the phenomenon in this area, and here it had a form, pace, and dimension all its own. Perhaps it is not surprising that we find the Oberland natives heading the campaign of the conservatives. Before describing the progress of the battle, let us acquaint ourselves with the personalities involved, in the order of their arrival in the Unterland.

The process of absorption of learned men from the Pressburg *yeshivah* into the communities of the Unterland began with the choice of R. Meir Eisentädter, Maharam Ash, as the rabbi of Ungvár. He was appointed in 1835, during the lifetime of the Hatam Sofer, who died in 1839. We have already seen that he wished to follow in his rabbi's footsteps, with respect both to educational matters and to the authority to enforce the religious laws.[10] However, the authorities' verdict on this topic was issued at the beginning of the Austrian neo-absolutist reign, in 1850, immediately after the suppression of the Revolution. The discussion of these issues was theoretical, and dealt with the state of affairs in the country as a whole, without reference to events in the rabbi's locale. By the time local events demanded a reaction, at the end of the decade, Maharam Ash was no longer alive; he died two years after the opinon was given, in 1852. His son, R. Menahem, inherited his position. The latter remained loyal to his father's ways, and we will find him among the leaders of the pious at the outbreak of the controversy.[11]

Toward the end of the decade under discussion, in 1858, R. Hayyim Sofer was accepted as the rabbi of Szentpéter, a small town close to Miskolc. R. Sofer was born in Pressburg, but was not a member of the Hatam Sofer's family. His father, R. Mordechai Ephraim Fishel Sofer, had studied with the Hatam Sofer while the latter was still rabbi of Mattersdorf, and later, in Pressburg, became his friend and confidant throughout the Hatam Sofer's lifetime.[12] R. Fishel Sofer behaved like a Hassid, in the classic sense of the term. He held no rabbinic position, and lived on the meager earnings of his wife and her inheritance. He spent his time on Torah learning, prayer, and righteous deeds, and devoted a great deal of time to teaching children of poor families on a voluntary basis. His sons and daughters grew up in this pious atmosphere. His sons were, like him, students of the Hatam Sofer, and five of them received ordination and became rabbis of important communities. Their character was molded by their father and mentor. He succeeded in implanting in them the ideal of exclusive pursuit of Torah study, which should be pursued even at the price of extreme poverty. This ideal entailed an explicit rejection of the hassidic way of life, news of which had reached even Pressburg, because of the waste of study time involved.[13] All the more so did it reject the call by the *maskilim*, even the moderate among them, for general studies to be pursued during one's free time. Nonetheless, the most talented and independent of the sons, Hayyim Sofer, whose biography we are now considering, struggled after the Hatam Sofer's death with the temptation to gain some secular knowledge, a temptation which he later considered the work of his evil inclination. According to him, he resisted this inclination with the help of his second teacher, R. Benjamin Wolf Löw, author of *Sha'arei Torah* (father of Jeremiah Löw), at whose *yeshivah* in Verbó he arrived at age eighteen.[14] His self-image as a penitent helps explain his zealousness in the anti-maskilic campaign about which we shall hear later. But a rejection of all compromise was one of the basic features of his personality. He proved this in the seven years after his marriage, when he remained unemployed and suffered hunger in order to remain faithful to his father's principles.[15] In 1851, his fortunes took a turn for the better, when he was appointed rabbi of the small community of Gyömöre, close to Győr, in the heart of the Oberland. Six years later, after publishing his first book, *Peles Hayyim*, he attained the rabbinate of the distant congregation of Szentpéter.[16]

Three years after R. Hayyim Sofer arrived in Szentpéter, R. Hillel Lichtenstein was appointed rabbi of Szikszó, a nearby village. R. Lichtenstein's history was more complicated, and his personality was distinctive.[17] He too was from the Pressburg area. He was born in 1814 in Vécs and studied in the Hatam Sofer's *yeshivah* from 1832 to 1837. After his marriage, he lived for thirteen years in Galánta, a small town not far from Pressburg, under the wing of his father-in-law, and gathered a group of disciples around him. Only in 1850 did he abandon his immediate environment, upon being chosen rabbi of Margitta, a town in

Transylvania, not far from Nagyvárad. He seems to have made an impression there, and a year later was chosen rabbi of Kolozsvár (Cluj, in Rumanian), the capital of Transylvania, a district which still preserved a certain degree of administrative independence within the framework of the Hungarian state. Unrestricted settlement by Jews in this city was permitted only after the Revolution of 1848. From then on, the community grew rapidly and showed great potential but, like many such communities, it lacked a tradition and was far from uniform in its level of religious observance. In order to lead it, one needed a certain amount of flexibility, tolerance, and restraint, qualities for which R. Lichtenstein was not noted.

According to his descendants and students, R. Lichtenstein had from his youth been extreme in his religious demands and independent in determining their nature and parameters. He tended to adopt every stringency, without regard for the difficulties involved, or the furor it would arouse among either his seniors or his congregants, whom he expected to depart from the norm. As long as this tendency was restricted to R. Lichtenstein's personal behavior, it did not arouse opposition; on the contrary, it earned him the reputation of an ascetic, an outstandingly pious man. However, when he was called upon to assume the role of halakhist, especially in a divided community such as Kolozsvár, where it was not clear if all the members even observed the basic religious laws, clashes were unavoidable. Those opposed to R. Lichtenstein wished to expel him from the city, and found a pretext to do so. The communities of Transylvania and their rabbis were under the jurisdiction of a government-appointed state rabbi; R. Abraham Friedman held the post at this time. He was the polar opposite of R. Lichtenstein; he was not accepted by the pious, because it was suspected, among other things, that he had gained his exalted position in a questionable manner.[18] R. Lichtenstein refused to accept his authority, and hoped to retain his office without the approval of the state rabbi. But the latter had the upper hand, and R. Lichtenstein was expelled from the town by the secular authorities.

According to contemporary newspaper reports, one of the causes for the clash between R. Lichtenstein and his opponents was his stringent ruling about fattened geese, and what we know of his method of adjudication makes this plausible.[19] Many Jewish households in Europe made extensive use of goose fat, from geese that were force-fed with corn or other grain for weeks before their slaughter. Some had reservations about this process, because of the suspicion that the gullet might be pierced during the fattening process, which would make the goose nonkosher according to talmudic law. The greatest halakhists of the sixteenth century, foremost among them the Ramah, upheld the accepted practice, on condition that the gullet be examined after the slaughter and found whole. This leniency had been accepted in the Hungarian communities of the Oberland from ancient times, and the Hatam Sofer found no reason to challenge it.[20] Examination of the gullet was one of the recurring jobs of every halakhist, making him personally responsible for the *kashrut* in his district. For a man like R. Lichtenstein, who wished to avoid anything savoring of prohibition, the desirable solution seemed to be to refrain from using this problematic food. In his eyes, the hardship this would daily cause his congregation was not to be weighed against the halakhic certainty gained. The fact that his master and teacher, the Hatam Sofer, had not challenged the leniency was of no import to him. We shall later find him challenging the leniency of another halakhist, R. Hayyim Halberstamm of Sanz, whom he came to know and admire.

After his dismissal from Kolozsvár, R. Lichtenstein stayed for a time in Nagyvárad, unemployed, until he was reappointed in 1854 to his former post in Margitta.[21] There he remained until he was chosen rabbi of Szikszó in 1861. We have little information about his years of service in Margitta. How he acted there—whether the people of this small place were readier to accept his stringent directives, or whether he had learned something from his previous experience—we do not know. A family tradition has it that at this stage he became acquainted with the Hassidim in the area, most of whom were the disciples of the *Admor* of Sanz, R. Hayyim Halberstamm. This acquaintance moved him to visit the rebbe's court, and we have later testimony to the ties between them.[22] The family tradition preserves a typical episode, which is connected to the first meeting of the two personalities. Upon reaching the house of the *Admor* of Sanz, the guest noticed that the walls of the rooms were plastered from one end to the other, in contradiction to an explicit law in the Talmud and Shulhan Arukh, which demands that a space be left unplastered, in memory of the destruction of the Temple. He did not hesitate to reprove the owner for this, and the latter accepted the reproof and corrected his error. In this case, R. Halberstamm had ignored a law that was not universally observed. But R. Lichtenstein even rejected an explicit directive of R. Halberstamm, who was also a noted halakhist. R. Halberstamm's ruling approved a leniency, which had begun to spread in his time, whereby non-Jews worked Jewish fields and ran Jewish businesses on the Sabbath, by virtue of a bill of sale making the non-Jew a partner in the business,[23] a leniency that allowed an entire stratum among the Jewish public, in Galicia and Hungary alike, to remain in business. R. Lichtenstein reproved anyone who had relied on this leniency, ignoring both the halakhic authority which had approved the leniency, and the economic loss for all involved.[24]

Those who only knew R. Lichtenstein from afar could consider him a hassid among hassidim. This began with the Szikszó period of his life, when he became the leader of a group that wished, like the Hassidim, to isolate themselves from the influence of modernity. But this similarity was only superficial. The inner world of R. Lichtenstein was far from that of the Hassidim. He had a favorite Yiddish saying: "The *Shevet Musar* [a book by R. Elijah Hacohn of Izmir] made me a Jew."[25] The founders of Hassidism wished to free themselves of exactly the oppressive spirit of asceticism that prevailed in books like the *Shevet*

Musar. R. Lichtenstein, in contrast, wished to infuse everyone who listened to his sermons with this oppressive spirit. Thus he wrote to R. Sussman Sofer, the younger brother of R. Hayyim Sofer, in 1860, his last year in Margitta: "I call heaven and earth to witness that if I succeed for half an hour to awaken the hearts of the idle masses, so that they cry . . . I hold this dearer than any inventiveness I discover while studying."[26] The "idle" of whom he speaks are not those who deviate from the traditional way of life, under the influence of modernity, whom he battled in the next phase of his life; they were Jews who were still immersed in the world of tradition but, by R. Lichtenstein's severe criteria, had many flaws in their lives and behavior.[27] He was imbued with the sense of a mission to bolster and entrench religious law, and he chose his methods in accordance with the changing conditions.

The third of the Hatam Sofer's students who played a role—and a decisive one—in the events which we shall describe below, was R. Moses Schick, Maharam Schick, who was remembered long after his two colleagues.[28] This was due to his great productivity as a halakhist, as evidenced by his books of responsa, for which he was considered throughout the rabbinic world, and not in Hungary alone, as the major student and successor of the Hatam Sofer. Indeed, his greatness in Torah learning was widely known even during the twenty years he served as rabbi of the small community of Szent György (Georgen), near Pressburg. His ability to serve as leader of a large segment of Jewry was revealed only in a later period. In 1861, at the age of fifty-four, he was appointed rabbi of Huszt, an important congregation at the other end of the state, near the Galician border, and in the course of subsequent events his gift for leadership emerged. Maharam Schick was a modest and retiring man. He closely followed the changing conditions and considered what could be done to halt the process of disintegration of traditional life; but he left the initiative to others. After the Reform Rabbinical Assembly in Braunschweig in 1844, he considered it necessary to excommunicate its participants, as had been done in earlier times to the Zadokites and Karaites. It was true that excommunication was forbidden by state law, but what could prevent the leaders of the time from publicly announcing the *halakhah* pertaining to secessionists, that is, that one should not allow them to share religious services, eat their food, or marry them? Maharam Schick presented his suggestions to R. Abraham Samuel Benjamin Sofer, the Ketav Sofer, who was ten years younger than he, and ranked above him only by virtue of his lineage and his position as rabbi of Pressburg. Maharam Schick expected the Ketav Sofer to take the initiative in implementing these ideas. This was a vain hope, however, and the excommunication of the reformers was never carried out.[29]

From Maharam Schick's halakhic correspondence throughout several decades, the impression arises that he never hesitated to answer any and every question. Nonetheless, he did not thrust himself into the public eye, and certainly did not battle for his ideas. Only great and unusual challenges could make him change his ways in his old age, and place him in the forefront of the battle for his faith. We shall soon learn the nature of these challenges.

We may assume that the congregations of Szentpéter, Szikszó, and Huszt, to which the three rabbis came in the late 1850s and early 1860s, still maintained their traditional character. They were relatively old, having been founded in the eighteenth century, and had not undergone upheavals. But in the Unterland—more precisely on the fringes of the Unterland—were congregations that had arisen or expanded only after permission was granted for Jews to settle in the cities in 1840. Among these were Kassa, Miskolc, and Eperjes. These cities played a central role in the rapid economic development of the region, and their Jews led this activity. Signs of the disintegration of tradition soon appeared along with this development, similar to the developments described in the interior.

Let us give some data about Eperjes. The congregation published a notice in 1858 of a vacancy for the post of rabbi. The reporter of the *Allgemeine Zeitung des Judenthums* notes alongside the notice that, given the nature of the congregation, the candidate must be "progressive."[30] According to him, the plague of "indifference" had spread throughout the congregation. This term was used in contemporary parlance for apathy towards all religious demands in favor of more earthly pursuits. A sign of the state of affairs, the writer notes, is the absence of a Jewish school in the city, and from other sources we know that quite a number of families sent their sons to *gymnasia*.[31] Leo Holländer, born in 1806, who was later to play a central role in the life of Hungarian Jewry, was educated in such an institution.[32] The newspaper article is corroborated by Hayyim David Lippe, a writer of Galician extraction who was employed by the congregation of Eperjes as a *hazzan* (cantor). In 1866 he described the background to the activities of the zealous, led by R. Hillel Lichtenstein, in six letters, written in Hebrew and German.[33] He denounced zealousness, but explained it as a reaction to the decline in religion and morality. This was manifest in the pretensions of the would-be *maskilim*, and in the open and unabashed abandonment of religious ways by the youth.[34] According to him, the situation was no different in the other two cities, Kassa and Miskolc,[35] and his testimony accords with the events occasioned by the building of new synagogues in those cities.

The need for new synagogues was a result of the increasing number of congregants. It gave those with a modernist bent an opportunity to express their preferences by giving a new face to the synagogue in keeping with the changing times and needs. The extent of the deviations from the traditional shape of the synagogues was the subject of debate and even controversy in Miskolc, as in most of the cities similarly situated. It was agreed that the *hazzan* would be accompanied by a choir on the Sabbath and festivals, hence the name "Chorschul" (choral synagogue) for a Reform synagogue. In Miskolc, the question of the placement of the *bimah* was also discussed. At one stage it was decided to leave it in its traditional place, in the center of the synagogue, but in the end it was moved forward (it is not clear whether it was actually moved close to the Ark).[36] According to the aged rabbi of the congregation, R. Ezekiel Fischmann, some were in favor of far-reaching changes, such as introducing an organ, which he rejected.[37] The rabbi had arrived from Moravia, and had served in the congregation from the time of its expansion in the mid-1830s, always taking care to preserve the tradition in public and private life. However, when the battle over the new synagogue erupted in the early 1860s, the breaches in tradition were already evident; shopkeepers opened their stores on the Sabbath.[38] The connection between the disintegration of religious life and the desire to restructure the synagogue was readily apparent in this city as well. Realizing the state of affairs in his congregation, R. Fischmann tried to find a modus vivendi with those who desired change. He decided not to oppose any innovations unless they deviated from explicit laws in the Shulhan Arukh. Indeed, when it became clear that the *mehizah* dividing the men and women's sections was too low to hide the female worshipers from the eyes of the males, as the law required, he succeeded in persuading those responsible to rectify the situation.[39]

R. Fischmann's attitude of compromise, which appeased the reformers, brought him into conflict with the conservatives, for whom the changes rendered the synagogue illegitimate. We do not know if these conservatives adopted their position on their own authority. It is clear, however, that their position gained the support of two rabbis in the immediate vicinity, R. Hayyim Sofer of Szentpéter and R. Hillel Lichtenstein of Szikszó. The village of Szentpéter lies close to Miskolc, and R. Sofer was officially subordinate to R. Fischmann. It seems that until the controversy over the synagogue erupted, harmonious relations had existed between them.[40] However, the village rabbi's inferior rank did not prevent him from reminding his superior what he considered to be the latter's religious obligations. Even before the synagogue was completed and the prayer service established, R. Sofer demanded of his elderly colleague that since the prayer service would be decided by the reformers, he should notify his congregation that he would not step into the building. R. Fischmann for his part reiterated the policy he had adopted, that if there should be some infringement of the laws of the Shulhan Arukh, he would not enter. Since he had succeeded in preventing such an infringement, he agreed to participate in the dedication, which took place shortly before the High Holy Days (September 1863) with great pomp and ceremony, in the presence of governmental authorities. The opening sermon was delivered by one of R. Fischmann's sons, who was the rabbi of a nearby community (Kecskemét).[41] He and his brother, R. Feish Fischmann, like their brother-in-law, Marcus Hirsch, were traditional rabbis who also had some general education and were moderate in their views (we shall meet the latter two later on).

Now R. Sofer became completely unrestrained in his opposition. He attacked the rabbi of Miskolc for his behavior, invalidated the synagogue, and decreed that anyone who entered it would lose his trustworthiness as rabbi, *shohet* (ritual slaughterer), or *hazzan*. He found a partner for his condemnation in the rabbi of nearby Szikszó, R. Lichtenstein, who a year earlier had called R. Fischmann "the elderly *gaon*, *Av Beit Din* of the holy congregration of Miskolc."[42] The rabbis Sofer and Lichtenstein no doubt knew each other from the time of their studies in the *yeshivah* of the Hatam Sofer of Pressburg,[43] and, since they were now in the same district, joined forces. The invalidation of the synagogue in Miskolc, and the controversy surrounding it, provided their first opportunity for such cooperation, with R. Sofer taking the lead. He forbade his flock in Szentpéter to eat of the slaughtering of the religious butchers of Miskolc,[44] who probably also served as precentors when needed in the disputed synagogue. Some of the inhabitants of Miskolc also heeded the decree of the zealot rabbis. They assembled in the old synagogue, which remained standing. The peace of the congregation was seriously disturbed, and R. Sofer himself took an active part in the quarrel between the two sides, when he came to Miskolc and sermonized against the new synagogue, its builders, and visitors—among them R. Fischmann, the city's halakhic authority. For this he was brought to trial before the authorities, but according to him, his case was dismissed.[45] The controversy quickly spread beyond the congregation. R. Fischmann disseminated a circular called *Divrei Shalom ve-Emet* (Words of Peace and Truth), in which he attempted to justify his actions before the rabbinic community.[46] His rival, on the other hand, took the trouble to find kindred souls who would be willing to delegitimize the synagogue.[47] In the spring of 1864, he apparently succeeded in gathering some rabbis from the vicinity, among them the rabbi of Szikszó, R. Hillel Lichtenstein, in order to decide on the steps necessary to disqualify the new synagogue.[48] In the midst of their consultations on this issue, news reached them that distracted them from this local problem.

As we have seen, the idea of establishing a rabbinical seminary with the educational fund had been in the air from the time of the fund's establishment in the early 1850s. The Austrian neo-absolutist regime did nothing, however, towards implementing it. Now, in the first half of the 1860s, when the Austrian government was in retreat, and all awaited major political changes, among them the granting of equal rights to Jews, the idea of the seminary was also revived. Those who favored the idea convinced the authorities to convene a committee of rabbis and public figures to prepare a program for the proposed institution. Those invited to the committee were, without exception, members of the "progressive" camp, and it is no surprise that notice of the planned convocation raised fears, and angered the Orthodox of all persuasions. R. Hillel Lichtenstein and R. Hayyim Sofer, who of course rejected the idea of a seminary, no matter who would support and administrate it, were severely shocked, and since they were men of initiative, they set about frustrating the plan. Realizing that they could not act effectively on their own, they appeared before R. Jeremiah Löw in Ujhely in order to discuss what steps should be taken.[49] R. Löw had strong reservations about the pair in general, but agreed with them in rejecting the rabbinical seminary. After consultation, in which other rabbis from nearby communities took part, they decided to convene a rabbinic assembly in the city of Nyiregyháza, in order to create as broad a front as possible to frustrate the initiative in the capital. The assembly was held on March 15 to 18, 1864, with the participation of eighteen rabbis, among them R. Meir Perles of Nagykároly and Isaac Aaron Landesberg of Nagyvárad, who had perhaps even greater suspicions than R. Löw about the fanaticism of the instigators. The latter's participation aroused the astonishment of the public.[50] We have some vague information about an argument with one of the participants, apparently over the question of cultural isolationism.[51] Nonetheless, most of those present shared a common interest. All of them were heads of *yeshivot* and viewed the ancient institution as the proper framework for educating rabbis. The establishment of a seminary would impinge on or even threaten the existence of the *yeshivah*. They agreed to forestall the danger by sending a delegation to Kaiser Franz Joseph in Vienna, an idea that was favored by the great rabbis of the Oberland, and the rabbi of Pressburg, the Ketav Sofer, at their head. Only one doubter remained, R. Esriel Hildesheimer of Eisenstadt, who favored the idea of a seminary, and even called for its establishment, on the condition that it be headed by someone like him, who upheld the ideal of Torah combined with general education. It seems that R. Hildesheimer had his supporters among the community of Orthodox householders. His *yeshivah* taught subjects of general education as part of the curriculum and nonetheless, or perhaps because of this, enjoyed great public support. However, if any of his fellow rabbis agreed with R. Hildesheimer, he remained silent.[52] Hildesheimer's failure to join the delegation to the king emphasized his isolation and uniqueness, and his inability to serve as an example to his fellow rabbis. The delegation, led by R. Jeremiah Löw, came before the king on April 11, 1864, and managed to avert what it saw as the evil decree.[53] The plan for the seminary was abandoned for the time being.

The unity of the Orthodox camp in opposition to the seminary could not conceal the gap between the factions in other issues of accommodation to the needs of the time, as is revealed in the Miskolc controversy, which was not an isolated instance. Similar disagreements occurred in other cities as well. If, in Miskolc, R. Hayyim Sofer was the leading zealot, on the nationwide scene it was R. Hillel Lichtenstein. We have already noted his fire-and-brimstone style of oratory, designed to reduce his listeners to tears of penitence. In this way he is reminiscent of the revivalist preacher, familiar to us from other religious denominations. At this stage he developed a new goal, in addition to his original mission of bringing individuals to penitence: that of enlisting his listeners in the conservative's battle against the reformers; this now became his primary goal. During R. Sofer's battle in Miskolc against the builders of the new synagogue and the rabbi of the city who had acquiesced in their project, some of the Jews of Miskolc came to Szikszó, R. Lichtenstein's seat, for a fair. According to an unimpeachable source, R. Lichtenstein delivered a speech to the people of Miskolc, in which he denigrated the events in their city and insulted their rabbi and teacher.[54]

The accepted rabbinic code of behavior prohibited rabbis from interfering in the affairs of each other's congregations. This was how the term *mara de'atra*, the title given the rabbi, was interpreted: the exclusive authority in that place. If it became known that an infringement of the religious laws was occurring in one community or another, the rabbis in other places could raise their voices for the purpose of *migdar milta*, that is, to shore up the breaches in religious life. There were obviously no clear guidelines for determining the extent of the breach or its nature; this depended on the views and personalities of those involved. R. Sofer and R. Lichtenstein viewed the changes enacted in the synagogues of other congregations as breaches that demanded their intervention. The latter, in particular, was infused with a sense of mission, and felt called upon to make the public repent. We find him preaching in public, in his demagogic manner, wherever he happened or meant to be. The groups of conservatives in the various congregations apparently began to view him as a potential partner in their battle.

We have already mentioned the city of Makó in the south, where the progressives embittered the life of their rabbi, R. Solomon Ullmann. The rabbi died in 1862, but the struggle over the nature of the congregation did not end. The administration of the congregation was in the hands of the progressives, and under their leadership the synagogue became a *Chorschul*; the administration appointed a rabbi who would agree to this change. The conservatives invited R. Hillel Lichtenstein to be their guest, if not in the hope of changing the state of affairs in the congregation, then at least to boost their morale. R. Lichtenstein arrived in the week of *Parshat Kedoshim* (spring, 1864). His followers from other congregations were invited to join the audience for the Sabbath sermon. Since the occasion seemed likely to become a public demonstration against the congregational administration, the members of the administration were determined to prevent this. By virtue of their connections with the governor of the district, they succeeded in keeping the unwanted guest from the city. He and his group of followers spent the Sabbath in a village nearby. According to the opinion published by the administration, from which we know the details of the episode,[55] the thrust of R. Lichtenstein's sermon was the admonition: "To dedicate their lives in peace and tranquility to the worship of God, and not, God forbid, to teach their sons any kind of craft, or allow them to study secular sciences, because they would no doubt be estranged from religion as a result."[56]

This was indeed the tone of the sermons that R. Lichtenstein gave from the 1860s onwards, both orally and in writing. He ceased being a fire-and-brimstone preacher, whose main battle was against the evil inclination, which tempts the Jew throughout the centuries not to fulfill his role of worshiping the Lord and observing the commandments. The vicissitudes of the times had battered the walls of tradition to such an extent that the efforts of the individual to resist the evil inclination were no longer sufficient. It was necessary to build a barrier that would protect the flock of the faithful from the evil winds that blew in the world. The best way to do this was by prohibiting any intellectual pursuit outside of Torah learning for, as R. Lichtenstein and his circle understood it, the breach in traditional life began when Jews opened themselves to non-Jewish ideas and disciplines. The necessary remedy was therefore to isolate oneself from these, especially now, at the turning point in Hungary's history marked by liberation from absolute Austrian rule, a process that began at the same time as the arrival of R. Lichtenstein in Szikszó. This was the signal for increased activity among Jews of a generally modernist, if not actually reformist, tendency. This activity prompted an energetic reaction from people like R. Lichtenstein; we have already witnessed the cooperation between him and R. Hayyim Sofer in the Miskolc controversy, and later in their attempts to avert the establishment of a rabbinical seminary. R. Hayyim Sofer was the initiator in the controversy in Miskolc and R. Lichtenstein his second-in-command. They continued to cooperate on various occasions from then on.

However, R. Hillel Lichtenstein now had another permanent partner in thought and deed, his son-in-law, Akiva Joseph Schlesinger. R. Lichtenstein had given his daughter to Akiva Joseph in marriage a short time after arriving in Szikszó, and from then on the son-in-law lived in his father-in-law's house, and worked hand-in-hand with him.[57] Schlesinger was born in Pressburg in 1837, and received most of his training from the rabbi of that city, Abraham Samuel Benjamin Sofer, the Ketav Sofer. He also studied with Maharam Schick, while the latter was still rabbi of Szent György. Both his rabbis granted him ordination shortly before his marriage,[58] and he was considered a talented and promising young man. But there was an unusual episode in Schlesinger's youth: he spent some time in Nikolsburg, during which time he encountered and became drawn to secular culture. According to information provided by his critics in Pressburg, the young man even took on the manners of the would-be intellectual upon his return from Nikolsburg, behavior that aroused the mockery of his acquaintances.[59] The effects of this youthful experience left their impact on Schlesinger's writings, and not positively. In hindsight, it appeared to him as a painful aberration and, in the way of penitents, he attempted to save others from the sin that had led him astray.[60] He no doubt shared his turmoil with his father-in-law. R. Lichtenstein had of course long ago rejected secular studies, but his son-in-law could attest from his personal experience to the havoc that such learning could cause among many of his contemporaries. He was younger than his father-in-law by twenty-three years, and his youth and student days had occurred after the disintegration of traditional society began in Hungary in the 1850s. As stated, he himself had experienced the attraction of secular culture; and, if a miracle had happened to him and he had retreated in good time, he saw many of his contemporaries, and especially the students of the established *yeshivot* who, from the time they tasted of non-Jewish learning, followed it to their perdition.[61] The inevitable conclusion was that any contact with secular knowledge should be avoided, including the study of the language or languages whose knowledge was a precondition for studying these sciences. The language of general culture at that time was German, and so the conservatives vented their anger at its study and use, particularly by rabbis and other preachers, in the synagogue or outside it. From their point of view, a rabbi who gave a sermon in German was tacitly permitting his listeners to do as he did and learn the language. The struggle against the abandonment of Yiddish or Yiddish-German for German thus coalesced with the campaign against aesthetic changes in the synagogues. However, this amalgamation made the target of attack much broader than the reformers alone, for the use of German was not restricted to those who had abandoned the tradition. As we have seen, even the faithful and pious had become accustomed to using it, at least in the communities of the Oberland, including Pressburg, which most considered a bastion of Orthodoxy.

Chapter 7

Pressburg as the Target of Zealot Arrows

Pressburg was considered the pride of Orthodoxy because it was identified with its great rabbi of the previous generation, the Hatam Sofer. He had insisted that tradition in his congregation be preserved, both in halakhic content and in cultural terms. The Hatam Sofer had good reason for writing in his testament about the choice of his successor after his demise: "Only a famous rabbinic scholar should sit on it [the rabbinic seat] . . . and he should abjure the literature of the heretics and should not sermonize in the vernacular."[1] He was fortunate to have his son, the Ketav Sofer, R. Abraham Samuel Benjamin, inherit his post; his son was both willing and able to adhere to the style of his father's sermons. However, the sermon was merely a symbol for the belief that all practices of daily life, private and public, should be preserved without change.

This wish was frustrated because of the vicissitudes of the period, which began at the time of the Ketav Sofer's accession to his father's post in 1839. A year later, as we have mentioned, permission was granted for Jewish settlement in the urban centers of the land. The Jews of Pressburg, who had hitherto been confined to a few streets on the edges of the city, which were governed by one of the magnates, could now move their households, stores, and factories to the inner city.[2] Formal and informal communal supervision over their religious behavior diminished, or even disappeared entirely. The famous *yeshivah* of the Hatam Sofer continued to function under his son, but families who preferred to send their sons to non-Jewish educational institutions could do so without interference.[3]

An episode described in the sources is emblematic of the rabbi's diminishing authority over his congregation. In 1850, with the beginning of the new Austrian neo-absolutist reign, a secondary school for the sciences opened in Pressburg, under municipal supervision, and students of the various religions were accepted. The leaders of the religious groups represented in the city were requested to give their blessing to the new enterprise, and were called upon to meet with the students of their religious persuasion, in order to prepare them for their studies. So we find the Ketav Sofer gathering the Jewish students of the school to the synagogue, admonishing them about the proper conduct towards their non-Jewish colleagues, but also concerning their duty to observe the customs of their religion in the strange environment.[4] This event is reminiscent of a famous scene in the life of R. Ezekiel Landau, author of the *Noda' bi-Yehudah*, who was constrained, by order of Kaiser Joseph II, to bless the first Jewish conscripts, and who fulfilled his duty with tears streaming down his face.[5] The attendance of Jewish students at a non-Jewish school was no doubt a source of grief to the Ketav Sofer, no less than the conscription of Jewish boys into the army was for the *Noda' bi-Yehudah*. But duty could not be denied, and we later find the Ketav Sofer ready for compromise in the educational field: The authorities were prepared to recognize the *yeshivah* as an institution authorized to grant ordination, on the condition that general studies would be added to the religious curriculum. It is clear that the Ketav Sofer's agreement was more a matter of compulsion than of desire.

At that time, of course, only a minority of parents sent their sons to non-Jewish educational institutions. However, the attitude toward secular studies, including mastery of the non-Jewish languages of the environment, changed even among those loyal to the tradition—including the descendants of the Hatam Sofer. The Hatam Sofer's daughter was married to R. David Zvi Ehrenfeld. They wed their daughter to R. Abraham Glasner, the Ketav Sofer's outstanding student, and he joined their household after the wedding in 1849. The talented young man, who had some general education, made a vow that he would devote himself exclusively to Torah study for three years after his marriage. And this is what he wrote in his diary a short time after his wedding:

About half a year ago, my pious mother-in-law, long may she live, with my father-in-law, long may he live, in agreement, came to me and said that they saw that I did not occupy myself with secular studies, and they irked me by saying: Why do you not occupy yourself with other things as well? At least go to study Hungarian and the language of culture (German) with taste and discernment, for this is the sum of man, and you cannot achieve anything without these two languages.[6]

He quotes their argument that even if he wishes to engage not in business but in the rabbinate: "You yourself know what people demand of their shepherd—they do not wish him to be a Torah scholar but a spokesman of his nation, and for him to orate pleasantly in the non-Jewish language."

Whether voluntarily or not, the Ketav Sofer submitted to the spirit of the times. He realized that his sermons, like those of other preachers of the old school, did not satisfy those with a modern education. A minority within the congregation also demanded the initiation of prayer services in the style found in other places, with nearby Vienna as a model for imitation.[7] In order to prevent a more serious deviation, the Ketav Sofer decided to appoint a rabbi of the educated Orthodox type as his assistant, one whose sermons would withstand the test of Orthodoxy with respect to their content, while in terms of their form, language, and style, they would satisfy those with modern tastes. He first approached R. Esriel Hildesheimer of Eisenstadt,[8] and when negotiations with him fell through, his choice fell upon R. Feisch Fischmann, the rabbi of Kolozsvár, the son of R. Ezekiel Fischmann of Miskolc.[9] R. Fischmann had a reputation as an inspiring preacher, one who spoke in high German while the content of his sermons was rooted in traditional Judaism, and who won over his hearers to its values and principles. R. Abraham Glasner, the son-in-law of the Hatam Sofer's daughter mentioned above,[10] was chosen to replace R. Feisch Fischmann in Kolozsvár. He was said to be similar to his predecessor.

These two appointments, of R. Fischmann in Pressburg and of R. Glasner in Kolozsvár, aroused the ire of R. Hillel Lichtenstein. He was not appeased by the fact that the two were generally held to be God-fearing. On the contrary, this fact made matters worse in his eyes. As he states, he admonished R. Fischmann prior to the latter's acceptance of the post in Pressburg: "I told him: Your motives are no doubt pure, but what will the students do, for they won't learn your diligence in Torah and your enthusiastic prayer from you—but to study secular matters, that they will learn from you."[11]

Before we once again follow R. Lichtenstein and his son-in-law's sentiments and deeds, we have reason to ask how the Ketav Sofer reconciled his choice of a man like R. Fischmann with his father's last testament, which stated clearly that one "should not preach in the non-Jewish languages." We have no direct answer to this question from any of those involved. However, from the Ketav Sofer's intimates, who later defended him against the attacks of his opponents (in the pamphlet *Ketav Yosher Divrei Emet*), we learn of the prevailing apologetic spirit. According to them, the Hatam Sofer's rejection of vernacular preachers was due to the heretical ideas they were likely to espouse, rather than to the question of the language itself. Proof of this was the Hatam Sofer's good opinion of R. Eleazar Strasser, the rabbi of Vágujhely, who was known to speak only German.[12] Times had changed, and R. Strasser's type became widespread, and his sermonic style the norm. Under these conditions there was no reason to have reservations about those who used German in their sermons.

The reaction of R. Hillel Lichtenstein and his son-in-law, R. Akiva Joseph Schlesinger, to this interpretation of the Hatam Sofer's position, was a loud battle cry. They understood the Hatam Sofer's admonitions not as good advice, whose applicability waned with the changing times, but as a halakhic decision that was binding for all time. They culled all the Hatam Sofer's comments on this topic, and appointed themselves the executors of his spiritual estate. They viewed all those who failed to adhere to the literal interpretation of his statements, including his son and successor, and other members of the family, as rebelling against the rabbi's authority, unworthy of being called his students. They themselves, who made great efforts to fulfill the Hatam Sofer's words in their strictest sense, were to be considered the guardians of his spiritual heritage.

This daring position was expressed in three letters that R. Lichtenstein sent to Pressburg, and which are included in his book *Responsa Beit Hillel*, responsa nos. 34, 35, 39. The earliest of the three is no. 39, the last mentioned, dated the summer of 1863. The name of the addressee was omitted by the editor of the responsa, Hayyim Jacob Lichtenstein, the grandson of the author, and not by chance. The author uses scathing language to the addressee, who is none other than the Ketav Sofer. The letter opens with a fiery protest against the attempt to justify the use of the vernacular by preachers, "in order to bring them [the people] closer to the Torah and to place them under the wing of the Shekhinah." The use of these means is invalid on principle, "for how can your heart be circumcised with a knife used for idolatry."[13] The Hatam Sofer's testament and one of his responsa (*H.M.*, no. 197) are cited in order to prove that the use of vernacular is prohibited. The responsum is addressed to the leaders of Némeťkeresztur, and deals with a ritual butcher who had acquired a bad reputation. The Hatam Sofer instructed the butcher, among other things, "not to read secular books," and en passant admonished his questioners for not having a rabbi, encouraging them to choose a "rabbi who would show the ways of God to God's nation. That he should not God forbid be one of those who writes falsehood, and reads secular literature, and who speaks other languages, for it is forbidden to accept halakhic decisions from someone like that." Now, however, the situation has deteriorated, says R. Lichtenstein in his letter, and rabbis "who are considered righteous and of our kind" are the ones who speak other languages. "If at times it seems that they cause many Jews to mend their ways and repent, this is a bad omen for Israel, a punishment for our many sins, because this causes the nation to have faith in them." The concrete background to these paradoxical statements becomes clear in the continuation—the choice of R. Fischmann as rabbi of Kolozsvár, a man whose "reputation goes before him as a completely pious man—woe unto us, for the damage he has caused in our district would not be believed if it were told." The damage he created is, of course, the legitimacy he gave to the use of non-Jewish languages, proving that it is possible to be God-fearing and scrupulous in the observance of the commandments while still absorbing elements of the surrounding culture. Kolozsvár was saved when R. Fischmann was called to be preacher in Pressburg, but before he left, he saw to it that someone of his type be appointed in his place: R. Abraham Glasner. He also was reputed to be a pious man, despite having a general education and preaching in German. R. Lichtenstein's request of the Ketav Sofer was—and this is the objective of the letter—that he prevent his sister's son-in-law from being appointed to the post in Kolozsvár: "To warn him, advise him, and command him in whatever way possible that he return the letter of appointment, giving whatever reason he wishes, so long as he not come under any circumstances." In the continuation, R. Lichtenstein called the Ketav Sofer "my master and rabbi, the glory of Israel and its pride," but in the same breath adjured him in the name of his father, the Hatam Sofer, to do as he says. He hinted that it was clear to him that R. Fischmann's arrival in Pressburg was not to the Ketav Sofer's liking, but "even if my master and rabbi, may his light shine, cannot protest in his congregation against the permissibility of non-Jewish languages, let him stand at our side and rescue us."[14]

Presumably such a hurtful and insulting letter did not merit a reply, and it is clear that no one except its addressee knew of its contents. R. Abraham Glasner arrived in Kolozsvár and, as expected, encountered the opposition camp. His family members endeavored to help him, and his brother-in-law, R. Samuel Ehrenfeld (who was later called the Hatan Sofer), turned to R. Lichtenstein, as an influential rabbi in the district, to testify to the good character of the new rabbi of the city. His uncle, the Ketav Sofer, had begun this work, and R. Lichtenstein was requested to finish it. R. Ehrenfeld's letter has not been preserved; we learn of its content from R. Lichtenstein's answer (number 35 in his responsa). It is sufficient to quote the opening sentence in order to perceive the tone of his words: "The Lord preserve me from this request and all relating to it, for I am heedful of our Sages' statement in the first chapter of BT Sanhedrin, that someone who appoints a judge who is not worthy is akin to one who plants a tree for idolatry . . ."[15] He poured out his wrath on Pressburg, "which was always a major city in Israel. Woe, how it has now become a whore . . . to take upon themselves a preacher who preaches in the language of the nations in a holy place where the angel of God trod, and who warned against doing so." If in his letter to the Ketav Sofer, R. Lichtenstein still gave him the benefit of the doubt—perhaps he was forced to allow such preachers into Pressburg—now he claimed that the Ketav Sofer and his adherents should have opposed the appointment, to show that it was done without the approval of the rabbis. As for the request to write to Kolozsvár and help the rabbi, on the contrary, he says he is considering doing the opposite: writing to reveal his negative opinion of R. Glasner. Were it not for an incident in which the two had clashed publicly, and his fear that people would think that a personal grudge was the reason for his opposition, R. Lichtenstein would have done so.

A short time after this correspondence with a member of the Ketav Sofer's family, R. Lichtenstein made another attempt to influence events in Pressburg. In a letter of 14 Kislev 1864, he approached the head of the congregation, Kalman Bettelheim, and attempted to convince him to act in accordance with the testament of the Hatam Sofer.[16] R. Fischmann, he claimed, must be made to preach in the Yiddish with which the general populace is familiar, upon pain of dismissal if he does not follow orders. The author revealed in his letter that at first he had recommended the appointment of R. Fischmann, who showed "signs of purity, and was one of those who strove for piety and purity." That is, R. Lichtenstein recognized R. Fischmann's high level of religiosity, and indeed, his religious enthusiasm was a byword among his contemporaries. But in R. Lichtenstein's view, these religious merits became negative traits if they were combined with openness to the surrounding culture, even if this was limited to adopting the language of the environment.

At that time, R. Lichtenstein's son-in-law, R. Akiva Joseph Schlesinger, began activities corresponding to R. Lichtenstein's attempts to impose his authority and personality. He chose to operate in a way that suited his talents as an able writer and sharp polemicist. He produced three literary compositions: two short ones in Yiddish-German, *Na'ar Ivri* and *El ha-Adarim*, which appeared in 1863, and a much longer one (150 pages), in Hebrew, *Lev ha-Ivri*, which appeared a year later.[17] The close cooperation between father- and son-in-law is discernible both in their shared goal—to establish their view prohibiting secular studies, and the knowledge of languages that is a prerequisite to such study—and in the major tactic used by both to achieve their aim. Schlesinger cited the prohibition over and over, using the Hatam Sofer as his source, just as his father-in-law did. *Na'ar Ivri* opened with a translation of the Hatam Sofer's testament into the local idiom, and the bulk of the pamphlet is comprised of its detailed explanation. *Lev ha-Ivri* is presented as a commentary on the testament, and it is structured around the clauses of this document. If the link between these is tenuous, the intention of invoking the Hatam Sofer's name is obvious to all.

This reliance on the Hatam Sofer seems to have been of personal and biographical significance to Schlesinger. Throughout *Lev ha-Ivri*, he speaks of the Hatam Sofer as if he had actually been his student, and only occasionally does he remember to say that to his sorrow, he did not merit the privilege of studying with the great rabbi.[18] He was two years old when the great rabbi died, and was therefore able to learn Torah only from the great man's son, the Ketav Sofer. But now he felt obliged to act in concert with his father-in-law against his master and teacher, a serious action in the world of rabbinic tradition. The problem troubled Schlesinger, and he sought to grapple with it. It was not difficult for him to find a precedent in the words of the Sages: "Where there is a desecration of God's name, one does not concern oneself with the honor of the teacher." He quotes this well-known statement of the Sages in his defense, as well as some others of a similar nature. But there was still reason to ask why he should not argue with his teacher privately; who granted him the right to differ with his master publicly? He answers: "And why do I speak publicly? For many admonished [him] secretly, and it is now obligatory to admonish publicly, as Maimonides states in the sixth chapter of *Hilkhot De'ot*: If he does not recant privately, one shames him in public and publishes his sin abroad."[19] Here Schlesinger admits that he sees himself as working in collaboration with his father-in-law R. Lichtenstein. The latter had admonished the rabbi of Pressburg in private, and his son-in-law now does so in public. It is clear that Schlesinger received his father-in-law's sanction to release himself from any sense of obligation to his rabbi and teacher. R. Lichtenstein's name is not mentioned in *Lev ha-Ivri*, but the author often speaks of "a great one," upon whom he relies, and the identity of this person is unquestionable. His father-in-law, whom he considered an outstanding leader of the generation, serves as a counterweight to his master and teacher. But his true mainstay is the figure of the Hatam Sofer. He calls him from the dead in order to support the student who sets out to disagree with his teacher.

The first part of *Lev ha-Ivri* was published anonymously. Its author was a young man, not yet thirty, with no position or reputation. His name on the book would have detracted from, rather than added to, its weight. However, his sharp words made an impression, and his readers identified their origin—the school of R. Hillel Lichtenstein. Some thought the latter to be the author.[20] In any event, the publication was seen as a daring attack by the zealots, not only upon the various types of reformers, but even on their God-fearing opponents, who disagreed with them about the means to be taken against Reform. If the first group reacted by a mocking shake of the head, the spokesmen for moderate Orthodoxy in Pressburg felt the need to respond to the zealots and to put them in their place. We have already heard of their rejection of the extremist interpretation of the Hatam Sofer's words—this is the main content of the pamphlet *Divrei Yosher ve-Emet*, published in Pressburg—and of their scorn for Schlesinger on account of the sins of his maskilic youth. However, the writers of the pamphlet also settled accounts with R. Lichtenstein, for giving his flighty son-in-law cover, and for his part in the composition of *Lev ha-Ivri*.

No more than a year passed, and it became clear that the publication of the anonymous *Lev ha-Ivri* was only the opening volley in a more general battle that R. Hillel Lichtenstein decided to wage in support of his principles.

Chapter 8

The Fruits of Zealousness
The Judicial Decision of Michalowitz in 1866

In the summer of 1865, Hillel Lichtenstein issued a public pronouncement containing nine clauses, each of which attacked one of the changes that had been introduced in many congregations throughout the country during the preceding decades. Some of these, such as the lowering of the curtain separating the men's and women's sections, designed to hide the women from the eyes of the male worshipers, contravened the laws of the Shulhan Arukh. Already in the late 1850s, Israel David (Margoliot-Jaffe) Schlesinger, the author of *Meholat ha-Mahanayim*, had designated moving the *bimah* close to the Ark, setting up the marriage canopy in the synagogue, and the like, as imitations of foreign worship, and had applied to these practices the prohibition against following the ways of the gentiles. In his pronouncement, R. Lichtenstein cited this source. The first of the list of prohibitions was against "preaching a sermon in the language of the nations"; he went so far as to obligate the hearer "to leave the synagogue and go outside." No source was given for this directive, but the basic prohibition against preaching in the language of the nations relied on the words of the Hatam Sofer, discussed above. There is good reason to believe that bringing this prohibition to the attention of the public was the main purpose of the pronouncement. It was, at any rate, its major novelty.

We have the text of the document, and the accompanying letter that was sent to R. Eliezer Sussman Sofer, R. Hayyim Sofer's younger brother, who at the time was rabbi of Kiskúnhalas.[1] The addressee was requested to sign the announcement in his name and that of his *beit din*, but not to publicize it until the sender should succeed in gathering at least fifty signatures, for otherwise the effort would be self-defeating. We do not know R. Eliezer Sussman Sofer's answer. His religious position was not much different from that of the initiator. We find him, several years earlier, asking R. Lichtenstein for guidance in leading his congregation.[2] But R. Sofer's congregation was located near the capital and was not immune to the winds of change. Could the rabbi endorse prohibitions which he could not uphold in his own congregation?[3] It is a fact that R. Sofer's signature is also absent from the list of signatories to the second version of the pronouncement which, in contrast to the first, was published abroad, as we shall see. We know of three other rabbis, aside from the rabbi of Kiskúnhalas, who received the pronouncement: R. Judah Leib Eisentädter, rabbi of Szobránc; R. Hayyim Bezalel Panet, rabbi of Tasnád; and Maharam Schick of Huszt. The first two responded positively, while Maharam Schick voiced reservations and sharp criticism.[4]

Maharam Schick admitted that the deterioration in the state of the tradition necessitated action, but the nature of this must, in his opinion, be determined by the guidelines of the *halakhah*. R. Lichtenstein absolutely disqualified those synagogues that deviated in their structure or prayer service from the accepted norm, and determined it is forbidden not only to worship there, but even to enter their portals. In contrast, Maharam Schick discussed in detail the various questions that arise concerning the use of these buildings: Is it permissible to enter them, at least while no service is going on? Should one be lenient with a synagogue that adheres to traditional lines in respect to the worship, or not? He even permitted praying there in case of need.[5] In other words, these synagogues had not changed their nature and lost their holiness in his eyes because of the deviations of their builders and those who used them. Moreover, he actually reprimanded R. Lichtenstein for calling these synagogues places of idol worship. "How can you say this?!" he exclaimed. Even if they were built in violation of the *halakhah*, they were built "in the name of God and in order to pray there to the Lord . . . God forbid, it is contrary to His wish to say this."[6]

But the major thrust of Maharam Schick's arguments was directed against the prohibition against preaching in German, which R. Lichtenstein was so interested in establishing and having affirmed.[7] As a student of the Hatam Sofer, Maharam Schick could testify that although the rabbi denounced those who preached in the language of the nations, he intended only those whose sermons deviated in their content from the accepted tradition—exactly corroborating the testimony of those who had been intimates of the great rabbi of Pressburg, of whom we heard above.

Maharam Schick displayed independence even with respect to the Hatam Sofer's own pronouncements. R. Lichtenstein referred, among other things, to the Hatam Sofer's responsum (*Even ha-Ezer*, part II, no. 11) in which he asserted that the ancients had also been masters of the non-Jewish language—that is, standard German—and had deliberately introduced changes in it in order to create Yiddish-German. In this way, they had heeded one of the eighteen unbreachable decrees of the Great Court in Jerusalem on the eve of the destruction of the Temple, recorded in the Palestinian Talmud, in Tractate Shabbat, chapter 1, which instituted "the change of language," obliging Israel to be separated from the nations in its language. Maharam Schick saw no reason to challenge the historicity of this artificial construction. His arguments were purely halakhic: (1) The commentators on the Palestinian Talmud do not agree that the term discussed actually means a change in language in the sense adduced; (2) A prohibition mentioned in the Palestinian Talmud and not in the Babylonian Talmud is not absolutely binding. Thus, unwittingly, the student called attention to one of the methods his master had used to defend the accepted custom: readiness to deviate from the generally accepted interpretation of the halakhists in order to adduce support for an accepted practice from the literary sources.[8] The Hatam Sofer was interested in preserving Yiddish-German as the Jewish language, and strived to find supporting sources for this endeavor. Maharam Schick did not accept his proof from the Palestinian Talmud, either because he was more critical in his reliance on the sources,[9] or because the desired goal, the preservation of Yiddish-German, was less important in his eyes.

Recently, Meir Hildesheimer[10] published a letter sent by Maharam Schick to R. Menahem Eisenstädter, rabbi of Ungvár, which reflects a later development of events. We learn from it that Maharam Schick showed the text of his response to R. Lichtenstein to two important colleagues in the area, the rabbi of Ungvár, and the rabbi of Ujhely, Jeremiah Löw, before sending it to R. Lichtenstein. This indicates that he attached great importance to his debate with R. Lichtenstein. The former rabbi appeared to agree with him at the time, but later retracted, as we shall see; while according to Maharam Schick's testimony in this letter, R. Jeremiah Löw fully endorsed the criticism of R. Lichtenstein's opinion, and it stands to reason that his reservations did not escape R. Lichtenstein. We should not be surprised to discover, however, that his important colleagues' criticism did not deter R. Lichtenstein; he merely changed his tactics. This was consistent with his character: He was a man of great self-assurance, who acted with a sense of mission, and without questioning the propriety of the methods he used to achieve his ends.

When the number of desired signatories for the pronouncement was not reached,[11] R. Lichtenstein decided to call a conference of those upon whose support he could rely. So was born the famous conference in the town of Michalowitz, which took place in November 1865, about half a year after the distribution of the pronouncement.

This conference has been dealt with extensively in the scholarly literature, and most recently by N. Katzburg.[12] These are the essentials: The number of participants was twenty-four. Only fourteen of these were rabbis of congregations; the others were judges in the *batei din* which the rabbis headed. Let us remember that R. Lichtenstein, in his letter accompanying the pronouncement, requested the signatures of the rabbi and his *beit din*, which means that such collective approval was counted as one vote alone. The number of those who endorsed the decision of the Michalowitz conference was therefore far below the quantity desired to establish its authority, and all the more so in terms of quality. Only two participants held respected positions in terms of the size of their congregations and their standing in the Torah world: R. Menahem Eisenstädter and R. Hayyim Sofer. The absence of the rabbis of Huszt and Ujhely certainly did not escape the attention of those present and all others who had an interest in the affair.

Nevertheless, the initiator of the conference estimated correctly that a decision promulgated by the conference, even if the participants were relatively few, would be preferable to a pronouncement with the same number of signatories. A pronouncement could be considered the opinion of one person, which others endorsed. On the other hand, the decision of the *beit din* of a conference was presented as the result of debate and deliberation by many, as the text reads: "We debated and studied the matter with reference to the law and the [conclusions] are clear in light of the views of our Holy Torah, without emendation."[13] Actually, the only debate was over a side issue: whether the prohibitions should be enforced by the pronouncement of a ban. This was alluded to in the text of the decision ("it would have been appropriate to pronounce a ban in this matter"). Akiva Joseph Schlesinger, who was present at the conference, although he had no position and was not counted among the signatories, also attested to this debate.[14] He also recalled—although ten years later, after leaving the country to live in Eretz Israel—that the question of whether it should be prohibited to send children to school was also debated.[15] Those assembled refrained from these two steps because of their fear of the secular authorities, and no trace of the debate about schooling is found in the text of the decision. The body of the document, with its nine clauses, is the work of R. Lichtenstein; the clauses are identical to those of the original pronouncement, with only minor changes.[16]

In contrast, the ideological preface and the emotional address to the reader in the document's introduction and conclusion were greatly augmented. These stressed that the rules set forth were not merely pious customs, for which "it is not worth creating a breach, let alone a controversy. It should be known henceforth that these are essentials of Torah and transgressions of them are considered the accoutrements of idol worship." Prominence was similarly given to the responsum about linguistic isolation of "the great master of rabbinic literature, rabbi of Israel in the last generation, the light of the Diaspora, our master and teacher, the Hatam Sofer," which served as the basis for the decision: His words are cited in detail and with emphasis.

The tactic of changing the pronouncement into a judicial decision succeeded. Within a short time after its publication, dozens of names of rabbinic figures from nearby districts were added, until the number reached seventy-one, the number of members of the Sanhedrin in Jerusalem in ancient times. According to Akiva Joseph Schlesinger, it would have been a simple matter to add even more signatures, but this was not done in order not to impair the document's impact as a court decision, and specifically, that of the Great Court.[17] Among the new signatories were well-known rabbis, including Yekutiel Judah Teitelbaum of Sziget, Menahem Mendel Panet of Dés, the brothers Jacob and Shraga Tennenbaum, the rabbis of Putnok and Csát, and others.[18] The problem was that the names of other leading rabbis were missing, among them some who had participated in the Nyiregyháza assembly, like the rabbis of Ujhely, Nagyvárad, and Nagykároly. Their absence must be interpreted as an expression of their reservations about the extreme rulings. They were not the only ones to look upon R. Hillel's assumption of authority over community affairs with disfavor, as we learn from his grandson, the author of his official biography. The grandson confirms that his grandfather composed the text of the decision, adding: "and some of his friends became his enemies because of this."[19] In other words, even among his friends there were those who did not agree with the predominant extremist tendency. However, as is typical of events at the time, this dissenting opinion was not voiced publicly, thus creating the impression that the spirit of Michalowitz, and the ruling that emanated from it, were a product of the consensus of all the rabbinic authorities, at least in the counties of the Unterland, and no one—whoever he may be—could legitimately oppose them.

This state of affairs is attested to by the well-known response of Maharam Schick to his student, Wolf Sofer, who lived in Zalaszentgrót. The use of German was a fact of life there, but now the student found himself in a quandary as a result of the Michalowitz ruling.[20] In his response, Maharam Schick explained at length why the prohibition against German was justified. It constituted a barrier to the study of the secular sciences which, experience had taught, brings about a weakening of faith and laxity in the observance of the commandments. But Maharam Schick exempted from this prohibition one who had already withstood the test, and now uses the knowledge of languages and secular sciences "in order to expand the limits of holiness and to draw the frivolous to God's Torah and to fear of Him." (As will be remembered, Maharam Schick claimed in his debate with R. Lichtenstein that this was also the view of his master, the Hatam Sofer.) Ostensibly, his student could rely on this leniency. But Maharam Schick seemed to contradict himself in his closing words: "This was my opinion about sermons in German, but my colleagues outvoted me and decided contrary to my words, and I must accept their words with fear and trembling, and God forbids us to disobey them." This means that, after the fact, he retracted his decision in deference to the rulings of the Michalowitz conference. Why then did he refrain from signing the "judicial decision" even after it was promulgated? This question occupied ultra-Orthodox groups and continues to do so to this day. They consider the decision as binding, and are perplexed that the great halakhist, who concurred with the ruling at least ex post facto, did not join the list of signatories.²¹ The question is relevant from a purely historical perspective as well.²²

Maharam Schick's letter to R. Menahem Eisenstädter, which we now have before us, seems to solve the problem.²³ It emerges from this letter that what prevented Maharam Schick from signing the ruling was its claim to be based on the authority of the Hatam Sofer, as if the ruling was simply a corollary of the great rabbi's testament. Maharam Schick cites the words of the Talmud (BT Berakhot 27b): "Someone who says something which he did not hear from his teacher causes the Shekhinah to depart from Israel." He considered the decision to be more stringent than the Hatam Sofer's directive. Maharam Schick did not dispute the right of contemporary rabbis to expand the prohibition, according to the prevailing conditions and needs of the hour. However, this should be presented as a decree necessitated by circumstances, a *migdar milta*, as it is called in the sources, without blurring the boundary between such a decision and the rulings of talmudic law and halakhic authorities—and this was an additional reason for not signing it.²⁴ It thus emerges that he concurred with the ruling, but not for the reasons given by the signatories. And so he indeed states in his letter to the rabbi of Ungvár: "Even though I cannot sign the decision mentioned above, I nevertheless endorse it and uphold it to anyone who asks me about it."²⁵

If a great and independent halakhist such as Maharam Schick submitted to the verdict of the majority, all the more so less important figures. This was true in particular for those who held positions in the congregations: rabbis, preachers, ritual butchers and the like, who, even if they themselves did not support the decrees, had to consider public opinion. They were likely to be disbarred from their posts if they ignored the prohibitions. Indeed, we hear from Miskolc that after the Michalowitz ruling, ritual butchers refrained from praying in the controversial synagogue.²⁶ According to Hayyim David Lippe, this is what happened in the Kassa congregation as well.²⁷ In his own congregation, Eperjes, a scandal erupted, for R. Lichtenstein disqualified the slaughter of those butchers who served as precentors in the "illegitimate" synagogues. R. Lichtenstein's followers had to rely on the butcher shops of the nearby village, Sebeskelemes, whose rabbi, Leibisch Jolesz, submitted to R. Lichtenstein's directives (unwillingly, according to Lippe).²⁸ This was not only an insult to the members of the congregation, but also created great financial loss, since the tax on meat was the major source of income for the congregation.

The ascendancy of the zealous tendency, culminating in the publication of the judicial decision, at times brought in its wake not only battles of ideas, but also a struggle for survival on the part of an individual or a public sector. R. Akiva Joseph Schlesinger tells that one of the signatories to the decision "permitted a ritual butcher to go to their synagogue for purposes of his livelihood, in contradiction to the ruling."²⁹ A person who was "great in Torah ... Mordechai Leib Klein of the congregation of Liptószentmiklós," addressed such a request to

Maharam Schick. His livelihood and that of his ten children depended on his giving private lessons to householders, which obligated him, as he understood it, to continue attending a synagogue that was apparently disqualified by the Michalowitz ruling.[30] R. Aaron David Deutsch of Balassagyarmat dealt with a similar question.[31] Both halakhists express their understanding of the material and spiritual dilemma of the petitioners, but do not consider it sufficient reason to be lenient.

The geographical locations from which these questions originate prove that, although the jurisdiction of the Michalowitz ruling was the Unterland, its echoes reached all parts of the country and troubled the peace of all believing Jews. It is likely that R. Hillel Lichtenstein hoped that certain rabbis of similar mind in the Oberland, like R. Judah Aszód of Szerdahely, would add their signatures to the verdict. According to a tradition that certainly has a grain of truth, R. Lichtenstein claimed that, after the death of R. Aszód, the latter came to him in a dream and told him that he had been judged in heaven for not having endorsed the decision.[32] R. Lichtenstein certainly did not hope for the general approval of the rabbis of the Oberland, for all his own and R. Schlesinger's activities were aimed to keep the compromise with secular culture that had gained a foothold even among the God-fearing in the Oberland from penetrating to the traditionalist Unterland districts.

However, the ruling was formulated in a general way, without limits of time or place, and its signatories arrogated to themselves the authority to obligate all the Jews of the country to obey their directives. This no doubt aroused the anger of the rabbis of the western districts, whose opinion had not only not been sought, but who were even presented as sinners, primarily because of the language they spoke. We learn from R. Esriel Hildesheimer that some of these rabbis held preliminary contacts with a view to issuing a joint announcement, in which they would protest the arrogance of the initiators of the ruling, and at the same time advise the public of the lack of any halakhic basis for most of the claims in it.[33] Hildesheimer even composed a draft of such an announcement, but his potential partners apparently hesitated to act. The draft was published as an appendix to Hildesheimer's article, which was published in Mainz, outside the boundaries of Hungary, in *Israelit*, and under his name alone.[34]

Hildesheimer analyzed the ruling clause by clause. His critique is similar to Maharam Schick's reaction to the prohibitions in their first incarnation. Both examined the clauses of the prohibitions in light of halakhic principles, but Hildesheimer went further in his critique. Maharam Schick found halakhic support for forbidding prayer in a synagogue that was not built according to strict halakhic principles, for example, if the *bimah* had been moved close to the Ark. Hildesheimer, for his part, determined that this prohibition has no source in the Talmud or in halakhic precedent, and therefore need not be heeded.[35] A similar conclusion was reached concerning the choir which, so long as it does not include women, is completely permissible,[36] against the view of Maharam Schick, for whom every *Chorschul* was illegitimate. As for the use of non-Jewish languages in sermons and the like, for which the ruling relied on the Hatam Sofer, Maharam Schick, as will be remembered, had explained his master's statement carefully, saying that, as he understood it, the Hatam Sofer permitted those who had proved that this knowledge had not flawed their faith to preach in German. Hildesheimer lacked this information, but, on the other hand, he did not consider himself subject to the Hatam Sofer's directives, except insofar as they rested on halakhic sources. He therefore rejected this prohibition, as he did the other prohibitions of the Michalowitz ruling that had no basis in the Talmud and in the hakakhic adjudicators.[37]

Close analysis reveals a basic difference between the attitudes of the two personalities to the ruling. Both of them categorized its directives as *migdar milta*, rulings added to protect the law, based on the needs of the time. As such, Maharam Schick felt it incumbent upon himself to take them into consideration. For the same reason, Hildesheimer felt it his right to reject them, and doubly so. The rabbis of the Unterland could not impose their decrees on congregations in districts that were not represented in their conference. And as for the issue itself, just as the Unterland rabbis were convinced that the future of Judaism depended upon isolation from the surrounding culture, so it was clear to him that the future lay in accommodating to this culture.[38] Hildesheimer was not alone in this awareness. As we have seen, the acknowledgment of the surrounding culture had long since become a fact of life in the Oberland communities. Hildesheimer was unique only in his courage in protesting the ruling. Nevertheless, as we shall see below, many public figures rallied to him when the struggle began between the "progressives" and the zealous over the nature of the national organization of Jewry to be recognized by the government after the Emancipation in 1867, which took on national dimensions.

The Michalowitz ruling also attracted much attention among the non-Orthodox Jewish public, whose members of course did not acknowledge the authority of the conference over them. At first the rumor spread that the issue under discussion was the emancipation of the Jews, and that the Orthodox had, as it were, attempted to subvert it.[39] But even when the clauses of the ruling became known, the general public could not remain indifferent to it. It was clear from the various community conflicts that the zealots viewed the changes instituted in the synagogue as undesirable, and that the extremists among them even refrained from attending such synagogues for this reason. However, to call the *Chorschul*, which was meant to serve as a place of public prayer conducted according to the Jewish tradition, a place of idol worship or the like, was a terrible insult and even a slur on the honor of Heaven.[40] This was indeed the spontaneous reaction of Maharam Schick, as we have heard. Protests against these and similar expressions were made by the opponents of the extremist Orthodox groups in the continued struggle between the camps, without the extremists' retracting their statements. That estrangement between the camps could reach this level was a dire omen for the future when, because of political circumstances, the Jews would be required to create an overall organizational framework for their public life.

III

On the Eve of the Congress

Chapter 9

Emancipation and the Idea of a Nationwide Jewish Organization

On December 20, 1867, the Jewish Emancipation Law was passed in the lower house of the Hungarian Parliament, and two days later it was approved by the upper house. This is the text of the law: "It is declared that the Jewish inhabitants of the land have the right to enjoy all civil or political rights on an equal footing with the Christian inhabitants."[1] Many consultations by government officials, public debates in Parliament, and similar discussions in the press in all its branches, preceded this historic decision.[2] The passage of the bill in the current session of Parliament was assured, following the compromise with the Austrian rulers which had been reached in February of the same year. The leading members of the Assembly had demanded approval of the bill a year earlier, and some had supported the idea as early as the 1840s. One such personage was Francis Deák, the architect of the policy of compromise with Austria, who at this historic hour was at the height of his popularity. Second to him was Baron Joseph Eötvös, a writer and intellectual of stature, who served as the Minister of Education and Religion in the liberal government of the time. Eötvös had recommended granting equal rights to the Jews in his book, *The Emancipation of the Jews*, which appeared in 1840, at a time when the Jews were just beginning to extricate themselves from their inferior social and economic position.[3] In the quarter century that had passed in the interim, they had taken a giant step forward. Most of the anti-Jewish laws, which had circumscribed their areas of activity, their places of habitation, or their choice of profession, were abolished one after another. One of the last to be abolished, in 1860, was the prohibition against purchasing property.[4] The improvement in their legal position was matched by their progress in the economic sphere, their social integration, and their adaptation to the surrounding culture. The legal changes accelerated this process in all spheres, while this advancement expedited the legal steps taken for their benefit. Nonetheless, the Jews remained devoid of any political rights and were prevented from participating in the elections to Parliament, and the like. Their achievements in other spheres highlighted their inferior civil position, which was a source of humiliation and frustration. Many circles in Hungarian society, intellectual and political alike, identified with the Jews, and government representatives repeatedly announced that the planned Emancipation Law was not a grant or a gift, but an equitable act and the rectification of an injustice.[5] The representatives of the Jews, for their part, declared at every possible opportunity, that they saw no need—nor were they willing—to act further on their own behalf, and that the enactment of the law was the affair of the legislative body, and its concern.[6]

Despite the express desire of all the parties concerned, passage of the law was delayed, because its exact wording was a subject of controversy. There were those, Francis Deák among them, who maintained that it was best to word the law in the negative, that is, to state that the civil and political rights of the inhabitants of the country should not depend on their religious affiliation.[7] However, Deák himself entertained the idea of simultaneously enacting a law that would restrict the freedom of immigration of all foreigners, not specifically Jews. This indicates that his real concern was about the number of Jews who could be expected to immigrate to Hungary from neighboring lands.[8]

Some of the difficulties of formulation stemmed from the relationship of the state to religion in general. A statement that civil and political rights are independent of a person's religious affiliation would be interpreted as a declaration by the state of its uninterest in the religion of its citizens, that is, as advocating its separation from the churches—an idea that a few radical circles upheld, but which was far from reflecting the view of the majority of the public, and contradicted the reality in Hungary. Important public functions were in the hands of the churches; most of the educational institutions were under their jurisdiction, and the registration of the population, as well as marriage ceremonies were conducted by church officials. The Jewish communities and their rabbis were also authorized to fulfill these functions for their members. Moreover, there were differences in the status and position of the different religious bodies: Most of the population were members of the Catholic Church, which considered itself the original state religion. It reserved for itself certain privileges even after the Evangelical and Greek-Orthodox churches (of which there were two, one Serbian and one Rumanian) were also classified as "accepted" religions. This term was not applied to the Jews. They were members of an "acknowledged" religion. The members of the "accepted" religions could move from church to church, but this was not the case for those whose religion was only "acknowledged." This meant that a Jew could convert to Christianity, but a Christian could not convert to Judaism. Jews hoped, on the one hand, that the inferior status of their religion would be abolished with the Emancipation.[9] On the other hand, they feared that if the lawmakers were to be firm in this demand, the Emancipation Law would not enjoy the support of devout Christians. Those with a secular bent, such as Deák, deliberated whether the granting of emancipation to the Jews—which meant that the state relinquished its exclusive relationship with Christianity—was not a suitable opportunity for the enactment of civil marriage. But this idea too was rejected, because it was feared that the addition of such an anti-church measure would endanger the chances of enactment of the Emancipation Law.[10] In the end, the law was passed in its limited version. It granted equal political rights to the Jews, without ignoring their religion and without changing its status. This was in accord with the viewpoint of Eötvös, who was responsible for overseeing the execution of the law. Eötvös, in contrast to his friend Deák, was a Christian by conviction, a faithful member of the Catholic Church, who had a clear conception of the proper relationship between the state and the churches that enjoyed its protection.[11]

Eötvös's idea of the relationship between a religion, or religions, and the state, was destined to influence the fate of Hungarian Jewry after the Emancipation, which we will later follow. Let us therefore clarify the nature of this theory. Eötvös identified with the motto of the French count Charles Montalembert, one of the central figures of the liberal Catholic movement in his country. He knew Montalembert personally, and had corresponded with him from the mid-1850s.[12] This motto was "a free church in a free state," alluding to the possibility of identifying with liberal principles while at the same time remaining loyal to the essential doctrine of Catholicism—in contrast to the stance of the church leaders, who viewed the two ideational systems as inherently contradictory.[13] The conflict between the liberalist doctrine, which upheld the right of the individual and group to construct their own intellectual, social, and political world, and the demand of the church to be the ultimate arbiter on all these issues by virtue of tradition and authority, seems obvious. However, as we know, the gates of ideology are never closed, and we find, particularly in France but also outside of it, ideologues who were successful at intellectual hybridization, by which they resolved such contradictions to their satisfaction.

Eötvös was concerned with the contradiction between the freedom given to the citizen in a liberal state to take part in the formation of the government, by choosing his representatives to the legislative body, and his position in the church, where he was totally passive. The heads of the ecclesiastical hierarchy decided not only on questions of faith, but on all church matters: They managed its funds and appointed priests, without consulting those who would be subject to them. Moreover, the church was accustomed to relying on the power of the secular arm, and with its help organized the educational system with which it was entrusted. Eötvös envisioned a solution whereby the lay members of the Catholic Church, as distinct from the priesthood, would form an organized body. The elected representatives of this body would cooperate with the ecclesiastical hierarchy and with the state government.[14] The example of the Protestant churches, which had unions of this sort, served as a model, the desire to emulate them having arisen some time earlier among the faithful in the Catholic Church, as well as the two Orthodox churches in Hungary, the Serbian and the Rumanian.[15] Since Eötvös was Minister of Education and Religion in the liberal government and an enthusiastic adherent of the idea of church autonomy, he began to act upon this idea.[16] He succeeded with respect to the Rumanian Orthodox Church and began to act in his own church as well, but here he encountered difficulties. Such reform in the Catholic Church meant changes in the structure of a church with a long tradition, which commanded enormous assets and whose representatives held positions and honors in society at large, as well as in the governmental hierarchy. Because Eötvös died soon after, there is no way of knowing whether he would have succeeded in overcoming these difficulties in the end.[17] It is thus no surprise that, when the enfranchisement of the Jews made it necessary to determine the government's attitude to their religion, the minister wished to grant its adherents the right of independent self-organization, following the example of the other religions.

As indicated above, many months before the Emancipation bill became law, the public, Jewish and non-Jewish alike, was certain that its approval in both houses of Parliament was only a matter of time. It was therefore appropriate to consider what would be the legal status of the congregations once their members had become citizens of equal status with all other citizens of the land. This question was the topic of a discussion between the Minister of Education and Religion, Joseph Eötvös, and the leaders of the Jewish community of the capital, shortly after the appointment of the independent Hungarian government, in the wake of the compromise with Austria in February 1867. According to contemporary sources, this conversation occurred when a delegation of the community presented itself to Count Eötvös, to congratulate him on his appointment as Minister of Education and Religion.[18] It was agreed at this meeting that the leaders of the Jewish community of the capital city would present a memorandum to the minister in which they would present their picture of the future of Hungarian Jewry after the emancipation.

Who first raised the idea of the memorandum was later the subject of controversy. The opening sentence of the memorandum states that it was written in response to the "gracious application" of his honor the minister.[19] Those among the Orthodox who disagreed with the content of the memorandum claimed that it was the members of the delegation who wished to establish a national organization for Hungarian Jewry, and that they were the ones who urged the minister to request their opinion, in order to present their program to him.[20] The memorandum lists the defects in Jewish community life caused by the lack of a legal basis for their activities.[21] There are no rules that state the rights of the members of the communities in choosing their leaders, nor any that define the authority of the appointed leaders. This invites arbitrariness and injustice by aggressive members of the community, or on the part of the representatives of the local government, who are called upon to settle differences on issues of principle and clashes between individuals or groups within the community. The interference of the authorities in internal Jewish affairs brings in its wake unintentional injustice, caused by the secular authorities' ignorance of Jewish law, worship, and customs. A vacuum exists also in respect to the rights and obligations of the officials appointed by the congregation—rabbis, teachers, and others—and if this vacuum allows these officials to be shortchanged, it also leaves room for rabbis to act on their own discretion, as in the case of the delegation to the Kaiser, an event which the authors of the memorandum point to as a negative example. The memorandum's authors consider the lack of a supra-communal Jewish organization, authorized to set the rules of conduct for the congregations, and to serve as a judicial authority in cases of intercongregational clashes, as the source of all evil.

There was also a financial interest in forming a national organization. As will be remembered, an educational fund existed, consisting of the fines levied upon the Jewish communities in the wake of the Revolution. The fund had remained in the hands of the secular authorities, who used it as they wished. The authors of the memorandum tacitly assumed that the authority over the fund would be transferred to the officials of the newly formed national Jewish organization.[22] Needless to say, the national organization was intended to represent all Jews to the authorities, in similar fashion to the role of the churches, according to Eötvös, to whom the memorandum was directed.

The question was raised as to whether this proposal accorded with the wishes of the Jewish public. The authors of the memorandum declared that they did not consider themselves authorized to speak in the name of the half a million Jews living in Hungary. They therefore requested that the minister convene an assembly of the representatives of all the Jewish communities in Hungary, in order to decide the issue.

The memorandum was formulated in a very diplomatic fashion, and could almost be considered self-contradictory. The penultimate paragraph stated that the authors restricted themselves to a description of the malady that had spread in the body of Judaism, while the remedy could be prescribed only by "a council of the elected representatives of all the congregations in the state." This meant that the proposed assembly would debate, and decide upon the proper means to remedy the situation. In the last paragraph, however, the authors of the memorandum put forward their own view that the remedy would be the establishment of "a central representative organization of the entire Jewish public,"[23] and that the assembly would be convened in order to carry this out. The first statement was meant to placate public opinion by suggesting that the elected representatives would be free to suggest remedies of their own, while the latter section implied that the remedy could only be achieved by the establishment of a national organization.[24]

The authors of the memorandum, with Dr. Ignaz Hirschler at their head, were members of the elite of the Jewish community, at least in terms of their successful integration into Hungarian society. Hirschler was a famous physician, a first-rank expert on eye diseases,[25] and his colleagues had reached similar levels of achievement in their fields. Their status as leaders of their congregations did not necessarily reflect their personal involvement in the religious life of the community. Their identification with the ideological and practical aspects of religion was superficial, unlike their interest in the fate of the communities, which faced a crossroads with the coming of emancipation. When their physical proximity to the center of government and their contacts with its authorized representatives afforded them the opportunity to influence the course of events, they did not hesitate to take the initiative, with the hope that their actions would retroactively gain the approval of all those concerned.

Indeed, they presented the memorandum to many leaders of the Jewish communities, and requested their opinions. However, unlike the closing paragraph of the memorandum, which ostensibly allowed for alternative suggestions by the communities, the accompanying letter presented the establishment of the national organization as the only topic on the agenda of the forthcoming assembly of congregational representatives.[26] The referendum did not, of course, include all the communities, and we cannot be sure that all of those addressed answered the question they were asked. However, from a survey of the sixty-two surviving responses, we can estimate the dominant reactions among the various sectors of Jewry, and get a picture of the chances for success of the proposed program.

The overwhelming majority of the respondents congratulated the authors of the memorandum for the initiative they had taken, and accepted their proposal without reservation. The analysis of the ills of the communities set forth in the memorandum accorded with their own experience, and the proposed remedy for the situation seemed reasonable. However, many among those who agreed with the content of the proposal commented that making it at this point was inappropriate, for it dealt with communal procedures to be implemented after the anticipated emancipation, and it would be better to wait until the legislation was approved by both houses of Parliament.[27] A more severe procedural complaint came from the leaders of the Pressburg community. They protested against the presentation of the memorandum to the government representatives before the responses from the communities had reached the initiators. The Pressburg leaders apparently assumed that the idea of establishing a central organization for Hungarian Jewry emanated from the authors of the memorandum, and these were accused of creating a fait accompli without authority or warrant.[28]

A certain rivalry between Pressburg and Pest had arisen as a result of events in the previous two generations. Earlier, until the Revolution of 1848, Pressburg had been the seat of the Parliament, and its Jewish community had enjoyed a position of leadership, both because of its proximity to the center of political activity and because of its internal life, its great rabbis and its famous *yeshivah*. But already during the years of Austrian rule, Pressburg had lost its political preeminence. The state was ruled by orders from the Austrian dignitary in Buda; and as for religious leadership, many communities, if not most, ceased to view conservative Pressburg as a model worthy of emulation. As we have seen, even Pressburg no longer maintained its uniform character. In any case, the leaders who signed the response, like K. Pappenheim and P. Bettelheim, espoused Orthodox principles, despite their openness to a certain amount of cultural influence. They saw a danger in the establishment of a central Jewish organization led by personages such as the authors of the memorandum, for in their view, such an organization could encourage the subversion of the tradition, which was already a problem. At this point, they contented themselves with a general reservation concerning the initiative, and announced their intention to reveal their opinions on the controversial questions, which the authors of the memorandum had attempted to obscure.

The anxiety of the conservative communities concerning the possible impact on religious tradition was expressed in other responses as well. The most negative response came from the community of Hunfalu (Hunsdorf). The leaders of the community announced that they were willing to participate in the planned assembly only on condition that its discussions would be categorically limited to administrative topics to the exclusion of any religious questions. As for the establishment of a central institution for Hungarian Jewry, they rejected it out of hand: "for, in light of the difference in religious views, the conscience of many is likely to be troubled."[29]

Other communities, in contrast, hoped that the assembly would assist them in the religious battle they were waging. Outstanding among these were the communities of Makó and Miskolc,[30] which had suffered from the activities of the zealous. The leaders of the small community of Göncz, near Kassa, came to an extreme conclusion. They were acquainted with the machinations of the zealots in the area and feared that the rabbis "who, despite the spirit of the times, set themselves against progress" would use their influence in the elections for the assembly as well, and would ensure that those chosen would be of their kind. Their suggestion was, therefore, that the members of the assembly should not be elected, but should be invited by Minister Eötvös, on the recommendation of the district governors.[31]

Chapter 10

The *Shomrei Ha-Dat* Society and the Assembly of Notables

Reservations about the initiative taken by the officials of the Pest congregation were voiced spontaneously in various conservative congregations. An organized reaction took shape at a gathering of Orthodox notables in the capital as early as the end of April. A report about this gathering was published in *Ben Chananja*, May 1, 1867.[1] Here we encounter for the first time mention of Albert Farkas, as the leading adviser on the plan of action to be taken. Farkas was an unusual phenomenon on the Orthodox scene.[2] He originated from Transylvania, had been educated in the Kolozsvár gymnasium, and had studied in the law faculties of Pest and Vienna. According to an unsubstantiated report, he had also studied in the Pressburg *yeshivah*. He was known as a writer, translator, and publicist in the Hungarian language. It was difficult for his contemporaries to understand his involvement in Orthodox public life, about which we shall hear below, and this is apparently what led Leopold Löw to assume that his marriage to the daughter of a zealously Orthodox family from the capital caused him to join the circle of Orthodox activists.[3] Actually, as we shall soon see, there are indications of Farkas's sincere identification with the Orthodox struggle, arising from a vision of the destiny of traditional Jewry in the modern world. This trend of thought had some adherents among contemporaries, even in Hungary. Its opponents deemed it "romantic"—and not as a compliment.

At the gathering in the capital, Farkas warned the participants that their initial inclination, to reject the idea of an assembly of community notables, was not realistic, for it had the support of the minister. This information was corroborated by R. Esriel Hildesheimer, with whom the Jews of Pest had consulted about the steps to be taken. In his answer, the rabbi of Eisenstadt revealed that two months earlier he had heard from a source close to the minister that the latter had decided to pursue vigorously Jewish issues in general, and in particular to put the education fund to use. Hildesheimer understood this to mean that the plan to found a rabbinical seminary would once again be raised. He felt that the Orthodox should demand that the seminary be founded on the principle of "Torah and *derekh eretz*." However, since he knew that most Hungarian rabbis rejected this idea, he could only withdraw from any further activity.[4]

In the end, the letter that the Orthodox group presented to the minister contained no concrete suggestion, confining itself to criticism of the aforementioned memorandum.[5] The letter claimed that those who had presented the memorandum had no authorization, even from their own community, to act on behalf of Hungarian Jewry. In pointing to the ailments of the communities, they had exaggerated, according to their subjective inclinations. As for their proposal to establish a national organization as the remedy for the situation, and, moreover, to entrust the educational fund to the hands of this organization, the authors of the memorandum had decided in advance on questions that only the planned assembly would be authorized to discuss. The Orthodox would be willing to participate in this assembly only if it were guaranteed that those who initiated the assembly would not impose their ideas upon the other members and the general public. They therefore demanded that first a steering committee be formed, composed of an equal number of "believers in the old and in the new" ("óhitü mint újhitü"). This committee would decide which topics the planned assembly would be authorized to discuss, would set up procedural rules, and—most importantly—would announce in advance whether the assembly would function as an advisory forum or as a legislative institution.[6]

In order that the Orthodox gathering and its presentation of the opposing memorandum should not seem to be a private initiative like the first memorandum, the participants circulated the text of their statement and requested that the officials of the conservative congregations return it with their signatures. The signatories proclaimed that upon hearing about the memorandum presented by the leaders of the Pest congregation, they were concerned that decisions, concerning both religious matters and the autonomy of the congregations, would be made by laymen. Therefore they request of anyone competent to do so, to act in their name, "in the present and future, before the exalted government, on any issue touching upon the interests of Orthodox Jewry."[7] One hundred and twenty congregations returned this signed statement.[8] Unfortunately, the names of the congregations were not given, and we therefore do not know from which circles the statement derives its authority. Gathering the signatures took time, and the counter-memorandum could therefore be presented to the minister only in September,[9] five months after the gathering was held to decide upon its composition and its circulation.

It becomes evident that the participants in the gathering did not wish to rely on ad hoc steps of this type in the future. Thus the idea was born of establishing a permanent organization, *Hevrat Shomrei ha-Dat*, whose literal translation in both Hungarian and German is Guardians of the Faith Society (in Hungarian,

Hitör, in German, *Glaubenswächter*).[10] Farkas's role both in composing the counter-memorandum and in founding the society proves that the groups responsible for these initiatives were identical. He appears as temporary secretary of the society in the appeal that its founders sent to the Jewish public to join its ranks, after its by-laws were certified in 1868 by Minister Eötvös's office.[11] He seems to have been a salaried officer, while M. Trebitsch and Samuel Abeles, who also signed the appeal, the former as temporary chairman and the latter as temporary treasurer, held voluntary positions.[12]

The statutes of the society were presented to the minister's office for certification on September 14, 1867,[13] that is, shortly after the protest document was submitted in the name of the one hundred and twenty congregations. The purpose of the society was defined as defense of the "Jews of the old faith [óhitü] as a whole, and of its parts." A second aim was "the dissemination of the Hungarian language among the Jewish nation," and the third, support of the journal *Magyar Zsidó*, that is, "the Hungarian Jew." The request details the statutes of the society, the composition of its institutions, the system for electing its central administration, to be located in the capital city, the conditions for accepting new members, and the like.[14] The only condition of acceptance was a declaration that the candidate identifies with the statutes of the society; his personal religious behavior was not under examination. It is true that the administration decided by majority rule on all new members, and that it required the approval of the religious council, about whose nature and composition we shall hear shortly. Moreover, even an established member could be expelled from the society if two thirds of the members find that "he is no longer worthy of membership." However, the guidelines for these decisions were not spelled out in the statutes, and their absence cannot be coincidental. It is clear that the founders of the society foresaw that their membership would also include those who, despite their deviating to some degree from tradition in their private lives, would be ready to support the struggle against its opponents in the public arena.

The adherence of the society to the Orthodox line is expressed in the proposal to establish the religious council mentioned above.[15] This would be composed of the greatest and most venerated of the Hungarian rabbis, elected by a two-thirds majority of the members of the central administration. The appointment of the members would be for their lifetime. With the demise of one of them, the surviving members would choose a substitute. Two paragraphs in the statutes are devoted to defining the function of the rabbinical council. Paragraph 7 establishes that the role of the rabbinical council is "to propose to the society suggestions and fateful decisions," while paragraph 8 speaks of questions relating to "religious laws and national customs," regarding which the rabbis' decisions carry absolute authority. The difference between the two categories is not sufficiently clear. In any case, it is clear that the lay leadership defined for itself a certain arena in which the rabbis did not have absolute authority, and decisions were made at the discretion of its members. Nonetheless, by granting the religious council the right to guide it with advice and wisdom in worldly matters, and even obliging itself to accept their rulings in heavenly matters, the lay leadership to a large extent ceded its independence in favor of the religious and spiritual authorities, and not inadvertently, but intentionally. Unlike their Neolog rivals, who apparently wished to narrow the rabbis' sphere of activity to the minimum, the Orthodox leaders broadened their sphere of authority. In actuality, the religious council was never chosen, but not because its authority was nullified, but because the rabbis found a way to enforce their authority without being chosen by the householders.

As stated, the statutes of the *Shomrei ha-Dat* society were presented to the office of Minister Eötvös in mid-September 1867. They were certified only on March 18 of the following year.[16] In the meantime, two critical events had occurred: At the end of December 1867, the Emancipation Law was passed, and in February 1868 Eötvös convened the Assembly of Notables and gave it the task of preparing the Congress. As will be remembered, the convening of such an assembly was another proposal made by the Orthodox in their countermemorandum to the minister. But they made it a major condition that the delegates to this assembly would be equally divided between themselves and those whom they considered their rivals, and this condition was far from being fulfilled. From among the thirty or more delegates, very few were men both of standing and of an Orthodox persuasion, such as Kalman Pappenheim of Pressburg and Leo Fischer of Herend. The question of how Eötvös arrived at this list of delegates, which provoked no small amount of criticism, has occupied historians of the period. L. Venetianer believed that the minister acted on the advice of Ignaz Hirschler, one of the leaders of the Pest congregation, who initiated the chain of events by his contacts with the minister.[17] But this explanation is only a conjecture, which relies on the fact that Eötvös and Hirschler were acquainted as fellow members of a social club in the capital city. A realistic description of the progression of events was given in *Israelit* of March 18, 1868, while the assembly was being held. Eötvös had turned to friends and acquaintances and asked them to present him with a list of intelligent and educated personalities (*Männer von Intelligenz und Bildung*) who would be suitable for the planned assembly, from which he could choose those to be invited to the assembly.[18] The concept "educated" (*Bildung*) meant mastery of at least one of the languages used by the general public, German or Hungarian, thus excluding those who spoke only Yiddish. Indeed, this type, which still represented a substantial percentage of the Jews in the state, was not included in the list of those invited. Only chance decided who from among the intelligent and educated was eventually chosen to be a delegate. There is no doubt that the Jewish leaders in the capital, who were already in contact with the minister, were among the "friends and acquaintances" who were asked to suggest candidates for the assembly, and there were those who suspected them of acting unfairly in favoring people with a reformist tendency.[19] But there was no certain information concerning the religious positions of many of those invited, especially from the provinces. These became clear only at the meeting held in Dr. Hirschler's house just before the assembly,[20] and during the assembly itself, and not without surprises.

The assembly convened on February 17 with a programmatic address by Eötvös, which received much attention, and with just cause.[21] In it, he defined the historical significance of the Emancipation from the government's point of view—it thereby gained four hundred thousand citizens (others spoke of half a million). But the government does not ignore the fact that these citizens are members of a special religion: "The government reserves the right to supervise the mosaic faith just as it does all the other religions."[22] This supervision is carried out by uniting all the members of each religion under a general organization. The government can impose such an organization upon the members of a religion under the law—Eötvös was no doubt referring to the example of the *consistoire* which Napoleon imposed on the Jews of France—but experience shows that people are satisfied only by joining institutions that they have created. The citizens of the state are therefore requested to establish their national organization, and the role of the present assembly is to outline the course of action to be taken in order to implement this program.

Eötvös's declaration of principles at the first meeting with the members of the assembly was actually no more than a brief summary of his views about the necessary relationship between religion and state, which we discussed above. The Orthodox members of the assembly could learn from his words that the forum that they had been called upon to join was not created by a plot or an initiative by their rivals, the "Progressives." But this did not prevent them from having reservations about the way in which the assembly was conducted, nor about the plan to convene the great Congress to lay the groundwork for the national organization.

At the very beginning of the debates, two members of the assembly protested spontaneously over what was said, although they spoke only on their own behalf. Israel Grün of Transylvania thought that there was no point in having joint discussions, given the differences between the reformers and those—like him—who adhered unswervingly to tradition, and that it would be better if representatives of the two groups would first consult among themselves.[23] Sigmund Kraus of Körösladány, a small town in the center of the country, went even further. He produced a written proposal, which he read to those present. According to him, Hungarian Jewry is divided into two religions, with different principles and laws. Those loyal to the original Judaism believe that the Torah and commandments, in all their details and niceties, are a product of Divine revelation, and their theoretical and practical authority are not open to question or change. The members of the other religion deny these truths.[24] If the minister wishes to achieve his goal, he must first take some sort of referendum among the Jews, in order to ascertain which of them belong to the old religion and which to the new. The representatives of the two religions should then convene separately, so that each might establish its own national organization. These were very blunt words, but they did not divert Eötvös from his plan. He declared that the laws of the state recognize only one Judaism, and the assembly, just as the planned Congress, must proceed on the basis of this assumption.[25]

Willingly or not, the Orthodox members accepted this state of affairs and actively participated in the debates of the assembly. The discussions began on February 17, and ended on March 1. The assembly was assigned three tasks: (1) to formulate the principles for selecting the representatives of the communities to the future Congress; (2) to propose a constitution for the national organization that would include, among other things, rules for the administration of the individual congregations; and (3) to create guidelines for congregational schools. The outline for the electoral process was to be handed over for ratification by the government through the agency of Minister Eötvös, while the clauses dealing with the other two topics were to be the basis for debate at the Congress, and its decisions would then be enacted into law.

Since the assembly had a definite majority of delegates with a modernist trend, its decisions reflected their tendency. Their leaders nonetheless claimed to have taken into account the views of the conservatives, while rejecting the demands of the extremists in their own camp.[26] The Orthodox noted during the debates that they planned to present different proposals from those of the majority.[27] But apparently the members of the majority deluded themselves into believing that those with reservations would acquiesce to their proposals in the end, because they had been partners in their formulation.

It is also likely that there was not complete solidarity among the Orthodox themselves. This is not surprising, since they did not come as an organized group, and were probably not acquainted with each other before they met at the assembly. But there is another explanation for the vagaries of their position. The group did not function completely on its own initiative. Testimony from various sources indicates that some well-known rabbis, among them the rabbis of Pressburg and Ujhely, were present in nearby Buda throughout the discussions of the assembly at Pest.[28] Their rivals claimed that the members of the *Shomrei ha-Dat* had invited their rabbis to provide guidance to the Orthodox representatives in reacting to the emerging proposals.[29] The correspondent for *Israelit* denied this, and claimed that the Orthodox personages had arrived there spontaneously, in order to forestall the anticipated threat to the religious values dear to them.[30]

In any case, two days after the assembly ended, on March 3, the Orthodox once again sought an audience with the minister, with a new memorandum in hand.[31] In it they declared that they planned to prepare different suggestions from those of the majority on all topics pertaining to rules for the congregations and matters of education, for the Congress. For the present, they requested amendments to the rules governing the electoral procedure for the Congress.[32] According to the majority proposal, the country was to be divided into districts, with each district choosing a number of representatives proportional to the number of Jewish residents, two hundred and twenty representatives in all. In determining the number of Jews in each district, the assembly based itself on the most recent census of 1857, taking into consideration the demographic changes that had occurred in the interim. This method left room for subjectivity, and for preference to be given to areas that were known to be Neolog strongholds, such as the capital, as opposed to areas with a conservative Orthodox population. The Orthodox delegation requested that these points be corrected in the proposal that awaited the minister's approval.

Another of their requests pertained to the issue of compensation to the representatives for their time at the Congress, to be taken from the educational fund. The assembly had refrained from deciding this matter, leaving it to the upcoming Congress. The Orthodox claimed that if the candidates were not certain of such compensation for the time they would be away from home, the wealthy would volunteer; thus their stratum of the congregations, which tended toward Neologism, would have an advantage from the start. They therefore requested that the minister decide in favor of financial compensation from the fund.

A third point by which the Orthodox minority proposal deviated from the one that lay before the minister related to the question of the participation of rabbis as voters or delegates to the Congress. The original proposal denied the rabbis the role both of voters and of candidates, ostensibly to restrict the issues debated in the Congress to administrative topics, and to keep any religious questions off the agenda.[33] When this decision aroused spirited protest, first and foremost by the Orthodox rabbis, as we shall see, the authors of the proposal hinted that it was actually the Orthodox who had demanded this; they for their part had conceded on this point, in order to arrive at a compromise text of the proposal at the end of the assembly.[34] There is substantiation for this claim in the fact that the Orthodox delegation protested only against denying voting rights to the rabbis. According to their proposal, rabbis could be voters, but not candidates: This was the decisive question—whether the members of the Congress would be only laymen, or whether there was a place also for religious leadership, in all its various forms. The protest against denying the rabbis a forum in the Congress thus went counter to the wishes of the Orthodox minority, no less than to those of the Neolog majority. The issue of rabbinic participation in the Congress created a confrontation—although not an overt clash—within the Orthodox camp itself, which was not uniform or monolithic.

The protest against the absence of rabbis at the Congress came, as we shall see immediately, from the educated Orthodox rabbinic circles, the leader of which was considered to be Esriel Hildesheimer. The idea of sitting together with laymen, many of whom they thought of as transgressors, deterred the old-fashioned rabbis.[35] They preferred that others do their job. We know that the rabbis who were in contact with the Orthodox members of the assembly were of this type, and it seems likely that the concession, barring their participation as voters or candidates, was made with their agreement. The Neologs for their part did not need much persuasion in order to exclude the rabbis, since their tendency was to limit the authority of the rabbis, including those of their own camp. Thus the original decision was made with the consent of both sides. However, on second thought, the Orthodox realized that the participation of the congregational rabbi in the voting process would encourage his flock to follow in his footsteps and to choose the desired candidate. So the Orthodox delegation added this request to the other requests made of Minister Eötvös. The minister promised the members of the delegation that he would look favorably on their memorandum, and even repeated his declaration that he would not allow the majority to suppress any religious minority, conservative or Reform. In matters of faith every person has the individual right of choice.[36]

Two weeks after this conversation with the representatives of the Orthodox faction, the minister made an additional gesture of reassurance. On March 18, his office approved the statutes of the *Shomrei ha-Dat* society.[37] The request for approval had been sitting in his office for over half a year, and it does not seem unreasonable to view his favorable response as a gesture of conciliation. The organizers, Trebitsch, Abeles, and Farkas, could now circulate the statutes of the society and enlist members.

The following is part of the text of the society's address to the public, which was written in Hungarian in flowery, if not pompous, style: "Our brethren! We have founded the Jewish Hungarian *Shomrei ha-Dat* society in order that it serve as a refuge for religiosity that rests on the old faith, one of the solid bastions of Hungarian nationalism and patriotism." The proclamation then goes on to promise aid and succor to the weak and despairing, while placing its trust "in the three heavenly firmaments, which are *the natural order, the righteous law of history, and the divine revelations of the human spirit*" (emphasis in the original). The continuation incorporates the term "the Divine Torah" and the translation of the verse "O house of Jacob, come ye, and let us walk in the light of the Lord"[38] (both in quotation marks). In other words, all those who are loyal to the divine Torah should join the society.

It is doubtful whether many of the readers understood the ideas underlying the opening paragraph. The reliance on the natural order and the judgment of history, and especially the revelation of the divine nature in the human spirit, were all alien to Jewish tradition, to the defense of which the new society wished to enlist its adherents. There is no doubt that this pompous formulation came from the pen and mind of Albert Farkas, whose conceptual world was modern. He was certainly not the only one whose support of the old Judaism relied on ideas taken from foreign sources, maskilic and romantic. For the simple readers, the attraction of the manifesto was in its conclusion, where attention was directed to the "enthusiastic recommendation of the elders of the guardians of our faith," namely three rabbis, the rabbi of Pressburg, Abraham Samuel Benjamin Sofer, the rabbi of Ujhely, Jeremiah Löw, and the rabbi of Ungvár, Menahem Eisenstädter, whose recommendations were appended to the manifesto and the statutes of the society.[39]

As will be remembered, the rabbis of Pressburg and of Ujhely are mentioned among those who were in Buda during the debates of the Pest assembly, and it is likely that the rabbi of Ungvár was there as well. In any case, the three of them were the pillars of rabbinic leadership by virtue of their personalities, their offices, and their genealogy. As stated above, the statutes of the *Shomrei ha-Dat* society called for the establishment of a council of five rabbis, in order to make it known that the society would follow the directives of religious authorities. The three rabbis who signed the recommendation are not presented as members of the council. These were to be chosen by the body of householders, which had yet to be formed. The three famous rabbis volunteered their testimony that the founders of the society were "men of repute . . . God-fearing and reverent."[40] These rabbis welcomed the founding of the society which, they averred, upholds goals that are worthy of encouragement and support. It has two purposes: to raise the banner of the Torah and to encourage the fulfillment of its commandments, as detailed in the four parts of the Shulhan Arukh, and to fulfill the responsibility deriving from the position attained by Hungarian Jews with the Emancipation. The first obligation that derives from this is the dissemination of the Hungarian language among the Jewish public.

This last recommendation was only lip service, as anyone who was familiar with traditional Jewish life understood. We know from Wolf Pappenheim, who was a confidant of the Ketav Sofer, that the rabbi signed the letter of recommendation as if under duress, knowing that his recommendation encouraging the dissemination of Hungarian was a falsehood.[41] The rabbi of Ungvár, whose name appeared at the head of the signatories of the Michalowitz ruling forbidding the use of any language but Yiddish, made himself the object of scorn and ridicule by now recommending the spread of Hungarian. Nonetheless, most of the criticism and ridicule came from the Neologs or educated Orthodox.[42] It seems that to those immersed unconditionally in the traditional world, this type of pretense was a necessary evil, because of the ambivalent situation in which the Jewish nation found itself in the Diaspora. It is a fact, at any rate, that the clearly discernible flaw in the recommendation of the rabbis did not impair its efficacy. Under the aegis of their recommendation, the *Shomrei ha-Dat* society began its career, just as the Assembly of Notables ended, and when the public struggle between the conservatives and reformers gained ground and reached unprecedented dimensions. The statutes of the society, together with the recommendations of the rabbis, were distributed to people who were considered ready and able to coordinate the activities of the society in their areas. The letter accompanying the pamphlet explained how to establish local chapters in the area, how to gather donations and levy dues, and the like. Albert Farkas signed the accompanying letter, and he deserves the credit for the organizational success of the society.[43]

At the same time, the administration of the society gained an unexpected backer. As we recall, the statutes of the society stated that it would publish a weekly with the title *Magyar Zsidó*, that is the "Hungarian-Jewish" newspaper. This newspaper, edited by Farkas, began to appear on September 10, 1867, without the name of the society appearing on the masthead, probably because the society had not yet been certified by the government. From June 1868 at the latest, Sigmund Kraus appears as the editor, and the *Shomrei ha-Dat* society as the publisher.[44] In other words, Kraus had meanwhile become an active member of the society, although he had no part in founding it. His independent stance at the Assembly of Notables had drawn attention to him, and it is no surprise that the founders of the society welcomed him into their ranks.

Kraus's blunt words at that venue about the two religions that were, as it were, struggling with each other within Hungarian Jewry were a total surprise. He had not been known beforehand as holding such extreme views. Indeed, there were indications to the contrary. Kraus had occasionally written for Leopold Löw's *Ben Chananja*, a forum that the Orthodox had good reason to beware. In one of the first issues of the journal, in 1858, Kraus reported on the graduation ceremony of his congregation's school,[45] which he had a part in founding (as he had in the congregation itself). The ceremony opened with prayers by the female students in German, an action that could only be considered at that time of Austrian rule over Hungary, as a prominent sign of accommodation to foreign cultural values. In a minor publication of 1859, Kraus debated with Leopold Löw on an historical subject—the origin and activities of the Great Assembly, the institution which preceded the tannaitic period in Second Temple times.[46] He upheld the traditional view that the role of the Great Assembly consisted of buttressing the Oral Law, which had originated at Sinai. Nonetheless, the very fact that he used history as the basis for his thesis, and saw Leopold Löw as a worthy opponent, put him, as it were, outside of traditional society.

A poem was published in an appendix to this small publication, which in its later Hebrew translation was entitled "Rose of Jericho."[47] In its German original it was called "A Bar Mitzvah Speech," meaning that it was designed to influence a bar-mitzvah boy. The title "Rose of Jericho" is taken from an article in *Ben Chananja* which dealt with the properties of that plant.[48] According to the article, with the flowering of the rose, its seeds scatter to the winds, and wherever these fall, an exact copy of the original grows; moreover, this process of scattering and renewal repeats itself indefinitely. The author of the article, Moritz Horschetzky, added that this natural phenomenon can serve as the symbol of the destiny of the Jewish nation; after it was uprooted from its homeland and original setting it struck roots in all the places where it arrived, for it was chosen to be the bearer of a great idea and to maintain its purity. The article inspired two other authors, Leo Jeiteles and H. Zirndorf, to give this metaphor and its moral poetic expression. The last verses of the two poems allude to the success of Israel's mission, a success that is now rewarded with the entrenchment of the messenger among those at whom its mission was aimed.[49] Kraus became the third of this group to glorify the path of the Jewish nation by this metaphor. The application of the metaphor to the situation of Israel was of course conditional upon identification with the idea of mission, upheld by those who supported the idea of Israel's acculturation within the nations, from the most extreme Reform position to the most outstanding representative of modern Orthodoxy, namely R. Samson Raphael Hirsch. Kraus was a follower of the latter, as arises from the conclusion of his poem. In contrast to his two predecessors, who leave Israel in the Diaspora with the conclusion of its mission, Kraus envisions its return to its land, when the words of the prophet "and the wolf will lie with the lamb" will be fulfilled, as will the vision of Friedrich Schiller that "all beings will be brothers." This bathetic ending is not a necessary conclusion of the Rose of Jericho metaphor. Its purpose is only to highlight the belief in the messianic coming, which an Orthodox Jew could not deny. In any event, this ending was only a sort of appendage to the main part, and its significance was not necessarily discernible to every reader. A reading of the poem gave the impression that its author was a maskilic Jew, who had preserved his belief in the divine mission of the Jewish nation, and expressed this in terms of modern thought.

How was Kraus regarded by the majority on the eve of his entry into the public arena as an extreme champion of the Orthodox? For this we must rely on indirect testimony, which is contained in a biographical sketch from the pen of Ignaz Reich in his *Beth El* of 1865.[50] Kraus was born in the city of Győr in 1815. His grandfather, R. Abraham Schick, was the rabbi of the congregation,[51] but the grandson was educated there under difficult economic circumstances. He received both a Jewish and general education in the congregation's local school, and had only a brief taste of *yeshivah* study. He taught himself his mastery of Jewish sources and his comprehensive general knowledge. He earned his living for several years as a teacher, and was rescued from his poverty after settling in the city of Körösladány, where he came under the patronage of the local magnate Wenkheim, and worked as a tenant and purveyor, with great success. A small Jewish community was established through his efforts, but he became known outside his community as well for his generous personal and economic assistance to his fellows and for his occasional participation in literary journals and pamphlets. This was sufficient for him to be included in Reich's book, which was devoted to a description of the lives of "outstanding Israelite Hungarians." As for his religious position, Kraus is painted in Reich's sketch as an Orthodox Jew who scrupulously adheres to religious law and custom, but also interacts with society, Jewish and Christian alike, and takes part in the political, cultural, and religious aspects of public life. This breadth of spirit was apparently interpreted as a tendency to compromise, although it was actually the result of absolute confidence in the principles of his faith, which in time of trial he was ready to defend with tenacity and devotion.

When the man's true position became known, with his appearance in the Assembly of Notables, he became a most desirable ally for the members of the *Shomrei ha-Dat* society. Kraus set his mark on the journal he edited. The first editor, Farkas, chose as his motto a statement by Eötvös: "In matters of religion, the majority cannot rule." This statement provided the moral justification for the Orthodox struggle, but it gave no practical guidance. Kraus exchanged the motto for a saying whose origin is unknown, and which was perhaps his own creation: "Wenn Überzeugungen auseinander weichen, muss die Scheidung den Streit ausgleichen." In free translation: "When beliefs and ideas clash, the problem will be solved by separation." Since his enthusiastic speech at the opening of the Assembly of Notables, in which he claimed that the division of Judaism into two religions should be recognized, for they cannot coexist within a single organization, was known to all—he himself made sure to publish his own words verbatim,[52] and they were extensively quoted in the press[53]—there was no mistaking the meaning of this motto. The slogan that the two rival camps must have separate organizations was thrown into the public arena. The slogan went against the policy of the government, and even the declared position of the leadership of both camps. Indeed, it aroused astonishment and opposition. The idea of the unity of the Jewish nation, of all Israel being brethren, was deeply rooted in public consciousness. Simon Bacher, a Hebrew writer and poet who lived in Pest at the time and served as a reporter for *Ha-Magid*, reprimanded Kraus for inciting to division instead of pursuing peace and seeking unity.[54] Similarly, the anonymous correspondent for *Israelit* asked, while reporting on the marginalization of the conservatives in the decisions of the Assembly of Notables: Will they, God forbid, force us to follow the divisive advice of Sigmund Kraus?[55]

However, as a dogmatic view of the principles of Judaism grew, the sense of unity was undermined. It is not surprising, therefore, that Sigmund Kraus found additional support from a circle that deliberately and consciously nourished the dogmatic conception, the school of R. Samson Raphael Hirsch in Frankfurt.

Chapter 11

Tensions and Fluctuations in the Orthodox Camp

An article appeared in the April-June 1868 issue of *Jeschurun*, edited by Hirsch, entitled: "Elucidation of the Majority Platform of the Hungarian-Jewish Assembly of Notables Concerning the Organization of the Communities and Schools." Its author was ostensibly a member of the *Shomrei ha-Dat* society. The editorial board noted that the text of the article was a memorandum, to be presented to the appropriate minister and members of Parliament, which had in the interim been submitted to the journal for publication. These details alone are sufficient to make the alert reader scent a hoax. At this stage, the matter was exclusively in the hands of the minister, without involvement by the Parliament. Moreover, the style of the article is considerably different from that which a Hungarian Jew would adopt in addressing the minister or members of Parliament.[1] It is clear that the article was written by Hirsch himself: He wanted to influence the course of events in Hungary, but did not wish to appear to be interfering in events outside his jurisdiction.[2] Indeed, Hirsch repeated one of the central arguments of the alleged Hungarian memorandum in an article he published later, and identified it offhandedly as his own.[3]

Hirsch criticized the majority proposals of the Assembly of Notables for the organization of the congregations and schools. These proposals had been published in two separate pamphlets, and their fundamental points were widely circulated in the press.[4] The proposals rested on the double assumption, which was also the assumption of the minister that (1) every Jew should be required to belong to a congregation and (2) only one congregation could be allowed to exist in any one place. At the same time, the authors of the proposals were aware of the difficulty in maintaining the unity of a congregation when its members are divided on the form public worship should take, and consequently on the type of religious officials: the rabbi, the precentor, and the teachers in the schools, all of whom guide religious life and education. The authors considered the solution to lie in granting every minority the opportunity to establish subinstitutions within the congregation. A modernist minority, which was not satisfied with the old-fashioned prayers and rituals in the synagogue, nor with the sermons and rulings of the old-style rabbi, could establish its own ritual framework, and if it wished, could choose a modern rabbi or preacher for itself. A punctiliously traditional minority, which would not enter the "reformed" synagogue and could not rely on the rabbi who officiated there, could build its own *beit midrash* and employ a halakhic authority according to its own taste, to guide and supervise the institutions associated with it.

This solution aroused the ire of the guardian of the faith, in whose voice R. Hirsch spoke. This solution, he argued, puts the situation of the Orthodox minority in a Neolog congregation and the situation of a Neolog minority in an Orthodox congregation on an equal footing, while in reality these are radically different. The Neolog minority, if allowed to establish its own house of prayer, and to choose the preacher to serve in it, would have its religious demands satisfied. As for the other services offered by the Orthodox congregation—the kosher butcher, for example—if a Neolog wishes to, he can avail himself of these, or if not, he need not. On the other hand, establishing a separate synagogue and appointing a halakhic master fulfills only a small part of Orthodox religious needs. The Orthodox require many religious services: kosher slaughter, a ritual bath, and a school. The author claims that a disparity exists even with regard to education, for the Neolog can shun the Orthodox school or attend it, but the Orthodox Jew has no such option for he will not have his children educated by Neolog teachers.[5] In another context, I have dealt with the nature of this argument, which carries a strong aroma of Orthodox arrogance (see chapter 1). In any event, this is a unique kind of argument, and Samson Raphael Hirsch attests to his authorship of it on another occasion as well.[6]

The arguments about the difficulties of an Orthodox minority in a Neolog congregation are of a practical nature, and the author himself acknowledges that it may be possible to overcome them. But the author of the article had an argument of principle as well, familiar to us from the battle Hirsch waged in his own congregation. According to the proposed arrangements, the congregation would remain united on the organizational level, despite its religious split. Membership taxes, Orthodox and Neolog alike, would be credited to the same account and would serve to support both kinds of institutions. The Orthodox taxpayers would willy-nilly be partners in supporting institutions and projects they abhor. In halakhic terms, they would be considered to be abetting a sinful act; if the law of the land constrained them to do so, this would constitute an impingement on the freedom of conscience of its citizens.[7]

As will be remembered, Hirsch wished to rescue the God-fearing in his own city from this dilemma by obtaining an exemption from taxes, to be calculated according to the percentage devoted to the illegitimate institutions. In Hungary, a neater solution could be offered by separating the Orthodox from the Neologs, as had been done in Székesfehérvár, where Hirsch himself was involved. He alluded to this incident in his article, stating that it should serve as an example for the entire country.[8] In order to convince the government to give its consent, Hirsch used Kraus's argument that Judaism has effectively been divided into two religions, a thesis with which he agreed. According to Hirsch, the chasm that divides the Orthodox and Neologs is deeper than that which divides two Christian churches, the Catholic and the Protestant, for example. Just as the state does not require that these unite under one framework, it should not make such demands of the factions within the Jewish community.[9]

When we say that Hirsch followed Kraus, we refer only to the Hungarian arena, where Kraus's argument concerning the existence of two religions preceded Hirsch's. It is clear that Hirsch provided the inspiration in the relationship, and that Kraus was influenced by him. We have no evidence of personal contact between them, but if we take into account Kraus's broad intellectual horizons and his awareness of all that was taking place in the Jewish world, there is no doubt that he was familiar with Hirsch's writings and followed his public battles. Indeed, Hirsch presented the doctrine of the two religions in much greater detail than did Kraus. We do not know whether Kraus identified the author of the article in *Jeschurun*. He certainly knew that it was not written by one of the members of the *Shomrei ha-Dat* society, all of whom he knew well. He of course viewed the author as a welcome supporter and advocate. We know that the article was circulated in Hungary in its original language and in a Hungarian translation,[10] and no one could have been more interested in this happening than Kraus, who now coordinated the propaganda machinery of the *Shomrei ha-Dat* society. In any case, although it was not at the time the basis for the declared policy of the society, the idea of division began to penetrate into the arena of Jewish public opinion in Hungary.

At the same time that Hirsch's article criticizing the Neolog proposals appeared, R. Esriel Hildesheimer published an entire book on the subject.[11] Their positions on this issue were understandably different. Hirsch looked at events from afar, while Hildesheimer, as the rabbi of an important congregation in Hungary, was actively involved in events. As he says in the introduction, his book was written in response to individuals who turned to him in confusion and asked him what was to be expected in light of the preparations for the Congress.[12] In addition however, an analysis of their respective positions reveals the differences between their thought processes and mentalities. In light of the roles these personalities will play henceforth, at times in harmony and at times in tension, it is important to describe these thought processes.

Hirsch was an abstract thinker, while Hildesheimer dealt with concrete situations. The idea that the Orthodox would in essence be supporting sinners by contributing to a joint treasury did not occur to Hildesheimer. His main concern was that, according to the proposed statutes for the congregations, and in particular because of the authority that the district and national organization would acquire, the leadership of the communal institutions would fall into the hands of the rich and powerful. They would exploit their power to diminish the status of tradition, which was upheld primarily by the common people. He found a horrifying example of this in the history of the Jews of France and Württemberg, whose centralized structure had served as a model for the Assembly of Notables.[13] Hildesheimer did not oppose the idea of the Congress, which would gather the representatives of all of Hungarian Jewry. He only wished to ensure that the delegates be chosen from among the adherents of tradition, whom he considered the majority and mainstay of the public. If the majority of the Congress consisted of this type, it would be able to direct matters to the desired outcome. However, he was well aware that the authors of the proposal, presented in the name of the Assembly of Notables, intended to achieve the opposite result. Why do they propose disqualifying rabbis from serving as members of the Congress? Only because their opponents are afraid to contend with those who could foil their plans. He apparently believed that the Orthodox minority's agreement to the compromise of granting only voting rights to the rabbis had been forced upon them. And why was mastery of either Hungarian or German a condition for being a delegate to the Congress? Only in order to exclude those who write only in the holy tongue.[14] Hildesheimer discerned a similar intention in the number of delegates assigned to the various districts. He of course knew of the lack of clarity surrounding the demographic statistics, but suspected that the authors of the proposals had exploited this lack of clarity in their favor. This was especially evident in the large number of delegates assigned to the Jews of the capital, a Neolog stronghold. It is typical of Hildesheimer's practicality that he took a sort of private census, via correspondence with the leaders of the communities, in order to bolster his claims factually.[15] Hildesheimer, like the Orthodox minority, viewed as an injustice the absence of a decision to compensate the delegates for the expenses incurred in connection with their attendance at the Congress.[16]

Hildesheimer shared the opinion common in Orthodox circles that the idea for the Congress, including the program of the national organization, was the initiative and plan of the leaders of the capital, deemed more than once by the Orthodox: "the errant city."[17] In any case, once the minister had given the order to convene the Congress, they had to take it seriously. The conservative Jewish public was accustomed to acting with respect to the heads of government, and it would not have occurred to them to disobey a minister of the state. At this stage no one questioned the authority of Eötvös to act as he did, even though this was a new regime, in which the distribution of authority among the various government officials was not sufficiently clear, as we shall see. The Jewish public had no doubt that Eötvös's orders were authoritative. However, the meaning of the order could be questioned. And thus Hildesheimer set out to prove that Eötvös had only expressed his wish that the Congress deal with the problems that disturb the life of the communities, while the solutions proposed by the notables were their own. When the destructive nature of these solutions became clear, the public had to reject them out of hand.[18]

On one point, Hildesheimer spoke for many, and not only those in his own Orthodox camp. This was the exclusion of rabbis from voting and being elected to the Congress. As soon as this proposal became known, it was criticized by various sides.[19] Hildesheimer's circle acted to annul the proposal. On June 15 a memorandum, signed by thirty rabbis, was presented to the office of the minister, which protested in their name and in that of their colleagues against denying them the right to vote and be elected to the Congress.[20] R. Shalom Kutna, the rabbi of Kaposvár, a small town near Eisenstadt, appears to have been the formulator of the protest. A strong sympathy of minds existed between Kutna and Hildesheimer,[21] and Kutna no doubt acted in consultation with his colleague. The memorandum expresses the rabbis' feeling of humiliation at being considered clerks ("indentured servants" in the popular jargon), at the beck and call of the lay leaders of the communities, because they are salaried officials. Actually, the rabbi's authority does not emanate from his appointment by the congregation, but from his being ordained as a guardian of the faith by his teachers. How can one think of excluding the rabbis from discussions about the structure of congregational life and the guidelines for schooling, when the supervision of all these is of the essence of their religious office? The memorandum argues that the claim that by excluding rabbis from the Congress, religious conflict will be avoided is a false hope. Although the rabbis have refrained from taking part in the preparations for the Congress until now, quarrels over religious questions have nonetheless grown unprecedentedly.

The numbers of signatories to the protest doubled afterward.[22] Unfortunately, the list of signatories has not been preserved, but it no doubt included rabbis from the entire spectrum of opinion. There was a consensus among all the rabbis on this matter at least. The memorandum also mentioned the issue of denying voting rights to teachers, but in a mild tone, while the protest about the rabbis was stated in a sharp and aggressive tone, which the minister could not ignore.[23] In the end, rabbis not only voted but were chosen as candidates, and in no small number, and they set their stamp on the Congress, as we shall see.

The tension between the rival camps, attested to in the memorandum, grew as the date of the Congress approached. It was set for December 10, the first day of Chanukah. The elections for the delegates from the congregations were scheduled for November 20, and a notice issued by the office of Minister Eötvös laid down the procedural guidelines.[24] The right to vote was granted to all Jewish citizens who had paid congregational taxes. A committee was to be set up to investigate the eligibility of anyone who applied to vote. This committee would be appointed by the officials of the congregations or in an assembly of all members. This was the case in a large community, where the number of members was sufficient to elect one or more delegates. In the smaller congregations, which could only achieve the number needed to elect a delegate by joining forces, the composition of this committee was the responsibility of the district governor, who consulted with the representatives of the congregations involved. Anyone who wanted to take part in the elections was required to present himself before the investigating committee and prove that he had the right to vote according to the stated conditions. Needless to say, these preparatory stages in themselves gave rise to disputes and clashes, at times on a personal and local level, but for the most part against the background of religious conflicts, from which only a few congregations were exempt. The composition of the committee was not insignificant, for its members, and particularly its chairman, could play a major role in deciding if the person before them would be able to participate in the elections.

The Hungarian language has a special term for electioneering, *korteskedés*, and with good reason. In Hungary, as in England, elections had been held under aristocratic rule as well. These took place in an atmosphere of celebration and hoopla, in which it was easy to influence the voters—if not by actual bribery, then by other illegal temptations. With the extension of voting rights to non-aristocrats following the achievement of Hungarian independence, the political culture did not change. The elections continued to be held in this circus-like atmosphere, with all that implied for the propriety of the elections. As the old saying goes: As the Christians behave, so do the Jews. When the members of the congregations were called upon to participate in the elections for the Congress, they adopted the Hungarian style of propaganda. It was raucous and slogan-filled, and gave cause for the adherents of each camp to suspect the members of the other of using improper methods in order to turn the elections in their favor.

The struggle did not take place on the local level alone. As we have heard, the weekly *Magyar Zsidó* had appeared as the official organ of the *Shomrei ha-Dat* society since its statutes were ratified in March 1868. At the same time, a group of activists and intellectuals headed by Dr. Hirschler organized themselves as "The Central Committee of the Assembly of Notables," with the declared objective of fighting the *Shomrei ha-Dat* propaganda. The founders of this organization did not feel the need to request government approval. In a secret letter, they requested people throughout the country whom they viewed as sympathetic to establish branches of the committee in their areas. They announced the acquisition of a journal that would serve their common interests, the *Izraelita Közlöny*. This journal had been in operation since 1864, under the editorship of its founder, Adolph Fenyvessy, and he was now willing to turn it into an organ for the advancement of the Neolog cause.[25]

The establishment of this committee is illustrative of the nature of the campaign in general; the Orthodox acted first, and the Neologs reacted. This was not accidental. The Neologs deluded themselves into thinking that their objective could be accomplished without further efforts on their part. They believed that their ideas were synonymous with those of freedom and progress, which were upheld in society in general. They viewed the Congress as the culmination of the process of emancipation, as did its initiator, Minister Eötvös himself. They considered the Orthodox to be lagging behind the historical process, vainly attempting to halt its progress.

This mood of exaltation was expressed in a sermon by R. Meir Zipser, our acquaintance from his days as rabbi of Székesfehérvár, who now, in the year before the Congress, was rabbi of Rohonc, one of the old but small congregations in western Hungary. Such a congregation chose its delegate together with the other small congregations in the district, after determining which of the inhabitants had the right to vote. Such a gathering took place in Rohonc in mid-October 1868, about one month before the elections. The rabbi of Rohonc used this opportunity to apprise those gathered of the significance of the occasion. He compared it to a holy gathering in the Jerusalem of ancient times, where the Israelites who brought the first fruits thanked the Lord for being free men who could enjoy the fruits of their labor on their own land. Blessed is this generation, said Zipser, which has reached a similar status by achieving equal rights within the state. The Congress which is about to open is a true expression of this new condition.[26]

In order to appreciate the deep chasm created between the different sectors of the Jewish public in the wake of emancipation, let us turn our attention to R. Menahem Mendel Panet, the rabbi of the city of Dés, in Transylvania. At a gathering similar to that in Rohonc, R. Panet decreed a public fast day, explaining that the process of elections to the Congress would necessitate taking a census of the Jewish population, which is forbidden, and which had brought about a plague in the time of King David.[27] In his emotional sermon, R. Menahem Mendel revealed that the expected results of the Congress frightened him no less than the prospect of plague. The Neolog leaders would hold sway over the Orthodox, and would be able to turn them, as riders do their horses, in whatever direction they want. By means of this metaphor, the preacher attempted to convey his message to his audience, calling upon them to avert the evil decree by prayer and fasting.

R. Panet's reaction was typical only of his circle, the circle of zealots in the Unterland, who were also wary of the educated Orthodox in the west, as is clear from the ruling of Michalowitz, which the rabbi of Dés signed. It is typical that he attempted to avert the evil decree with fasting and prayer, while the people of the *Shomrei ha-Dat* society used more rational methods, such as enlisting the faithful through propaganda and organization. The leaders of the *Shomrei ha-Dat* society in the capital were well aware of the differences between themselves and the zealots in the north, but did all they could to overcome these gaps, without being particular about the methods taken, and with good reason. The rabbis and hassidic leaders in the north ruled over the Jews in their districts, and only with the support of this public, which made up a large part of Hungarian Jewry, could they reach the desired majority in the Congress. It was important to find an entry to the hearts of this group. The public relations and propaganda of the society were written, as we have seen, in German and Hungarian, languages which the Jews of the north did not know, and which were considered a sign of alienation from Judaism. In order to remove the language barrier, the public relations literature of *Shomrei ha-Dat* was translated into the Yiddish spoken in the northern districts.[28]

But, as stated, much depended on the position that the rabbis and hassidic leaders would adopt. Two of the three rabbis who recommended the founders of the society and its goals to their followers, R. Jeremiah Löw and R. Menahem Eisenstädter, served in northern congregations, the former in Ujhely and the latter in Ungvár. R. Löw's influence was limited, because of his outspoken and spirited opposition to Hassidism, which was spreading in his day.[29] We heard above of the rivalry between him and the rabbi of Liszka, Zvi Hirsch Friedman, who served as a hassidic rebbe to many. The leaders of the *Shomrei ha-Dat* society wanted the support of both, and they negotiated directly with the rebbe. We learn of this from two letters written by the rebbe in the summer of 1868, the first to one of the leaders of the *Shomrei ha-Dat* society, and the second to the Ketav Sofer of Pressburg.[30] In both he explained his refusal to join the supporters of *Shomrei ha-Dat*. Although he was a partner in the struggle of the God-fearing against the establishment of a rabbinical seminary, in his view more than that ought to be attempted.

R. Friedman understood from the representative of the *Shomrei ha-Dat* society who turned to him that the society accepted the mandatory education law, which would also obligate Jews to send their children to school. In his view, this decree was no less severe than that of the seminary, and the society must attempt to abrogate it, and to demand that schooling for Jewish children should remain voluntary, and not mandatory. In response to his addressee's claim that it would be difficult to explain such a demand to the government, he replied that just as the society demands abandoning the idea of a seminary for being contrary to the Jewish faith, so it should demand exemption from obligatory schooling in the name of religion. In his view, there is a prohibition against allowing schoolchildren to learn anything other than Torah, and against teaching them a foreign language: "Anything that is not the holy tongue is like the serpent's venom." The *Shomrei ha-Dat* society's failure to act to retain the *heder* as the exclusive educational institution for Jewish children prevented the hassidim from joining its ranks.

A second reason for R. Friedman's opposition was the fear that the leaders of the society, who were "Ashkenazim," would tip the scales against the "Sefardim," that is, the hassidim, in the power struggle taking place between the two in the north. Indeed, this was the main theme of his letter to the Ketav Sofer, in which the rabbi of Liszka felt the need to justify his refusal, and that of the hassidim, to join the society. As for the problem of the schools, perhaps there was no way of escaping the decree, and one must say: "We were coerced . . . and an evil decree may in time be annulled," but concerning the latter issue: "If it is not explicitly guaranteed to preserve . . . the religion of every Jew according to his custom, Ashkenazim according to their custom and Sefardim according to their custom, we must take care of ourselves, for we have been afflicted with all sorts of assaults . . . and we have already heard from outstanding masters [rabbis] calling us followers of Shabbetai Zvi, may his name be cursed."[31] These words are a clear echo of his conflict with R. Jeremiah Löw, who was a signatory to the recommendation given to the *Shomrei ha-Dat* society. If the Ketav Sofer, who headed the list of those who recommended the society, would guarantee the hassidim equal status with the Ashkenazim, and the society would make an effort to avert the decree of mandatory education, the hassidim would be ready to join the society.

We do not know if any further correspondence took place between the two. However, approximately two months after this correspondence, a notice appeared in *Israelit* about an additional effort to enlist supporters in the north, through the mediation of the third of the rabbis who had approved the society, R. Menahem Eisenstädter. According to this notice, the rabbi of Ungvár convened thirteen local rabbis in his city in order to enlist their support for the society. The *Allgemeine Zeitung des Judenthums* reported that the rebbe of Liszka was one of them, and the correspondent noted that the participants made their participation dependent on the condition that the two rabbis to be appointed to the anticipated religious council of the *Shomrei ha-Dat* society, in addition to the three who had originally approved it, would be from among the hassidim.[32] This report is quite believable. The inclusion of hassidim on the rabbinic council would enable them to influence the activities of the society. This council was never chosen, but the *Admor* of Liszka was appropriately compensated for the requested position, as we shall see.

While the contact between the members of *Shomrei ha-Dat* and the rabbi of Liszka, and the rabbi of Ungvár's activity among the rabbis, were local and more or less private initiatives, the society's involvement in the controversy in the city of Kassa demonstrates that its members did not shrink from public and—to their critics—even dubious actions, in order to achieve their goals. A controversy erupted in Kassa under circumstances familiar to us from the community of Miskolc. In Kassa too, a synagogue was built in response to the growth in the number of Jews in the city, and it was decreed invalid by the zealous, who adhered to the decrees of the *beit din* of R. Hillel Lichtenstein and his followers. The dispute reached the ears of the Minister of Education and Religion, and he sent a representative to mediate between the factions. This office was given to Mordechai Marcus Hirsch, the rabbi of Ó Buda, the son-in-law of R. Fischmann of Miskolc. He, like his father-in-law, was a moderate Orthodox Jew who had not yet despaired of mediating between the extremes, either on the local scene or on the national scale.[33] When his mission to Kassa was unsuccessful, he published the recommendations that he had presented to the government. There he referred to the claim of the zealous, that they are forbidden to use the general synagogue because of the famous ruling of Michalowitz. R. Hirsch expressed his dissenting opinion, that the ruling expressed the view of individual rabbis, and had no authority over the general public. In this opinion he relied, inter alia, upon Hildesheimer's article in *Israelit*, in which the latter had attacked the ruling.[34]

This opinion was published after the *Shomrei ha-Dat* society had been ratified by the government, from which time on its leaders considered themselves the spokesmen of the Orthodox throughout the country. They composed a dissenting opinion to that of R. Hirsch, rejecting Hirsch's claim, and declared that the Michalowitz ruling is obligatory as long as it is not nullified by a greater *beit din*, that is, a convocation of all the rabbis in the country.[35] Here, in an official document, the leaders of *Shomrei ha-Dat* took a position on a question that was the subject of sharp controversy within the Orthodox camp itself: Do the directives of the Michalowitz ruling carry absolute authority? True, the critical reader could discern from a close reading that they were not completely sincere. A hint was insinuated between the lines that they were not expressing their own ideas, but were acting as the spokesmen of the extremists in Kassa.[36] But this tactic did not work well; if their words appeased the zealots in the north, they aroused the anger of the leading opponent of the ruling in the west, R. Esriel Hildesheimer.

This is revealed in Hildesheimer's letter to Sigmund Kraus of late July, which was published in Hildesheimer's collected correspondence, and in two letters by Kraus to Hildesheimer, which are still in manuscript.[37] One of these preceded Hildesheimer's letter, and the other was written in response to it. The two men were not personally acquainted, but had corresponded for some time. It transpires that there had been an attempt to enlist Hildesheimer into the leadership of *Shomrei ha-Dat*, and he had refused.[38] In Kraus's first letter he declares his complete agreement with Hildesheimer's doctrine, whose major tenet is moderate but conscious acculturation to the environment. He is also convinced that this will be the wave of the future, after experience will demonstrate that neither the new seminaries (he no doubt referred to those of Breslau and Padua) nor the old *yeshivot* alone fulfill the needs of the time. However, to create this situation, a set of statutes for the congregations must be established, which would ensure complete freedom of conscience without external pressure. This goal can be achieved by eliminating the danger of Neolog domination. This is possible only if all of the God-fearing unite, ignoring differences on questions of religion and education. He himself views the spread of Hassidism as a danger to Judaism, no less so than that of the heretics, and regrets that no one has dared to oppose it apart from R. Jeremiah Löw. But in practice it is necessary to unite, even if only for appearance's sake. He admits that such a pretense involves no small amount of self disavowal (Selbstverleugnung), but it does not entail reneging on principles, for even God himself, so to speak, appears in apparently inconsistent fashion in accordance with changing circumstances.[39]

Hildesheimer's letter makes no direct reference to Kraus's missive. Most of it is a criticism of the *Shomrei ha-Dat* society's statement to Minister Eötvös about the controversy in Kassa. He categorically rejects the use of pretense in order to achieve the desired goal. Hildesheimer rebelled against the surrender of the *Shomrei ha-Dat* to the extremists in the north. He took it as a personal affront as well, for he had made it known publicly that the ruling of the *beit din* lacked any halakhic basis, and Marcus Hirsch had relied on this position in his memorandum. Now, the *Shomrei ha-Dat*'s endorsement of the ruling in effect disqualified his opinion. The claim that the concession to the hassidim is necessary in order to contribute to the unity of the reverent is not sufficiently cogent to lead him to "repudiate his public activity throughout the past thirty years of his life."[40] Moreover, this concession would not achieve its goal. If he moves closer to the hassidim of the north, he will estrange others—those who adhere faithfully to the original halakhic decision, and refuse to accept new laws from rabbis who lack authority. Hildesheimer also protested the affront given by the *Shomrei ha-Dat* to the honor of R. Marcus Hirsch. They had invalidated his credentials for judging the Kassa controversy, calling him a Neolog. But Hildesheimer, who had sat with him in a *beit din* called to decide a similar controversy in Szombathely,[41] attests that he had defended the rights of the Orthodox minority against the schemes of the Neolog majority. Has the time come when anyone who does not accept the Michalowitz ruling will be called a Neolog? In his conclusion, Hildesheimer wished to know who was responsible for the *Shomrei ha-Dat* opinion. Had the spiritual patrons of the society, the rabbis of Pressburg, Ungvár, and Ujhely, seen the statement? "I would be very surprised if the rabbi of Ujhely would agree, or even the rabbi of Pressburg." Perhaps the hands of Trebitsch and Farkas had been in the affair, written this weighty document on their own initiative, and submitted it to the minister? If so, this raises many questions.[42]

In his reply, Kraus did not hide behind the rabbis, who were certainly not involved in the affair, nor behind the laymen.[43] He took upon himself full responsibility for the statement to the minister, from which we learn that by now he was an active partner in the management of the society. He had nothing to add to what he had written in his previous letter in defense of his two-faced position, aside from emphasizing its overriding necessity. The extremists in Kassa, among whom were not only hassidim, but also mainstream Orthodox Jews, had to be appeased: "These people must be treated like children, and must be brought to true awareness in indirect ways." He can only hint at his true opinion, his vehement opposition to the ruling and everything connected with it. "It is very sad if a person cannot and is not permitted to be open, but what can one do? The goal is holy, and it seems that in such a case trickery is permissible—so at least Maimonides teaches us."[44]

Aside from the overt controversy about the means that were justifiable in order to achieve the goal, there was also a hidden but essential difference between the two debaters, Sigmund Kraus and Esriel Hildesheimer, concerning the nature of the goal. Sigmund Kraus was convinced that traditional Judaism could be saved only by distancing itself from those who deviate from it, either in thought or in deed. His image of the Orthodox camp was of people with a full awareness of the essentials of Judaism and a punctilious observance of the commandments. He therefore imposed these strict criteria upon the delegates who were to represent Orthodox Jewry in the Congress as well. He appealed to those voters whom he considered close to his view to give their vote only to candidates who are known not only to observe the Sabbath and *kashrut* and the like, but also to agree with Orthodox principles—ranging from acknowledgment of the Bible and Talmud as eternally valid revelations, to the belief in the messianic coming and the resurrection.[45] It is not surprising that Kraus sought in confederates circles where these criteria were understood.

Hildesheimer differed. Although he was an unflagging fighter for the preservation of the tradition in its entirety, both in theory and in practice, he did not think that all Jews could be called upon to declare their identification with this position. He demanded only one condition for the legitimacy of the Jewish community: that the religious leadership that determines the nature of its institutions be entrusted to faithful hands, according to the traditional criteria. This held for an individual congregation, and concomitantly for the national organization that was to be created in the wake of the Congress. By moderating his conditions for religious adherence, he hoped to increase the number of supporters of the Orthodox delegates to the Congress, and because of his cultural openness in the sphere of education in general and in regard to the training of rabbis in particular, he also hoped to pacify the moderates among the Neologs. In a speech before the elections for the Congress he declared openly that he did not wish to divide the nation.[46]

The official position of *Shomrei ha-Dat* apparently tended towards Hildesheimer's. Following the establishment of branches of the society in the peripheral cities, the central management had attempted to maintain contact with them via circular letters. The goal was to encourage the faithful to stand fast against

Neolog attempts to bring them over to their camp.[47] After the dates of the elections for the Congress were publicized, the first to be held on November 2, and the second on December 10, the leadership felt it proper to circulate a list of the desirable traits which a candidate should have. A candidate must be one with a strong religious bent, that is, unequivocal adherence to the Written and Oral Law. This is an indispensable condition. Aside from this, attention should be paid to "refinement of character, to social position, and to intelligence."[48] They thus hoped for the election of leading householders—not rabbis—known to be immersed in the world of tradition, but demanded no detailed examination of their dedication to its details, unlike Sigmund Kraus. Just as there was no consensus between the members of the administration about the traits demanded of the candidates to the Congress, so were there differences concerning the goal those candidates chosen would be obliged to pursue. Kraus's slogan, which declared separation to be the only solution, continued to be the banner of the *Magyar Zsidó*, the official organ of the *Shomrei ha-Dat* society. However, the official leadership did not obligate the candidates to accept this principle. The circular letters did not touch upon the question of the ultimate goal, but expressed the awareness that most Hungarian Jews tended towards Orthodoxy, and the society's direct aim was to ensure that the number of delegates would reflect this reality. If the majority of the members of the Congress were of an Orthodox bent, they would be able to establish the national organization on Orthodox principles as they understood them.

The letters, which at this stage were circulated constantly, were directed toward this goal of attaining an Orthodox majority in the Congress. The activists of the society were called upon to rouse the indifferent in their hometowns from their apathy. They were warned against the scheming of their rivals and the government officials, who are on the latter's side. The inexperienced or timid were instructed how to act, to whom to turn and the like, in order that no vote that could support an Orthodox candidate would be wasted.[49]

By directing the elections from the center, the members of *Shomrei ha-Dat* hoped to counterbalance the advantages of the Neologs, who were generally from the economically privileged leadership strata. Many of them were professionals: doctors, lawyers, and the like. As such, they had easy access to the local representatives of the government, under whose supervision the elections were held. In places where many villages were united into one electoral district, the government had a direct impact on events by appointing the committee which would determine who was eligible to vote. Those of means in the congregations could exploit their position, and put pressure on those who depended on them economically, and there is good reason to think that such cases did actually occur.[50] The managers of the *Shomrei ha-Dat* society attempted to neutralize these elements through persuasion, by appealing to religious sentiment no less than by their sophisticated use of organizational means. As the date of the elections approached, a year after the beginning of their activity, they could boast of having become a determining factor on the Jewish public scene. An indication of this was their becoming a target of scorn and abuse for their opponents, a focus of identification for their supporters and friends, and an object of admiration for neutral observers.[51]

Chapter 12

The Conference of Rabbis in Buda in Advance of the Congress

The elections were held as scheduled. Both sides, especially the Orthodox, suffered disappointments at the local level. However, the true distribution of power on the national level became clear only at the Congress. The views of some individual delegates were not known. But, before we proceed to the opening of the Congress, we must take note of an unexpected development, a major conference of rabbis in Buda, a meeting that greatly influenced the direction taken by the Congress.

The idea of this conference occurred almost inadvertently, even for the leadership of the *Shomrei ha-Dat*. It was first aired in public by the most senior of the rabbis, R. Abraham Zwebner Schag, the rabbi of Kobersdorf, one of the seven oldest communities in Burgenland. R. Schag circulated a letter among the Hungarian rabbis, dated 12 Elul 1868, inviting them to gather in the city of Vác, situated near the capital, on the twenty-first of the same month.[1] He conceived of it as a forum for consultation about the steps to be taken to thwart the Neologs, who wanted "the rod of the wicked [to] rest upon the lot of the righteous." The author went on to give details about his proposal:

And do not be carried away and say the *Shomrei ha-Dat* society ... will be our salvation, for although the most honored and revered leaders conferred of their glory upon them, this is not the time to be silent ... they erred in their vision, and do not say there is guidance in all they say, for if you examine their words you will find that the guidance becomes falsehood [a play on the Hebrew words *qesher* and *sheqer*], and this great error was by their hand because they did not do as fitting in this great matter according to the majority of the nation of Israel, and did not fulfill the words of our Sages, "only if all [the judges] are present is it a binding decision."[2]

It seems at first glance that R. Schag found fault with certain actions taken by *Shomrei ha-Dat*, but his major protest was clearly directed against the three rabbis who authorized the *Shomrei ha-Dat* to act on public issues without consulting other Hungarian rabbis. The invitation to a rabbinical conference was meant to remedy this flaw.

R. Schag's letter made a deep impression. He was one of the major disciples of the Hatam Sofer, a halakhic authority for many, modest and self-effacing. Faced with his inability to repair the breakdown of tradition in Hungary, he decided to go to Israel (at the end of his life).[3] When his letter reached the central office of *Shomrei ha-Dat* in the capital, the secretary of the society responded by adding an appendix to a circular letter which was about to be distributed. Farkas did not hide the consternation with which the leaders of the society received the astonishing broadside by R. Schag.[4] It was an attack on the honor and authority of the leading rabbis who had endorsed the society, and could serve to undermine its very foundations. To demonstrate the serious consequences of this action, he noted that the Neologs were rejoicing over the disunity within the Orthodox camp. But he also promised that steps had already been taken to correct the fault, no doubt a reference to the attempts being made to persuade R. Schag to retract his accusations. This was quickly achieved. Less than two weeks after the publication of his letter, R. Schag published a statement that canceled all that was written in the first letter, with an apology to all those who had been injured by it; but he offered no explanation as to his original motives, or what had caused him to retract.[5]

Nonetheless, a close scrutiny of the statement reveals that the first letter was written after contact with a certain rabbi, who related things he had heard from "important notables" regarding the activities of *Shomrei ha-Dat*. It seems that some of the Orthodox opposed the *Shomrei ha-Dat*, but did not dare to confront them openly. They exploited R. Schag's innocence and used him to propose the conference of rabbis, which was intended to restrict the movements of the *Shomrei ha-Dat*. R. Schag's honor suffered, but he had the satisfaction of seeing the *Shomrei ha-Dat* itself adopt the idea of the conference of rabbis. He heard from R. Aaron David Deutsch, who was close to *Shomrei ha-Dat*, that they too had thought of a conference of rabbis.[6] It is likely that the idea had entered their heads, but they decided to act on it only in the wake of R. Schag's appeal. With the acceptance of the idea by the *Shomrei ha-Dat* society, it began to take shape. The conference was scheduled for after the High Holy Days, in order to allow time for preparation. The location was moved to the capital and invitations were sent to those rabbis whose participation was desired.[7] The participants were requested to encourage other appropriate rabbis to join them.

Approximately one month after the rabbis were invited, on Tuesday, *Parshat Toldot*, 1868, a letter was sent to the branches of the *Shomrei ha-Dat* society with an invitation to a "nation-wide convocation" of its members.[8] Unlike the rabbis' conference, which was decided upon only shortly before the actual event, the convocation was provided for in statutes of the society. Among its purposes was the election of various officers—the president, secretary, and others—who until now had been acting only on a temporary basis. It was also designed, as stated in the invitation, to choose the five important rabbis to sit on the religious council, which until now had existed only on paper. The proximity of the two conferences created a certain conflict between them, and not only in terms of timing, as we shall see. The rabbis' conference was to begin on November 24, 1868, apparently with no time limit. It continued to sit into the first two days of December, which were the first two days of the society's meeting. The date of the latter meeting was chosen to coincide with the closing of a fair being held in the capital in the last days of November. It was convenient for those who had attended the fair to put aside their business matters at its conclusion and devote two days to the needs of the Jewish community.[9] The dates of both conferences were between the November date set for elections to the Congress and its planned opening on December 10. Of course this factor determined the content and atmosphere of both gatherings, in particular that of the rabbis' conference.

They met in Buda, the ancient part of the capital city, in which a traditional Jewish community had been active as early as the period of Turkish rule, in the sixteenth and seventeenth centuries. The royal bathhouse, one of the largest and most splendid buildings in the city, was chosen as the venue. It was easier to house the two hundred rabbis in Buda than in Pest, whose Jewish community was known for its progressive nature. It took great organizational efforts to see to the needs of almost two hundred people, many of them elders of the generation, for two weeks. This job was placed in the hands of the *Shomrei ha-Dat* society. As for the management of the conference, they contented themselves with proposing a set of procedural regulations,[10] although behind the scenes they undoubtedly exerted their influence on the course of events.

Both aspects of this situation are apparent in the choice of president and recording secretaries, who wrote the protocols in German and Hebrew.[11] The rabbi of Pressburg, the Ketav Sofer, was chosen as president of the conference, unanimously and by acclamation.[12] It is clear that his standing as the first and foremost of the rabbis was accepted by all. His two deputies were chosen from among several candidates, by secret ballot. The members of the conference were asked to write six names on a piece of paper: the two receiving the most votes would be the vice presidents, and the remaining four would serve as recording secretaries of the protocols. R. Jeremiah Löw of Ujhely and the *Admor* Zvi Hirsch Friedman of Liszka became vice presidents, and R. Esriel Hildesheimer and his friend R. Shalom Kutna were chosen as the first two recording secretaries.[13] It is hard to imagine that this result, which gave appropriate representation to the various sectors of the Orthodox public, came about without a guiding hand. Let us remember that the Hassidim agreed to support the *Shomrei ha-Dat* at the conference of rabbis in Ungvár, on condition that two of them be elected to the projected religious council. Apparently the choice of the *Admor* of Liszka as vice president was a partial payment of this debt. The choice of Hildesheimer and Kutna as recording secretaries was perhaps a result of their mastery of German, necessary for writing the protocols. But they also represented a sizable sector of the Orthodox public, that which supported a selective cultural accommodation, according to the conditions of time and place.

At the beginning, it seemed as if the differences of opinion between the camps with regard to cultural accommodation would not create an obstacle to joint action. The opening speech of the president of the conference, the Ketav Sofer, which was sermonic in style—according to Hildesheimer it was full of subtle homiletic points—ended with an emotional call to pursue peace and conciliation. The members of the meeting who reported the events, R. Hildesheimer and H. Pollak, gained the impression that the Ketav Sofer was striving to mediate between the extremes, "and that he would not refuse to support progress on a traditional basis," as the latter put it.[14] However, a different tone dominated the speech of the vice-president, the *Admor* of Liszka. He declared that there was no place for change in the life of the nation, regardless of circumstances.[15]

Hildesheimer ignored these words, and, in his activist fashion, took the initiative to advance the objective alluded to in the president's speech. He argued that the conference must define its purpose and advertise it in public, for two reasons: (1) The householders in their communities would wish to know why the rabbis were absent from their communities; and (2) It is no less important to inform the authorities of what is happening at such a major conference, which is partly closed to the public. He therefore proposed the text of a declaration, whose substance was as follows: The conference strives to create a bridge between the different religious sectors of the Jewish community. It strives to find a way to raise a generation that would shed glory on Judaism, adhering to the written and oral law as codified in the Shulhan Arukh, while taking into consideration the requirements of culture and education, according to the needs of the homeland.[16] Hildesheimer was ensured in advance of the support of forty participants, twenty percent of the members of the conference. To his surprise, their support was not required, for his suggestion was enthusiastically received. Many were prepared to vote for it and endorse it on the spot. Only the consideration that it was not fitting that such an important decision seem to have been made so offhandedly prevented this. A committee of twenty people was appointed to examine the proposal and to decide on its official formulation, in the presence of the author of the proposal, who apparently served as the chairman of the committee. Aside from friends and sympathizers such as Kutna and Gottlieb Fischer, old opponents also sat in the committee, with R. Hayyim Sofer, now rabbi of Munkács, at their head. Hildesheimer was astounded at the tolerant and congenial atmosphere in which the examination of the proposal was conducted. Only one change of substance was made: Jewish customs were granted the same status as the laws of the Shulhan Arukh, which were mentioned in the proposal as the basis for Jewish observance. This addition came at the request of the members of the committee from the Unterland. As will be remembered, one of Hildesheimer's criticisms of the Michalowitz ruling was that it gave customs equal rank with halakhic rulings. This was therefore a concession on his part, which he justified with the claim that it allowed the proposal to be passed unanimously. "Moreover, in principle we too admit that customs have some validity,"[17] that is, each community has its own customs.

When the amended version was brought before the forum, it was received with general enthusiasm. It was printed and circulated abroad, and ostensibly set the predominant tone for the conference. On that same day, Hildesheimer recorded the details of the events, describing how even the eldest of the Unterland rabbis came to him and congratulated him for his initiative.[18] This was a great day in his life, or so at least it seemed at the time. He believed that he had convinced those who opposed his doctrine, which was based on the idea of "Torah and *derekh eretz*," that in the existing circumstances it was the only way. In reality, this unanimity was illusory. The first crack in this unity came from the left of Hildesheimer's position. His proposal stated that one of the purposes of the conference was to bring the different religious sectors of the community closer to each other. But a group of rabbis was not satisfied with this statement, and H. Pollak, who reported for *Neuzeit*, was one of this group. According to his report, the members of this group demanded that a notice be sent by the conference to the communities stating that this conference was not a demonstration against the Congress, which was soon to be opened, but on the contrary, its purpose was to mediate between the different positions and to conciliate their representatives. This proposal did not win a majority, and moreover it was decided that any minority opinion would be null and void, and would not even be mentioned in the protocol. In reaction to this decision, this minority stopped participating in the conference.[19]

Hildesheimer's disappointment was not slow in coming. It arrived at the moment that the conference was called upon to switch from abstract discussion to a dialogue on the concrete questions that were expected to be raised at the Congress. It was the vice president, R. Jeremiah Löw, who forced the plenum to open this discussion.[20] On Sunday, November 29, the fifth day of the meeting, he surprised the assembled by announcing his resignation from the office to which he had been appointed, in order to return home for reasons of pressing public business. When he was pressed to retract, he revealed what was really on his mind. He lamented the uselessness of continuing the conference, which was not fulfilling its role of guiding him and the other delegates to the Congress in the position they should take about issues relating to "our holy religion." These were the organization of the communities and the educational institutions, including the seminary for ordaining rabbis and training teachers. He found it difficult to decide these issues on his own, and was ready to act according to the decisions of the majority.

The issue of the seminary, which had long been a bone of contention between the factions in the Orthodox camp, was thus thrown into the arena, and effectively ended the illusion of unity. The representatives of the two factions, R. Esriel Hildesheimer on the one side and R. Hayyim Sofer on the other, were both present. They now clashed, although for the moment they were not called upon to express their opinions on the topic itself, but merely to determine how the conference would reach a decision. R. Sofer suggested that those present be divided into groups of about twenty people, and that these would reach conclusions within a number of hours, and would present them to the plenum: It would make the final decision without delay. The author of the suggestion was convinced that this procedure would produce an unequivocal rejection of the seminary, even if it would take place under the management of someone like R. Esriel Hildesheimer.

Hildesheimer, on the other hand, was convinced that the composition of the conference did not adequately reflect the broad support for the idea of the seminary among the public, the householders as well as the rabbis. He therefore suggested conducting a sort of referendum among the district rabbis: The conference would choose a committee of about thirty people, which would organize the referendum, and its results would be binding upon the delegates to the Congress. But Hildesheimer begged in vain for a discussion of his proposal; no one listened. The meeting decided to forgo even the procedure suggested by R. Sofer. The question of the seminary was put to a direct vote, and Hildesheimer was not even allowed to present his reasons for advocating the seminary, which had supporters among those present as well. He could only announce his resignation from the conference in protest. He was accompanied by some of those who supported his views, or who were angry at the arbitrary manner in which the forum was conducted.[21] Only senior rabbis, such as R. Meir Perles, the rabbi of Nagykároly, or R. Israel Isaac A. Landesberg, the rabbi of Nagyvárad, could afford such a public protest against those who dominated the scene. Many young rabbis, who according to Hildesheimer tended to support him, did not dare to cross the older rabbis and these did not hesitate to make them toe the line.[22]

After the exalted mood of the first days of the conference, Hildesheimer's final trial was a fall from a pinnacle to an abyss. This dramatic change of sentiments calls for an explanation. It seems to indicate that Hildesheimer was and remained a foreign element in the country, even though he had lived there for more than a decade and a half. He did not understand his native veteran rabbinic colleagues. They were ready to sign a declaration about the need to include general cultural values in the traditional educational framework, especially when it would pacify the government, without considering themselves bound to act in accordance with it. Hildesheimer, moreover, displayed a lack of comprehension of the relationship between the junior rabbis and their seniors—those who were considered prominent—in the conference, and in the country in general. He poured out his bitterness in a letter to R. Samson Raphael Hirsch and requested that Hirsch come to his aid. One of his major complaints was directed against the senior rabbis, who displayed not even a spark of parliamentary spirit.[23] In other words, he expected that a free give-and-take would take place among the two hundred participants of the conference, in which everyone would speak his mind freely, and that the votes would be counted without giving greater weight to the views of those with special status. In reality, he confronted a hierarchical structure, which in theory recognized the principle of majority rule, but in practice subordinated those of lesser status to those of greater. Hirsch did indeed respond, but Hildesheimer's hope that Hirsch's support would help him in his struggle in Hungary also proved illusory.

Hirsch devoted an article in his *Jeschurun* to the state of affairs among Hungarian Jewry, and described it as divided into three sectors. He expressed his certainty that the moderate sector, represented by the rabbi of Eisenstädt and his circle, was the one responsive to the needs of the hour, and would prevail in the end.[24] There were indeed circles in Hungary that followed Hirsch's doctrine, on both its levels—the readiness for cultural acculturation, but under the auspices of the seceding Orthodox community, whose representatives we have already encountered above. However, Hildesheimer's rivals, if they took note of this doctrine at all, adopted only part of it: They saw him as a supporter and example worthy of emulation in his battle for the independence of the Orthodox community; as for his advocacy of cultural accommodation, even if they did not denounce it openly, they considered it an outgrowth of conditions in Germany and inapplicable elsewhere. During the first days of the rabbinic conference, Hildesheimer expected that it would create a sort of modus vivendi between those who supported accommodation and those who opposed it; instead, the conference became the arena in which its opponents triumphed over its supporters.

The rejection of the idea of the seminary prior to Hildesheimer's departure was not the final word in this confrontation. Although we have only fragmentary information about what occurred in the conference from this moment on, the reliability of one of these items, concerning general studies for *yeshivah* students studying for ordination, is confirmed by its author, the Ketav Sofer, rabbi of Pressburg. Knowing that the government was interested in encouraging general studies among the rabbis, he announced to the members of the conference that if the government issued an order about this, it will be considered a "law of the kingdom," which must be obeyed. They would then have to appoint professors to teach general studies in addition to the regular *yeshivah* curriculum.[25] But the authority and prestige of the Ketav Sofer as the president of the conference was not sufficient in this case. His vice-president, the *Admor* of Liszka, got up and declared that all a rabbi needed to know was the Latin alphabet, in order to be able to sign his name on an official document in German or Hungarian. Indeed, a declaration was passed at the end of the conference, that forbid not only the establishment of a seminary, but also its substitute, the inclusion of a course of general studies within the *yeshivah*.[26] The report about the exchange of words between the president and his deputy was spread abroad, but, as usual with these things, with a certain amount of distortion.[27] The statement about "the law of the kingdom" was omitted, and the idea of inviting professors to teach general studies in the *yeshivah* was attributed to the Ketav Sofer. When this version was printed in the official newspaper of the *Shomrei ha-Dat, Magyar Zsidó*, as well, the Ketav Sofer felt the need to set the record straight.[28]

A minority protest assembly of rabbis who had not been invited to the rabbinic conference took place in another part of the city, Ó Buda, at the same time as the conference in Buda.[29] Among them were Orthodox moderates like Marcus Hirsch, and some rabbis with an overt Neolog tendency, like Samuel Kohn, a preacher in the great synagogue of the Pest congregation. Those assembled protested against the rabbinic conference's usurpation of authority in attempting to impose its decisions on the public and its rabbis, as had the Michalowitz conference three years previously, under the aegis of R. Hillel Lichtenstein. They meant the comparison with R. Lichtenstein in a pejorative sense, but to those who followed the actions of the conference in Buda and adhered to its decisions, the comparison could have been considered a compliment. Indeed, in the minds of the succeeding generation, the two conferences were juxtaposed as two links in the same chain of events. The Buda conference finally sealed the debate about accommodation, and whenever the issue of the seminary or of the need for general education arose, opponents had a ready answer; a conference of two hundred rabbis had given their decision a long time ago, and no Orthodox Jew had the right to challenge them. It was quickly forgotten that the decision was not the result of open debate, and that many of those present—according to the two eyewitnesses, Hildesheimer and Pollack, almost half of those present—were forced to agree.[30] As usual, it was not the historical facts but the myth that obscured them that determined the course of events.

As stated, we have no testimony from those present about the final days of the conference in Buda, but the isolated data we have enable us to reconstruct the events with almost complete certainty. First, let us note the dates. These were the last days of November and the first days of December, approximately two weeks after the elections to the Congress, which took place on November 18. The results of the elections were already known by this time, and the members of *Shomrei ha-Dat*, with their great talent for organization, collated this information. About two weeks before the elections, they had sent a circular letter requesting all of their branches to inform the central branch immediately—preferably by telegram—after the counting of the votes, of the identity of the delegates chosen in their areas, and whether they were Orthodox or Neolog.[31] The results were disappointing. The central branch of the society reacted to the news in a circular letter of December 2, and noted that in many districts the Neologs had won by virtue of stratagems and the application of pressure, and that the Orthodox voters must appeal to the Congress about the results, to the extent that they have proof to support their allegations.[32] But they certainly did not delude themselves that these appeals would have the power to alter the essential balance of power.

The hope of achieving an Orthodox majority to control the Congress had thus been thwarted by the time of the rabbinic conference. The danger that the Congress would make decisions contrary to the doctrines of Orthodoxy, to which the government would grant the force of law, now appeared real and immediate. Moreover, the clash with Hildesheimer and his colleagues at the beginning of the conference almost caused the moderate conservatives, and even some of the undecided, who were ready to support Orthodoxy, to consider themselves rejected. In their annual report, which was issued on the eve of the rabbinic conference, the leaders of *Shomrei ha-Dat* boasted that, thanks to their policy, which seemed at times to be self-contradictory, they had succeeded in uniting all branches of Orthodoxy, from Ungvár to Eisenstadt.[33] But this sophisticated policy was now revealed to be a complete failure. Hildesheimer's prophecy, that the *Shomrei ha-Dat* would find themselves captives of the people of Ungvár alone, had come true.

In any event, anyone with a modicum of sense saw that there was no hope of defending the Orthodox position, as it had coalesced during the rabbinic conference, within the framework of the Congress. So the idea arose of taking the bull by the horns, and notifying Minister Eötvös himself that Orthodox Jewry would not acknowledge the legality of the decisions of the Congress, unless they were in accordance with Judaism, as interpreted by its halakhic authorities. It was therefore necessary to compose a memorandum that would present this bold decision in the proper way. While an entire committee had composed the declaration Hildesheimer suggested, only one man was chosen to formulate this weighty and important declaration, and he was not one of the rabbis who participated in the conference, but one of the leaders of *Shomrei ha-Dat*, who ostensibly only organized the meeting. This person was our acquaintance, Sigmund Kraus.[34] We will not be far amiss if we assume that the task fell to him because he was among the originators of this initiative, and that he was responsible not only for the style, but also for the content of the declaration.

The memorandum opened by mentioning the declaration that was circulated by the rabbinic conference in order to reduce tensions in the communities, especially in the wake of the elections for the Congress. However, asserted the memorandum, the existence of two camps throughout the country, guided by different religious principles, is a fact. This is a somewhat moderated version of the doctrine of two religions that Kraus had long since held. In order to define the nature of Orthodoxy, Kraus used a term from the school of Hirsch, *gesetzestreu*, "faithful to the law," that is, to the religious law, the observance of which, in all its details and minutiae, defines the basic identity of the Orthodox Jew. Therefore, the rabbinic conference requested of the minister that he agree to the appointment of a committee from among the great rabbis, to consider every decision of the Congress, which would not be submitted for governmental approval until it received their sanction, or was amended to their satisfaction. Up to this point the memorandum was worded as a request, addressed to the minister. In the final paragraphs, however, the right of imposition of rabbinic supervision is phrased as an unequivocal demand: "Only on this condition can we grant legal recognition to the decisions of the Congress."[35]

The reporter for the *Allgemeine Zeitung des Judenthums*, who cited the contents of the declaration, inquired if the authors of the memorandum realized the implications of their demand of the minister.[36] The latter had decided to convene a Congress on the basis of elections by members of the faith, in order to ascertain their desires, and—as we know—in order to serve as a counterbalance against the excessive influence of the "priesthood" over the leadership of the nation. Now the representatives of the "priesthood" wish to neutralize the expression of the will of the people at its very inception. What could the minister's response to this be? It is indeed likely that Sigmund Kraus, who well knew the ways of the world, and was well informed as to the minister's view, knew that the answer would not be positive. Nonetheless, a declaration by the great rabbinic conference, which still presumed to represent Orthodoxy as a whole, could serve as a basis for the demand that it be recognized as a separate group, to whom the decisions of the Congress would not apply. This was, in the final analysis, Kraus's idea from the very beginning of his public involvement. But if he was undeterred in his demand for rabbinic supervision of the Congress, some of those who participated in the debate over the ratification of the memorandum were more hesitant. It seemed to them a direct provocation against the minister appointed over Jewish affairs, and it was not like the conservatives to defy those in power.

We learn of the debate over the ratification of the memorandum from one of the participants in the conference, R. Efraim Fischel Sofer, the rabbi of the community of Hajdunánás and the brother of R. Hayyim Sofer. In a much later stage of the battle for the independence of the Orthodox communities, R. Sofer was reminded of a sermon which Maharam Schick had given "during the rabbinic conference in 1868, where there were more than two hundred rabbis, great minds and righteous men among them. The *gaon* Maharam Schick (may his deeds protect us) opened his mouth and mentioned the *mishnah* in Tractate

Sotah (8, 6)." The *mishnah* alluded to describes the procedures taken during wartime against those who would flee the battlefield in fear. R. Sofer concluded his words with the sentence: "and all the great ones were in awe of the holy words which emerged like flames from his pure heart."[37] There is no doubt that this emotional speech by Maharam Schick was given during the debate over the memorandum to Minister Eötvös. It can only be interpreted as a reference to the battle against the will of the minister, something that cast fear into the hearts of some of those present.

R. Sofer's words are the only testimony to Maharam Schick's presence at the Buda conference. Maharam Schick was a modest man, and did not assume a leadership role. However, when things reached a crucial stage, and there were those who wished to retreat out of fear of the government, he intervened and called for self-sacrifice for the sake of religious values, as he understood them, without concern for the possible outcome. Kraus found in him a patron and partner, and we can speculate that this was where the contact between them was established, which soon developed into a close tie.

Before the rabbinic conference closed on December 3, the meeting of the *Shomrei ha-Dat* society convened in the society's premises in Pest. While, as we have seen, the organizers noted the number of participants in the rabbinic conference, it stated only that there were many at the *Shomrei ha-Dat* convocation.[38] Most were apparently merchants from the outlying towns, who happened to be there for the Buda autumn fair at the end of November, and who devoted the first two days of December to community affairs.[39] They ratified the report of the leaders of the society on their past activities, and authorized them to continue.[40] Meir Trebitsch could now sign as president of the society and Albert Farkas as the secretary of the society, without the title of "temporary." But special attention should be given, not to what the conference did, but to what it did not do. The appointment of the religious council of rabbis was on the printed agenda of the conference. But there is no mention of this, either in the summarized report on the conference sent in a circular letter, or in the detailed description given in the official newspaper of the society, *Magyar Zsidó*.[41] Indeed, this committee, whose appointment and functions were outlined in the statutes of the society, was never chosen, and the reason for this omission is clear.

Since the rabbinic conference preceded the conference of the *Shomrei ha-Dat* society, and it chose its own leadership, it thereby demonstrated the rabbinic leadership's independence of the householders. It is true that the president of the conference was chosen only for the duration of the conference, and there are no traces of a continuation of its activities thereafter. Nonetheless, it would have been very strange had the small conference in Pest had the presumption to appoint to the council five rabbis from among those who had participated in the great conference, which acted on its own initiative. The authors of the statutes of the *Shomrei ha-Dat* society had taken an example from the local congregations. Just as they chose a rabbi, and authorized him to guide the congregation and supervise it by virtue of his appointment, so did the national organization of householders, the *Shomrei ha-Dat* society, intend to act towards its rabbinic council. But by advancing the rabbinic conference, which was not on the original agenda, the society unwittingly promoted the rabbis' independent stance on the national level. The rabbis no longer needed the authorization of the householders. They drew their power from their sense of mission, of concern for the religious welfare of the entire nation. Moreover, even among themselves the rabbis did not wait for legitimation by their colleagues: They considered it a time of crisis, a time of danger for religion, a time when one does not stand on formal details, and anyone who felt he could act to save the situation did so. Indeed, although the memorandum intended for the minister was signed by the president of the conference—the rabbi of Pressburg, the Ketav Sofer—the one who decided that it should be signed and sent was Maharam Schick, the rabbi of Huszt, who had no official position. Similarly, Meir Trebitsch was elected president of the *Shomrei ha-Dat* society, but the one who determined its modus operandi, and who from then on worked hand in hand with Maharam Schick, was Sigmund Kraus, who had no official position in the society, and attached himself to it as its standard bearer and ideologue.

IV

The Congress

Chapter 13

The Composition of the Congress and Its Chances of Success

The Congress opened one week after the close of the rabbinic conference and the *Shomrei ha-Dat* society meeting, on December 10, 1868, the first day of Chanukah, 1868. It was held in Pest, in the meeting halls of the district council of Pest, which were now put at the disposal of the two hundred and twenty elected representatives of the Jewish community. This was an unprecedented event, which gained the attention of the general Hungarian public and, needless to say, of Jews throughout the world. Minister Joseph Eötvös, the initiator of the Congress, emphasized the uniqueness of this event in his festive inaugural speech.[1] He was not referring mainly to the government's summons of the representatives of the Jewish communities—this had a precedent in the convening of the Sanhedrin in Paris by order of Napoleon exactly sixty years before. Indeed, many of those versed in the history of the Jews in Europe were reminded of this event when Eötvös's initiative was announced. For Eötvös, this gathering was unique in that it provided the opportunity for Jewish representatives to lay the groundwork for their own national organization, an opportunity unavailable in other countries where such organizations existed (in France and some German states). In these places, when the state saw the need for such an organization, it imposed a predetermined constitution, in all its details, upon the Jews, without seeking their opinion. Despite this, the minister left no doubt that the state had interest in the proceedings of the Congress; it was perceived as more than just a voluntary enterprise.

In granting emancipation to the Jews, the state recognized the existence of the Jews as a religious entity, comparable to the churches (whether with equal or different status was not stated). The state reserved the right to supervise the various kinds of Christian churches by way of their national organizations. State supervision of the Jewish congregations had also been customary, but since no organization linked one congregation to another, such supervision had been carried out by the local governments, which directly intervened in Jewish internal affairs.

Now it was incumbent upon the Jewish community to establish a national organization—both for its own good, to ensure its self-government, and for the good of the state, to lighten the burden of state supervision.

In practice, the Congress was called upon to fulfill three functions: (1) To formulate a set of regulations for community life. (2) To establish a national organization to implement these regulations, and to determine the relationships that should prevail between the communities. A special set of rules was needed to set up educational procedures. The state had decided that attendance at school was compulsory—this law too had been enacted at the minister's initiative—but allowed the religious bodies to carry out the law within their own systems of education. Here too, the rules served to facilitate both implementation and state supervision of education. (3) To prepare procedural guidelines for future congresses. The present Congress must of necessity operate according to the guidelines formulated by the office of the minister, guidelines copied for the most part from the procedural regulations of the Parliament. Eötvös mentioned that the preparations for orderly conduct of the Congress had already been made by the Assembly of Notables, and these could serve as the point of departure for the debates in the Congress. The memorandum of the rabbinic congress in Buda, in contrast, was not mentioned. We do not know if the minister responded to it directly, or whether he simply ignored it in his opening speech, indicating thereby his rejection of the request included in it.

The minister's words were greeted by loud cheers, but only a few of these reflected genuine agreement. The audience sat in two wings of the hall: those called the "Progressives" sat on the right, and those called the "Orthodox" on the left—a paradoxical arrangement that prompted not a few joking remarks. The opening session took place on a Monday morning, but the delegates had already gathered in this hall on Saturday evening for preliminary consultations. The Progressives arrived first—according to R. Esriel Hildesheimer, the Orthodox were delayed because of the Sabbath[2]—sat on the right side of the hall, and retained their places throughout the Congress.

This separate seating of the camps was not accidental; it apparently came about at the initiative of the Progressives. Had the delegates sat together, the division into two camps would not have been so obvious to the eye, and it is likely that the voting on certain issues would not necessarily have followed the sectoral allegiance determined in advance. According to Hildesheimer, whose report after the close of the Congress is one of our most important sources for reconstructing events, there were about thirty to forty moderates among the Progressives, who could have been expected to support a moderate Orthodox line.[3] According to him, it was Dr. Ignaz Hirschler, whose stature as an acknowledged leader was clear to all, who succeeded in locating everyone who could be thought to support the Progressive line, and enlisting them as avowed members of the camp at whose head he stood. This membership was concretely expressed by joining the Progressive club, patterned on the permanent clubs founded by the delegates to the parliaments of Hungary and Austria. Hildesheimer even attributed the relative success of the Progressives in the elections to Hirschler's organizational diligence.[4] This hypothesis contradicts the testimony of contemporaries who, as we have seen, praised the organizational talent of the *Shomrei ha-Dat* society, and who claimed that its opponents were only good at producing slogans about the need for progress and the like.

In reality, the progressive trend was nourished by the general spirit prevailing in society and the state at large, in the wake of Hungarian political independence and the rise of liberalism, one of the results of which was the granting of emancipation to the Jews. The national organization of the Jews to be set up by the Congress was seen as the final stage of Jewish integration into the Hungarian nation. The appearance of the majority of voters for the Congress in the capital, under the leadership of Dr. Hirschler, is described by a contemporary: They gathered in small groups, dressed in the Hungarian national costume, and so marched in formation to the voting booths.[5] The Hungarian national costume had been the preferred means of expressing patriotism during ceremonies and public occasions ever since the time of the Hungarian national awakening, in the second third of the nineteenth century. Its use by the Jews during the elections to the Congress indicates that they considered this occasion a step towards their acceptance into Hungarian society, an achievement whose price was of course a far-reaching renunciation of the signs of their Jewish identity. The short time between the granting of emancipation and the convening of the Congress certainly contributed to the progressive tendency and worked against the conservative Orthodox. The optimism of Progressives was well grounded. Nonetheless, they were far from achieving all their desires. The two wings of the house were divided in the election of the president, to which we will come shortly: One hundred and seventeen were in favor of the Progressive candidate, Dr. Hirschler, and ninety were in favor of Leopold Popper, the Orthodox candidate. Hildesheimer rightly claimed that this was not a sufficiently clear majority to serve as a basis for decisions of public importance of the first rank.[6] And according to the correspondent for *Israelit*, who no doubt expressed Hildesheimer's view, the Progressives reached even this number only by enlisting the hesitant and doubtful, which they did largely by applying pressure at the hands of Hirschler and his circle. According to this source, the Progressives succeeded in creating an atmosphere of ridicule and scorn for the Orthodox, until it took a certain amount of courage to join their camp publicly.[7]

The Orthodox camp therefore relied on the delegates who had unequivocally promised their voters to put before the Congress the conservative position, as it took shape during the elections. But we have already seen that even the Orthodox voters were not homogeneous, and accordingly their representatives to the Congress were of several types, according to their origin and background. The article in *Israelit* listed two types, which were actually three. Approximately fifteen were hassidim, and a similar number were of the traditional Jewish type without being linked to Hassidism. The other two-thirds of the camp, about sixty in number, were described by the article as faithful to the doctrine of Torah and *derekh eretz*, whose outstanding spokesman in Hungary was R. Esriel Hildesheimer.[8] Indeed, in his report, the rabbi of Eisenstadt presented himself as the recognized leader of this large group. According to him, the members of the group debated whether or not to present themselves publicly as a separate faction—distanced from the Progressives because of the religious gap between them, and from the conservative Orthodox because of the cultural gap that separated them.[9] Considerations of principle and tactics led to a decision against separate organization. Firstly, a public split in the Orthodox camp would weaken it vis-à-vis the Progressives. Secondly, many of the outstanding rabbis of the country, including R. Abraham Schag, R. Hayyim Sofer, and Maharam Schick, were among the conservative faction. They were too universally respected to be challenged publicly by an Orthodox group.

The Orthodox "club" that organized at the Congress thus numbered ninety-eight members, and chose as its chairman R. Jeremiah Löw, who could serve as an intermediary figure between the two factions of the camp.[10] To outsiders, the Orthodox camp appeared for the present as one unit. However, the great respect of its members for the rabbis reveals a weakness of their activities at the Congress. The great rabbis were also delegates to the Congress, their voice being of equal weight to each of the other two hundred and twenty delegates. However, their words had greater authority, at least to those who adhered to tradition, by virtue of their religious authority. Moreover, we know that, as in the days of the Assembly of Notables, at least a few rabbis situated themselves near the Congress in order to attend the consultations of the Orthodox club, even though they had not been elected by the public. A tradition of the descendants of the Ketav Sofer asserts that, despite his refusal to be elected as an official representative of his community, the Ketav Sofer felt obligated to spend the duration of the Congress close by, and that he took part in the decisions of the Orthodox club.[11] It is known that R. Hillel Lichtenstein left his seat in Kolomea, Galicia, where he had been rabbi for two years, and stayed close to the Hungarian capital for the duration of the Congress,[12] accompanied by his son-in-law, R. Akiva Joseph Schlesinger.[13] The great weight attributed to those with religious charisma of course contravened the parliamentary rules, according to which the Congressional debates were ostensibly held. Some admitted this openly. In presenting the Orthodox program for community organization, Sigmund Kraus declared that there are matters in which the majority does not rule, but only the opinion of those with authority counts. At times, he said, votes are not counted, but weighed.[14]

More or less open tensions prevailed between the various factions of the Orthodox camp. However, the major drama that viewers from near and far followed closely was the confrontation between the two camps, the Progressives and the Orthodox. The first act of the drama centered around the choice of a president and his deputies. Already during this act, viewers could discern the intention of the majority leaders to exploit their advantage even beyond the formal rights it granted them. The first sign of this became apparent when the eldest of the delegates was called upon to conduct the meeting at which the permanent president would be elected. In the preliminary consultations on Saturday night, R. Abraham Schag was granted the title of the eldest member of the Congress, but on Monday morning, with the conclusion of Minister Eötvös's speech, Leo Holländer was brought to the podium. He was the representative of the community of Eperjes, had been one of the outstanding public personalities in Jewish public life for decades, and was one of the pillars of the Progressive camp. Holländer certainly was better suited to preside over the session, but in terms of his age he was only third in line, and assigning him this role was an arbitrary action, which wounded those older than he, who belonged to the Orthodox camp.[15]

Heated debates preceded the choice of the permanent president of the Congress.[16] It was clear even to the Orthodox that the president of the Congress would be chosen from among the Progressive majority, but they wished to prevent the election of Dr. Hirschler, whose activities prior to the Congress exemplified the vigorously anti-Orthodox tendency. They proposed Leopold Popper, the representative of one of the northwestern districts, a well-known philanthropist, who esteemed Torah and culture and was observant in his private life, as their candidate. Hirschler won a majority in this vote, one hundred and seventeen against ninety. The Orthodox now felt obliged to support Popper for the vice-presidency. Two candidates vied for the task of second vice-president—Kalman Pappenheim, one of three representatives of the Pressburg community, and Mór Wahrmann, one of many representatives of the capital. Pappenheim was a respected man, and adhered to the Orthodox line, in accordance with the tradition of his family and with his position as the chairman of the community he represented. Within the Orthodox camp, he was one of the confidants of R. Esriel Hildesheimer, and a vigorous opponent of the factional tendency, as we shall see. Wahrmann was the grandson of R. Israel Wahrmann, who had served as the first rabbi of Pest during the years 1796–1826, at a time when the community still held its traditional character. The grandson, in contrast, already represented the new generation, and his attitude to Judaism was similar to that of the other Progressive politicians. Wahrmann had a legal education, was a successful businessman with political aspirations, and we shall meet him again later. He won the office of second vice-president in the contest with Pappenheim. It may be assumed that, had the Orthodox agreed to support the presidency of Hirschler, they would have received a vice-president of their own in return. Given their relative power in the Congress, one of the vice-presidents should, in all fairness, have been from the Orthodox camp, as the *Israelit* reporter argued. Such an arrangement would have served to moderate the differences between the camps. The unwillingness of both sides to compromise obviated this possibility, and both were destined to suffer the consequences of their actions.

Nonetheless, there was still hope at that time, or so at least the moderate Orthodox believed, that a modus vivendi would be found between the two factions. The Congress did not confine its debates to the three topics that the minister had placed on the agenda. Many members of the Congress, and of the Jewish public at large, thought that a gathering of the representatives of Hungarian Jewry would provide an opportunity to advance issues of public importance. It was not an easy task for the presidency to refuse requests of this sort, without hurting the feelings of the suppliants. The president was unable to refuse one request: a proposal to deal with the problem of the desecration of the Sabbath, caused by holding the weekly fairs in the cities and towns on this day. The request for the debate came from Lipot Mittelmann, the representative of one of the northwestern districts, who was not of the Orthodox camp. His suggestion was that the Congress approach the central government with a request to move the fair days from the Sabbath to one of the weekdays.[17] This issue was debated in the Congress—although behind closed doors—for two full days, and with much gravity. The first speaker was Esriel Hildesheimer, who was favorably surprised at the very fact that this topic was raised at the Congress.[18] He himself had previously attempted to solve this problem, and he even proposed an amendment to Mittelmann's suggestion. He felt that it was necessary to request that the seasonal fairs, held in the major cities and in the capital, also not conflict with the Sabbath and Jewish festivals. He described at length the psychological duress of the believing Jew, who is forced to desecrate the Sabbath in order to support his family, and even found reasons to justify the request from the perspective of society at large, and of the state: The Jewish economic contribution is beneficial to the entire population. Since the state granted the Jews complete citizenship, it is obligated to consider the demands of their religion, and their freedom of conscience.

During the debate, in which some of the prominent members of the Progressive camp participated, it became clear that there were no ideological and emotional differences between the camps with regard to their concern over the decline in status of the Sabbath. Even two reformist rabbis—Dr. Meir Zipser, whom we remember from his battle in Székesfehérvár, and Jacob Steinhardt, who took Aaron Chorin's place in Arad—emotionally expressed their apprehension in the face of the situation.[19] There is no reason to doubt the sincerity of the speakers. Even rabbis of their kind must have felt that with the desanctification of the Sabbath, the main foundation for their activity was crumbling under their feet. They would willingly have supported an amelioration of their situation, in the spirit of the suggestion that Mittelmann had made, which gained the enthusiastic support of Hildesheimer, were it not for hesitations about its practicality. Most of the participants in the debate gave the proposal no chance of success: The right to determine the fair days belonged to the local authorities, and the central government could not interfere. The delegate Joseph Popper, from the city of Miskolc, could illustrate this. In a joint effort, he and the Jews of his city had obtained a ministerial order to move the fair days in the cities of the district from Saturday, but the city officials steadfastly asserted their right to be the determining factor in this issue, and the order was canceled.[20] And in the town of Dunaföldvár, where the local council acceded to the request of the Jewish community, the population reacted with unbridled provocation against the Jews, until they themselves requested a return to the old system, for fear of pogroms.[21] R. Steinhardt warned against turning to the government on this matter in the name of Judaism. Jewish emancipation did not solve the question of the position of the Jewish religion, whether it remained an "accepted" religion alone, or whether it had become an "acknowledged" religion, of equal status with Christianity. Before this question was decided, clarifications and struggles with potential opponents would be necessary. A demand that the government concern itself with the special needs of the Jewish faith would begin the debate prematurely and endanger the desired outcome.[22] And indeed, equal status for Judaism was achieved only a generation later, in 1895.[23]

The Sabbath debate was not on the official agenda of the Congress, and therefore it is mentioned in the protocols of the Congress only in an aside.[24] We owe thanks to the reporter of *Israelit* for a detailed description of the debate on this topic, for it is of some historical interest. It emerges from the debate on this issue that there was some shared religious consensus between the representatives of the two camps, a sentiment expressed by the last of the speakers, Kalman Pappenheim. Pappenheim did not add anything to his predecessors' statements on the issue itself, but described the deep impression that the serious attitude of all the participants in the debate had made upon him, and found support in it for his view, which he continued to voice ever since, that there was no call for a split in the Hungarian Jewish community: "There may be different viewpoints, but with good will we can reconcile them."[25]

There were attempts to extricate the Congress from this split, in which each camp was entrenched behind predetermined positions. We hear of men of good will with a foot in both camps, who attempted to mediate between them, whether on their own initiative, or with the backing of others, many or few.[26] A public attempt at reconciliation came from an unexpected quarter—Sigmund Kraus. Acting in the capacity of editor of *Magyar Zsidó*, he surprised his readers by changing the motto of the newspaper, beginning with the issue of December 28, 1868, two weeks after the opening of the Congress. Instead of the slogan announcing the necessity of a split between the two camps, the banner now carried the translation of the verse from Isaiah 57:19: "Peace, peace to him that is far and to him that is near, sayeth the Lord." In a long article in the same issue, he explained his sudden change of heart. In following the debates since the beginning of the Congress, he had become convinced that there was almost total consensus among the members on three principles: (1) observance of the sacred religion of our ancestors, as explained in the Written and Oral Law; (2) dedication to the principle of freedom of conscience in the broad sense of the word, this principle being as sacred as the former; and (3) the obligation to preserve the unity of the Jewish nation in Hungary. How could the first two principles be carried out, in light of the existence of conflicting interpretations of the demands of the Written and Oral Law? To this the author, after a certain amount of ideological sophistry, replied that each minority would be given the opportunity to care for its special needs within the framework of the united congregation. The Orthodox minority in a progressive community would be able to maintain a synagogue faithful to its spirit, and to appoint a butcher and judge to its taste. Each congregation would thus preserve its unity and at the same time would obligate itself to join local associations composed of congregations in a given district, which would facilitate contact with the authorities and enable these to supervise the activities of the congregations, in accordance with the minister's requirements as outlined in his inaugural speech.

The alteration of Kraus's slogan, which signaled a change of position from one extreme to the other, aroused astonishment. Two newspapers, the *Allgemeine Zeitung des Judenthums* and the *Congress Zeitung*, queried how it was possible to trust a person who could change so drastically overnight.[27] Kraus's explanation was far from convincing, for the proposals of the majority of the Assembly of Notables included the right of the Orthodox minority to see to its special needs within the framework of a united congregation, and this was categorically rejected by the minority. As we remember, the anonymous article in *Jeschurun*—the work of R. Samson Raphael Hirsch—came out against this compromise with a flood of explanations, with which Kraus identified, and which he made sure to publicize.[28] What had changed since that time, and what moved him to repudiate his ideas in a manner that made him appear vacillating and weak of character?

In order to understand Kraus's move we must take several facts into account. First of all, we must note that Kraus also published his article as a separate pamphlet, and dedicated it to Leopold Popper, the first vice-president of the Congress: "The man of peace, a true lover [*treue Anhänger*] of Judaism and of its spiritual development."[29] This means that Kraus hoped to find allies among the observers of tradition in the Progressive camp on the basis of the program which he outlined in his article. Second, and this is the main point, Kraus certainly did not act on his own authority, for the *Magyar Zsidó* was the official organ of the *Shomrei ha-Dat*. The newspaper could publish differing viewpoints, so long as they remained within the boundaries of Orthodox ideology, but taking a position concerning the central question of the Congress could not be an individual prerogative. We have no way of knowing whom Kraus consulted before presenting his far-reaching proposal, but we can find motives for requesting a compromise in the course of events.

With the opening of the Congress it became clear once and for all that the Orthodox were in the minority. It was widely believed in Orthodox circles that the very idea of the Congress was the brainchild of the leaders of the Pest congregation and that they were the ones who persuaded the minister to act on it. However, they realized from the minister's speech at the inauguration of the Congress that he identified with the idea of the Congress at least after the fact, and saw in the planned organization of communities a useful and necessary tool for governmental supervision of the congregations. And the centerpiece of the planned organization, as envisioned by the Assembly of Notables, was a center with its seat in the capital, which (like the central *consistoire* in Paris) would govern communal life in the state. This center was destined to fall under the influence of the leaders of the Pest community, both because of their wealth and status, and because of their proximity to the foci of political and judicial power. This vision of the future cast fear into the hearts of those loyal to tradition. Kraus's new plan was intended to forestall this danger. Indeed, it should be appreciated not only for what it included, but primarily for what it did not: that is, the center in the capital which would rule over the local congregations. Instead, he proposed having district centers as the medium of governmental supervision over the congregations; in exchange for forgoing the national center, the Orthodox would be willing to content themselves with separate institutions for their needs within the united congregational framework. At the time, this compromise seemed the lesser of evils.

This readiness for compromise was rooted, of course, in the assumption that the Congress would approve the statutes that the majority proposed, and that the minister would be willing and able to make them into law. However, even at this stage, doubts were voiced concerning the minister's right to do so. Kraus published a series of articles in *Magyar Zsidó*, from the pen of one Dr. Wilhelm Neumann, who claimed that the minister's demand that the communities join in a national organization had no basis in the laws of the state.[30] Leopold Löw also advanced this claim with detailed argumentation, in a small book which he published prior to the Congress. Löw accused the sponsors of the Congress of giving away the congregations' most precious treasure, their autonomy, for illusory advantages, castles in the air.[31] This aroused the anger of the patrons of the Congress.[32] The authors of these claims gravitated towards the radical faction, which had begun to oppose the government, whose power rested on the centrist wing of the political powers in the state. The Orthodox who led the campaign against the Progressives in the Congress were far from this radical position. These were Esriel Hildesheimer and his close friends on the one hand, and the prominent members of the Orthodox club led by Jeremiah Löw on the other.

If we stated above that Kraus could not function without the agreement of the heads of *Shomrei ha-Dat*, these in turn depended upon the rabbis' opinions and viewed themselves as subject to their authority. As we know, the religious council of *Shomrei ha-Dat* was never appointed, but the three rabbis who approved the establishment of the society, the rabbis of Pressburg, Ujhely, and Ungvár, were privy to the debates, the latter two as delegates to the Congress, and the Ketav Sofer in a voluntary capacity. Among the delegates were also other great rabbis, including Maharam Schick and R. Hayyim Sofer. It is clear that those who sought a compromise with the Progressives acted with the sanction of the rabbis—if not all, at least some of them. We hear from the son of the Ketav Sofer, that the authors of the proposal for compromise with the Progressives came and went in his father's house in Pest.[33] Even the lay leader of this congregation, Kalman Pappenheim, was one of the outspoken supporters of the compromise. Kraus's surprising proposal no doubt gained the blessing of the rabbis, and it seems likely that it was not his own product. For himself, Kraus supported the idea of separation, because of the essential dogmatic difference between the Orthodox and their opponents, following the doctrine of R. Samson Raphael Hirsch. Unlike Kraus, however, the great rabbis of Hungary did not concern themselves with abstract considerations such as this. For them, the danger of Neolog domination of congregational life, perhaps to the extent of suppressing the observant and preventing them from observing their religion in their customary manner, was the crucial factor. When the idea arose of establishing separate institutions for the observant within a united congregation in exchange for abandoning the idea of a center that would exercise control from the capital, they saw it as the solution to a pressing situation. And indeed this time appeared to them as a time of crisis, because of the danger of open confrontation with the government. It comes as no surprise that Kraus was ready to defend the program. This is not the first time that we meet him acting as required by circumstances, not in accordance with his inner sentiments, although this time he left himself open to sharp criticism and to attacks on his character.

The desire of the leaders of the Orthodox campaign in the Congress to prevent head-on confrontation with the minister is evident in many steps they took. Kraus's proposal was a sort of last-ditch compromise in the event that the Congress would accept the program proposed by the majority. But the Orthodox leadership did all it could to prevent this. Already at the second session (which was conducted by the oldest member, as the Congress had not yet managed to choose a president), a delegate from the Orthodox camp by the name of Israel Grün stood up and declared, in the name of his colleagues, that their participation in the Congress was conditional upon observance of the guidelines that

Minister Eötvös had set, which specified that the forum would deal exclusively with organizational issues, excluding any topic relating to religion.[34] Grün, an educated man who knew German and Hungarian equally well, was the delegate of the Transylvanian communities. He was nevertheless loyal to the Orthodox line and no doubt acted in accordance with the views of the rabbis.[35] Indeed, immediately after the president was elected, in the fourth session of the Congress, he presented a document signed by twelve members, which delineated the conditions laid down by the Orthodox for recognizing the authority of the Congress to make binding decisions: (1) In order that the Congress be considered autonomous, it must act according to an agenda of debate acceptable to all. Its first step must be an examination of the clauses of the regulations that Minister Eötvös's office had prepared for the Congress. (2) Since the purpose of the Congress is to reconcile two opposing positions, decisions cannot be taken by majority rule. Equal weight should be given to majority and minority decisions.[36]

From Hildesheimer's brief statements, we know that this document was discussed in the Orthodox club, but he and his group of intimates did not support it. They too believed that only compromise between the two sides would ensure the success of the Congress under the circumstances, and they hoped for dialogue with the opposing side regarding the concrete questions on the agenda. They considered the demand to abandon the principle of majority rule from the outset too extreme and even provocative.[37] The result would be a stalemate on every controversial question, and the Congress would become a barren forum. It may not be too cynical to assume that this was actually the goal of the authors of the proposal: to paralyze the Congress, and thus to avert what they regarded as an evil decree that would emerge from it.

Hirschler's reply indicates that more far-reaching suggestions were made in the debate on the proposal of the twelve members. There were those who categorically rejected the order of debate which was imposed from above, and claimed that this Congress would do better to formulate procedures for future Congresses, and refrain from discussing the topics for which it had assembled.[38] Needless to say, the president and the great majority of the Congress rejected these ideas. They accepted the set of regulations prepared in the minister's office as the legal basis for the Congress. Following this principle, the president allowed himself to rely on one of its clauses in order to reject the proposals mentioned above, as well as similar proposals that arose in the course of the debates;[39] that clause stated that no protest against the decisions of the Congress would be acceptable. Hirschler decreed that any proposal that opposes the written rules of procedure is to be considered a protest, and must be rejected outright.

In order to appease the Orthodox, the president promised to supervise carefully the implementation of the minister's directive to limit the debates in the Congress to organizational issues alone: "As for religious views, religious institutions, issues of prayer, ritual customs, and ceremonies in the congregations, the Congress will make no decisions whatsoever."[40] According to Hildesheimer, these words were received with enthusiasm and great joy, especially in his own camp.[41] In reality, this happiness was misplaced, for the two camps had different conceptions of what the term "religious" entailed. Hirschler was sincere in his declaration. Nothing was said in the Congress about religious issues in the limited sense of the word: the principles of faith and the laws of worship. But in the Orthodox view, these matters far from exhausted the concept of "religious." For them, matters concerning the organization of the congregations, and all the more so the educational institutions, which Hirschler and his group considered to be outside the realm of religion, could raise questions of religion and religious law, no less than matters concerning the synagogue and other forms of worship.

As we recall, the demand of the conference of rabbis in Buda was that the determination of which issues fell under the category of religion would be in the hands of its representatives. Respected members of this conference now sat in the Congress. Either on their initiative or independently, R. Kalman Weiss, the representative of one of the northern districts, presented this idea to the members of the Congress, with a change of formulation. It came as a reaction to a complaint by one of the representatives of the capital about the Orthodox, who create difficulties in debates in the Congress because of their fear that these will impinge on their religious conscience.[42] R. Weiss declared that the Orthodox are indeed full of fears, and rightly so, for of what avail are the promises of Minister Eötvös and the president of the Congress, that questions of a religious nature would not be decided in this forum? Are these two respected people authorized to determine which questions are of a religious nature and which are not? The consciences of devout Jews will not be still if a way is not found to present these issues before a forum of authorized rabbis, either by gathering them in an assembly for this purpose or by written referendum.[43] This was of course an impractical proposal, which even the Orthodox camp could not take seriously, although its basic thrust was certainly to its liking.[44] Dr. Hirschler could easily reject the proposal, by saying with a touch of humor that it would mean setting above the Congress a sort of upper house, to which it would be subordinate.[45]

Chapter 14

The Inevitable Clash

Observers both within the Congress and from the outside were well aware of the Orthodox camp's resolve to paralyze the Congress by all sorts of appeals. Sharp-eyed reporters as well as their opponents in the Congress often took them to task for this.[1] R. Esriel Hildesheimer himself called their battle "guerilla warfare," and justified it as a last resort necessitated by President Hirschler's repressive actions.[2] Hildesheimer's expression was certainly appropriate, for the attacks by the Orthodox during the first stages of the Congress did not deal with the controversial issues; they were attempts to escape confrontation or delay it, in the hope that help would come from some unexpected source in the interim. When this did not materialize, there was no escape from confrontation. Clashes occurred already in two of the three committees appointed by the Congress. These two were assigned the task of preparing the platform for the debates concerning the statutes of the congregational organizations and concerning the regulations for the educational systems.[3] The third committee was assigned the formulation of procedures for future Congresses; since these never met, its activities are of no historical interest. Each committee had twenty-five members, who reflected the division of power between the two camps in the Congress: Fourteen were of the Progressive camp, and eleven were from the Orthodox. Joseph Popper, Leo Holländer, and Jacob Steinhardt were outstanding among the Progressives, and Sigmund Kraus, Kalman Pappenheim, and Manó Eisler among the Orthodox members of the committee for the congregational organizations. On the education committee we find Abraham Hochmut, Samuel Kohn, and Meir Zipser from the Progressives, and Esriel Hildesheimer, Feisch Fischmann, and Israel Grün from the Orthodox camp. The committees were chosen at the tenth session, on December 30,[4] but the Congress began to discuss their proposals only a month later, on January 28. In the interim, the Congress recessed part of the time, and during the remainder dealt with topics of no historical interest.

    We have only fragmentary information about the discussions in the committees, but the results suffice to indicate that neither camp succeeded in bridging the gaps. Instead of a single text agreed upon by both sides, the Congress received two (in the case of the committee for organization of the congregations, even three). It is clear that the arguments and counter-claims that were voiced in the Congress had already been raised in the committees themselves, but in the plenum the arguments were publicly aired, in front of the entire world, and the goal was no longer to mediate between the different approaches, but to decide between them. It is not surprising that the tension that prevailed in the committees was multiplied many times over in the plenum. It led to accusations and outbursts which made it difficult for the two camps to continue to sit together.

Priority was given to the debate about the organization of the congregations. The Progressive platform on this topic preserved the essentials of the outline of the program that had been published a year earlier, after the Assembly of Notables, with majority consent.[5] The platform categorized the Jewish congregation as an organization whose function is to supply the religious needs of the mosaic-rabbinic (*mosäisch-rabbinisch*) community, without delineating the nature of those needs and without describing the institutions necessary to fulfill these needs. The only institution mentioned is the office of rabbi, but again without defining the authority and functions of this official. Only one congregation could exist in any place, and membership would be mandatory. However, should part of the congregation be unable to satisfy its needs with the existing congregational institutions, it would have the right, under certain conditions, to set up alternative institutions in accordance with its views. This paragraph allowed for the creation of variations in religious ceremonies within the framework of one congregation, thus averting the danger of coercion of conscience. A district organization would unite the individual congregations, and above the district organizations, a center to be located in the capital, which would represent the Jewry of the state, both externally and internally, as the supreme institution in settling local conflicts or intercongregational ones.

If we contrast the clauses of this platform with that of the Orthodox, the depth of the rift between them becomes clear.[6] For the Orthodox, the Jewish community in Hungary consists of "those loyal to the principles of faith, and the teachings of the religion of Moses and the Talmud as they are formulated in the Shulhan Arukh." Moreover, the Orthodox platform listed the institutions which the congregation is obligated to maintain: "a rabbi, school, *mikvah*, ritual butcher, cemetery, etc." According to this platform, the congregation encompassed all the Jews of the area and membership in the congregation was mandatory.[7] The minority—whether to the right or left of the majority—could maintain separate institutions of its own, but the Orthodox minority would enjoy total independence of the religious leadership of the majority, since it could not accept its authority.[8] Another important limiting clause, not mentioned in the Progressive platform, stated that the variations in the religious ceremonies would not go further than that which had already been accepted in Hungary[9]—and we shall immediately see the practical implications of this condition. The Orthodox platform also mentioned a district congregational organization,[10] but not a national one. This was consistent with the spirited Orthodox opposition to this institution, discussed above in the context of Sigmund Kraus's reasons for changing the banner of the *Magyar Zsidó*.

In reality, the Orthodox platform was no more than a detailed version of Kraus's article, and was entirely his work. Indeed, he presented it to the Congress, with an accompaniment of oratory and sophisticated explanations.[11] Since this was a formal proposal to the Congress, the question again arises here, what authority did Kraus have for his proposal? His Orthodox colleagues in the committee certainly supported him. Indeed, one of them, Manó Eisler, saw fit to present his own proposal,[12] which differed from Kraus's only in containing certain additional details designed to ensure the independence of the Orthodox on religious issues within the united congregation. As for Kraus's astonishing compromise—that the Orthodox would remain within the framework of the congregation—Eisler was in full agreement with him. The concession was more difficult for Eisler than for Kraus. Eisler was strongly influenced by Hirsch's doctrine, as the wording of his arguments in the many discussions throughout the Congress attests.[13] Eisler was also in personal contact with Hirsch, and when he succeeded in establishing an Orthodox congregation in his city of Galgóc, after the Congress, Hirsch made haste to congratulate him on this achievement.[14] Now, however, as he sat on the Congressional committee, he endorsed Kraus's view, that the circumstances necessitated acceptance of the framework of the united congregation. They would not have acted thus without the more or less explicit agreement of the rabbinic leadership of the Orthodox club.

As stated above, the readiness of the Orthodox for compromise stemmed from the desire to avoid conflict with the government, personified by Minister Eötvös. This becomes clear from an exchange of words between Kraus and his rival, Joseph Popper, the spokesman of the Progressives on the committee. The argument focused on the proposed center in the capital, which was meant to represent Hungarian Jewry to the government. In presenting the committee's majority platform to the Congress, Popper claimed that the center was needed for its own sake, adding that practical wisdom dictates its establishment: If Jews do not set it up, the minister can do so by his command.[15] Kraus had a ready answer to this argument. This suspicion, he said, is unfounded, given the attitude of the central government to the institutions of district governments in other spheres. It respects the rights of the districts to long-held judicial and administrative autonomy, and in fact the central government entrusts them with responsibility for supervising education within their districts. There is no reason why it should not allow district governments the right of supervision over

Jewish institutions, as specified in the Orthodox proposal.[16] In other words, the Orthodox thought that on this point they would enjoy the minister's support. The comparison to other functions of the district governments substantiated this claim, as did the fact that the minister had not voiced a decided opinion about the center in the capital, in contrast to the issue of the unity of the congregations. Regarding the latter issue, he had proclaimed on several occasions that the law of the state recognizes only one Judaism, and that the members of this religion must have a single organization.[17]

If they were forced to remain under one roof with the "sinners," the Orthodox wanted to ensure, first of all, that they would be able to live their lives according to their tradition and conscience. To this end, their platform upheld the independence of their institutions within the framework of the congregation. Second, they wished to create an obstacle to any new forms of worship that might seek legitimacy as variants of Judaism. In other words, Neolog forms of worship would be tolerated, but not Reform, which at that time had not yet become rooted in the country, although there was no lack of potential supporters, overt or covert.[18] Third, they wanted the entire community to acknowledge that it was subject, at least in principle, to the tradition in its entirety. For this reason the first paragraph defined the community as one loyal to the Written and Oral Law, as detailed in the laws of the Shulhan Arukh. In light of this apodictic demand, the actual tolerance that they exhibited towards the Neologs seems contradictory. Ever since the Neolog movement had begun, Orthodox spokesmen had argued and complained that all changes, major or minor, ran counter to the laws of the Shulhan Arukh. This overt contradiction between the two paragraphs of the Orthodox platform provides insight into the true significance of the demand that acknowledgment of the authority of the Shulhan Arukh be the primary condition for partnership with the Progressives. They could not—and did not—hope that in order to maintain unity, the Progressives would from now on make the Shulhan Arukh their guide, or would abolish the reforms they had instituted in the synagogues and religious ceremonies. If these were forbidden in Orthodox eyes, their creators considered them completely permissible, and even required by current circumstances. The Orthodox demanded acknowledgment of the authority of the Shulhan Arukh not to change the behavior of the Neologs, but to quiet their own consciences.

Ever since the boundaries of the traditional society had been breached, first in the western countries and then in Hungary, the Orthodox had found themselves in a crisis of conscience. The Jewish community now included also those who no longer observed the commandments, whom it would formerly have ejected from its midst—an action the Orthodox believed was called for even now. Since there was no possibility of doing so, a conditional tolerance was called for. So long as the transgressors gave no ideological arguments for their actions, they were classified as sinners, whose evil inclination had led them to transgress; the gates of repentance were not locked against these, and they could remain within the community. This interpretation, which was conscious and more or less explicit, served as the justification of the Orthodox attitude in western countries towards the sinners/strayers, and their comrades in Hungary adopted this stance almost unconsciously.[19]

However, the problem became more sharply defined at the time of the Congress, when the Orthodox confronted a consolidated camp. It is true that the spokesmen of this camp claimed that the differences of opinion between them were not on questions of religion, but the convening of the Congress in order to create a sort of constitution for Hungarian Jews forced the authors of this constitution to open with some sort of definition of the Jewish religion. This task was given to the organizational committee, and it became a subject of dispute between the representatives of the two camps, who no doubt acted in consultation with their leaders regarding this pivotal issue. The Progressives suggested using the complex term *mosäisch-rabbinisch*, that is, the rabbinic-mosaic faith. This formulation characterized Judaism vis-à-vis Christianity, but it lacked any descriptive content. For this reason the Orthodox were not content with it, and resorted to the classical pair of terms, Written and Oral Law. In order to emphasize their obligation on the level of practice, they specified the interpretation and details given in the Shulhan Arukh. This subservience to the laws of the Shulhan Arukh was of course not to be taken literally. The great rabbis who stood behind this demand knew well enough that even they themselves did not slavishly follow the Shulhan Arukh in their halakhic decisions. First of all, these are not always unambiguous, and second, the halakhist sought corroboration for his decisions throughout the halakhic literature. Moreover, some of the great rabbis in the Congress, those who had signed the ruling of R. Hillel Lichtenstein, were accused by their colleagues of having strayed from the injunctions of the Shulhan Arukh, not towards leniency but towards stringency. The Shulhan Arukh was therefore mentioned in the introduction to the constitution of the Jewish community not to regulate communal behavior, private and public, but to make it clear that the only legitimate basis of the Jewish religion is the *halakhah*, as consolidated in the Shulhan Arukh. Even if the entire Congress had accepted this definition, it would not have had the power to halt the deviations from a halakhic way of life, either in private or in public affairs. It was intended, as stated, only to allow the Orthodox to live with the deviations of others of their community without pangs of conscience. There is no way of knowing if the Progressives' consent to this declaration would have saved the Congress from failure. Additional obstacles existed, first and foremost the question of the seminary. Nonetheless, such acceptance would have created a more conducive environment for a give-and-take over the various details, which began with the presentation of the two programs to the Congress.

When it became clear that the definition of the Jewish religion remained a

154 • The Congress

subject of controversy between the representatives of the two camps within the committee, the Orthodox decided to make acceptance of their definition a precondition for their agreement to continue to participate in the Congress. With the conclusion of the presentation of both programs and their explanations, and before the debate over them began in the expanded forum, the Orthodox presented the following declaration, signed by eighty-eight members:

> The undersigned, whose entire wish is to assist significantly the work of the Congress, which is to begin now, consider it incumbent upon themselves to present the following proposal, in order to quiet their conscience and the conscience of their electorate.
>
> May the honored Congress decide that no statute pertaining to the organization of the congregation or schools become a subject of debate and study in the Congress unless it be recognized, in principle, that only the directives of the Torah and Talmud, as they are interpreted in the Shulhan Arukh, can be used as its exclusive foundation.
>
> Duly noting the fact that no member among the members of the Congress denies or can deny the validity of these directives, we believe that we can certainly expect our urgent proposal to be accepted.[20]

The Congress was thus confronted with two demands: to accept the definition of the term "religion" given by the Orthodox minority in the committee, and to make it a criterion for the acceptability of the statutes that were to be debated in the Congress. Had this proposal been accepted, the question would have arisen: Who, if not the great rabbis who were authorized to do so, could tell the Congress whether any of the suggested statutes pertained to paragraphs of the Shulhan Arukh? Actually, this was a resurrection of the old demand, that the rabbis be given authority over the members of the Congress, over and above their authority as representatives. As we recall, when it was made explicitly, this demand was rejected by the president of the Congress, with the argument that the assembly would thus forgo its parliamentary independence. Now, when the demand was made only indirectly and in order to defend the freedom of conscience of those involved, he too took a diplomatic tone. He defined the Orthodox demand as "determining the terms of our religious dogma, determining the boundaries of the mosaic faith."[21] The Congress is not authorized to do this, for it is not a synod, that is, a gathering of rabbis. And even were the Congress authorized to do so, it would not consider it a necessity, for it is known to all that "all the congregations of Israel in our homelands exist on the basis of the traditional principles of the rabbinic-mosaic faith." Thus Hirschler not only rejected the proposal, he decreed it ineligible for discussion, as being outside the sphere of authority of the Congress. Hirschler's reply was anticipated, even by the authors of the declaration. The proposal was apparently made only to prove to all, and particularly to the governmental authorities, that the Congress was advancing towards a situation which would involve intolerable coercion of conscience, which would force the Orthodox to draw the expected conclusions and leave.

This far-ranging conclusion is not to be attributed to all eighty-eight signatories. As we shall see below, only about half of them, forty-eight in number, drew the practical conclusion and left the plenum. A small minority, Hildesheimer's group, refused to sign in the first place. This is not surprising, since the gap between Hildesheimer and the leadership of the Orthodox club had widened already at the stage of choosing the committees. As we know, he was chosen as a member of the educational committee and participated in consultations about the position the Orthodox should take within its framework in the future. At this juncture, the issues of the rabbinic seminary and of secular studies in the *yeshivot* arose again, topics on which he and his intimates opposed the leadership of the club. The result was an open clash with his opponents in the Orthodox club itself, a sort of continuation of the clashes that had occurred in the rabbinic congress in Buda. Hildesheimer's opponents were the same, R. Hayyim Sofer and R. Menahem Eisenstädter and others. In his final report on the progress of the Congress, Hildesheimer poured out his bitterness over the moral pressure exerted upon those who straddled the fence, in language similar to that he had used during the conference in Buda.[22]

Hildesheimer of course supported the minority program for the organization of the congregations, which was now on the agenda. The issue at hand was which of the two proposals would serve as the platform for the paragraph-by-paragraph discussions in the Congress. While it was clear that the plenum would not vote for the minority proposal, Hildesheimer believed that, in a detailed discussion of each paragraph, it would be possible to convince the majority of the Congress to include changes in the platform that would enable the Orthodox to live with it.[23] We cannot know if this expectation had any chance of being fulfilled. When the overwhelming majority of the Orthodox camp presented its ultimatum, that every proposal made to the Congress must pass the test of compatibility with the directives of the Shulhan Arukh, the opportunity for dialogue ended, for it excluded the possibility of compromise, in which each side would emerge partially satisfied.

The challenge contained in the declaration of the eighty-eight members did not go unanswered. The members of the rival camp saw the declaration as an act of arrogance on the part of the Orthodox, as an impingement upon the authority of the Congress, and even as an aspersion cast upon the faith of the Progressives and their religious intentions. Jacob Steinhardt responded very sharply at the same session, and Leo Holländer continued the attack in the next session.

Steinhardt was, as stated above, one of the pillars of the Progressive party and religiously in the left wing of the Neologs. As the rabbi of Arad, the home of Aaron Chorin, perhaps the least traditional congregation, he had to grapple with the growing alienation from religious life; we have already heard of the sorrow he expressed at the disintegration of Sabbath observance. He wished to ensure the continuity of Judaism in future generations by accommodating the spirit of the times, although not by outright reform.[24] He rejected the Orthodox claim that a failure to make congregational life subject to the laws of the Shulhan Arukh would leave an opening for the establishment of Reform communities. To counter this argument, he noted that experiments of this type, which had occurred with the onset of the Revolution of 1848, had long ago disappeared, and that it had thus been proved that they and their like could not find fertile ground in Hungary. Moreover a movement in the opposite direction, towards Orthodox zealousness, had since begun among Hungarian Jews. Here Steinhardt moved on to a counterattack, pointing to the assembly that had passed the Michalowitz ruling, what preceded it, and what followed. With the mention of the zealots, the orator broke from objective argument and adopted an emotional tone of accusation. The Orthodox published material inciting against their opponents, he said; they were the ones who called their rivals' synagogues places of idol worship, and they were the ones who attempted to expel from the community of believers anyone who took the slightest step outside of the boundaries they had erected. Why have the Orthodox made the Shulhan Arukh the criterion for loyalty to Judaism—they are the ones who have abandoned it, by adding stringencies and prohibitions of their own to its directives. Steinhardt was a gifted speaker, and when he began his polemic against his opponents, the arguments came to him effortlessly, as if of their own accord, and he indiscriminately showered his opponents with invective. In his passion, Steinhardt quoted the words of the Palestinian Talmud about the "pious fool" who sees an infant drowning in the river and delays in saving it, because he has to take off his *tefillin* (phylacteries) first.[25] He meant to refer thus to the zealots, who adhere to external rituals at the expense of ethics and spirituality, but his listeners understood him to be characterizing the entire Orthodox camp. It is no surprise that he aroused a stormy reaction, and many of those who were affronted left the hall with loud protests.[26]

As if the heat from Steinhardt's speech were not enough, Leo Holländer's speech two days later added fuel to the fire.[27] As we remember, Holländer was the most senior of the Progressives in the Congress. He nostalgically recalled the 1840s and 1850s, when many rabbis accepted various changes, such as those in the synagogue practice, and—according to him—relative tolerance prevailed even towards actual reform. He was baffled not only by northern zealousness, which he had observed from close by as a resident of the city of Eperjes, but also by the general strengthening of the Orthodox and their demands for independence, accompanied by estrangement from the rest of the public. Whence did this all come? He attempted to answer this question in light of a notice published recently, in which R. Samson Raphael Hirsch of Frankfurt had exhorted the rabbis of the Congress not to work towards compromise, but to stand firm on the right of the Orthodox to maintain separate congregations.[28] The source of this notice is not clear. Sigmund Kraus had published a Hungarian translation in *Magyar Zsidó* of an article by Hirsch in *Jeschurun*, written at the behest of Hildesheimer after the Buda conference. This article ended with the declaration that Orthodox Jewry could continue to exist only within the framework of a separate congregation.[29] The aforesaid notice might have come in the wake of this article. But it is also very likely that Hirsch, who closely followed the confrontations between the factions in the Congress, exhorted his rabbinic colleagues not to miss the chance to achieve the Orthodox independence he championed. Be that as it may, Holländer, the old Hungarian patriot, was angry that someone who was not a citizen should interfere in an internal Hungarian Jewish quarrel. He hinted at attempts by foreign elements to influence events in Hungary, hints his hearers perhaps understood, but which puzzle the contemporary reader. But his barb regarding Hirsch's interference was clear and hurtful: "Aren't our traditional rabbis learned and wise enough to set their own paths, without copying them from Bismarck's policy?"[30] In the atmosphere of Hungarian nationalist enthusiasm that hovered over the Congress, a worse accusation could not be made against the Orthodox. They were extremely sensitive and vulnerable on this subject. Their loyalty to the country's rulers and its laws was not mere lip service, but this was insufficient in the general nationalistic atmosphere, which demanded cultural and linguistic identification and conformity. This the Orthodox, particularly in the conservative sectors, could not fulfill. As a reaction to the insult, the moderate Orthodox left the plenum, but after an apology by Holländer, they returned to their places.[31] Those who had already left the hall in response to Steinhardt's speech, however, were confirmed in their decision to leave the Congress entirely; they could now add the insult they had suffered at the hands of Holländer to the reasons for their decision.

The notice of resignation, signed by forty-eight members, was presented as early as the next session, which took place on the same day. The notice stated with sorrow that the proposal made by the signatories two days earlier, that the Shulhan Arukh be recognized as the basis for the statutes to be endorsed by the Congress, had not been accepted. Moreover, these precious principles were publicly mocked: "Insulting attacks were also made against our entire party, and false accusations were flung against our loyalty to our precious homeland as devoted citizens." The last paragraph of the notice had practical importance. It stated: "You will easily understand, our esteemed members of the Congress, that we cannot presently participate in the Congressional debates, and we must protest most vehemently against the decisions that are likely to be made under these conditions."[32]

The chairman of the session, Dr. Hirschler, attempted to refute the claims of the signatories and opened a debate on their justification. He immediately understood the practical implication of the notice. He seized upon the term "presently" and understood from it that the signatories intended not to forgo their membership in the Congress, but only to absent themselves for the time being. He therefore treated them as members requesting a leave of absence from the Congress, and permission was granted. He rejected their protest against any future decisions, relying on the clause that invalidated any protest against the decisions of the Congress. He therefore proposed ignoring the notice and proceeding with the issues on the agenda.[33]

Although all the Orthodox were affronted by the two orators mentioned above, and even more by the consistent inflexibility of the president of the Congress, who used technicalities to reject any proposal for change, their reactions were far from uniform. Even the thirty-two members of Hildesheimer's circle, in whose name he wrote his report at the end of the Congress, did not follow a uniform line.[34] On the one hand, Hildesheimer refrained from signing the demand by the eighty-eight members that the Shulhan Arukh be the basis for any decision taken by the Congress, while a third of the members of his group did sign; moreover, four of them followed through and joined those who left the Congress.[35] On the other hand, there were more than twenty members outside Hildesheimer's group who signed the petition and nevertheless did not absent themselves from the discussions. Among these were Israel Grün and Sigmund Kraus, and their behavior is a mystery. The reality they faced was a complex one, and it was difficult to determine whether it was preferable, in terms of the individual or public interests of the Orthodox, to stay or leave.

Chapter 15

A Rump Congress and a Divided Orthodoxy

Since the Orthodox had not resigned their membership in the Congress, Dr. Hirschler apparently thought that their departure was merely a form of protest, which could and should be ignored. He did not heed the deep fear that had fallen upon the Orthodox leadership, the apprehension that the Neologs would be able, with governmental assistance, to rule their lives. The entire Orthodox camp, both the minority under the leadership of Hildesheimer and the majority led by R. Jeremiah Löw, now perceived the state government, represented by Minister Eötvös, as the front on which their attention must concentrate, and with which they must do battle, if necessary.

After the paragraph about the Shulhan Arukh was finally rejected in the plenum vote on the statutes of the congregational organization, Hildesheimer requested an interview with Minister Eötvös, and presented himself at the head of a delegation of ten.[1] Hildesheimer listed the Orthodox grievances against the presidency of the Congress: It acts arbitrarily, and even contravenes the directives and promises of the minister himself. In response to the minister's invitation to state their concrete demands, the members of the delegation advanced two: (1) The names of the institutions necessary for preserving the religious nature of the congregations should be mentioned explicitly; and (2) The idea of a national organization should be abandoned, for it impinges on the autonomy of the congregations. The report in *Israelit*, which is our exclusive source for this interview, and which, if not actually written by Hildesheimer, was certainly composed under his guidance, praises the minister for his cordial reception of the members of the delegation. Nothing is said of any promises or commitments. There is indeed no indication of any intervention by the minister to advance the Orthodox causes in the Congress; according to the mandate and authority which Minister Eötvös gave the Congress, he was not allowed to interfere in its activities.

From a note published in *Israelit* alongside the report about the departure of the forty-eight members from the Congress, it appears that Hildesheimer acted of his own accord, for he believed that those members who left imagined that their absence from the Congress would release the districts they represented from adherence to the decisions of the Congress.[2] In reality, those who left, or at least their leaders, knew that the act of departure was not enough. They also planned to turn to the minister, not in an interview, but with a written protest much more forceful and aggressive than the demands that Hildesheimer's delegation had made.[3] The memorandum that was presented to the minister on February 16, that is, two weeks after the uproar in the Congress, not only protests the actions that led to the signatories' departure, but describes the stages of the convening of the Congress, during which their rights were infringed. Although the Orthodox are the majority of Jews in the country, it said, they are assigned the status of a minority in the Congress. Moreover, even as a minority, they deserve some consideration by the majority, for the issues at hand are religious ones, which are matters of individual conscience in which majority rule does not apply; each person must follow his own belief. This is the doctrine and the undertaking of the minister himself. The presidency of the Congress has ignored all this. The memorandum lists all the incidents in which the attempts of the Orthodox to guarantee their rights and their freedom of conscience were denied. Thus far the complaints are levied against the actions of their opponents in the Congress, and the minister is the addressee for these complaints, however, the memorandum also lists abuses for which the minister himself is responsible. He had imposed upon the Congress the rules of debate that allowed the president of the Congress to reject any protest or appeal by the Orthodox. Towards the end of the memorandum, the very legality of the goal of the Congress—to establish a national organization for the members of the Jewish faith by limiting the independence of the congregations—is called into question:

We also wish to bring order to congregational affairs, but founded on religion on the one hand, and on the basis of free will on the other. We have no reason to sacrifice the autonomy of our congregations, in light of the fact that there is at present no law of the state that obligates the congregations to do so.[4]

Therefore, if certain parts of the memorandum were addressed to the minister as the power expected to redress injustice, near the end it reminded him that there were authorities higher than himself. First, the authors of the memorandum declared their conviction of the minister's willingness to prevent their opponents from imposing upon them a harmful central organization—a willingness they had no reason to believe existed—but ended by saying: "We are convinced that the legislative institution of our homeland, which is founded on the constitution, will not legalize that which is incompatible with human dignity. We are convinced that the crowned king of Hungary, who is sworn to uphold the constitution, will not ratify such laws."[5] These sentences were a transparent hint that the authors were ready to do battle, but first offered the minister a way to avoid confrontation. They delineated their concrete request in the paragraph preceding the warning: that his honor the minister postpone the debates of the Congress until the signatories consult on these vital matters with their constituencies.[6] Acceding to this request would, of course, have meant that all the minister's efforts would come to naught. This being the case, the chance for solving these problems in a peaceful manner approached zero.

The question arises here: Who wrote and who inspired the memorandum whose contents we have analyzed? The question has three elements: (1) In order to compose a document of this sort, the author must have had a full command of German or Hungarian and to be accustomed to legal terminology; (2) In order to set forth the essential arguments, the author must have understood Hungarian politics and the balance of power between its institutions, which had only recently been established after the upheavals of the past years; (3) The main point—the decision to wage open war against the minister, with unforeseeable results, required great courage and a readiness to accept the consequences of such action. If the great rabbis who controlled the Orthodox club knew German—Hungarian was not even a possibility—it was only a passive knowledge. They understood the written word but were unable to express themselves in writing. The staff of the *Shomrei ha-Dat* society were no doubt at their disposal, and they could also be assisted by those educated members of the Congress who, despite their education, identified with the Orthodox line. One of these was Sigmund Kraus—who for some reason did not join those who left the Congress, but who most likely agreed with them—and he was not unique. We have already met Israel Grün as the representative of the Orthodox club in the plenum. We shall also meet Isaac (Ignác) Reich, who was similar to Sigmund Kraus in several ways.[7] Reich was a successful businessman in the southern city of Temesvár, was active in Orthodox circles, had wide contacts outside the Orthodox sphere, and nonetheless elected at the opening of the Congress to sit together with the conservative rabbis. He did not speak up at the debates, but did in the consultations, for otherwise he would not have been assigned a central role in the Orthodox leadership, as we shall see later.

Such people could have served as advisers in evaluating political data, which were crucial to the success of the struggle that was soon to begin. This is not to say that some of the rabbis themselves were not capable of independent assessment. R. Jeremiah Löw, who in his capacity as head of the Orthodox club was expected to direct the policy of the party, was considered sharp-witted and well versed in worldly matters, including questions of supreme importance in the political world. However, if R. Löw's knowledge allowed him to evaluate the situation before him in depth, at the point of deciding between the various alternatives he is—and he will be on other occasions—hesitant and indecisive, reluctant to take responsibility.[8] He required support and he apparently received it from his colleagues, R. Hayyim Sofer, Maharam Ash, the Ketav Sofer, and first and foremost, Maharam Schick.

Maharam Schick's presence at the Congress was almost imperceptible. The writer Friedrich Liebig, who described the outstanding members of the Congress, did not devote a single line to him. This is not surprising, for Maharam Schick took no part in the debates and was not one of the vocal protesters, such as R. Hayyim Sofer.[9] For himself, he felt distressed and anxious, and later said that he shed more tears during the Congress than when mourning the destruction of the Temple on the Ninth of Av.[10] As becomes clear from his description of the progress of events, he took an active part in the consultations in the club before leaving the Congress in protest, for he includes himself among the active participants: "We saw ... we approached our adversaries in peace," and so on.[11] Actually, he was the leader of the group: Leadership of the Orthodox camp fell to him as a given with the end of the Congress, and this can be explained only on the assumption that his personal authority had withstood the test of the fateful decisions made during the Congress. This authority was rooted in his absolute belief in the righteousness of Orthodoxy, which alone merited the name Judaism. This faith, and his courageous nature, which we have already witnessed during the Buda conference, made him worthy of standing at the head of the camp, and of leading it to battle without fearing anyone.

Justice demands that we note that the members of the Orthodox minority who did not accept the leadership of Maharam Schick and his colleagues and continued to participate in the discussions of the Congress, did not do so because of a lack of faith or courage. Although he differed from Maharam Schick in his background and personality, their leader, R. Esriel Hildesheimer, could be compared to him in the strength of his faith and his dedication. What divided them was their evaluation of the situation. Hildesheimer believed that, although the Progressive proposal for the structure of the congregational organization would serve as the platform for discussion, it would be possible to insert changes which would satisfy him and his friends. As evidence for this evaluation, he pointed to the debate over the second paragraph of the congregational statutes, in which the Orthodox demanded a list of the institutions with which the proper congregation must be equipped: a synagogue, kosher butcher, ritual bath, and so on. After a protracted and thorough debate, the Progressives won by a margin of sixty-five votes to forty-four. No more than thirty Orthodox members were present, meaning that fourteen of the Progressives had been won over to their view. Had the conservative Orthodox not left the plenum, their votes would have decided the issue.[12] But his was a futile call. The departure of the majority of the Orthodox was an established fact, and those who remained were an insignificant minority. This is evident in the debates over the two topics that still remained: the rules for the conduct of future congresses, and educational issues, including that of the seminary to train rabbis for ordination. The debates on the first topic were meaningless, for no other congresses convened, and nothing further need be said about them. The educational issue and all that it encompassed was of both contemporary and future significance, but the Congress did not have sufficient time to give it the attention it deserved.

The Congress lasted much longer than expected and cost an enormous amount, for the congregations paid the expenses of the delegates for the duration of their stay at the Congress. The time wasted in futile argument aroused much public criticism and undermined the status of the Congress even in the eyes of its creator, Minister Eötvös. He, of course, followed its progress: Clerks from his office were present at times in the discussion halls, and the open meetings were reported on, not always favorably, in the general press. For this or other reasons, Minister Eötvös requested that the Congress finish its work as soon as possible.[13] The Congress was left with only three days in which to discuss the proposals of the education committee, which had worked a month and a half in preparing them. Fortunately, we know the essentials of the committee's work from the detailed report in *Israelit*, written under Hildesheimer's guidance, although not actually by him. On the basis of this report, and of the protocols of the Congress, we can reconstruct the main issues on the committee's agenda, which were finally resolved in the brief debate in the plenum.

The committee addressed the question of whether the Congress should make it mandatory for the congregations to maintain special Jewish schools for the education of their children. At Minister Eötvös's initiative, a mandatory education law had been passed, applying to all children up to age twelve. The local authorities—the city, village, and town councils—were in charge of the children's schooling, regardless of their religion. This requirement could also be fulfilled by attending church schools, as most children had done prior to the enactment of the law. The Jewish community too, was now allowed to establish institutions for its children. The Congress was faced with the question of whether it should obligate the congregations to exercise this right. Most of the members of the committee were of the opinion that Jewish education was the only means to ensure the next generation's commitment to Judaism, and advised the Congress to decide in this spirit.[14] But some had reservations about this recommendation, and they came from both sides of the Congress. The non-denominational school was designed to imprint the children of the various religions with one national culture. Those who were in favor of Jewish absorption into Hungarian society argued that the Congress should not create an obstacle to interdenominational education, and that Jewish schooling should remain voluntary and not mandatory.[15] Surprisingly, the conservative Orthodox concurred with this opinion, and pretended that their reason for preferring the nondenominational school was to destroy the barriers between Jews and "the rest of the citizens of our beloved homeland." They accused the supporters of the special Jewish school of wishing to strengthen these barriers—this was stated explicitly in the memorandum they presented to Minister Eötvös.[16] However, it becomes clear in the continuation what really frightened them in the idea of special Jewish education: it would be entrusted to Jewish teachers with a modern education, likely to "uproot from the heart of the growing youth all religious feeling,"[17] in the words of the memorandum. The conservatives considered the Jewish school the most dangerous enemy of the traditional education of the *heder*. Now, with school attendance mandatory, they preferred to obey the law by putting their children in the hands of non-Jewish teachers for several hours a day, and leaving their religious education to the *heder* for the rest of the time.[18] Since the conservatives were absent from the sessions of the Congress at this stage, only the true adherents presented the arguments in favor of the nondenominational school, and they were overruled by the majority, which decided in favor of separate Jewish schooling.[19] This debate grants us insight into the mentality of most of the Progressive members of the Congress: They still considered the Jewish community a separate entity, and were far from advocating unrestrained assimilation into the surrounding environment.

The last topic that occupied the Congress was the question of the seminary. This occasioned the sharpest controversy, as had become evident already at the stage of the appointment of the education committee. Those who supported the Congress's establishment of the seminary wanted to split the committee into subcommittees, one of which would deal with the topic of the seminary.[20] This would mean, in effect, that whether to establish the seminary was no longer in question; only its academic structure need occupy the committee. This demand was based, among other things, on the fact that the educational fund founded by the order of Kaiser Franz Joseph, was intended for the establishment of a rabbinical seminary. The Congress therefore would only be fulfilling the royal command. Opponents of the seminary succeeded in foiling this stratagem. The education committee was not split, and the establishment of a seminary was debated in it as an open question. The opponents of the seminary presented a formal objection on the grounds that Minister Eötvös had promised, and the president of the Congress had declared, that any topic relating to religion was outside of the purview of the Congress, and would not be put on the agenda. Could any topic be more concerned with religion than the training of rabbis for their offices, which determines the nature of communal life under their leadership?[21] Had the opponents adhered to this formal, preliminary argument, they would never have had to relate to the question of what form that institution would take, and what its character would be. Most surprisingly, the chief spokesman of the opposition, R. Esriel Hildesheimer, addressed this question specifically. He even admitted that, were he sure that the seminary program would be founded on the study of the Talmud and other relevant sources in the spirit of true Judaism, that is, Orthodoxy, and that the secular studies included in this framework would be of secondary importance, not only would he not oppose the establishment of the seminary, but he would consider it the means to ensure the future of Judaism.[22] To substantiate his apprehensions, he pointed to the graduates of the rabbinical seminaries in Padua, Paris, and Breslau, whom his personal experience had led him to consider bitter fruits, the like of which should not be encouraged.[23]

Hildesheimer's candor in explaining his opposition is a testimonial to his character, but casts doubt on his tactical skills. By abandoning the formal claim denying the authority of the Congress to deal with the seminary issue, he allowed his rivals to argue with him on the substantial question of the necessity for, and desirability of, the seminary. In response to his critique of the graduates of the seminaries, his opponents pointed to the failure of the *yeshivot* to train rabbis who have a common language with their flock, rabbis who could serve as leaders and sources of influence. By including secular studies in his *yeshivah*, Hildesheimer himself had proven that he was not satisfied with the type of rabbinic training available in Hungary.[24] And by entering into an argument over the nature of the seminary, Hildesheimer undermined the essential claim of the Orthodox, that the topic itself was out of bounds. The president ignored the Orthodox protest. The Congress not only decided to establish the seminary, but also saw its decision as the pinnacle of its achievements.[25]

With the final decision on the seminary, the sessions of the Congress came to a close. At the time, it seemed that the Progressives had emerged with the upper hand. They had succeeded in preserving the unity of their camp, and had therefore been able to enact the essentials of the program they had envisioned. The Orthodox on the other hand had split into factions in the course of the debates. Most of them only showed their strength in appeals and protests, and the minority, which was ready for compromises, was too small to force the majority to compromise with it. But the decisions of the Congress were, for the moment, only suggestions. They required the ratification of the government in order to become law; the Progressive victory was not, therefore, the final word.

V

In the Aftermath of the Congress

Chapter 16

The Battle over Ratification of the Statutes

When the Congress adjourned, its members presented themselves before Minister Eötvös with a short memorandum in hand. After announcing that the Congress had fulfilled the task assigned to it and had formulated the statutes that were henceforth to govern Jewish communal affairs, the memorandum added that these regulations are insufficient to guarantee the independent self-rule of the community. Therefore it presented the following request to the minister:

It is requested that the minister take action in order that a law be enacted in the next session of the Parliament that will guarantee the Jewish community the same right of self-rule and the same civil rights ... that belong to the other religious communities in the land, which are called accepted religions according to the law.[1]

There is no obvious logical connection between the beginning of this memorandum and the end. Why should the right of a religious community to self-rule depend on its status—what difference did it make whether it is considered an "accepted" religion, like the Christian religions, or only an "acknowledged" one, as Judaism had hitherto been classified? This category affected only interdenominational relationships. The members of the accepted religions could transfer from one community to another. For example, a Catholic could become a Protestant and vice versa. However, a member of an acknowledged religion, that is, a Jew, could convert and join one of the Christian denominations, but a Christian could not convert to Judaism and join its community. As we have seen, emancipation did not remedy this situation.[2] The Progressive members of the Congress, who considered the activities of the Congress the culmination of the emancipatory enterprise, apparently thought that Parliamentary ratification of the statutes of the Congress would afford the appropriate occasion to remedy the injustice. They were confident of ratification, and expected the amelioration of the status of Judaism to be a sort of by-product of this legislative step.

170 • In the Aftermath of the Congress

This was not the outlook of the Orthodox. As we know, they had concluded the memorandum of protest that they presented to the minister upon leaving the Congressional sessions by expressing their confidence that the legislature, which acts in accordance with the constitution, and the king who is sworn to uphold it, would not enact laws that force Jews who are faithful to tradition to act contrary to their conscience.[3] The battle between the two camps was now moved to a new front, the legislative arena. In order to follow this battle we must describe the legislative institutions and their functions at this historic hour.

A new, unprecedented order was established in the country in the wake of the compromise with Austria in 1867. The old aristocratic order had been abolished in the Revolution of 1848, but the revolutionary idea of replacing it with a parliamentary democracy could become a reality only with the end of Austrian rule, and with considerable alterations to the original revolutionary vision. The revolutionaries wanted to sever themselves totally from Austria and the House of Hapsburg, but did not achieve complete success. According to the compromise of 1867, Hungary remained tied to Austria in matters of foreign policy, and Kaiser Franz Joseph of the House of Hapsburg maintained his seat in Hungary as well. However, here he was a constitutional monarch, sworn to rule according to the laws of the state legislated by both houses of Parliament. The representatives of the public sat in the lower house, the major legislative body, and the king chose the members of the government from among them, but his choice required the approval of the majority of the house. In the first years of the new regime, the government was formed by the central party, standard-bearers of compromise with Austria, of which Eötvös was one of the pillars. The opposition party, which was more left wing, criticized the government not only for its policy of compromise with Austria but also for the slow pace of reform in the country, among other things with regard to the relationship between religion or religions and the state. It contended that the principle of liberalism demands severing any link between the two—granting freedom to the citizens of the state to organize in religious bodies as they desired, to change religions, and even to divest themselves of any religion, without interference by the authorities. These ideas had reached Hungary from radical circles in western Europe, although they were not practiced anywhere aside from the distant United States. Although these ideas were aired throughout Hungary, they did not have the power to change reality. The churches, whose institutions and personages were actively integrated into state and society, maintained their position in the new regime.

Eötvös did not attempt to initiate anything for which a precedent did not exist. Since the Protestant Church had an existing national organization representing the local communities, he wished to establish similar organizations for other religions, including the Jewish religion, according to this example. The idea of freedom of religion that reverberated in public opinion negated the very existence of religious organizations, but the long-standing Protestant organization retained its standing, and no one questioned its right to exist. In contrast, the new Jewish organization, just now being created, was portrayed as an anachronism whose time had passed. In the summary of his report on the Congress, the reporter for the *Allgemeine Zeitung des Judenthums* characterized Eötvös's plan as the establishment of a state church organization (*staatlicher Kirchenorganismus*), something that had no place in modern times.[4]

These political and ideological data largely determined the outcome of the battle waged between those involved, each side acting according to its interpretation and evaluation of reality. What were the reactions of those involved to the situation created by the adjournment of the Congress?

R. Esriel Hildesheimer felt the need to publish a detailed report of the actions taken by himself and the members of his faction.[5] This was, in essence, a sort of brief defending their stand in remaining at the Congress, contrary to the majority position, a stand apparently unjustified by the outcome. This was written before the holiday of Purim; in his introduction the author admitted that the events described were not likely to increase the joy and merriment of the season. He nonetheless concluded by expressing his certainty that the decisions of the Congress that endanger religious life in Hungarian Jewish communities in general, and institutions of Torah learning in particular, would not be ratified without provoking the appropriate reactions. These eternal values "will of themselves arouse their defenders, and the avengers of their blood [*goalei ha-dam* in Hebrew]."[6] But he no longer felt himself worthy or capable of being counted among them. When he was called to Berlin to serve as the rabbi of the Orthodox minority in the community, he responded willingly. He left Hungary even before the end of 1869.

Not all the Orthodox shared Hildesheimer's sadness and pessimism. A long article was published in *Magyar Zsidó*, March 7, by an anonymous writer whose identity we shall immediately discover. He claimed that in some ways the turn taken by events in the Congress could advance the interests of Judaism, for they would finally clarify the situation as it really was. They would serve as a warning against similar experiments intended to "unite by force religious factions that are essentially opposed to one another."[7] As the author proved from the words of the progressive rabbis Jacob Steinhardt and Meir Zipser, the unity to which the Congress aspired did not relate only to the organizational aspect, as these spokesmen claimed. In their debates with their rivals, the rabbis focused on religious doctrine, presenting their doctrine as superior to and more beneficial than that of Orthodoxy.[8] However, no proof is needed that the Neolog doctrine represents a deviation from traditional Judaism. It is sufficient to examine the situation in the Neolog congregations, such as that of Arad, the seat of R. Steinhardt, or that of the capital city of Pest. In the latter, the leaders of the congregation built a splendid synagogue, with an organ that played on Sabbaths and festivals, but did not concern themselves with maintaining the institutions necessary for practicing the most elementary commandments: *kashrut*, family purity, religious education, and the like.[9] The writer went even further and announced that even if the issue were only organizational unity, the situation was unacceptable to the pious. In such an organization, leadership positions would be open to all, no matter what their religious behavior. However, the *halakhah* disqualifies a religious transgressor from any public appointment, regardless of the type of appointment.[10] The observant Jew would also not be able to contribute his part to the maintenance of institutions that do not meet his religious criteria. Unity can then be achieved only by force, which involves clear impingement on religious freedom. Can such a thing be done in a state founded on a constitution that grants equal rights to every person?[11] The author reiterated the argument of the Orthodox manifesto of protest, that in essence the Congress had no legal basis and added that events showed that it lacked contact with reality. The two factions of the Jewish community that had been assembled could not live under one roof. The situation prior to the Congress should be reinstated, that is, granting autonomy to each congregation, while instituting reforms according to the principle of freedom of conscience. A minority in the congregation—whatever its size—that cannot find religious satisfaction in congregational institutions should be permitted to resign from it and to organize itself as a separate public body.[12]

The editor of the paper, Sigmund Kraus, felt that the demands put forth in the article went further than the conditions he and his colleagues had made for accepting the decisions of the Congress. They were willing to remain in one congregation together with the Neologs so long as their religious needs would be met within its framework. They also did not oppose a supra-congregational organization within the county framework. Kraus therefore noted in the margin of the article that past concessions had been made for the sake of peace and hoped-for unity. When the opponents in the Congress revealed that they wished to do battle, the concessions became obsolete, replaced by principled demands from a trustworthy and authoritative source.[13]

The article won extravagant praise from R. Samson Raphael Hirsch, and he reprinted it verbatim in his *Jeschurun* as soon as it appeared.[14] He felt that the article was worthy of publication because it "sheds clear and penetrating light on the conflicts dominating contemporary Jewish experience, and not only in Hungary but also in large circles outside it."[15] The praise was perhaps also designed to remove suspicion that he himself had written the article. Surprisingly enough, not more than two months had passed when Hirsch revealed himself to be the author of the article (a fact that has nonetheless escaped his bibliographers to this very day). As we shall see, in order to gain support for its opposition to the ratification of the Congressional decisions, the leadership of the

Shomrei ha-Dat society sent the proposed statutes to prominent rabbis in other lands, seeking their opinion as to whether they were compatible with traditional Jewish principles.[16] A group of nine Orthodox rabbis in Germany joined forces to sign a joint opinion.[17] The text of the opinion was also presented to Hirsch, who added this postscript to his signature: "The undersigned devoted a detailed study [*eingehende Studien*] to the debates of the Jewish Congress in Hungary and reached conclusions that accord with those stated above, and he even published them recently in the journal he edits."[18] Hirsch did not have to study the decisions of the Congress, for he followed the debates and formed his basic position earlier than his colleagues. Although he can be identified as the author of the article by its content and style, there is no better testimony than the admission of the author himself. The article attests to the importance that Hirsch attached to developments in Hungary, so much so that he intervened personally, in the most literal sense. And the publication of the article is not the only instance of this intervention, as we have seen and shall yet witness.

Let us now turn to the Orthodox assessment of the situation after the adjournment of the Congress. They were fearful of the decrees to be expected with the ratification of the statutes, and they reacted almost instinctively by turning to the person they considered responsible for religion in the state, the King. They no doubt remembered the rabbinic delegation to Franz Joseph, only a few years before, which had brought about cancellation of the plan to establish a seminary.[19] They ignored the changes in the king's status that had occurred in the interim. The reporter for *Israelit* reminded them of these: In 1864, Franz Joseph had ruled in Hungary as an absolute monarch, and controlled every aspect of life; now he is a king without authority, whose signature on the decisions of the legal government is merely a formality.[20]

The idea of turning to the king apparently arose immediately with the adjournment of the Congress, in consultations between several rabbis to decide upon the steps to be taken to further the struggle. In a letter from Maharam Schick to R. Jeremiah Löw of March 21, 1869, one month after the close of the Congress, the author refers to "the letter that I wrote from Pest to the honored rabbi that it is fitting and necessary to urge all the rabbis . . . that the time has come to go and plead before the king . . . and we requested in this letter . . . that his honor be at the head."[21] It is true that R. Löw had previously headed the delegation. However, although he maintained his position as the head of the camp throughout the Congress, at its close he left with reservations about the behavior of his colleagues. They took a negative approach, while he would have wanted that "we for our part propose the necessary enactments." Maharam Schick replied that he agreed and that this could easily be remedied. The statutes that had been passed in the Congress should be reformulated so as to make them compatible with Orthodox views. And indeed, he had already done so, as he stated: "And while I was in Pest I also requested of the rabbi of Kollin that he take the time to formulate procedures as necessary and proper, and I do not know if he did this." Who is this rabbi of Kollin?

An announcement appeared in the *Allgemeine Zeitung des Judenthums* of May 18, 1869, that in his great fervor to counter the outcome of the Congress, R. Samson Raphael Hirsch had sent his son-in-law, R. Joseph Guggenheimer, the rabbi of Kollin, Bohemia, to assist the Orthodox in their struggle, and that he, Guggenheimer, was composing the documents required for this purpose.[22] This surprising announcement, which fits the pattern of Hirsch's previous involvement in the conflict in Hungary, is unwittingly verified by Maharam Schick. He and his conservative colleagues directed the campaign, but they required someone who was literate in German to formulate a document or set of regulations.

Ever since the establishment of the *Shomrei ha-Dat* society, its staff had served as a sort of operational arm of rabbinic policy. However, at this critical hour at the close of the Congress, several rabbis, including R. Löw, distanced themselves from the society, for unknown reasons. As we recall, R. Löw was one of the three rabbis who had originally recommended the founders of the society and its goals, while Maharam Schick, who was not one of its original supporters, was now called upon to defend it to R. Löw: "Now I have come to urge regarding the *Shomrei ha-Dat* society, that we be wise and establish it properly, for it must be preserved and we must support it, in my humble opinion, and *many do not want it.*"[23] The *Shomrei ha-Dat* themselves later admitted candidly that, with the adjournment of the Congress, many congregations from whom they had expected assistance held themselves aloof from the society and abandoned it to its problems.[24] Perhaps their former supporters felt that the *Shomrei ha-Dat* had led the Orthodox into a battle that had ended in failure and disappointment.

The Orthodox front was clearly in danger of disintegration. It was saved thanks to the spontaneous leadership of Maharam Schick, who fully comprehended the situation, and began to take action and enlist others. The letter mentioned above testifies to his clarity of vision. He recommended seeking an audience with the king—and this took place without his participation—but he certainly did not see this as the ultimate answer; his attention was focused on the repercussions of the expected ratification of the statutes of the Congress. The congregations would be expected to organize themselves according to the regulations, and to choose representatives to the planned district organizations, and when "the congregations will cooperate and heed . . . and vote . . . they will never again recover, and will be brought like lambs to the slaughter."[25] In order to avert this danger, the Orthodox must prepare their own organizational regulations, and if the rabbis themselves cannot do so, they must resort to the services of those who can. Maharam Schick's recommendation to bolster the *Shomrei ha-Dat* society emanates from his recognition that success in the public campaign would depend upon an organizational apparatus. If some of his rabbinic colleagues felt that the *Shomrei ha-Dat* society was a thorn in their side, for whatever reason—and it appears that not all those active in the society were the most pious of men[26]—Maharam Schick decided to ignore this, and to judge the society according to its goals and usefulness.

According to all indications, the idea of approaching the king was not initiated by the *Shomrei ha-Dat* and was carried out without its participation. As stated in Maharam Schick's letter, the idea arose among the former members of the Congress, and one of the group, Ignác Reich, took it upon himself to lay the groundwork for this event. The delegation wanted to present itself before the king with an authorization in hand from as many communities as possible, empowering it to act in their name. A form was distributed for this purpose, to be signed by the heads of the communities, affirming that the delegation spoke on their behalf, in petitioning the king to refuse to ratify the statutes of the Congress. The form was attached to a letter explaining to the addressees why this step was necessary.[27] Both practical and theoretical reasons were listed: the establishment of district and national organizations would inflict an unproductive burden on the congregational coffers; taxes of Orthodox members of a community would be used to maintain institutions from which they would derive no benefit; moreover, forced participation in the maintenance of institutions they consider illegitimate will impinge on their religious consciences. This last argument had not hitherto been heard in Hungary and it bears the stamp of R. Samson Raphael Hirsch's doctrine, further proof that his son-in-law, R. Guggenheimer, was involved in this initiative. The names of the *Shomrei ha-Dat* members do not appear on the circular letter. The signatories to the authorization were requested to send it to the personal address of Ignác Reich. The letter was distributed at the end of March, about two weeks before Passover, and the signatories were requested to return it during the intermediate days of the holiday at the latest. The matter was urgent, since elections for Parliament were to be held at the beginning of April, and the king was to come to Hungary for the festive opening of the legislature on the twentieth of the month. This was the opportunity for the delegation to present itself before him. A meeting of rabbis was held shortly before this date in order to appoint the delegation.[28] The members of the delegation were chosen from among those who were present at the meeting: the rabbi of Pressburg, the Ketav Sofer; Rabbi Menahem Eisenstädter of Ungvár; R. Aaron David Deutsch, the rabbi of Balassagyarmat; and R. Menahem Katz of Deutschkreutz.[29] R. Jeremiah Löw did not come to the meeting despite the importunities of Maharam Schick, and it is not clear if Maharam Schick himself was there. If he was, he behaved in his usual modest and retiring manner, and was not chosen as a member of the delegation.

The audience with the king took place at the royal palace in Buda on the twenty-fourth of the month. There is no authorized information about what was said at the interview. The official organ of the *Shomrei ha-Dat* society, *Magyar Zsidó*, which probably had reliable sources of information, was reticent. It described only the ceremonial aspects of the occasion. The rabbis requested permission to cover their heads in order to make the obligatory benediction upon seeing the face of a king. One of them blessed the king with long life, and another presented the petition to him together with an explanation of its content. One of the householders in the delegation then spoke. From reports in other newspapers, it appears that R. Menaham Eisenstädter blessed the king in the name of the delegation, while R. Aaron David Deutsch presented the petition and explained its contents. Ignác Reich was the householder who spoke. He had played a role in obtaining the audience, through his connections in the royal court; he had made his fortune by supplying horses for the kaiser's army and had even received a medal of distinction from Franz Joseph. As one well versed in such matters, as well as being devoted to the aspirations of Orthodoxy, Reich was well equipped to present its concerns to the king.[30] However, the audience yielded no real benefits. The reporter for *Israelit*, who signed as M. H. (none other than Markus Horovitz), had from the beginning pointed to the difference between the state of affairs at the present time and when the first rabbinic delegation had gone to Vienna five years before. Folklore filled in the gap between the hoped-for results and the disappointment—a myth was created in which the king was overcome with emotion, and promised that he would not allow an Inquisition to take place in his land.[31]

According to the notice in the press, the Orthodox also contacted Eötvös at this stage; his answer to their request was an unequivocal and forceful refusal. He rejected the claim of religious coercion by pointing to rabbis like Marcus Hirsch and Meir Zipser, who were considered to uphold tradition but had not found fault with the decisions of the Congress. Eötvös did not yet realize the depths of the chasm that split the Jews of Hungary, and that conflicts trivial to him were of great weight to them. He labored ceaselessly to gain royal ratification of the statutes of the Congress, and on June 14, Franz Joseph did indeed sign the statutes at his royal seat in Vienna.[32]

However, even the king's approval did not grant legal status to the statutes; in order to be considered law, they had to be officially published together with the minister's signature.[33] This took time: In a letter of mid-August, Eötvös, who spent the summer months in Karlsbad to improve his health, urged his office manager to hasten the process. This letter reveals the minister's assessment of the situation at that juncture:

As for the Jews, I request that you see to it that the decisions of the Congress be enacted as soon as possible, which I believe needs only my signature on their publication. The Jews have inherited the wisdom of Solomon in that they always recognize when a matter is closed, and that is what will happen with the efforts of the Congress after they are enacted. Until this happens, though, we shall have no peace.[34]

The minister's directive was implemented, and in early September we hear that the statutes have been ratified and that their publication has begun.[35] This meant that a central organization, composed of the representatives of the congregations, was to be established in the twenty-six districts. Authorized personnel from among the governors or high-ranking officials were appointed for this purpose, and were assigned the task of encouraging the congregations to hold elections to choose their representatives.[36] This created the situation that Maharam Schick had foreseen, which posed a dilemma for the observant in the congregations with no apparent way out: The government officials demanded their participation in the elections, in order to implement the decisions of the Congress, while propaganda disseminated during and after the Congress led them to believe that the aforesaid statutes contradicted the principles of the faith. Given this situation, many leaned towards accepting the inevitable, thus fulfilling Eötvös's prediction that the Jews would accept after the fact what they had first opposed.

In a letter of late October 1869, R. Menahem Eisenstädter described to his colleague, R. Hayyim Sofer, what was happening in his congregation of Ungvár. The "commissar," that is the authorized official, chose representatives for the district organization over the protests of "the heads of the congregation and most of the members of the congregation."[37] The writer feared that a similar thing would happen in other places: "In each place there will be people who will choose whomever they want, and we will achieve neither objective." This meant—as the addressee, R. Hayyim Sofer, understood—that the district representation would be established in any case, but it would be composed of undesirable elements. Therefore the option of accepting the decree and participating in the elections should be considered seriously. On November 22, 1869, R. Hayyim Sofer was asked by one of the congregations whether it would not be better to accept the laws of the Congress rather than take the risk of a split "of one camp into two camps, that one entity will be two."[38] His response in both cases was a demand that they refuse, and be prepared to suffer the expected consequences. "It is better that the observant go into exile, God forbid, than to accept of their free will laws that destroy the faith."[39] R. Hayyim Sofer judged his fellow Orthodox by the yardstick of his own character. He was ready for self-sacrifice—indeed, it might be said that he sought the occasion for it.[40] His senior colleague, Maharam Schick, who at this stage became a full partner in the activities of the *Shomrei ha-Dat* society, took a different approach. The policy of the society was to accept the laws of the Congress, and make a maximal effort to avoid head-on confrontation with the authorities.

The leaders of *Shomrei ha-Dat* succeeded in extricating themselves from the crisis they suffered with the end of the Congress. A general meeting of the society was held on June 1, 1869, partly to appoint a new vice-president.[41] A single candidate was proposed for the post, Ignác Reich. He was not only chosen unanimously, but was given the title of first vice-president, and was appointed to administer the central branch in the capital. The publications of the society would be signed by the president, Meir Trebitsch, and the first vice-president, Ignác Reich. While the rabbinic council was not chosen on this occasion either, the society committed itself to continuing to consult authoritative rabbis in the future. Maharam Schick later confirmed that at this stage he was cooperating with the society.[42] Since we know that he was interested in strengthening the society, it is clear that Ignác Reich's appointment, if it was not made at his initiative, certainly had his approval. Although Reich had worked without a link to the society and perhaps even against it, now, with the adjournment of the Congress, he became its central pillar. He breathed new life into its activities and set his mark on its style of campaign, while enjoying the patronage of Maharam Schick, who was considered the leading rabbi. On the other hand, Reich's entry into the administration of the society led to Kraus's withdrawal—at least temporarily—from the society's activities. From July 19 he ceased to appear as the editor of the *Magyar Zsidó*; the newspaper was run according to the policy of the administration of the society, and without the slogan calling for compromise. A new banner appeared in the August 20 issue: "There is no peace, sayeth the Lord, for the wicked." We do not know what passed between those involved, but it seems likely that Kraus, who had already been burned once when he changed his tune, did not wish to seem fickle.

Shortly after the appointment of Ignác Reich as vice-president of the *Shomrei ha-Dat*, the society took the important step of turning to the rabbis of Europe to solicit their opinions about the statutes of the Congress. As stated, Maharam Schick acknowledged that he was consulted about this step.[43] The original intention was to use the opinions to reinforce the petition asking that the king refuse to approve the statutes. The responses were impressive, for all of them pointed to incompatibilities between the statutes and Orthodox doctrines. But the responses came too late: Most of them arrived in July, and the king gave his approval in the middle of the previous month. Nonetheless, the responses were brought to the attention of the king, with the hope that they would perhaps move him to retract his ratification. When this did not help and the authorities began to implement the statutes at the end of August, the leadership of the *Shomrei ha-Dat*, in its new format, went out to the unavoidable battle.

At the end of August or beginning of September, a short circular, signed by the president and vice-president of *Shomrei ha-Dat*, was sent to the heads of the congregations. After a declaration that the signatories consider the addressee to be a conscientious Jew, who will do all he can to avert the danger expected from the antireligious laws of the Congress, it stated: "We have consulted on this matter with experienced and famous diplomats and jurists, and to a man they demonstrated to us that this set of regulations is not law and has no legal validity except to those who accept it via their participation [in the elections]."[44] To the letter was attached a declaration to be handed to the commissar of each district in response to his demand that they participate in the election of representatives to the district organization. The declaration stated that, on the basis of the principle of freedom of conscience, the members of the community refuse to accept laws that contradict the principles of their faith, as set out in its basic book, the Shulhan Arukh.[45]

As in previous cases, the *Shomrei ha-Dat* fed their adherents the text of the opinion they were requested to express. But at this opportunity they did more. The announcement that statesmen and jurists had rejected the legality of the statutes of the Congress was an attempt to reassure those involved that their refusal to participate in the elections in accordance with their religious conscience would not violate the laws of the land.

The battle of the elections for the Congress was to all intents and purposes renewed.[46] Once again the members of the *Shomrei ha-Dat* were the most active. They addressed each sector of the Jewish public in language they understood, and put forward one stipulation: The observant must refuse to accede to demands that they participate in the election of representatives to the district organizations.

A proclamation signed by twenty-six well-known rabbis was sent to the educated.[47] The conclusion provides the clue that its author was none other than Maharam Schick himself: "And at the proper time, God willing, we shall take time to formulate rules for the congregations of Israel according to the basic principles of our Torah, in order that all of Israel find its proper place."[48] This statement parallels the paragraph in Maharam Schick's letter to R. Jeremiah Löw both in content and style.[49] And indeed, the quiet and decisive voice of the author as we know him from other of his writings reverberates throughout the proclamation, which is constructed logically and written in restrained language.

The proclamation opens with the pronouncement, partly halakhic and partly homiletic, that a person must see to it that his fellow man not suffer financial— or all the more so, spiritual—harm, which would be the outcome of accepting the laws of the Congress. The members of the Congress have "denied the Shulhan Arukh, which is the foundation, and which collects all the laws of the holy Torah." The author is willing to judge most of the participants in the Congress leniently, assuming that they acted for lack of knowledge, for "the light of God's holy Torah did not shine upon them . . . for they did not learn it from their childhood." But the greatest rabbis from many lands, among others, have testified to their wrongdoing. The next phrase is the proof that the idea of addressing these rabbis was also the fruit of consultation with Maharam Schick, for he writes, "and we have already sent the laws of the Congress to all the great rabbis of Europe." The responses are now before the king, "and perhaps our master the Kaiser will nullify the laws of the Congress entirely." However, even if the king should uphold them, they will not become laws, for the reason stated in the letter of *Shomrei ha-Dat*, which the proclamation reiterates in slightly altered form. The conclusion is that no legal obligation exists in terms of state law to participate in the establishment of the organization called for by the Congress, and religious law forbids doing so. The proclamation ends with the promise quoted above, that proper statutes would be prepared in place of these invalid ones. The essential reason for sending the proclamation was only to give rabbinic endorsement to the step taken by the *Shomrei ha-Dat* society.

Detailed arguments for rejecting the statutes were listed in a pamphlet of eighteen paragraphs, inserted as an appendix to one of the issues of *Magyar Zsidó*.[50] The pamphlet spread over five folio pages in closely written handwriting. It is apparently a summary of the opinions of many halakhists who examined the statutes of the Congress and found them in conflict with one or another *halakhah*.[51] Most of the remarks were similar to those already voiced by critics during the Congress, but some were the result of precise or even pedantic scrutiny; if these had been the statutes of a legitimate congregation, it seems likely that they would have been defended. The addressees of this pamphlet were of course the learned men of the community, whose support for the cause of *Shomrei ha-Dat* was vital.

Another tone entirely dominates the proclamation in German that was disseminated together with the circular. If the latter was meant to advise the observant how to proceed in rejecting the laws of the Congress, the former was meant to explain to the common people why they should reject them.[52] According to the proclamation, two religions exist within the Hungarian Jewish community, that of the Shulhan Arukh and a religion called "the rabbinic-mosaic religion." The laws of the Congress are intended for the latter, but these are sinners, transgressors of the Sabbath, and consumers of non-kosher food. A minister of a free state cannot force those loyal to the Shulhan Arukh to live together with the others. Those loyal to the Shulhan Arukh must organize in a separate camp, and thus place themselves outside the jurisdiction of the laws of the Congress. The proclamation promises that steps to establish an organization for the Orthodox would soon be taken in accordance with the laws of the land. Meanwhile, the observant in each and every district must unite and choose from among themselves someone who will act as a liaison with the central committee of *Shomrei ha-Dat* in order to further the common goal. The idea of a separate Orthodox organization conceived by Maharam Schick is not presented here independently, but as the means for releasing the Orthodox from any obligation to observe the statutes of the Congress.

An entire package of the opinions of European rabbis about the laws of the

Congress was published as a propaganda tool to convince the "hesitant among Hungarian Jewry."[53] Originally intended to influence the king, they were now used to win over the common people. These opinions were indeed impressive. Even Lazare Isidore, the chief rabbi of France, whose *consistoire* served as the example for the organization envisioned by the Congress, found a flaw in the statutes.[54] He felt that they were likely to impinge on the conscience of the Orthodox. It later became clear that this opinion was written only after pressure was exerted upon him.[55] But the rabbis of the other lands, in particular of Germany, the origin of most of the opinions, responded willingly and unwaveringly to the request of the *Shomrei ha-Dat*. Their leaders, R. Jacob Ettlinger of Altona and R. Isaac Dov Halevi Bamberger of Würzburg,[56] were among the most spirited fighters against the Reform movement in their land, and it is clear that they viewed the statutes of the Congress, if not as actually reflecting Reform principles, at least as opening the way to Reform. It is thus no surprise that they were no less opposed than their colleagues in Hungary. Other rabbis took their cue from these two great rabbis, while R. Samson Raphael Hirsch could take pride in having preempted the other rabbis by giving his opinion before being asked.[57] His son-in-law, Joseph Guggenheimer, took this opportunity to present Hirsch's doctrine. Guggenheimer declared, as one who was familiar with Hungarian reality, that the split within Hungarian Jewry was a fact, and enforcing its unity by governmental decree would mean coercing the Orthodox to deny the principles of their faith.[58]

The members of *Shomrei ha-Dat* for their part knew that the danger of coercion had not passed, and that the split was far from certain. They worked towards separation but did not wish to seem responsible for it. As hinted in the short introduction to the collection, they had a double purpose in publishing this manifesto: It was meant to prevail upon those sitting on the fence to stop hesitating and join the Orthodox camp; and it was meant to prove to general and Jewish public opinion in Europe "who is to blame for this terrible rent within the 'House of Jacob.'"[59] The introduction ends with the prophecy that Orthodox Jewry, which is based on the eternal divine Torah, will continue to exist even when its rivals, "whether they be charlatans who emerged from [the Congress] or government ministers who hate Israel, will be lost from the world and their names will be plunged into the eternal void."[60] The last sentence could only be interpreted as a declaration of war on Minister Eötvös. Who would have thought that the day would come when the old warrior for Jewish emancipation would be denounced by Jews as a Jew-hater! This occurred because the *Shomrei ha-Dat* finally despaired of finding a sympathetic ear in the minister, and they did battle with the only means at their disposal. And the minister picked up the gauntlet and responded in kind.

Approximately one month after the publication of the opinions of the European rabbis, Eötvös sent a ministerial order to the municipal and district authorities, which stated: Since his office has received reports about propaganda being distributed among the Jewish public against enactment of the laws of the Congress, the district rulers are ordered to summon the heads of the congregations and their rabbis and to impress upon them the serious implications of these actions. After their ratification, the statutes of the Congress are no different from other laws of the land, except in that they pertain to the members of the Jewish faith alone. They are mandatory for all Jewry, and refusal to obey them or attempts to foil their enactment carry the same punishments as transgressing any other laws of the land.[61] This formulation was no doubt meant to refute the argument set forth in the publications of the *Shomrei ha-Dat*, that the statutes are valid only for one who joins the Progressive community for whom they were formulated.[62] The hidden confrontation between the Orthodox leadership and the minister was now open and, contrary to expectations, the former were to emerge with the upper hand.

Chapter 17

The Parliamentary Decision
Orthodoxy's Purim Miracle

As we shall see, the Orthodox celebrated their victory as was fitting, its spiritual leaders, rabbis, and preachers endowing it with metaphysical significance. They took God's deliverance of his loyal subjects from travail as a sign of the justice of their path. Although a historian must ignore this sort of interpretation, he must nevertheless concede that the Orthodox public's generally steadfast position against what it considered an attempt to make it apostasize played a central role in the outcome of the struggle. The opponents of the Orthodox could claim that the incitement initiated by the *Shomrei ha-Dat* was responsible for the stubborn refusal of the common people to accept the laws of the Congress, and as we know, Minister Eötvös shared this assessment, but this was not the impression of disinterested observers, whose views were expressed in the general press.

There was a sharp turn in general public opinion in favor of the Orthodox at this stage. If at the opening of the Congress the Neologs had enjoyed widespread sympathy because of their tidings of progress, and the Orthodox were depicted as relics of the past worthy only of ridicule or pity, the tables were now turned.[1] Although such fluctuations in public opinion could occur for no apparent reason, in this case there are reasonable explanations. When the Congress opened, the two camps appeared more less equally powerful, and sympathy was naturally given to those whose appearance, manner, and bearing closely approximated the taste and views of the representatives of public opinion. By the end of the Congress, the Progressives emerged as the winners and the Orthodox as the underdogs. As such, they would have aroused sympathy even without identification with their claim that the proceedings at the Congress contravened the principle of religious freedom, an idea that had begun to penetrate contemporary society without any connection to Jewish issues.[2]

We can better comprehend this unlooked-for assistance by following events in the Parliament. On July 10, 1869, Daniel Irányi, one of the leaders of the opposition, introduced a bill for religious freedom, that is, the abolition of all restrictions on civil rights that emanate from a citizen's affiliation with any religion.[3] The bill in essence proposed complete separation of church and state, including the abolition of the privileges enjoyed by the Christian churches in general and the Catholic Church in particular. Implementation of the law would have necessitated transferring all the functions that the churches had hitherto filled to the state, and first and foremost would have introduced civil marriage. The state of affairs in Hungary, especially the balance of political power in the land, made the passing of such a bill a distant dream. Nonetheless, the idea won much sympathy in Parliament and in public opinion. The idea charmed contemporaries, who had won relative independence for their state by their espousal of ideas of liberalism and progress. More than a few of the members of Parliament had spent the years of Austrian rule in exile, and some of them had even wandered to the distant United States. These were great supporters of religious freedom, as they knew it from philosophical writings or as they had encountered it in real life. Therefore they held serious and weighty deliberations in the Parliament about adapting Irányi's idea to the Hungarian situation.

The concept of religious freedom arose again in various contexts in parliamentary debates in the following months. One such debate concerned funds for Catholic institutions, which had hitherto been in the hands of the government and which, according to Eötvös's plan, were to be turned over to the autonomous Catholic organization. These were similar to the Jewish educational fund, which was to be transferred to the management of the planned national organization after the ratification of the statutes of the Congress. The leader of the opposition expressed doubts as to whether such an organization had the right to exist. He complained that Eötvös had acted on his own initiative in presenting the statutes of the Congress to the king for approval, before the legislative assembly was given the opportunity to discuss them. The speaker also threw out a rhetorical question to the parliamentary floor: Had there been any point in convening the Congress in the first place, since it had only intensified the conflicts between the two factions of the Jewish community, which were divided on religious issues?[4]

And so, almost inadvertently, the Congress became a subject of debate in the legislature, when someone felt it his duty to respond to the opposition member. This was none other than Moritz Wahrmann, the vice-president of the Congress, who had been elected as a representative from the capital a year earlier; he was the first—and for the time being, only—Jew to win such a post after the Emancipation. Wahrmann opened his speech by noting this fact, and concluded from it that he was uniquely qualified to explain to the Parliament what had occurred during the Congress.[5] According to him, the Congress had convened with the approval of most of the Jewish public. He described its opponents as being opposed to any change: "They do not aspire to leave the ruined ghetto walls, for they do not want to breathe the air of freedom and their eyes cannot bear the brilliance of the light."[6] A national organization would allow the Jewish community to deal with its internal matters autonomously, to obviate the necessity for the government intervention that had been customary until the Emancipation. As for the educational fund, Wahrmann had a quasi-legal explanation. He reminded his audience that the money originated in a fine that the Austrian commander had imposed on the Jews as a punishment for their participation in the Revolution. Turning it into an educational fund did not mean taking property from the government and giving it to a private institution, but returning property to its rightful owners, that is, the Jewish community.[7] Minister Eötvös had thus acted properly in convening the Congress and in implementing its conclusions, except for one particular—he should have submitted the statutes of the Congress for parliamentary ratification before presenting them to the king. The leaders of the Congress had requested this of the minister at the conclusion of the Congress, and the speaker read the text of the request to the Parliament.[8]

There is reason to believe that Wahrmann was prepared for this speech, for he had in his hand the text of the Congress's request to Eötvös. The remarks of the opposition member and Wahrmann's response were made on February 16, 1870. It was known at that time that the *Shomrei ha-Dat* society had presented a petition to the legislature, in the name of one hundred and fifty congregations, to exempt the Orthodox from the statutes of the Congress, and a number of the larger congregations presented similar requests on their own initiative.[9] A parliamentary debate on this topic was therefore to be expected. Later, the Neologs expressed their regret that they had not presented a counterpetition, that is, a brief in defense of their position.[10] They apparently relied on the fact that one of their leaders, who had served as vice-president of the Congress, was a member of the legislature, and that he was the most suitable person to refute the claims of the Orthodox. The critical remarks by the opposition leader about the Congress provided Wahrmann the opportunity to say his piece defending the Congress, before the topic was put on the agenda of the house. But this speech completely missed its mark. It aroused negative and even hostile reactions, which turned the tide of opinion in the legislature to the Orthodox side.

The first mistake that Wahrmann made was assuming that the members of the legislature were not well versed in the subject being debated, and that the information he dispensed would be the deciding factor in forming their positions. However, not only was the controversy within the Jewish community covered extensively by the general press, but the interested parties undertook an intensive propaganda campaign in anticipation of the expected debate in the legislature. We hear from one of the participants in the debate that both sides had inundated the members of the house with a flood of propaganda material and importuning telegrams.[11] The first speaker to respond to Wahrmann, Mór Jókai, the greatest writer of the time, displayed considerable familiarity with the subject. He was also active in public life, and a member of the opposition party in Parliament.[12] Jókai took Wahrmann to task for arrogating to himself the right to explain the issues of the Congress to the Parliament because he was the only Jewish member. For this very reason he should have remained silent, since as a representative of one side in the controversy he could only present his faction's view.[13] After categorizing Wahrmann as the defense attorney of the Neologs, Jókai took upon himself to serve as the defense attorney of the Orthodox. He reminded his audience of the injustice done to them during the preparations for the Congress and throughout its sessions, and listed the cities from which information had recently been received of pressure put upon the Orthodox, with the aid of the government, to organize according to the statutes of the Congress.[14] The author well understood the dogmatic issues entailed in acknowledging the Shulhan Arukh as the basis of Judaism,[15] and claimed that in all such matters a person must be permitted to decide according to his conscience and the government should refrain from any intervention.[16] The speaker sharply reprimanded Wahrmann for describing Orthodox Jews as ignorant and rebels against the light; the famous author asserted that he was acquainted with Orthodox individuals who were "enlightened men, educated and dedicated patriots" no less than their rivals.[17] As proof of the rapprochement between the Orthodox and the Hungarian nation, he noted their renunciation of the special Jewish school in favor of the interdenominational school,[18] without of course understanding the motivation behind this gesture.

The reporter for *Neuzeit* mocked Wahrmann for forgetting where he was, and speaking before the Parliament in the style to which he was accustomed from his appearances in community halls.[19] Jókai's response proved that Wahrmann's speech had not furthered Neolog interests. And this was not the end of the matter: Jókai's colleague at the extreme left, Albert Németh, followed suit, and did so in a tone that insulted not only Wahrmann and his party, but the entire Jewish public.[20] In noting the source of the educational fund, Wahrmann had compared it to the property of Count Batthyány, the prime minister at the time of the revolution, which had been confiscated by the Austrians, and had later been returned to the family by the independent Hungarian government.[21] What nerve to mention both matters in the same breath, protested Németh. Batthyány was a national hero, and among the thirteen leaders of the revolution that the victorious Austrians had executed. In contrast, the Jews were fined, not as they now boast, for having spilled their blood for the sake of the homeland, but for supplying merchandise to the revolutionary army, not without making a tidy profit on the deal.[22] To this remark, which had some anti-Semitic overtones, Németh added another, which was meant solely to cast aspersions on the loyalty of the Jews to the Hungarian nation. In 1861, when the

Hungarians were still battling the political suppression imposed by the Austrians, the emperor's government in Vienna announced an obligatory government loan. The Hungarian Parliament for its part forbade its citizens to participate in this loan drive. Who paid no attention to this prohibition? The Jewish plutocrats in Budapest, that is, people of Wahrmann's sort, who were unsure which side would win in the struggle between the Austrians and the Hungarians, and therefore continued to serve the Austrians.[23]

This exchange of accusations between Wahrmann and his critics took place, as stated, on February 16, by which time the Orthodox petitions had already been submitted to the parliamentary committee for its opinion. The text of the petition has not reached us, but we shall refer below to a pivotal statement contained in it, and its general substance is conveyed in the committee's opinion,[24] and in Francis Deák's favorable speech, which tipped the scales in its favor.[25] We learn from Deák's speech that the Orthodox were shrewd enough to include in their petition the opinions of the European rabbis, who had determined that the congressional statutes contradict the basic principles of the Jewish faith in its traditional garb. But the main argument for the Orthodox claims rested on the principle of religious freedom, and on the assumption that the Parliament identified with this principle and expected the government to propose a law establishing it. It was not yet clear what form this law would take and how it would accord with social and political reality. One conclusion was nonetheless to be drawn from this principle, namely, that in matters of religion and faith the state has no right to use its powers of coercion. Since the Orthodox declared that the principles of their faith differ from those of the authors of the Congress statutes, the legislators could not force them to accept the statutes. This was the essence of the parliamentary committee's opinion, and consequently of Francis Deák's supporting speech. The Parliament approved the committee proposal unanimously, which is not surprising: The opposition had already stated its views in the wake of Wahrmann's speech a month earlier, and now Deák endorsed them. Although he held no ministerial post, Deák was a member of the ruling party whom many considered the most intelligent man of his generation and an oracular figure in questions of public ethics. The Orthodox could boast that their cause was supported by the greatest of writers, Jókai, and the greatest of statesmen, Deák. But they almost completely ignored the real causes of their victory: the date of the event, March 18, the date of *Shushan Purim* that year, was what counted for them. It was clear as day that a new miracle of Purim had taken place. This was stated in the public announcement of the *Shomrei ha-Dat*, and it was presented as such in the sermons of preachers at the time and in the stories passed on to later generations.[26]

Before we continue to follow the actions of the Orthodox, upon whom we will henceforth focus, let us note two actions taken by the defeated minister Eötvös, and one action of the disappointed members of the Congress. The minister accepted the decision of the Parliament, and on April 2, two weeks after it passed, distributed a directive to the appropriate authorities, instructing them to continue establishing the organization of the congregations according to the statutes of the Congress, but to refrain from any attempt to coerce members of the congregations who refuse to participate.[27] In the course of the same week, on April 7, the minister submitted to Parliament a bill for religious freedom,[28] a step that of course was not a direct consequence of the Jewish issue, but which had important implications for Jewry. The bill was a far cry from what the supporters of religious freedom had anticipated. It guaranteed freedom of worship to members of all religions and abolished any link between legal and political rights and religious affiliation. On the other hand, the law did not nullify any of the privileges of the various Christian churches, and did not even abolish the difference between "accepted" and "acknowledged" religions. Similarly it did not relinquish the obligation and right of the state to supervise religious matters, via contacts between the authorities and the leadership of the religious bodies. In light of this, the position of the Jewish religion at this time remained inferior: A Jew was permitted to convert to Christianity, but a Christian could not become a Jew, and marriages between members of the two religions were forbidden as well. The organization of the congregations according to the statutes of the Congress ostensibly created a body that would parallel the churches. However, not only did the Parliamentary decision to free the Orthodox of the obligation to join it mar its completeness, but its reservations about the minister's right to act on the congressional decisions without consulting Parliament raised doubts about its legal status.

A correct reading of the situation moved the former members of the Congress to approach the Parliament in December 1870 with a long memorandum.[29] As early as May they had asked a large number of rabbis in western Europe if the statutes of the Congress contradicted the accepted principles of Jewish faith.[30] The answers of the thirty-three rabbis, all of whom affirmed that the statutes adhered to the principles of the faith, were appended to the memorandum, signed by Ignaz Hirschler, which was no doubt the product of a team of experts. This appendix misled its contemporary readers and serious future historians into thinking that it was intended to counterbalance the opinions given by the Orthodox rabbis and to move the legislature to rescind its decision of March 18.[31] But the authors of the memorandum were not naïve. They knew it was impossible to counter the Orthodox claim that they were bound by the decisions of their own rabbis, not by the opinions of those they considered to lack authority.

A careful reading of the memorandum and of the cover letter by Wahrmann, which accompanied the copies distributed to all the members of the house, reveals the true intention of the campaign.[32] The leaders of the Congress were now pushed to a defensive position: The Orthodox petition had described the organization that arose in the wake of the Congress as "a Jewish body with dogmatic principles of faith differing from those that were hitherto accepted in Hungary."³³ From this it was easy to conclude that "this new religious body should not enjoy the rights granted to Jews in Hungary from time immemorial."³⁴ The opinions of the thirty-three rabbis were intended to refute this claim. They attested that the statutes of the Congress are in line with the accepted principles of Judaism, and there was therefore good cause to request retroactive parliamentary ratification of the organization that was formed in the wake of the Congress. The memorandum and Wahrmann's accompanying letter mention the possibility that the Orthodox will establish their own national organization.³⁵ If this happens, the memorandum states, the legislature will be faced with the following question: "Should it recognize two independent and equal Jewish religious bodies in the state? This question can only be answered positively."³⁶ The remarkable point of this statement is the concern, not that the Orthodox organization would be deprived of its rights in favor of the Neologs, but the opposite, that the Neolog movement, ostensibly the newcomer, not lose its position and rights because of its deviations from the old. According to Wahrmann, the changes the Neologs have made are not fundamental: "We have not introduced any changes in the essentials of our faith and have not deviated from the accepted religious ceremonies. Therefore we have not established a new religious community, and we have no intention of establishing such a community in the future."³⁷

The memorandum expands upon the history of the controversy with the Orthodox. According to this version, it emanated not from differences on questions concerning the principles of faith and religion, but from disagreements as to the amount of authority to be granted to rabbis in public leadership. The Orthodox give their rabbis, whose conceptual world is limited to what they learned in the *yeshivot*, the right to decide all public issues. In contrast, the Progressives wish to preserve the right of the public to mold its life according to its understanding, under the leadership of rabbis rooted in Jewish tradition but also immersed in contemporary culture. This is the gist of the problem, as proven by the fact that the uncompromising clash between the two camps centered around the education of the rabbis: The Progressives wanted to entrust this to the hands of an institution, the seminary, that would be founded upon the synthesis mentioned above, while the Orthodox totally rejected such a synthesis.³⁸

Despite the criticism the memorandum leveled against Orthodox doctrines, it was not intended to convince them, nor to prevent them from adhering to their beliefs. For the time being, the Progressives were satisfied to receive recognition for their position, and this was, as stated, the purpose of their appeal to the legislature. But at the end of the memorandum, they included the request they had already made at the end of the Congress, that with the ratification of the statutes of the Jewish organization, the Jewish religion be granted a status equal to the Christian religions.³⁹ They now added a new argument to support their request: The Emancipation law was intended to put the Jews on par with other citizens of the state; what kind of equality is it when the religion of others is "accepted" and theirs is only "acknowledged"?[40] But logic is one thing and reality another. The memorandum sat before the committee of experts until March 30, 1871, and we shall see below what it recommended to the legislature.[41] The committee ignored the request to put the Jewish religion on an equal footing with Christianity; Judaism remained a second-class religion for another two-and-a-half decades.[42]

Chapter 18

The Orthodox Organization and Its Founders

The memorandum of November-December 1870, sent by the leadership of the Jewish Congress, as well as Moritz Wahrmann's cover letter, mention a separate Orthodox organization as a theoretical possibility. In reality, preparations for such an organization had already begun on August 9, at the assembly of the representatives of the Orthodox congregations held in Pest. The obliviousness of the members of the Congress to this fact can be explained against the background of the obstacles that stood in the path of Orthodox self-organization. As we have seen, Maharam Schick realized the need for such an organization as a counterweight to the decisions of the Congress, as soon as it had adjourned. The idea gained favor among Orthodox circles even before the legislature released them from the jurisdiction of the proposed national organization, on March 18, 1870. As early as March 16, an anonymous author contributed to *Magyar Zsidó* a set of proposed statutes of the putative Orthodox organization, and the editorial board discussed the details with utmost gravity. In the April 7 issue, a month after the legislature's decision, a call to the public appeared on the first page of the paper, entitled "Organize!", and signed by the secretary of the society, Albert Farkas. He emphasized that as long as the isolated congregations stood alone against the national organization established by the Congress, they would always be inferior, and he expressed his doubts as to their ability to preserve their independence for any length of time.

As we have heard, similar doubts had already disturbed Maharam Schick. The leaders of *Shomrei ha-Dat* were of the same mind, and acted to remedy the situation. They requested Minister Eötvös's authorization to convene a gathering for the purpose of establishing a national organization of the Orthodox congregations.[1] The minister's response was delayed—it arrived only on June 18—and provides information about the grounds for the request. This was based on the decision of the legislature, which released the Orthodox from the jurisdiction of the Congress organization. At the same time, it relied on the minister's declared position that it is incumbent upon every religious community to organize itself as a public body, in order to regulate its internal affairs and to facilitate governmental supervision. Since the legislature had recognized the Orthodox as a separate religious community, it was bound by this obligation, and ready and willing to discharge it. It follows logically that the Orthodox community should now convene a Congress of its own, under conditions like those of the abortive general Congress. The demand probably embarrassed the minister, and this is the likely reason for the delay in his reply.[2] The minister did not accept the Orthodox extreme interpretation of the legislature's decision. He understood it to release the Orthodox from the obligation to join the Congressional organization, but not to constitute an authorization to convene a Congress of equal standing. However, if the Orthodox wished to gather and consult on their common interests, it was their right, as it is the right of all citizens of the state, according to the principle of freedom of congregation.

The correspondence between the president of *Shomrei ha-Dat*, Meir Trebitsch, and R. Hayyim Sofer, in mid-April 1870, indicates that the leaders of the society had prepared the program for the meeting even before receiving permission from the minister's office, and wished to ensure the support of the leading rabbis in advance.[3] They announced that "these statutes will not be proposed until they are purified like silver by the great ones of our time, may they live,"[4] that is, that this time the rabbis would examine all the proposals, as they had demanded, and only after their approval would the statutes be presented to the assembly for discussion. R. Hayyim Sofer rejected the program, for practical reasons as well as ideological ones. He did not believe that the representatives of the congregations would be able to agree, and viewed their stay "in Pest for a good long while" as a waste of the public's money. Nor did he consider granting supervision over the statutes to those called "the great ones of the time" a sufficient guarantee. According to him, half of these had "given a hand to the sinners, some openly, some in secret, and some straddling the fence."[5] R. Sofer even now remained faithful to his doctrine that Orthodox Judaism should be led by extremists like himself, who categorically reject any compromise, even at the price of losing "a few congregations," as he put it. Indeed, he refrained from participating in the assembly, even after it was convened.[6] But if he was steadfast in his opposition, others, with the Ketav Sofer and Maharam Schick at their head, who were no doubt informed of the program as he was, supported it.

And so, with the receipt of permission from the minister's office, a proclamation was sent to the congregations, or to the Orthodox factions within congregations, calling on them to elect their representatives for the assembly, which was set for August 9, 1870.[7] Unlike the elections for the Congress, where legitimacy depended upon adherence to specific rules, this time the congregations were permitted to conduct the elections as they wished. This was in any case a voluntary step, to be taken only by congregations that wished to be represented in the assembly; the promise was repeatedly made that membership in the planned organization would be completely voluntary.[8] Under these circumstances there was not—and could not be—insistence upon a minimal number of voters entitled to send a representative. Indeed, in the list of congregations that was published in *Magyar Zsidó*, which contains almost two hundred and fifty communities, we find congregations of hundreds of members alongside small and even tiny congregations, who for the most part joined together to send a single delegate.[9] The number of those attending also indicates this. While at the inauguration of the assembly there were only sixty-two delegates present,[10] over the course of time their number reached one hundred and thirty.[11] This data, provided by *Israelit*, whose report of the assembly is more objective and candid than that of the official organ of the *Shomrei ha-Dat*, agrees with Maharam Schick's later estimate: "Groups of outstanding people, more than one hundred, gathered from the congregations, and with the agreement of about thirty rabbis promulgated the statutes."[12]

We shall later inquire into the identity of the rabbis who participated, and the role they filled, but for the time being let us follow the activities of the assembly step by step. Although the assembly had no official status, its organizers took care to follow parliamentary rules as they had learned them from their participation in the Congress, and for good reason. They hoped to receive ex post facto government ratification of the assembly, as the founding convention of the Orthodox organization. Here too the representatives met a day prior to the official opening of the assembly for informal consultations, and agreed upon the general outline of the agenda, apparently ascertained who was the most senior of the group in order that he serve as chairman in selecting a president, and so on. The initiators, Meir Trebitsch and Ignác Reich, delivered their congratulations. They vanished from view after the official opening, but of course continued to act behind the scenes.[13]

R. Menahem Katz, rabbi of Deutschkreutz, was chosen as senior delegate on the opening day of the assembly, August 9, 1870, and after words of welcome he appointed a ratification committee, whose function was to examine the letters of appointment of the delegates. The meeting was adjourned for one hour, and during these sixty minutes the committee managed to approve the documents of the sixty-two delegates.[14] This amusing scene amply demonstrates that all the parliamentary flourishes of this assembly were only for appearance's sake; in reality everything was planned and conducted by those operating behind the scenes.

The senior delegate asked the plenum if it wished to appoint the president and vice-presidents of the assembly by individual vote or if acclamation would be sufficient. Sigmund Kraus and Emmanuel (Manó) Eisler, our acquaintances,

194 • In the Aftermath of the Congress

along with Leo von Fischer, were chosen by this short-cut method, the first as president and the other two as his vice-presidents. The newly elected president used the identical method in the next session to choose the members of the committees, one for the statutes of the organization of the congregations, one for education—as in the Congress—and the third to deal with the subject of the education fund, to which those assembled attached great importance. When the committees began their deliberations, the plenary sessions adjourned. It is not overly speculative to assume that the initiators of the assembly presented to the committees prepared drafts on the subjects of their deliberations; in any case, they finished their work within a short time. The entire assembly lasted only from August 9 to 24—excluding the two intervening Sabbaths, a total of thirteen days. Furthermore, between the formulation of the proposals in the committees and their presentation for discussion, they were submitted to the rabbis. This procedure also took time. On the other hand, this procedure, a unique feature of this assembly, was to some extent a shortcut, as stated by the delegate who opened the plenary discussion on the statutes of the organization. He wanted those present "to act with restraint towards the set of regulations and to accept it, since the great ones of the land have examined it and found it good."[15]

He neither stated explicitly nor hinted at who these "great ones of the land" were, and our sources do not provide a clear answer to this question. The manifesto that was published after the close of the assembly, simultaneously with the publication of the set of regulations, and the rabbinic opinion that was meant to endorse it, stated that of those who signed, "some of us were also parties to the consultations of the assembly committee and some of us were directed by God to the city."[16] Perhaps some of the signatories happened to be in the capital at the time, and joined their colleagues in endorsing the regulations;[17] it is more likely, though, that all the signatories were present during the assembly. Some of them were delegates from their congregations, and the names of at least five of them appear on the list of representatives of the congregations published in *Magyar Zsidó*.[18] However, it is clear that some of the signatories, and particularly the most prominent among them—Maharam Schick, Ketav Sofer, R. Aaron David Deutsch, R. Zvi Hirsch Friedman, the *Admor* of Liszka—did not come as delegates of their congregations. It appears that the members of *Shomrei ha-Dat* ensured the presence of some of the great rabbis at the assembly, both as patrons and as authorities, examining the proposals before their presentation to the assembly. These are the rabbis mentioned in the manifesto as those whom God directed to the city. They added to their ranks some outstanding rabbis from among the delegates, or perhaps merely requested their signatures at the close of the debates. In any event, they constituted only a minority of the rabbis who participated in the assembly, whom Maharam Schick counted as about thirty, while *Magyar Zsidó* numbered no more than twenty-four. One of these, Solomon Zvi Schick, rabbi of Karcag and a relative and student of Maharam Schick, reports that the householders in the assembly chose as president Sigmund Kraus, he too from the Schick family, "and the rabbis chose as their head my relative, the Gaon R. Moses Schick, may his merit protect us forever, and at the behest of these people, the assembled acted and went and formulated the statutes."[19] This testimony should be accepted only partially. It is clear that Maharam Schick played a significant role in the activities of the assembly, however, he does not seem to have been officially chosen as the head of the rabbis. If such an election actually occurred, the natural candidate for this title would be the Ketav Sofer, and his name indeed appears first among the signatories to the manifesto.

This subordination to the rabbis surrounded the debates with an atmosphere of tranquility. From the outset, there were few basic differences of viewpoint between the participants, and those in charge of wording the statutes succeeded in blurring any that remained.[20] This was the case with the question of the congregational schools. As we know, the Congress had made their existence mandatory, while their future was a matter of controversy within the Orthodox camp. The extremists wished to preserve the *heder*, and to fulfill the governmental educational requirements by sending their children to the non-Jewish schools. A sizable number of delegates were representatives of the northern hassidic congregations, and among the rabbis present was the *Admor* of Liszka, the most extreme of the extremists. The assembly therefore decided to support the interdenominational school,[21] a decision that even boosted their liberal and patriotic image in general public opinion.[22] At the same time, they sanctioned the congregational schools by issuing guidelines for those that already existed.[23]

The statutes relating to the organization of the congregations made membership conditional upon recognition of the Shulhan Arukh as the basis for their regulations. The congregations were to be autonomous; in some places they would encompass all local Jews, while in others they would govern only a minority that had seceded from the Neolog majority. Moreover, individuals were permitted to join the Orthodox congregation outside their place of habitation. The statutes determined the procedure for the courts of arbitration that adjudicated both within a single congregation and between congregations. Any candidate for rabbi was required to have a certificate of ordination from three rabbis recognized in Orthodox circles.[24] What was completely missing from the statutes was any definition of the functions of the national organization; they merely stated that an office would be opened in the capital to serve the needs of the organization, and that several officials would be at its disposal.[25] The statutes were submitted for governmental and parliamentary approval after the adjournment of the assembly, and we shall later hear of their fate.

It was resolved that an executive committee of seven members be chosen in order to advance the affairs of the organization. In reality, only five were chosen, and no explanation was given for the discrepancy between intention and action. Those appointed were the president of the *Shomrei ha-Dat* society, Meir Trebitsch, his vice-president, Ignác Reich, and the three presidential officials of the assembly—Sigmund Kraus, Emmanuel Eisler, and Leo von Fischer.[26] It seems strange at first that this important committee lacked a rabbinic eminence. But as we have already seen, even in its earlier manifestation, the *Shomrei ha-Dat* society had relinquished the idea of instituting a rabbinic council, preferring to rest under the wing of the great rabbis of the time without spelling out their names. Indeed, the leading rabbi of the time played a greater part in guiding the path of the organization than before, for Maharam Schick himself launched the national organization. However, his aversion to any official title was as great as his initiative. It is also possible that two rabbis were asked to be among the seven members of the executive committee, but refused the position.

Although the leading rabbis did not sit on the executive committee, they worked in their own way to advance its cause. Their assistance was needed, for while the number of representatives of the congregations at the assembly was impressive, it was far from what the organizers had hoped for. The list of rabbis who attended was particularly disappointing. Absent were some of those who had been the most prominent in the struggle for Orthodox interests at the Congress. The absence of these gave the lie to the contention of *Shomrei ha-Dat* that the turning point in Orthodox strategy, that is, the decision to found a supra-congregational organization, was approved by all the great rabbis.[27] It was therefore necessary to convince those who were absent to approve the decisions of the assembly after the fact; this of course depended upon the cooperation of the colleagues of those who absented themselves. In a letter to R. Hayyim Sofer about five weeks after the close of the assembly, we find the Ketav Sofer openly reprimanding him for the failure of his flock in Munkács to accept "the statutes that were made in the councils, with the knowledge of the scholars and elders of the city Pest."[28] He also expected that they would gather "by hand," that is, raise money, "for the *Shomrei ha-Dat*, who are in financial straits . . . why should his flock stand by from afar, this is very strange, and a matter etc.," the unstated etcetera implying that it was a matter of evil counsel.

We heard already of R. Hayyim Sofer's motives for not taking part in the assembly. He believed it would not go far enough in isolating the Orthodox from their rivals. We shall later see what conclusions he drew from this position. An entirely different spirit moved R. Jeremiah Löw to absent himself from the assembly and to distance himself from its decisions, even after the fact. He returned from the Congress disillusioned. From what he stated to Maharam Schick, as Schick repeated in the letter discussed above,[29] it is clear that Löw attributed the failure of the Orthodox, as it appeared at the time, to their own defects. He did not endorse Maharam Schick's ideas for improving the situation. He also discerned a turn in the tide of public opinion. In a letter to R. Hayyim Sofer, he explained to the latter that extreme demands such as his would no longer find support in the Ujhely congregation. "With pain in my heart I must tell his honor that since the Congress, for our sins, the opinions of people here have changed."[30] Upon his return from the Congress, Jeremiah Löw decided on a policy of passivity. He was not moved from this decision despite the extraordinary efforts that were made to involve him after the founding assembly of the Orthodox organization, by Maharam Schick himself among others. We hear of these efforts in a letter R. Aaron David Deutsch wrote to Maharam Schick one week after the adjournment of the assembly.[31] According to R. Deutsch, Maharam Schick's words to R. Löw made a great impression, and he was only one of many who turned to R. Löw on this matter without, as we know, moving him from his position.

J. Rosenheimer, who served as the head teacher in the district school in Ujhely, reports in the *Allgemeine Zeitung des Judenthums* as late as July, 1872, of R. Löw's continued uninvolvement. According to him, the rabbi did not answer any of the applications made to him by the Orthodox office in the capital city.[32] All signs indicate that Rosenheimer, who excelled at detailed and precise reportage, was in contact with the rabbi's household, and perhaps in personal contact with the rabbi himself. He gives a reasonable explanation for R. Löw's behavior. As did many others, R. Löw believed that a law guaranteeing unlimited religious freedom was inevitable, and would soon be enacted. Such a law would retroactively nullify any act of the Congress and its aftereffects, and would allow the congregation freedom to organize itself on an entirely new basis. Hope of this anticipated situation provided R. Jeremiah Löw with the rationale for not taking part in the Orthodox organization, for he assumed it would soon be invalidated in any case. This explanation fits what we know of R. Löw's personality; he had supreme faith in his judgment, and was happy when his conclusions obligated him only to be an observer.

This seeming farsightedness of R. Löw was a trait unique to him. His Orthodox rabbinic colleagues acted according to what they saw: The national organization that the Congress had founded was becoming established, while the congregations that were potential members of the Orthodox organization hesitated or held back. The reasons for this attitude varied according to the composition and leadership of the various congregations, particularly in religious terms.

By this time, most of the congregations in Hungary no longer adhered uniformly to tradition. Even those congregations whose institutions carefully preserved their old nature, and most of whose members were devout, usually included some members who were, to one extent or another, non-traditional. They too were considered members of the congregation according to the law of the land. They remained involved in the congregation through their familial and social ties, if not because of their ties to religion as they perceived it. They were not deprived of the right to take part in molding the life of the congregation, and they saw no reason to forgo this right voluntarily. When such a congregation had to decide between joining the Congress organization or the rival Orthodox organization, the progressive minority did not think of tipping the scales in favor of the Congress. But this does not mean that it could not delay or even prevent the congregation from joining the Orthodox organization. The illustrious congregation of Pressburg provides an example of such tactics.

As we recall, the rabbi of Pressburg, the Ketav Sofer, reprimanded his colleague from Munkács for his congregation's failure to join the Orthodox organization.[33] But lo and behold, his own congregation was found to hesitate. Only at the end of January, 1872, almost a year and a half after the founding assembly, were the new statutes for the congregation formulated, and only in March were they presented to the government for ratification. This followed a bitter quarrel with those who opposed the Orthodox organization, despite the fact that the organization was the creation of their teacher and rabbi.[34] Pressburg was only one of the traditional congregations that hesitated to join the national organization. In an article in *Das traditionelle Judenthum*, February 22, 1871, entitled "'Status Quo,'" Emmanuel Eisler addressed an open question to three nearby congregations of this type, Eisenstadt, Vágujhely, and Tapolcsány: How did their inaction fit with their known loyalty to Orthodoxy?[35] Eisler could find an answer to his question in the upheavals that shook his own community, Galgóc, in which he took an active part. An allusion to this is found in the title of the article, "'Status Quo.'" The quotation marks indicate the novelty of the term, and the author explains that this concept is used by those who are anxious to justify their refusal to join the national organization. Reading between the lines, it is clear that he is referring to members of his own community.

The term "status quo" was to play a central role in the public struggle we are describing; let us therefore trace its creation. There is reason to believe that it first appeared during the controversy in Eisler's congregation. This controversy can be reconstructed by examining the claims of both sides, and an official document issued by the county prefect of Nyitra.[36] This document contains, no more and no less, the order of the synagogue prayer service on the Rosh Hashanah and Yom Kippur of 1871, a prayer service in which both factions—who were not capable of coexisting under one roof—were required, willingly or not, to participate. This controversy became an object lesson to all, demonstrating what absurdities factionalism causes when it becomes divisiveness for its own sake.

Galgóc was one of the oldest congregations in the district, its founders having emigrated from nearby Moravia as early as the eighteenth century. It was considered an established and traditional community in terms of religion, although at the period under discussion, some of its members no longer followed a traditional lifestyle. However, there is no evidence for a move to reform the synagogue service and the like, which was the usual reason for disturbing congregational unity. According to a contemporary, the issue of elections to the

Congress created tension between the rabbi of the congregation and Emmanuel Eisler. The rabbi, Jacob Fleissig, considered himself a candidate for the role of delegate to the Congress, but Eisler won the post.[37] We know Eisler from his activities in the Congress, upholding Hirsch's doctrine that the independence of the Orthodox community was a necessary condition for true loyalty to Torah. This doctrine suited Eisler's character, which shows signs of extreme pedantry. Eisler was outstandingly consistent as a fighter for the Orthodox cause, and it is no coincidence that he was chosen by the founding assembly of the Orthodox organization as a member of the executive committee, nor is it surprising to see him intent upon applying his principles in his own congregation. But here he encountered spirited opposition. A small minority of the congregation wished to join the Congress organization, and one of the more aggressive members even took an active part in organizing its district branch. The rabbi attempted to mediate between the two factions: On the one hand, all of them would declare that their lives are based on the principles of the Shulhan Arukh, in accordance with the Orthodox demand, for it had never entered anyone's mind to institute changes that contradicted its ruling. On the other hand, the congregation would join neither of the organizations. It is best to maintain the present state of affairs, or the "status quo."

This line of thought seems to have developed in other places as well, under similar circumstances. The Berlin reporter for *Jüdische Presse* wrote on July 7, 1871, that some congregations in Hungary have reservations about both parties, the Neolog and the Orthodox, and they call themselves neutral.[38] The term used in Galgóc apparently caught on more readily than the term "neutral," and became prevalent. Reacting to this new position, Eisler informed the government in the name of his supporters—estimated by his opponents to be about forty in number, out of a congregation of 190[39]—that they no longer considered the rabbi a reliable religious authority. They therefore wished to establish a separate Orthodox community. We do not know how Eisler succeeded in persuading those in charge of the justice of his case, but we do know that in the issue of March 9, 1871, the board of *Das traditionelle Judenthum* congratulated Eisler upon receiving permission to establish a separate Orthodox community.[40] Two weeks later, in the March 23 issue, Eisler published a congratulatory letter from R. Samson Raphael Hirsch, which expressed his delight over Eisler's success in seceding from the general congregation.[41] The rabbi of Frankfurt was probably not aware of the details of the incident; he apparently assumed that some religious-halakhic flaw had been found in the congregational institutions. It stands to reason that, had he known that the excuse for secession was a controversy over joining the national organization, he would not have considered it an occasion for congratulations. As we shall see, he differed from his colleagues, the extreme separatists in Hungary, on this question.

Eisler's struggle did not end upon receipt of permission to establish a separate congregation. He continued to keep the government occupied with the demand that his group be acknowledged as the mother congregation, with the right to claim the property of the entire community, despite being the minority. His arguments for this claim are not given, but are easy to guess. From the time when the division of the congregations appeared a distinct possibility, each side had accused the other of responsibility for what was considered by most a disastrous future. Although those pushing for division were mainly the Orthodox, they nonetheless claimed that not they but their opponents were the secessionists, for the latter forsook the customs of their ancestors, while they remained loyal to them. They should therefore be recognized as the mother congregation. Eisler, with his doctrinaire mentality, apparently made this ideological argument the basis for his legal claim: The Orthodox adhere to the old customs of the congregation and therefore they are its legal heirs. The major and perhaps only property of the congregation was the synagogue, and the legal battle now centered on it. Until the issue was decided by the courts, neither side wished to leave the synagogue to the exclusive use of its opponents, in order to prevent a de facto right of possession. Both groups used the building for prayer, and on Sabbaths they gathered at different times, under governmental supervision. This temporary arrangement was impossible with the approach of the High Holy Days. The Orthodox minority feared it would be forced to hold its prayer service outside of the synagogue and would thus lose its right of possession. Eisler therefore insisted on the right of the minority to use the synagogue, and suggested a division of roles between the precentors of both groups. Such a division was simple for those ceremonies that took place twice during the festival, such as the prayers on the two days of Rosh Hashanah, and it was necessary only to cast lots to determine which precentor would be first. Unluckily, the first day of Rosh Hashanah came out on the Sabbath and the blowing of the shofar took place only once. Fortune thus favored one of the sides and discriminated against the other, as it did regarding the prayers of Yom Kippur. The compromise document dealt with the minute details of the division of roles, in order to create the fairest possible division. This was Eisler's work, but it was signed by Johann Mauther, the county prefect of Nyitra.[42]

With the onset of confrontations in the Hungarian congregations in the wake of changes in the religious ceremonies, controversies about religious issues were more than once brought before the non-Jewish courts. This was considered scandalous—a desecration of God's name, as contemporaries put it. One of the arguments in favor of the Congress was that if an autonomous Jewish organization were created, it would provide for an authoritative Jewish institution to decide such questions. But the Congress only sharpened controversies and created more, instead of ending them. And so cases of non-Jewish intervention in internal Jewish matters became more frequent. The phenomenon was therefore well known. Nonetheless, the act of the county administration of Galgóc was exceptional, and not only because of its attention to details (who would blow the shofar, and so on). In this case the Orthodox side, which had declared its inability to live a shared religious life with the other side, had forced its opponents, with the aid of the government, to share the most solemn ceremonies of the year. This meant that the division was not caused by a religious chasm between the camps, but because division itself had become the main objective. Anyone unwilling to join the Orthodox organization was considered religiously disqualified by those who upheld the organization. This position coalesced in its final form only some time later. But the incident in Galgóc, brought about by Eisler's fanaticism, heralded this phenomenon. Evidence for this is provided by the fate of R. Jacob Fleissig, who refused to divide the congregation. The bickering within the congregation, which desecrated the holiness of the synagogue and insulted the rabbi, increased rather than disappeared in the months after the forced compromise of the High Holy Days of 1871. His opponents embittered the rabbi's life, until, in mid-February, 1872, he resigned, leaving himself and his family without a roof over their heads or a means of subsistence.[43]

Let us now leave the local and return to the national scene. As we recall, the memorandum of the leaders of the Congress had lain before the legislature since December 1870. In it, they had reiterated their justification of the actions of the Congress, and had requested ratification of its statutes. Although the memorandum did not demand the nullification of the March 18, 1870, law that released the Orthodox of the obligation to join the Congress organization, the Orthodox suspected that this was its intention, for it was well known that this decision was a source of annoyance to the initiator of the Congress, Minister Eötvös. The Orthodox presented a counter-memorandum intended to forestall any such eventuality, which rebutted the arguments of their opponents and reiterated their demand to release them from any link to the Congress organization and its statutes.[44] Both memoranda were submitted to a subcommittee of the legislature for its opinion, and both sides eagerly awaited its decision. Before the committee could finish its work, something happened that confounded all expectations.

On February 2, 1871, the sudden death of Baron Joseph von Eötvös was announced. The entire nation went into deep mourning over the death of the renowned author and original thinker, who had also been a leader of the party that had extricated the nation from the consequences of its failed revolution. The patriotic Jewish community participated in the national mourning for an additional reason. The man who had fought for Jewish equality and civil rights had departed. The Jewish and general press announced mourning ceremonies and eulogies in synagogues throughout the country.[45] The speakers who supported the Congress no doubt noted among his qualities also his activity in support of the Congress. We can only surmise the state of mind of the opponents of the

Congress, who viewed the deceased as the promulgator of one of the worst decrees to befall the Jewish nation in its history. There is no mention of Eötvös's death in the many sermons of the great rabbis that have been preserved, many of which were dedicated to national events—Jewish emancipation, coronation of the king, the convening of the Congress and the like. These circles, which viewed every event connected to their interests as an act of providence, no doubt also interpreted this event, from which they could hope for a change for the better, in this way.[46] But these musings were best kept silent.

The official organ of the Orthodox, *Das traditionelle Judenthum*, which could not refrain from mentioning the event, buried it in an article entitled "Der neue Cultusminister," that is, the new minister for religious and educational affairs.[47] It said of the deceased minister that those who mourn him are correct in doing so, for they differentiate between the man and his policy; the former is deserving of praise and the latter, the opposite. In an article published a few weeks later, on the other hand, the deceased was exonerated on all counts. He was not guilty of convening the Congress, since the evildoers of Israel had seduced him, and they alone were to blame.[48] The new minister, Dr. Tivadar Pauler, was congratulated by the author, who described him as a conservative Catholic, and emphasized the irony that these conservative circles are the ones that now bear the banner of religious freedom.

A sign of the change in favor of the Orthodox came two months after the death of Eötvös. On March 30, 1871, the subcommittee presented to the legislature their opinion of the two conflicting memoranda—that of the Congressional leadership and that of the Orthodox. The committee refrained from deciding in favor of either one, and adjured the new minister to delve into this difficult issue and present a reasonable solution to the legislature.[49] The legislature accepted this proposal, and the minister interpreted this as sanction to act on the matter as he saw fit. From his statements on various opportunities, and primarily from his actions, it was clear that he accepted his predecessor's view that the national interest mandated encouraging the religions of the state to organize into national organizations, in order to make their supervision easier. He deviated from this view only in regard to the Jewish religion. His predecessor had believed that a single organization would suffice, while he became convinced that such unity was impossible under the circumstances. Therefore he officially recognized the former heads of the Congress as representatives of the congregations that joined its organization, and simultaneously granted the founding assembly of the Orthodox a de facto official position. Accordingly, the minister presented the statutes of the future Orthodox organization for the approval of the king. The king's signature was affixed on October 22, 1871.[50] News of this reached the public shortly before Chanukah, eliciting the expected reaction of those who attributed significance to such matters.[51] Pauler, the devout Catholic, received the congratulations of the God-fearing for his generosity, and not only by residents of Hungary. Letters of thanks reached him from Willy von Rothschild of Frankfurt and from the rabbi of *Adath Jeschurun* in the city, R. Samson Raphael Hirsch. From England, Moses Montefiore and the Chief Rabbi, Nathan Adler, sent their congratulations. The honorable minister published these messages of congratulation in the official government newspaper.[52]

Chapter 19

The Fate of the Uncommitted
The Status Quo Congregations and Their Ostracism

With the king's ratification of their statutes, the executive committee of the Orthodox organization had good grounds to persuade the congregations to join their organization. The need to do so did not decrease. The organization's influence with the government, among other issues on the share of the education fund that the Orthodox would receive, depended on the number of congregations in their organization as opposed to the number in the rival organization. But even now the pace of enrollment remained slow, and the two journals of the organization, *Shevet Ahim* and *Das traditionelle Judenthum*, continuously exhorted the public on this issue.[1]

There were various reasons for the slow pace of enrollment in the organization. One was technical. The ability to join depended upon a congregation's formal self-organization: holding a meeting of its members, a protocol of whose decisions must be sent to the executive committee, and a copy of which was filed in the government office. In old and established congregations, which had their own rules, the members wondered why they should bother for something which was of no use to them. On the other hand, many of the smaller congregations, which had been established only in the last generations, functioned without a set of statutes, and they lacked not only the motivation, but also the technical means to institute a formal code. On previous occasions, when the *Shomrei ha-Dat* society wanted to claim empowerment by the congregations, it had provided them with the appropriate form, and they were requested only to return it with the leaders' signatures. But this time it was necessary to formulate a fairly complicated document. Members of the executive committee apparently attempted to help the congregations overcome this difficulty by giving guidance, and perhaps even by appearing in person or sending their representatives.² However, they focused on providing incentives for enrollment, by repeating the arguments and reasons that should obligate the isolated congregations to rise above local considerations and consider the needs of the community at large. A manifesto, meant for this purpose alone and signed by about forty rabbis, was distributed in March.³ The fact that there was a need for this, nearly half a year after the ratification of the statutes, is evidence of the executive committee's disappointment at the rate at which congregations joined the organization.

The manifesto recalls the memory of the "strong hand that God revealed to us in breaking the rods of the Congress," with the king's granting permission for the pious to organize themselves according to "the Torah, justice, and rectitude." The opportunity must now be seized, by establishing a set of regulations for each congregation and by their enrollment in the general organization. "And it is forbidden to neglect this and be dilatory, for if we dally in uniting . . . soon the people of the Congress will raise their hands and will again rule over us, for there is no escape from the Congress except by accepting the 'organization-statut,'" that is, the statutes of the Orthodox organization. This last passage gives the impression that each congregation was required to join either the Congress or the Orthodox organization. It would have been convenient for the Orthodox had the government demanded such a choice, for then all those who hesitated to join the Neolog organization would have joined their group. But such an order was not given. We do not know if Minister Pauler even considered this possibility, and if he did, he apparently dismissed it. It would have contradicted the principle of freedom of conscience, the principle that had released the Orthodox from subordination to the Congress organization. Now that two organizations existed, there was no compulsion to join either one of them. The authors of the manifesto were no doubt aware of the situation, but the threat of the Congress's domination over the pious—which did not necessarily have to come via state law—seemed to them the best means to motivate those who felt threatened to follow the Orthodox line.

The rabbis who signed the manfesto were from all areas of the state, from Munkács to Pressburg,⁴ and they ranged from the old Ashkenazi type, exemplified by R. Abraham Schag of Kobersdorf, to the hassidic rabbi Zvi Hirsch Friedman, the *Admor* of Liszka. The rabbi of Liszka was not the only hassid among the signatories: At least two more joined him, R. Yekutiel Judah Teitelbaum of Sziget and R. Menahem Mendel Panet of Dés, who functioned both as city rabbis and as hassidic rebbes. It is, nonetheless, a mistake to conclude from the signatures on the manifesto that the Orthodox organization was as popular among the hassidim as among other sectors of the Jewish public. The Sziget community refused to join the Orthodox organization throughout the lifetime of R. Teitelbaum—he died in 1883—and its refusal to do so caused one of the most raucous controversies in a period replete with dissension.⁵ The scope of the phenomenon of refusal to join and its background is revealed in the extensive correspondence of R. Aaron David Deutsch on this matter.[6]

R. Deutsch was born in Moravia. After concluding his studies in the *yeshivah* of the Hatam Sofer, he settled in Hungary, and from 1851 served as the rabbi of Balassagyarmat. He had a strong sense of public responsibility, and without having an official position in the Orthodox organization, he worked hand in hand with its executive committee.[7] His part in the attempt to influence R. Jeremiah Löw in favor of the organization has been mentioned above. He ended his letter to Maharam Schick on this matter with the sentence: "His honor the *gaon, Av Beit Din* of Ungvár, should also write to Liszka, for we must unite with the hassidic rabbis and give them honor."[8] About a half year later we find him writing to the rabbi of Liszka on the same matter.[9] This is rather surprising, for the *Admor* was one of the forty signatories on the manifesto that urged the public to join the organization. This means that such a signature did not necessarily constitute a commitment to act personally on behalf of the organization. Hassidim from near and far came to the rabbi of Liszka's home, and R. Deutsch requested that he "encourage them and adjure them about this," that is, that they join the organization. He requested the same of R. Menahem Mendel Panet, but in this case indirectly. The rabbi of Dés was regarded as a hassidic rebbe, but only of a minor degree, since he considered himself a follower of R. Hayyim Halberstamm, the *Admor* of Sanz. R. Halberstamm followed events in Hungary and at times took a stand on public issues of contemporary importance. R. Deutsch turned to Sanz, this time explicitly at the behest of the executive committee, and requested that the rebbe instruct the rabbi of Dés to encourage his hassidim to support the Orthodox organization.[10]

R. Samuel Shmelke Ginzler, rabbi of Visó, was not known to be a hassid, but his congregation in the Máramaros district was permeated with hassidism.[11] R. Deutsch maintained a correspondence with him, in which R. Ginzler set before him the hassidim's reasons for refusing to join the Orthodox organization; we learn the nature of these from R. Deutsch's answer, which alone survives.[12] One is purely a traditionalist response—our fathers did not have such an organization, so why should we?[13] Another reason was a flaw they found in the statutes of the organization, which made formal organization of the congregation mandatory, required written down procedures for electing officials and the like, but did not stipulate that the candidates must be Sabbath observers, as stated in the Shulhan Arukh, which disqualifies the non-observant from holding public office.[14] This claim carried a certain weight, but the main concern of the hassidim was apparently different: by joining the organization, they would be subject to the rule of its leaders in the capital city, and these were not of their kind, but Ashkenazim "with shaved faces"[15] and the like. And even though reliable people vouched for the present leaders' reliability, who could guarantee that their successors would be the same?[16]

Concerns about local factors also seem to have been behind the arguments against the organization. Hassidism had become rooted in the northern districts, but it was far from dominant. We already heard of R. Löw's opposition to the hassidim. Although he stood alone in his open and vigorous battle with the *Admor* of Liszka, he had friends and sympathizers in the attempt to prevent the encroachment of hassidic customs and ways. R. Hayyim Sofer, the Orthodox extremist, was one of them.[17] The general population, which clung to its traditional customs and prayers, also displayed a passive resistance to Hassidism, and viewed the hassidim as innovators. The *Admor* of Liszka lamented this, but accepted the reality. In his *beit midrash* he of course adhered to all the minute details of Hassidism, but when he prayed in the congregational synagogue on festivals and other occasions, he made no attempt to change the old customs.[18] The hassidim apparently suspected that in this hidden struggle between the doctrines, joining the national organization might tip the scales against them.

In his reply to the rabbi of Visó, R. Aaron David Deutsch attempted to assuage the fears of the hassidim on all the points raised in their arguments. Regarding the differences between "the customs of Ashkenaz or Sefarad," that is, those of the hassidim, there was no reason to fear: According to the statutes of the organization, each congregation would decide the nature of its religious life in special statutes, and the leadership of the national organization would have no right to interfere. By referring to the autonomy of the individual congregations, R. Deutsch wished to deflect the criticism over the status of those who desecrated the Sabbath. Congregations that wished to do so could disqualify religious transgressors from being appointed to public office. He left it to the reader to draw the conclusion that the organization would not exclude a congregation that did not wish to—or could not—act according to the stringency of the law on this matter. As for the concern that the organization might fall into disloyal hands in the future, he claimed that clauses in the statutes would prevent this.

The most important and interesting part of R. Deutsch's statement is his response to the argument of mere traditionalism. His answer to this can be summarized in one short sentence: What appears to be a novelty is, rather, a return to the previous state of affairs. R. Deutsch sketched a brief historical survey, a testament to his analytic skills, in support of this thesis. Did the preceding generations not formulate rules as needed? Certainly they did, and they could enforce them, and all the laws of Israel, by use of the ban. Then came a time when a governmental decree forbade the use of the ban. From then on, transgressors abounded, and controversies erupted in the congregations. Since the congregation lacked powers of enforcement, matters were taken to the courts and district rulers. Thus was born the idea of the Congress. It was meant to create an internal Jewish organization with coercive power, which would prevent Jews from turning to the legal and judicial institutions of the government. However, the Congress refused to accept the laws of the Torah as the basis for its constitution, and therefore the devout seceded from it, but requested government permission to form their own organization. "We are not powerful enough to tell the evil ones how to behave," but for ourselves we can grant the congregations powers of enforcement through the central organization. To this end, a passage in the statutes states that if an individual should refuse to follow the directives of the local *beit din*, the central office will appoint another *beit din*, where the recalcitrant one will be judged, willingly or not. The organization and its institutions were ratified by the government, and therefore the rulings of its *beit din* can be enforced by government representatives.[19] The purpose achieved by the ban in previous generations will now be attained with the aid of the organization. Thus far the historical analysis. At the end of the letter, R. Deutsch reiterated the dubious threat of the organization propagandists, that a congregation that did not join the organization would fall under the jurisdiction of the Congress.[20] In order to ensure that his letter had some effect, Deutsch requested that it be sent to the *Admor* of Sanz, stating that he himself hesitates to trouble him again on the same matter.[21] If his words had some impact, it was probably due to the support of authorities such as the rebbe of Sanz, for the theoretical arguments were beyond the grasp of most of the hassidim. Indeed, the hassidim remained isolated from the general Orthodox population, and at times even institutionalized their isolation by establishing "Sefardic" congregations in the country.[22]

We do not know exactly when it became clear to the general public that the Orthodox claim that the law of the land required each and every congregation to choose between the organizations, was invalid. It is clear that this happened. Many congregations, among them large and important ones such as Ujhely and Nagykároly, refused to join—Ujhely by the order of R. Löw, and Nagykároly under the leadership of R. Meir Perles.[23] The case of R. Meir Perles demonstrates that inconsistency was not limited exclusively to hassidic rabbis. He too had signed the manifesto that urged the congregations to join the Orthodox organization, but nonetheless refrained from doing so in his own congregation. Thus R. Perles, who was considered one of the greatest Torah scholars in the country, acted in a manner contrary to his binding signature.[24] This lack of commitment by some of the great congregations worried the national Orthodox leadership, and if it hoped for government intervention to force the congregations to join one or the other of the organizations, this was a vain hope. The government remained indifferent to the matter, and events in the city of Kassa indicated that they considered it permissible not only for a congregation to remain outside of the national organization, but even for part of that congregation to take an intermediate stance between the Neolog and the Orthodox, and create a separate congregation.

As mentioned, a struggle had been going on in Kassa between the two factions in the congregation even before the Congress, and the complaints of both camps were submitted to the Ministry of Education and Religion, and became the subject of articles in various newspapers.[25] In April, 1872, a verdict was finally given by Minister Pauler's office, which ruled that they should separate. The *beit midrash*, which both sides claimed, was given to the Neologs, but they were obligated to finance the building of a new place of prayer for the Orthodox.[26]

Before the power struggle between the two factions ended, a severe split occurred in the Orthodox camp itself, caused by the rabbi of the congregation, R. Abraham Katz (Seelenfreund).[27] R. Katz was the son of a prestigious and renowned rabbinic family and he himself had written both homiletic and halakhic works.[28] It is not sufficiently clear what flaw his opponents found in him, but it is clear that he did not have the support of the majority of the Orthodox faction. Nonetheless, he did not lack supporters in the congregation, and when they saw that there was no chance of reconciling the differences, they decided to set up their own congregation with him at its head. Some members of the Neolog congregation also joined this halfway creation after its establishment. The new congregation called itself *Adath Shalom* (the Congregation of Peace),[29] and not Status Quo, apparently to indicate that it was not created in reaction to events on the national scene, but in response to local conditions, and considered itself no less loyal to authentic Judaism than the majority from which it had seceded. This majority did not, of course, acknowledge the right of the minority to do this, and the case was presented to an arbitration court. Two rabbis from neighboring communities were chosen, each side naming one,[30] and they together selected R. David Silberstein. He was also a rabbi in the district at the time, but in contrast to the other two, he was a well-known rabbinic personality, because of his homiletic and halakhic writings and because of his contributions to public affairs (he went to the land of Israel, but returned to his native land several years later).[31] Even without his son's testimony later, during the controversy in Sziget, we would know that his opinion decided the issue.[32] The ruling denied the right of the secessionists to establish their own congregation.[33] The members of the secessionist group, as well as the Neologs, were given the opportunity to return to the Orthodox congregation. Whoever did not enroll with the Orthodox would be considered a Neolog, stated the ruling. This ruling was of practical significance for *shohetim* (ritual slaughterers) and halakhists, for if they were to continue to serve the secessionists, they would fall under the prohibition, "according to the ruling already made by the great ones of our time, may God preserve them, concerning the Neologs in several places in our country."

As a result of this ruling, R. Katz found himself the loser on both fronts. The householders could return to the Orthodox congregation, while he could not, since his position as rabbi of the congregation had already been given to another, and the court of arbitration had explicitly approved this.[34] Moreover, if he wanted to continue to serve the secessionists, his rulings would be rejected, as if he were one of the Neologs. It is no wonder that the rabbi refused to accept the ruling. He appealed it before authoritative rabbis and received a sympathetic hearing from some of them. R. Benjamin Z'ev Mandelbaum, the rabbi of Szatmár and one of the senior rabbis of the generation, testified to his integrity and his high level of scholarship, and R. Meir Perles of Nagykároly nullified the prohibition concerning his authority.[35]

The controversy quickly spread beyond the boundaries of Kassa. The opinions supporting those who upheld the secessionists were published in a special pamphlet (which is not extant), and the Jewish press in Hungary and outside it reported on the progress of events. The two newpapers of the executive committee of the Orthodox in the capital, *Shevet Ahim* and its German counterpart, *Das traditionelle Judenthum*, paid special attention to it.[36] These noted the great damage that could ensue from the confrontation in Kassa for the Orthodox cause throughout the country. Even though the *Adath Shalom* congregation was created by local factors, had it received the approval of halakhic authorities, it would have served as a precedent for Status Quo congregations everywhere. They therefore loudly congratulated R. Silberstein on his ruling, while abusing those who upheld R. Katz in every possible way. They did not spare even R. Perles, despite his high rank among the rabbis of the time. Maharam Schick also followed with concern the progress of events surrounding the confrontation in Kassa. R. David Silberstein's son related that after news of the appeals against the ruling became known, Maharam Schick turned to his father and asked why he did not publicly defend his ruling.[37] His father's answer was that he had done his share, and others should defend his ruling. Maharam Schick responded to the challenge: This is the background to his famous responsum about the Status Quo.[38] The responsum was addressed to R. Meir Perles, the most prominent among the opponents of the ruling, whose name the editors of the responsum omitted.

Maharam Schick complained to R. Perles of his inconsistent behavior. Formerly, he had joined forces with the rabbis of the country who warned "the children of Israel to be on guard and to take care not to fall into the trap set for them . . . and how is it that he now upholds the Status Quo?" Maharam Schick was certainly aware that previously R. Perles and his colleagues had been asked to decide between the Neologs and the Orthodox. Here, as if in passing and without hesitation, he identified the Status Quo congregations with the Neologs. Even if these are not "the messengers and agents of the Congress people, they stood idly by while we were attacked." This allusion to the verse from Obadiah (11) called forth an additional association from the Song of Deborah: "For they did not come to the help of the Lord against the mighty" (Judges 5:23). Maharam Schick depicted the Orthodox as "the legion of Torah and faith," while the Status Quoers, even though they did not actively aid the Congress people, also did not fulfill the commandment, "do not stand aside when the blood of your neighbor is spilled": "and if this is true for physical danger, all the more so in respect to spiritual danger and eternal life."

This serious accusation echoes the deep anger that was felt towards the Status Quo position, but is in fact an anachronistic description of a situation that only arose later on. No group existed during the struggles in the Congress that could be identified as the precursor of the Status Quo position.[39] The differences of approach in the Orthodox camp emerged only later, with the realization of the need for a separate national Orthodox organization; this idea actually took shape at the initiative of the author himself. This organization began its work with the founding assembly, which took place in August 1870, and from then on the pious were called upon to take an active part in it. This demand took on greater force after the king's approval of the statutes of the organization one year later. Thus, at issue was what could be termed religious policy; that is, steps that appeared to their planners necessary to ensure the well-being and completeness of the religious community. Maharam Schick wished to endow these steps with absolute religious authority, and did so by making a series of positive and negative commandments applicable to these steps, and the failure to take them. "Do not stand aside . . ." would apply to whoever does not bestir himself to save his comrade from falling into the trap of the Congress people. He thus abets sinners and transgresses the commandment of "do not put obstacles in the path of a blind man." The Torah had commanded placing a railing on roofs to prevent bloodshed, and Maimonides had extended this commandment to include "not putting obstacles in our house and in our land." "And who does not know of the obstacle of the Congress, that which they planned to do with evil laws? There is no other way to guard and make a railing but that which God has shown us—by organizing—and whoever delays will be called to account in the future."[40]

In his dispute with the authors of the Michalowitz ruling, led by R. Hillel Lichtenstein, Maharam Schick had claimed that they had erred in granting halakhic validity to decrees that they had enacted because of contemporary needs. It seems strange that he now did the same, without realizing his inconsistency; but at that time he had been unhappy with the decrees themselves, and could therefore easily point out the weak points of their arguments. In this case, he was no doubt convinced that his initiative in founding the Orthodox national organization was the only way to save Judaism, and thus the proofs for this were produced effortlessly from the wealth of sources at his command. Transposing the command "do not stand aside . . ." to the spiritual realm, and similarly extending the obligation to make a railing, are complete novelties, the result of free association alone. Both in earlier and later halakhic literature the two directives are understood to apply only to physical danger. This was a homiletical, rather than a halakhic method. Indeed, the first passages of Maharam Schick's responsum are not halakhic, but a sort of homiletical opening to stir the emotions. The halakhic discussion begins only in the fourth paragraph, which opens with the words: "Fourthly, I cannot refrain from explaining the obligation to accept the need for organization." Here he raises the concrete question whether and under what conditions the individual or public is obliged to accept statutes that were enacted, without the interested parties having participated in creating them. This question had been repeatedly discussed in halakhic literature from its beginnings, but, surprisingly, Maharam Schick is brief where it would have been appropriate to expand. He brings proof from communal law, where the individual cannot release himself from communal regulations. In the middle of the twelve lines of his discussion, he highlights Nahmanides' statement that it is a biblical injunction imposed on "the earthly *beit din*, and on anyone who is able, to uphold the Torah." And he adds: "Since the *beit din* is commanded to uphold and to decree, the public is required to obey." To prevent any possible misunderstanding that this refers only to the Sanhedrin, he alludes to Maimonides' statement that this means "every court that has the power . . . and as the Mordechai wrote in his commentary on the first chapter of BT Baba Bathra, the city officials are to be considered in their place of habitation as having the same status as the great ones of the time." The requirement to obey the *beit din* in each city is transferred almost unconsciously to the congregations of the land, whether or not they had authorized that *beit din*.[41]

In the remaining parts of the responsum, Maharam Schick rebuts R. Perles's rejection of the ruling against the secessionists in Kassa, and in particular condemns the religious functionaries of their congregation, with R. Katz Seelenfreund at their head. Maharam Schick also refers to R. Aaron David Deutsch's opinion against R. Perles, which preceded his own. The opinions of these two have not reached us, and it is therefore difficult to understand Maharam Schick's rebuttals. This is not a great loss, for they addressed only the local problem, and the importance of Maharam Schick's responsum lies in his pronouncements on the general issue. We will discuss its importance after hearing of the reaction of those he attacked, R. Meir Perles and his circle.

However, the progress of events in Kassa itself is also of interest. Although Maharam Schick's responsum, following that of R. Deutsch, reiterated and supported R. Silberstein's ruling, they had no real effects. The third congregation, which later was explicitly called Status Quo, continued to exist, and its rabbi, R. Seelenfreund, who was disqualified as a halakhist, not only continued to serve, but even succeeded in preserving his status as an equal among the Hungarian rabbis, publishing two more books after the confrontation in Kassa.[42] True, most of the letters of approbation that he received came from great rabbis in Poland, but his strong position is revealed by the cooperation given to him by important Hungarian rabbis over a serious halakhic problem. R. Katz was called upon to permit an *aguna* (a woman whose husband is presumed dead, but no witnesses to his death can be found) to remarry in 1881, and when he agreed, he requested and received the agreement of three of his colleagues, as was the custom: R. Joel Ungar, R. Isaac Billitzer, rabbi of Nagyida, and last but not least, R. Leibisch Jolesz of Sebeskelemes, R. Katz's replacement in the Orthodox community in Kassa.[43]

In reaction to Maharam Schick's responsum, R. Meir Perles and those who supported the secessionists retracted their rejection of R. Silberstein's ruling. The two newspapers of the executive committee were happy to print R. Perles's short letter:[44]

My comrade, the rabbi, *gaon, av beit din* of the holy community of Huszt, may he live, has encircled me with bundles of correct reasons . . . to uphold the organization statutes against all Status Quo communities. I saw that his reasons are well stated, and therefore I retract all that I wrote to the holy community of Kassa . . . and may it be as if my words were never spoken, and may no one rely on these words any longer.[44]

If Maharam Schick's argumentation is questionable, there is no doubt of his character and intentions, while R. Perles remains an enigma. Could he not discern the glaring weaknesses in the attack upon him? R. Perles had his own ideas about solving the problems on the public agenda, and even prior to the Congress, Sigmund Kraus had said that his doctrines were unique.[45] But he tired of fighting for them. In 1882, a minority in the Kolozsvár congregation seceded from the mother congregation and organized as a Status Quo congregation. The secessionists turned to R. Perles in the hope of winning his moral support. His answer was that both camps, the Orthodox and the Status Quo, "are new inventions of which our ancestors did not dream, and they are vanity." Every community that follows the path of its ancestors "is to be called a holy community, and it is forbidden to speak against them in even the smallest way and to be disrespectful. Unfortunately, the name Orthodox is borrowed from the Christians . . . and I feel great sorrow that the sons of our holy forefathers call themselves by the name of idolatry."[46] This is an unequivocal and harsh anti-Orthodox position, seen from the perspective of the Status Quo. But theory is one thing, and readiness to stand up for it is another. R. Perles emerges as a withdrawn person, for whom any public confrontation was a burden. It was sufficient that he encounter opposition, as happened with Maharam Schick, and he fled the battlefield.[47] It was the bad luck of the Status Quoers that their most eminent patron was this type of person. The Orthodox were lucky that their leader was the total opposite.

Maharam Schick was not eager for battle either, but when conditions forced him to do so, he battled with all his might. In admonishing R. Perles, he seemed to be mixing into a quarrel not his own. No one had asked him; he took the initiative. Moreover, almost in passing he sealed the fate of people and congregations whose religious status and behavior were impeccable, and whose only fault was that they did not accept his view and that of his circle, that the Orthodox national organization is the only and absolute guarantee for the preservation of Judaism. This opinion was supported by sources from the treasures of rabbinic literature, as was every halakhic responsum. Actually, as we have seen, the responsum deviated from the accepted rules of adjudication in at least two ways: the reliance upon examples from biblical events, and the transposition of halakhic concepts from the personal-individual-physical level to the public-organizational arena. But these deviations from the accepted patterns of adjudication seem to have strengthened rather than weakened the impression made by the responsum on all concerned. Analysis of the validity of the proofs was a job for scholars of the same rank as the author. For the average reader it was sufficient that the author, who was known to be one of the greatest rabbis of the time, equated the Status Quoers with the Neologs. And he did so, moreover, not merely with logical proofs, but with the pathos of one who issues decrees with the approval of God and of the community of the pious. The pious public is enjoined to detach itself from anyone who is not prepared to join it in order to ensure the future of the "legion of Torah and faith."

Although Maharam Schick's ruling responded to a local incident in the Kassa congregation, it retroactively became a sort of manifesto of the organizing Orthodox. It granted religious-halakhic authorization to the executive committee of the organization to compel those congregations or parts of congregations that did not want to join the Congress organization to enroll in their own organization. At first the committee believed that the government would force the congregations to choose between the two organizations. When this hope was not realized, the Orthodox used moral-religious pressure in place of government coercion. The public promise made with the publication of the statutes of the organization after the founding assembly, that membership would be voluntary even for congregations whose representatives were present at the assembly, was abandoned and forgotten. Now the Orthodox made membership an absolute religious requirement for anyone who wished to consider himself devout. This is the demand that Maharam Schick endorsed, and to which he granted religious-halakhic validity. Consciously or not, he thus helped strengthen a new tendency to define the place of an individual or community on the religious spectrum, not according to its views and behavior, but according to its institutional affiliation. This new doctrine came about unwittingly, as a consequence of the upheavals that shook Hungarian Jewry in the Congress era. It was a change that molded the public face of Judaism for generations to come.

VI

Looking Forward, Looking Back

Chapter 20

Theoretical and Practical Limits of the Schism

The events of the Congress and its consequences have been described in great detail. A comprehensive survey is now called for, in order to describe the changes created in Hungarian Jewish society, their nature and significance.

The initiators of the Congress, Minister Eötvös and his allies within the Jewish community, hoped to see the half-million Hungarian Jews, with their numerous communities—almost three hundred and fifty of them—subject to a central administration, which would be established with the active participation of its members. Judaism appeared to them to be a religion like all others, and like the other religious communities, its adherents should be required to conduct their own affairs, although with the approval and supervision of the state. It was well known that this community was no longer unified in its attitude to its religious heritage, and that bitter struggles were taking place between the rightists and the leftists in the congregations. In the view of Eötvös and his allies, however, this fact itself necessitated the establishment of a national organization, which would be authorized to create a mechanism to establish procedures and to make peace between the factions.

What actually happened was entirely different: Instead of one autonomous national organization with powers of enforcement, two national organizations arose, both of which lacked the authority to compel the congregations to join them. Only a congregation that voluntarily joined one of the organizations was bound to act according to its statutes and to accept the authority of its leadership. The state recognized each organization as spokesman for the public it represented, as if they constituted two separate religious bodies. The Orthodox seized on the fact of the division to claim that indeed two religions were involved, and that there is no common ground between their faith and that of the Neologs. The Neologs rejected this claim, and the state identified with their position, for its own reasons. State law recognized only one Jewish religion, and government spokesmen repeatedly proclaimed that they would have been happy had the two factions succeeded in reuniting under one organization. The government's agreement to the split may have been a result of peculiar circumstances, the most significant of which was the appointment of Minister Pauler after Eötvös's demise. Still, once this agreement was granted, it was accepted even by those who doubted the justice and practical wisdom underlying the decision. This is why the Orthodox claim that there were two separate religions remained mere rhetoric, government officials refused to draw any practical conclusions from it, and their attitude of reserve reflected the prevailing feeling among the Jewish and non-Jewish public alike, that Judaism as a whole remained one definable entity despite the split.

This state of affairs presented quite a few difficulties and dilemmas for the Orthodox administration. Let us give two examples: (1) its attitude to the establishment of the rabbinical seminary; and (2) its reservations about the struggle to achieve equal legal status for the Jewish religion—changing it from an "acknowledged" to an "accepted" religion. As we know, one of the decisions of the Congress was to establish a seminary to educate rabbis, to be financed from the education fund, which the king had intended for this purpose. In the original plan, this institution was intended to replace the *yeshivot* as the institution for educating rabbis, and for this reason the heads of the famous *yeshivot* made haste to foil it with their successful appearance before the kaiser. The Congress's decision seemingly did not affect the Orthodox, for they denied any religious link with the Neologs, and what legitimate interest could they have in the actions of another religious body? The Orthodox did have a strong argument in claiming that the education fund was created from the donations of all Jews, and that there was no justification for spending it on an institution that only some of them would use. However, had this been a financial matter alone, their demand would have been limited to a just allocation of the funds. In practice, they made a tireless effort to prevent the legislature's approval of the seminary, and for good reason.[1]

Their fear of the seminary now, after the division, was no less than it had been before it. The apprehensions that some congregations would appoint rabbis from among the graduates of the seminary did not ebb, nor did the even greater fear of the seminary's attraction for Orthodox youth—and this fear was justified, for much of the student body consisted of former *yeshivah* students.[2] The struggle against the establishment of the seminary did indeed fail, and not necessarily because the arguments of its Orthodox opponents were not cogent. Orthodox influence diminished after changes occurred in the Education Ministry. Pauler, who had favored them, vacated the post in 1873 in favor of August Trefort, Eötvös's brother-in-law and a member of the same party. Trefort had long been known for his emphatic demand that Jews adopt the Hungarian national language and culture.[3] The training of rabbis in a modern institution was likely to advance the desired cultural rapprochement, and Trefort was therefore an enthusiastic supporter of the concept of a seminary. In May 1877, he received the king's agreement to establish it with the money in the education fund. A year and a quarter later, he requested ratification by the legislature;[4] and when this was not forthcoming, he circumvented the legislative institution and established the seminary by administrative means.[5] This institution opened in 1877, despite strong protests by the Orthodox. Their stubborn struggle against the creation of the institution gives the lie to their argument about the existence of two religious communities, where one should not interest itself or intervene in the activities of the other.

The attempts of the Congress faction to transform Judaism into an "accepted" religion, a category that would give it equal status with the Christian denominations, failed. The inferior status of Judaism had practical implications: A member of the "acknowledged" Jewish religion could, as stated, become a member of the "accepted" religion, that is, convert to Christianity, but the opposite was forbidden. But the major drawback was emotional and theoretical. After the Emancipation, the Jews were considered citizens of equal status, and their self-respect was offended by the inferior status of their religion. If the members of the first generation of citizens accepted the situation, the members of the second generation joined forces in an attempt to change it.

Near the end of the 1880s, a movement arose under the banner of "Reception," that is, turning Judaism into an accepted religion.[6] The leaders of the movement were gathered from among intellectuals, academics, and writers, and Vilmos Vázsonyi, a rising political star, was especially outstanding. It was a novelty that people who did not represent the two organized camps would take the initiative in the public realm. The heads of the Neolog organization did not much like this phenomenon, but when they saw the public response to the youthful initiative, they abandoned their pride and joined the supporters of the initiative. This was not the case with the Orthodox organization, which was actually in the hands of one man, Ignác Reich. Reich continued the policy that had been consolidated at the time of the founding of Shomrei ha-Dat. In theory, he relied upon the views of the rabbis, but they were not public appointees, and he could decide with whom to consult and upon whom to rely. Reich had strong reservations about the Reception movement, the official excuse for this aloofness being that the movement had taken initiatives without consulting with the official representatives of the Orthodox camp. In this position he could rely on the opinions of well-known rabbis, such as the rabbi of the Orthodox congregation in the capital, Koppel Reich,[7] who viewed the successes of the Reception movement as a danger to Judaism. Making Judaism of equal status with the Christian religions could open the way for intermarriage, which had hitherto been prevented by law. But this view was not accepted by all: There were also rabbis and Orthodox intellectuals who believed that elevating the status of Judaism would outweigh the dangers inherent in removing the barriers between the two religions.[8] The significance of the Orthodox position for our purposes is that it demonstrates that the Orthodox were in fact considered, and considered themselves to be, an inseparable part of the general Jewish population. Thus, when the question of Reception arose, it touched them as well. The thought was never entertained that the Neolog religion would achieve "Reception" while Orthodox Judaism would remain only an acknowledged religion.

It was thus impossible to maintain a complete division between the Orthodox and the Neologs, even at the level of national representation. The relationship between the two national organizations was like that of Siamese twins, in which a movement by either of them forced the other to move as well. Nor did the congregations divide neatly into two distinct types, as we would expect according to the theory of two religions. The reality that was created in the wake of the division was much more varied. Some communities were paradigms of one model or the other. There were villages where all the Jewish residents were strictly observant and in contrast there were medium-sized cities that had only a Reform synagogue, in which the rabbi preached in Hungarian, and where householders felt free to determine the level of their observance of tradition. Congregations of these two types had no doubts about their organizational affiliation, the first with the Orthodox organization, and the second with the Congress organization—or the Neologs, as they were generally called. Even in congregations such as this, individual or public tensions and controversies could arise, but these were not over questions of principle, and membership in one of the national organizations provided a means for settling disputes with its judicial apparatus.

Peaceful congregations of both types existed, but they were few. The economic, social, and spiritual factors that divided Judaism on the national level generally acted on the local level as well. The reality of pious Jews living together with non-observant Jews created a problem, but did not necessarily call forth an institutional solution. The leaders of the traditional congregations continued to ignore the non-observant in their midst; when they multiplied and became a sizable minority, a de facto attitude of tolerance developed. It was sufficient that the traditional members were able to maintain the congregational institutions—synagogue, ritual slaughter, the rabbinate, and so on—in their traditional form. The deviant minority, for its part, did not always attempt to introduce changes in these institutions according to its taste, and only in extraordinary circumstances did it secede from the community in order to set up a separate Neolog congregation.[9] The non-observant who remained within the framework of the traditional congregation were free to decide if, and to what extent, to make use of the congregational institutions. They were of course obliged to contribute their share to the financial support of the congregation, and in turn preserved their right to participate in its administration. We have already seen that the statutes of the Orthodox organization did not oblige the congregations to make traditional observance a criterion for positions of leadership in the congregation. The authors of the statutes thus acquiesced in the existing practice, which contradicted Jewish law, but seemed to be a necessary evil under the circumstances.

A totally different situation obtained where the balance of power was inverted—where the majority of the Jewish population defined itself as Neolog, and the minority adhered to the tradition, à la Orthodoxy. This minority was not able, according to its understanding, to avail itself of most of the congregational facilities; even if the minority had faith in the local butcher, the meat he slaughtered was forbidden by rabbinic ruling. They also disqualified all other institutions of the congregation: the synagogue, the *mikvah*, baking of *matzah*, and the like. The idea that the Orthodox minority would maintain its own institutions within the framework of the congregation, a solution that had been suggested at one stage of the Congress by the Orthodox as well, had long since been dropped. The Pest community, whose large synagogue on Dohány Street was no longer used by the pious because of the organ that had been installed in it, decided at the beginning of the Congress to build another synagogue—on nearby Rumbach Street—for this minority.[10] This seems to be the only case in which a Neolog community supplied the needs of the Orthodox minority within it after the split. If its intention was thus to prevent the minority from leaving the mother congregation, it missed its mark. Budapest was one of the first places in Hungary where the Orthodox organized in a separate congregation, immediately after receiving governmental permission to leave the Congress organization.[11] The modus vivendi that was common in Germany under the name *Gemeindeorthodoxie*, where secondary Orthodox institutions existed within a Reform congregation, was not found in Hungary, even though the estrangement of the Orthodox from the Neologs was less severe in Hungary than that of the Orthodox from the Reform in Germany. The reason for this seems to be the existence of a central rabbinic authority in Hungary, which was capable of requiring anyone who wished to be counted among the Orthodox to separate completely from the Neologs.

The intensification of rabbinic authority in Hungary was the paradoxical result of the course of events since the convening of the Congress. Its initiators wished to base it on householders alone, as in the Christian communities, where the lay organizations served as a counterweight to the excessive influence of the ecclesiastical hierarchy. The Jewish partners in the initiative, the officials of the Pest congregation, perhaps thought in their innocence that the planned central institution would be similar to the local congregations, where organizational affairs were decided by lay officials. Even the Orthodox members of the Assembly of Notables, which the minister had convened to prepare the Congress, did not view this as a deviation from tradition—and rightly so, for the administrations of the congregations also turned to their rabbis only when unequivocally religious questions arose. Even the *Shomrei ha-Dat* society was planned essentially on this model. Its body and its administration were meant to be composed of householders alone. This body promised to choose a council of five rabbis, which would field questions of religion and law.

But the analogy with the local congregations was not complete. A body of householders existed within the congregation by virtue of their living in one place, while a supra-congregational group such as *Shomrei ha-Dat* had first to cohere from among individuals who had joined it voluntarily. This meant that its success in the public arena depended at the outset on large-scale identification with its declared goals. The founders of the society understood correctly that they themselves did not have the status and the prestige to enlist the general public in their efforts. They compensated for this by receiving the recommendation of three prominent rabbis, those of Pressburg, Ujhely, and Ungvár. Thus, from the beginning, Orthodox activity in the public arena was characterized by this duality of lay initiative, taken under rabbinic auspices. Eventually, the rabbinic side in this partnership gained the upper hand. The householders never chose the religious council that was to advise and assist them; and instead they established informal contacts with a group of rabbis who supported the society. At the same time, the rabbis' activities in the public arena expanded, for after protests by many of them—Orthodox and Neolog alike—they were permitted to serve as delegates of their congregations to the Congress.

The significance of this turn of events was completely different for each camp. The Neolog rabbis who attended the Congress acted as individuals, each according to his own abilities, without special standing among their fellows. They did not demand that special weight be given to their views in the consultations that preceded the Congress, nor to their statements during the debates. This was not the case on the Orthodox side. Here the laymen themselves, the founders of the *Shomrei ha-Dat* society, wished to gain prestige from the authority and status that rabbinic pronouncements enjoyed in Orthodox public opinion. However, once the way was open for rabbinic involvement in questions of public policy, it was impossible to limit this involvement. This became evident with the demand of R. Abraham Schag, the most senior of the rabbis, that a meeting attended only by rabbis should set guidelines for the Orthodox in anticipation of the Congress. This demand would have been interpreted as a challenge to the leadership of the *Shomrei ha-Dat* society, had they not succeeded in taking the sting out of the implied criticism by themselves volunteering to organize the meeting. Nonetheless, this meeting had an exclusively rabbinic character; the members of *Shomrei ha-Dat* could act only behind the scenes. Moreover, although the occasion for the gathering was the expected Congress, participation in it was not limited to rabbis who had been chosen as delegates by their congregations, and the agenda included questions that were not up for discussion at the Congress, but which interested the rabbis. Since the meeting did not derive its authority from the voters, but rather by virtue of the rabbis' being recognized halakhic masters, the decisions taken at the meeting took on the nature of halakhic rulings, which laymen had no right to question. As we recall, the majority voted to oppose not only the establishment of a special institution to train rabbis, even if it were to be a "kosher seminary" like that proposed by R. Esriel Hildesheimer, but also the addition of some secular studies to the curriculum of the *yeshivot*, as the Ketav Sofer had suggested. Thus, whenever such an idea was raised in the public arena from that time on, the ready answer was: "Two hundred rabbis have already decided to forbid it." This was the impact of the meeting upon future generations.

No less significant was the decision taken on the question at hand: How were the Orthodox delegates to the Congress to behave during its debates and discussions? These delegates were elected by the voters, and were therefore expected to discuss and vote on the questions according to their own understanding. However, the rabbinic meeting took it upon itself to set guidelines for this as well, and to demand that a rabbinic committee of its own choosing examine each and every proposal on the agenda of the Congress for its compatibility with religious requirements. This demand, of course, was contrary to the aims of the initiators of the Congress and its patron, Minister Eötvös, and of most of its Neolog delegates. For the Orthodox, however, this demand carried great weight: they could not ignore it, for their slogan was loyalty to religious heritage, whose authoritative interpreters were the rabbis. From then on, Orthodox politicians gave the appearance of relying on the views of the rabbis, for better or for worse. The leaders of *Shomrei ha-Dat*, and later the members of the executive committee, claimed to act according to the views of the rabbis, who had not been formally empowered by the public. The rabbis almost inadvertently gained authority to decide public issues without distinguishing whether or not they were appropriate for halakhic adjudication. Not only were the subjects of rabbinic scrutiny expanded, but the area of its jurisdiction was also enlarged: Decisions relating to individual congregations were replaced by rulings that obligated the pious everywhere. This transformation did not take place in a vacuum.

A sense of solidarity had evolved since the elections for the Congress, during which the Orthodox campaign was conducted by means of shared slogans, which were the work of *Shomrei ha-Dat*. This solidarity was strengthened, at first by the great rabbinic meeting, and subsequently through the echoes of debates in the Congress and the events that followed. When Maharam Schick ruled that the devout minority in Hungary was obliged to accept the view of the majority of the Orthodox, as if he was talking about a single congregation, he deviated from the letter of the law, but was only translating the spreading consensus to the language of *halakhah*. Finally, it may be said that the initiators of the Congress, with Minister Eötvös at their head, intended to create an institution of laymen as a balance against the excessive influence of the rabbis, but they achieved the opposite result within the Orthodox camp, where the authority of the rabbinic leadership increased at the expense of the householders.

Nonetheless, there was a great difference between the earlier isolated community and the present organization of congregations. The congregation possessed direct and indirect powers of enforcement over its members, which the management of the national organization did not have over the individual congregations. These were called upon by the rabbinic ruling to join the organization. If the devout in the congregation were only a minority, they were called upon to separate from the majority and to establish their own congregation, which would of course join the Orthodox organization. This demand was at times too difficult even for a congregation the majority of whose members were devout, if the minority gave up its desire to join the Neologs but protested against enrolling the congregation in the Orthodox organization. This situation was the main reason why some congregations preferred the position of Status Quo, and not a few rabbis whose hearts were with the Orthodox acquiesced in this compromise. The alternative was a division of the congregation, which was nevertheless the fate of many dozens of congregations, which split into two, and at times even into three, entities. This process was accompanied by arguments over the division of congregational property and the like, as exemplified by the course of events we followed in Galgóc and Kassa. Even more serious was the fact that such a split involved a painful estrangement between comrades, and more than once created an unhealed breach within a single family.

Chapter 21

The Painful Process and Its Aftermath

The relatively small Jewish congregation was a social unit where almost familial relationships prevailed between its members. Various societies were also active in these communities, most of them for pious purposes, associations for visiting the sick, and, at the least, a burial society, whose members volunteered to prepare the deceased for his last journey. Such societies created an intimate relationship between their members, and it is not surprising that the idea of disbanding because of the split in the congregation encountered resistance. Moreover, a division in the burial society meant giving up the right to be buried in the ancient cemetery where family patriarchs had been buried, a particularly great sacrifice for families with deep roots in the congregation.

Maharam Schick voiced these sorts of misgivings in his responsum to the members of the pious congregation in Bonyhád, which had split off from the Neologs and was now debating whether to go one step further and acquire a separate cemetery. He ruled: "There is certainly a great virtue in preserving the ancestral cemetery," and if it is possible to ensure that in the future too "everything will be done according to the laws of the Shulhan Arukh, and there will be no fear that a pious man will be buried next to a transgressor, then it is better to remain together with the Neologs."[1] He left it to the inhabitants to decide if there was a sufficient guarantee that the conditions mentioned would be observed. In other areas of life, Maharam Schick did not consider a promise to uphold the laws of the Shulhan Arukh as a sufficient condition for preventing a division. This meant that he felt that the situation was different regarding the burial society: the pious were strongly motivated to preserve unity, and the Neologs were ready to adhere to traditional customs. This analysis applied to Bonyhád as well, but it was nonetheless decided that the split would also extend to the cemetery.[2] However, special tensions prevailed between the two camps in this congregation, for local reasons. Similar circumstances led to a quick decision in other places as well. In Pressburg, where the Neolog minority was the one that broke off from the mother congregation, the secessionists felt they had no place in the Orthodox society, and acquired a separate cemetery.[3] In most places, however, the burial society remained united even after the split, a sign of communal cohesiveness that was only gradually undermined in the wake of the organizational division. In the large and important congregation of Nagyvárad (Oradea), the Orthodox majority agreed to grant the Neolog minority an equal share in administering the burial society. This arrangement fell apart towards the end of the century, when the minority tried to introduce non-traditional burial customs, such as laying wreaths.[4] A more serious impingement on the tradition ended such cooperation in Temesvár at about the same time. The Neologs permitted a non-Jew to be buried in the cemetery, over the protests of the Orthodox rabbi, the son of R. Solomon Zvi Schick. This matter was brought before the father, who strongly opposed estrangement between the camps but, faced with this action by the Neologs, saw no way of avoiding a split.[5]

The hesitations and delays over disbanding the burial society give us an idea of the boundaries of the division, which was far from unequivocal and all-encompassing. As early as the 1840s, in reaction to the Reform Rabbinical Assembly in Braunschweig, Maharam Schick had suggested that the reformers be treated as their ancestors in previous times had treated those who strayed from the path, from the time of Ezra the Scribe and up to the persecution of the Sabbateans: "to forbid eating of their bread and wine," as that of gentiles, and "since they are total non-Jews, they, their daughters and their sons are forbidden to us."[6] It is true that the government forbade excommunicating the apostates, but this did not release the halakhic authorities of their responsibility to announce publicly how the pious should act. At that time, Maharam Schick did not consider himself the leader of contemporary Jewry, and he made his suggestion to the rabbi of Pressburg, the Ketav Sofer. In any event, he referred to the Reformers in Germany, who had no followers in Hungary, and his suggestion was purely theoretical. Now, however, after the Congress, when the rabbis of Hungary, Maharam Schick himself at their head, felt bound to announce that almost half of Hungarian Jews were heretics, the question arose again in all its severity: Should we not treat the Neologs in practice as our ancestors did the deviant sects of their day?

Maharam Schick surely did not pass over the question, which begged to be addressed, and if he ignored it, his colleague R. Hayyim Sofer put it before him and all the rabbinic community. R. Hayyim Sofer had, as we know, composed an entire book on this topic, in which he detailed the religious laws that applied, in his view, to the body of transgressors. Needless to say, their bread and wine were forbidden, as was intermarriage with them; they also clearly were not to be given a Jewish burial. However, according to him, their sons were also not to be circumcised; in short, they were to be considered as having left Judaism, even though they had not converted to another religion.[7] Maharam Schick knew of R. Sofer's rulings, and he responded to them, perhaps as soon as they were published, in 1869.[8]

The debate between them was renewed in the early spring of 1872, during the month in which Maharam Schick gave his ruling on the Status Quo in his letter to R. Meir Perles. If that letter seemed to indicate that he wished to place at a distance not only those Neologs who were close to Reform, but even the Status Quoers, whose position was somewhere between the Neologs and the Orthodox, we learn otherwise from his letter to R. Hayyim Sofer: Unlike his colleague, he limited rejection of them and in no way considered them to have left the Jewish community. If in his previous letter to the Ketav Sofer he advocated ignoring the government prohibition against excommunication, and announcing that the pious community should distance itself from transgressors, as demanded by religious law, he now firmly based himself on the governmental order from which to reject his rival's views. And so he writes to R. Hayyim Sofer: "I am surprised, for has his honor—may he live—forgotten that by order of the king and his officers it is forbidden to pronounce the ban and excommunication, and we are commanded and bound to obey the king's orders, and it is said 'I obey the king' and it is said about an oath in the name of God."[9] He then refers to his teacher the Hatam Sofer, and writes: "and such an evil thing occurred already during the time of my teacher the Hatam Sofer, may his memory be blessed, and a rabbi demanded that they be put under the ban and excommunicated, and he answered thus, see Hatam Sofer, *Responsa*, V, no. 89." This description of the incident involving the Hatam Sofer is not accurate. The rabbi to whom the Hatam Sofer responded, R. Abraham Eliezer Halevi of Trieste, did not want to excommunicate the reformers, but to encourage government officials to suppress them through the intervention of the Jewish leaders of the time.[10] It was the Hatam Sofer who attested that, "if we had judicial power over them, I would favor ejecting them from our midst . . . and their sect should be considered like Zadok and Boetheus, Anan and Saul."[11] Indeed, this famous passage from the Hatam Sofer is usually cited as a supporting view by those in favor of total separation.[12] Maharam Schick, however, skipped directly to the end of the paragraph, which dismisses this possibility in practice, because of the government prohibition against excommunication ("all this seems to me theoretical and not practical without the permission and formal approval of His Glorious Majesty").[13]

As the letter continues, it becomes clear that Maharam Schick had other reasons for not accepting the extreme suggestions of R. Hayyim Sofer aside from the royal prohibition: "To refuse to circumcise the son for his father's wickedness seems a strange and cruel thing to the populace, and they consider it improper, and this would lead them to speak even more errantly against the rabbis of this generation."[14] It is necessary to consider general public opinion, which would not accept such drastic measures of exclusion, even if they are perhaps legally justified. Maharam Schick alludes to the fact that this is not the first time that he has expressed his view about behavior towards the Neologs after the split. However, he does suggest one limitation: "It seems that according to the law, we should not arrange matches with them because of the suspicion of *mamzerut*" (offspring of an illegitimate union).[15] His wording should be noted carefully. This is not a blanket prohibition against their children because the parents have left the fold. The problem with the children arises as a result of the unreliability of those rabbis who arrange divorces in non-Orthodox congregations. This doubt makes it necessary to examine each and every case individually, but is not a general prohibition against all the descendants of the Neologs.[16]

The question of marriage with the Neologs was a major issue for the Orthodox after the split, and Maharam Schick was not the only one to deal with it. R. Barukh Eckfeld was also questioned on this subject, and in his responsum he lists all the problems that are likely to arise as a result of such a marriage. Nonetheless, his conclusion is merely: "Whoever guards his soul will distance himself from this," which is only good advice and not a legal ruling.[17] Indeed, it is a mistake to attribute to the Orthodox rabbis a prohibition against marriage with Neologs. Marriage between the camps, at least from time to time, did not cease. R. Solomon Schick, who was an Orthodox rabbi, even differed with the policy that prevented rabbis from the *yeshivot* from serving in non-Orthodox congregations, and bitterly lamented the results of this policy. In the absence of authorized supervision of the laws of personal status in the Neolog communities, their genealogy is suspect, and the Orthodox suffer as well, for they continue to marry Neologs.[18] The author M. Ehrentheil, who held a position similar to that of R. Solomon Schick, mocked the Orthodox rabbis who flee any partnership with the Neologs, but who will not hesitate to sanctify a union between a Neolog and an Orthodox. Refusal to do so would involve forgoing the fee received for performing the ceremony, which depended on the size of the dowry.[19]

Maharam Schick's rejection of R. Hayyim Sofer's proposals reveals how great was the gap between Orthodox rhetoric, which decried the Neologs as founders of a new religion differing from authentic Judaism, and the Orthodox attitude in practice to the members of that religion. The members of the Neolog congregation were considered transgressors, unless it was proven that they continued to observe the commandments in their private lives (and there were some who did), and not members of another religion. And indeed transgressors, to wit, Jews who did not live traditionally, were found also in many Orthodox congregations, and there is no evidence of a difference in attitude to them on the basis of their congregational affiliation. The presence of these transgressors within the same social framework as the devout raised many halakhic questions that had to be answered: How reliable are they to be considered on religious issues; can they be counted in a *minyan* (quorum); does their touch make wine prohibited?[20] Questions that had arisen regarding Sabbath observance because of economic partnerships with non-Jews, which had occupied halakhists in former times,[21] now arose again and with greater severity regarding partnership with Jews who acted on the Sabbath as did non-Jews.[22] Halakhists relied on these earlier halakhic rulings and their answers in many cases depended on the extent of estrangement of the person from the tradition—whether he transgresses the Sabbath in private or in public, and the like. The question if he is a member of a Neolog or Orthodox congregation is never considered relevant. This is also the case regarding rendering religious services to transgressors, to the extent that they need them. The readiness of rabbis to arrange marriages (and of course divorces) is one example of this, and the willingness of *mohelim* (circumcisors) to circumcise the sons of Neologs is another. *Mohelim*, whether voluntary or professional, did not distinguish between one Jew and another. They circumcised Neolog children just as they did Orthodox children, taking no heed of the level of observance of the parents. Moreover, some professional *mohelim* agreed to the request of the Neologs to forgo the *mezizah* (ritual drawing of the blood), a step that was considered by the Orthodox to be a peculiarly Reform innovation. This happened at least in Budapest, and this practice of the *mohelim* was officially approved by a well-known halakhist, Hayyim Hirsch Mannheimer, rabbi of Ungvár.[23]

These details lead us to the unequivocal conclusion, that the ostracism—not a formal ban—of the Neologs by the Orthodox was not personal, but institutional alone. First and foremost, the prohibition applied to the institution for training rabbis, the seminary.[24] An Orthodox Jew should not send his son to study at the seminary, and the *yeshivot* were warned against becoming an educational vehicle for the seminary, for they should not be "fattening calves for idolatry" (in the words of Akiva Sofer of Pápa, the son of R. Simon Sofer, the rabbi of Cracow).[25] Needless to say, students of the seminary were disqualified from serving in any rabbinic post in an Orthodox congregation. Moreover, *yeshivah*-trained rabbis were forbidden to serve in Neolog congregations, and this prohibition applied also to the Status Quo congregations.[26] This injunction related not only to rabbis, but also to all sorts of religious functionaries, first and foremost the *shohetim*.[27] The meat slaughtered by a *shohet* for a Neolog or Status Quo congregation was forbidden to the Orthodox, no matter how devout the man himself was.[28] In addition, anyone who was persuaded to serve in any of the forbidden congregations lost his status as an observant Jew, and could not be reintegrated into an Orthodox congregation. His status was that of a transgressor, and only public repentance could clear his name.[29]

Those who most suffered from the split were the religious functionaries who served in congregations that became Neolog or remained Status Quo, and were faced with the choice of losing their reliability in the eyes of their colleagues, or leaving their posts and losing their means of livelihood.[30] The entire stratum of candidates for these jobs was indirectly affected. This was composed of many *yeshivah* students who were trained for no profession other than religious service, and the competition for the available jobs was enormous. The disqualification of more than half of the available positions greatly reduced the sources of potential livelihood for this group.[31] Of course, not everyone heeded the prohibitions and the prohibitors. Some ignored them without any pangs of conscience, and others gave various excuses, and were considered by themselves and by others to have been forced to do so by considerations of livelihood. The Neolog and Status Quo congregations had no trouble finding candidates to fill all the religious posts; while they could find rabbis from among the seminary students, many of whom had also studied previously in *yeshivot*, the *dayyanim*,[32] *shohetim*, cantors, and beadles and the like, were all former *yeshivah* graduates.

However, if in theory the division only affected those who held religious posts, in the course of time, public life in general was affected, although of course, there were differences from place to place. We heard from two witnesses from the center of the country, that towards the ends of the century the Orthodox and Neologs were still marrying one another, and that the Orthodox rabbis continued to assist them in doing so. However, an incident in a village in the Sabolc district in the north indicates that the pious in the village considered such cooperation insupportable. A butcher who held the post in the Orthodox community performed a marriage for a Neolog couple, and when this became known, the pious refused to eat of his slaughtering. R. Abraham Isaac Glück, author of the responsa *Yad Yitzchak*, justified their behavior.[33]

The institutional split created a growing estrangement between the two parts of the public. Of course, economic contact between them did not cease. The range of profession was not identical among the Neologs and the Orthodox: many professions were opened to the Neologs because of their superior education and their abandonment of numerous religious limitations; the Orthodox, in contrast, remained tied for the most part to the traditional occupations (this topic deserves a penetrating and exhaustive study). Nonetheless, both sectors were part of the middle class, whose economic basis was capital investment and entrepreneurship. This similarity guaranteed the continuation of commercial links between Neologs and the Orthodox. However, commercial contact was one thing, and social interaction and cultural ties were another. Regarding the latter, the institutional-religious split raised an almost impenetrable barrier between the two camps. This is what made the instances of intermarriage between the two camps quite exceptional.

During the third generation after the split at the latest, that is, during the lifetime of those born in the first decade of the twentieth century, of whom I am one, the Orthodox and Neologs already functioned as two separate social units, because of their adherence to different principles and to different religious lifestyles. Even someone who grew up in an Orthodox family like mine, which was not especially extreme or fanatic, was taught to consider the Neologs as members of a different religious community. I can testify that entry into a Neolog synagogue was considered no less taboo in our circles than a visit to a Catholic church. This estrangement was the product of two generations of struggle, education, and propaganda, a description of which is outside the historical scope of this book.

In summary it can be said that the two camps learned to be self-sufficient, each in its own way. This was made possible, first of all, by the growth of the Jewish population in the country. The Jewish population in Hungary at the outbreak of World War I was approximately nine hundred and fifty thousand. If we ignore for the time being those who belonged to Status Quo communities, and work on the accepted premise that the Orthodox and the Neolog blocks were more or less equal in size, then each one had almost four hundred thousand members (a number equal to four-fifths of the entire Jewish population of Germany during this period). Such a large population provided a broad enough base to maintain educational institutions and to provide religious leadership for the congregations; it also allowed for the establishment of publications that coalesced public opinion, a necessary condition for creating a broad sense of unity. Both camps relied on the services of the press—weekly for the most part—and encouraged a wide range of literary activity, of different levels. The intellectual activity in both camps was greatly stimulated by the tension with the opposing camp: in reacting to the opposition, each camp developed and formulated its own position. It can be said that both camps succeeded in the mission that historical circumstances bequeathed to them, with the division occupying center stage.

How did the spokesmen for the two camps view the split itself? Their positions were entirely different: The Orthodox leaders viewed the split as a positive event, a divine salvation of true Judaism, at a time when its enemies sought to eradicate it. These terms probably became mere rhetoric when mouthed by Orthodox politicians and propagandists, but for those who originally formulated them—Maharam Schick, R. Hayyim Sofer, and others—they were an authentic expression of their naïve faith.[34] This was anchored in the traditional view of the historical process as being guided by Divine providence. The fact that they themselves were active in creating this split did not affect their belief that they were acting as messengers of the Divine. From their unshakable faith in the righteousness of their path, they drew the courage and fortitude to condemn anyone who did not follow them.

The Neologs, with their rational mode of thought, could not appreciate or even understand the Orthodox position. They attributed it to the domination of religious fanaticism, that had begun with the activity of R. Hillel Lichtenstein in the mid-1860s. They asked again and again what flaw the devout could find in the Congress organization, whose task was limited to administrative affairs, and they rejected as unjust the Orthodox claim that their intention was to make the devout into heretics. The Neologs admitted that they had hopes that the national organization would serve to rescue the Jewish populace in general from its cultural isolation. But a certain amount of rapprochement with non-Jewish society was considered a clear necessity in the post-Emancipation era, a need that the Orthodox also acknowledged, at least to which they paid lip service. The Neologs wished to facilitate this process, among other things, because they knew that the non-Jewish public considered the isolationist, uneducated Jew to be a paradigm of the Jewish nation as a whole. After the split, the Neologs, to a dramatic and painful extent, lost their ability to influence the general Jewish population, so that it can be said that the establishment of their national organization left them with many unfulfilled goals.

If the Neologs had some compensation, for the Status Quoers the split caused only frustration and bitterness. This is a great irony of history, for they had no part in the quarrel; they remained as they had been before the split. Now they constituted a small minority (approximately twelve percent), wedged between the two big blocks.[35] It is true that even a small religious group can maintain itself and even flourish, if it has a special spiritual quality and a unique social profile. However, the Status Quoers did not aspire to create a religious style of their own. On the contrary, when the Orthodox decided during the Congress that the hallmark of Orthodoxy was an explicit declaration by a congregation that it bases itself on the Shulhan Arukh, the Status Quo communities also hastened to adopt this declaration. The problem was that after the Congress, the Orthodox added another criterion, namely membership in their organization, a demand that the Status Quo communities were not ready or willing to fulfill. These congregations were thus rejected also by those with whom they identified in religious terms. This rejection was expressed both verbally and practically: The Orthodox did not miss an opportunity to reiterate Maharam Schick's ruling that the Status Quoers were no better than the Neologs, and perhaps even worse, for they should have realized their obligations under the circumstances. The illegitimation of the rabbis who served in the Status Quo congregations affected these rabbis personally, and sometimes led to deliberate personal humiliation. In one case, a Status Quo rabbi who happened to be in an Orthodox synagogue was called up to the Torah, but he was denied his title as rabbi and religious functionary.[36] When R. Simhah Bunim Sofer, the author of the *Shevet Sofer*, the third in the rabbinic line in Pressburg, passed away, his students who served in Status Quo congregations did not attend, because the administration of the congregation did not notify them of the time of the funeral. The students got the hint that their presence was unwanted and that if they were to come at their own initiative, they would not be permitted to eulogize their teacher.[37]

The rabbis of the Status Quo congregations continuously complained of and protested their ostracism and humiliation. What sin had they committed in doing what rabbis of previous generations had done, each of them caring for the religious level of their congregations?[38] We hear from Maharam Schick himself, that at least in the first generation after the split, the rabbis were not considered personally flawed. In a responsum of 1878, nine years after the split, he wrote that it is likely that the Status Quo rabbis are "holy and pure . . . they are worthy and God-fearing at the head of their congregations." Their flaw lay in the fact that they did not see the future and did not understand that without the support of the national organization their congregations were destined to degenerate, as had happened already to congregations "that were full of Torah and God-fearing."[39] This prophecy, if it was not fulfilled in its entirety, did not completely miss its mark. It became clear with time that the Status Quo congregations had difficulty in preserving their religious character in their isolated situation. Some of them therefore changed their minds and joined the Orthodox, while others went in the opposite direction, and chose rabbis from among the more conservative of the seminary students.[40] In any event, this was a self-fulfilling prophecy, for the isolation of the Status Quo was imposed by the Orthodox policy makers, whose leader was the prophet of doom himself.

VII

The Schism, German Style

Chapter 22

Eduard Lasker, the Prophet of Freedom of Conscience

One of the greatest surprises to emerge from our study of the progress of events in Hungary was the extent to which R. Samson Raphael Hirsch was involved in the process of division, both in refining the ideology that underlay Orthodox separation from the general congregations, and in helping accomplish this goal. The Orthodox demands that emerged in the wake of the struggle in Hungary, and which Hirsch helped to formulate and advance, went farther than his original aspirations for his own city, Frankfurt. The demand was no longer that the Orthodox be exempt from paying taxes to maintain what they considered to be illegitimate institutions—the aim of Hirsch's battle in Frankfurt in his earlier years—but that they have absolute organizational independence.

However, if the idea of total separation crystallized in far-off Hungary, in Frankfurt and in the other congregations that followed suit, the unwanted bond between the Orthodox minorities and the mother congregations continued to exist. There were few such congregations—Mainz, Wiesbaden, Karlsruhe, Darmstadt—and they were relatively small. The Orthodox founded a sort of miniature *Adath Jeschurun* in these communities in reaction to the reforms introduced in the congregational institutions.[1] Another separatist congregation in Berlin, *Adath Israel*, was added in 1869. It too was created in the wake of reforms and changes in personnel, primarily in the rabbinic leadership of the congregation, in the mid-1860s. This event had great significance for the history of Orthodoxy, since Frankfurt thus emerged from its isolation. *Adath Israel* soon became the sister community of *Adath Jeschurun*, and not only because of its size and the rapid development of its institutions, but mainly because of its spiritual leader, R. Esriel Hildesheimer. After his disappointments in Hungary, he eagerly accepted the invitation to come to Berlin, where he acted with the same enthusiasm and devotion as he had exhibited previously, but this time without encountering obstacles and frustrations.[2] Contemporaries attributed *Adath Is-*

rael's quick consolidation to his presence, and the historian has no reason to question this assessment.

All the Orthodox communities mentioned above shared the same legal status. Those who joined them continued to be members of the general congregation, and were required to pay taxes to the congregational coffers, despite their financial support of the institutions of their subcommunity. They considered this unfair and a miscarriage of justice; we hear from R. Hirsch in April 1870, that repeated appeals against this situation had been made to the relevant governmental officials, but these had gone unanswered.[3] Only in Karlsruhe was the situation different, and events there gave Hirsch the opportunity to take a public stand.

Karlsruhe was the capital city of the state of Baden, which had a tradition of progressive liberalism. The other Orthodox communities were located in Prussia—this included *Adath Jeschurun*, since Frankfurt had been annexed to this large northern state after the Austro-Prussian War in 1866. The legal status of the Jews of Baden differed from that of their brethren in Prussia. The rulers of Baden had anticipated the other German states in granting citizenship to the Jews, but had also required them to organize themselves in a national organization. The supreme council of the organization was empowered to guide and to direct their lives, among other things by supervising the religious practices of the congregations.[4] This state of affairs was satisfactory as long as the members of each congregation were of the same mind, either in adhering to the traditional practices, or in enacting reforms with majority consent. This consensus collapsed in Karslruhe in 1868, when the leadership of the congregation decided to place an organ in the synagogue. In reaction to this, a group of Orthodox members organized in a separate community and its members refused to pay communal taxes.[5] The supreme council took them to court over this issue, but after prolonged litigation, they were acquitted. The state supreme court accepted the declaration of the Orthodox that, because of the assault on their religious conscience, they intended to leave the national organization of their coreligionists, and that any further ties between them and the mother congregation in Karlsruhe were now at an end. The committee denounced the seceders for their attack on communal unity, a serious accusation in light of the longstanding tradition of Jewish unity in the shared struggle for equal rights. The Orthodox community turned to R. Hirsch, whom they considered their leader and teacher, for moral support and encouragement. He responded to the challenge and developed the general outlines of the theory that was to serve him in the struggle for the right of secession, of which the episode in Karlsruhe was only the first step.[6]

The point of departure for his theory was the axiomatic belief that the Jewish community has persevered throughout the centuries thanks to the awareness of "those loyal to the Divine Law of the obligation to belong to the local congregation and to support it."[7] In their eyes, this obligation was no less important than the other religious commandments, such as Sabbath observance and *kashrut*, which cannot be performed unless one is willing to assume the financial burden involved. The obvious conclusion is that during its classic period the congregation had no need for the assistance of the state, nor for the means of enforcement available to its leadership. "Not in the name of the state but in the name of religious law, to which the leaders of the congregation, like its members, were subject, did the former turn to the latter, in the certainty that these demands would be fulfilled."[8]

This idyllic description of congregational life in the premodern period ignores the fact that, despite general identification with its values, the leadership did resort to means of compulsion, the most obvious of which was the ban, and that these were available because of the relative autonomy that the state granted the community. Moses Mendelssohn was aware of the fact that the traditional congregation used coercion, but he claimed that the practice was untrue to the authentic Jewish spirit.[9] Then along came his spiritual descendant, R. Samson Raphael Hirsch, who denied the very existence of such coercive measures. Whether Hirsch consciously ignored the explicit evidence to the contrary in the halahkic literature he knew so well is a question for his biographers, and need not concern us here. The motive for ignoring this evidence, though, is readily apparent. To Hirsch, the traditional congregation was an institution founded entirely on the will of individuals to observe the *halakhah*; only a community founded on this principle should be recognized as a legitimate congregation. The Orthodox minority in Karlsruhe was thus the congregation, and it cannot remain joined to its rival, or else it may seem as if *"Judaism equally grants the right to exist to those who deny religious law and to those who sanctify it"* (emphasis in the original).[10] The only cooperation between the two parts of the Jewish population in Karlsruhe that can continue is the maintenance of the institutions of charity and good works, both as a remembrance of their shared past and because eternal Jewish dedication to the good of mankind unites them.[11]

Hirsch also alluded to the fact that Orthodox Jewry in Prussia awaited a change in its status as well. Hildesheimer's *Adath Israel* in Berlin repeatedly requested that the government relieve its members of the requirement to pay taxes to a congregation whose services they can no longer use, according to the dictates of their religious conscience.[12] These efforts were in vain, and only in 1872 did the window of opportunity open, with a general revision of the state laws pertaining to churches and other religious bodies. Bismarck was conducting a cultural war against the Catholic Church at this time, with the aim of weakening its influence. Bismarck ruled the state at this stage, with the National-Liberal party as his power base, and the members of this party on principle supported the extension of individual rights as against the demands of the religious bodies. It was not known when these new laws would be presented for debate in the

Landtag, the Prussian Parliament, and what form they would take. In late summer of 1872, the rumor spread that the time for this was drawing near, and the Orthodox activists in Berlin prodded R. Hirsch to come and present the Orthodox position before the government officials concerned.

Hirsch reached Berlin several days before Rosh Hashanah (early October), 1872. Hildesheimer was absent because of an urgent family matter, and we therefore have a letter from Hirsch to his colleague in Berlin describing his accomplishments during his visit there.[13] He was told, he writes, by the two government offices with which he had contact, that there was no chance that the Jewish issue would be put on the agenda of the Prussian Parliament during the coming session, which was due to be convened in November of the same year. It had not been adequately prepared. For this reason, Hirsch urged Hildesheimer to encourage the leaders of his community to present their petition once again to the government, and to list their reasons for their desire to form a separate community. They should stand behind their demand to receive exemption from the taxes of a congregation that had deviated from the principles of their faith. Hildesheimer answered his friend between Rosh Hashanah and Yom Kippur, saying that the same arguments had been reiterated again and again to the government, to no avail, and that there would be no use in repeating them without adding new arguments.[14]

Contrary to the prediction of the government officials, the question of the right to secede from the congregations did arise in the parliamentary session of March 1872. These officials had not intentionally misled Hirsch; their response rested on a mistaken assumption. They were busy preparing a general legal framework for dealing with Jewish affairs. The existing statutes had been in force since 1847, and reform was necessary in light of the changes that had occurred in the interim. New territories with different laws pertaining to the Jews had been annexed to Prussia, and the intention now was to create a uniform legal system. Changes had occurred, moreover, within Prussian Jewry itself, among other things as a result of the coalescence of religious factions, which were at odds with one another, and had difficulty coexisting. The officials assumed that the right of secession could be dealt with only within the new framework of laws that were now in preparation. In reality, the question of secession arose in the context of the general revision of the state laws, which was on the agenda of the Parliament in its coming session.

The proposed laws were first discussed in the various committees, which were composed of representatives of the government and members of Parliament. One committee prepared the law of secession for the Christian churches, which stated that a Catholic or a Protestant who declares before a judge that he wishes to leave the church to which he had previously belonged would be released, under certain conditions, from any bond or obligation to it. The emphasis was on secession from the church, which was a national institution recognized by law, rather than the local religious community; a Protestant or Catholic could not secede from the local community and still remain a member of the Church. This condition was meant to ensure that the secession would be based on religious motives, and not on any secondary considerations, such as a quarrel with local religious appointees or the desire to rid oneself of a burden imposed by local conditions. The law of secession was thus based on the principle of freedom of conscience: No one should be required to belong to a religious institution in whose principles he does not believe. All members of the committee agreed that the Jew's freedom of conscience should be equal to the Christian's. It was therefore decided that, likewise, a Jew could not secede only from his local congregation but, in the absence of a national organization of the congregations, he must also leave Judaism.[15]

The proposed law of secession with the addendum regarding Jews was publicized in January 1873. It aroused mixed reactions among the Jewish public. Most Jews, at least according to official Jewish leaders, would have preferred that the requirement to belong to the congregation continue as before, because they feared a mass departure from the congregations, as we shall hear below. Now that secession was made conditional upon leaving Judaism, this fear subsided somewhat. Not many would decide to leave the congregation at the price of denying Judaism.[16] For those who opposed secession the aforesaid limitation was a sort of consolation; for the Orthodox who demanded the right of secession, however, it was adding insult to injury. By making secession conditional upon leaving Judaism, the proposed law denied the possibility of seceding in order to organize as a separate Jewish congregation. It is no surprise that the Orthodox were the first to react to the proposal. They published a memorandum (Denkschrift) in March 1873, ostensibly written in Berlin, but which was actually the work of R. Samson Raphael Hirsch of Frankfurt.[17]

It is possible that the text of the memorandum was sent to R. Esriel Hildesheimer or the Jewish activists in Berlin before its publication, since its putative origin in Berlin was meant to give the impression that they were responsible for it. Its true author no doubt wanted to prevent the issue from being interpreted as pertaining only to the struggle of *Adath Jeschurun*. Indeed, *Adath Jeschurun* of Frankfurt and *Adath Israel* of Berlin are mentioned in one breath as the two outstanding examples of Orthodox communities created because of the alienation of the mother congregations from authentic Jewish principles.[18] However, its basic arguments were applicable to any Orthodox minority existing within a Reform congregation.

The anonymous author of the memorandum was full of praise for the rulers of Prussia, for proposing a law freeing the individual from forced membership in a religious body with whose principles he could not identify. But, he asked, why were the Jewish citizens of the state excluded from the broadmindedness of the legislature? Why can a Catholic or Protestant leave his church without ceasing to be a Christian, while the Jew cannot leave his congregation without denying his Judaism?[19] The author attributes this discrimination against the Jew to the average legislator's lack of knowledge of developments within the Jewish community. They saw Judaism as a single and unified religion, and if they had heard something of the opposing forces that had developed in recent generations, they interpreted them as differences of viewpoint of the sort that may occur within any religious body, and not as schismatic divisions.[20] The memorandum then points to the establishment of the Orthodox congregations in Frankfurt and Berlin as proof of the error of this interpretation. The founders of the two communities took upon themselves the difficult burden of maintaining separate religious institutions because their religious conscience prevented them from relying on the services of the larger congregation. The memorandum attempts to explain the dogmatic differences between the Orthodox and their rivals. The former view the accepted religious customs as the product of revelation, and as Divine laws (the terms "Orthodox" and "gesetzestreu," loyal to the law, are used interchangeably in this memorandum, as in all the writings of R. Samson Raphael Hirsch). The Reform deny this principle of faith. And the conclusion is: "The differences between the various Christian denominations [*Konfessionen*] are no deeper than the differences between Reform Judaism and Orthodox Judaism characterized by loyalty to the Law."[21] Therefore, just as the proposed legislation permits a Christian to leave his religious community if he ceases to identify with its principles, so it must permit the Reform Jew to leave an Orthodox Synagogue, and the Orthodox Jew to leave a Reform Synagogue.[22]

The author of the memorandum acknowledges the concern that permission to secede would allow individuals to evade the burden of maintaining the congregations, and that this would endanger their existence. But, he asks, why should greater suspicion fall upon the Jew than upon the Christian? He considers this a character assassination of the Jewish people, a sort of "moral yellow star," which reason cannot accept.[23] On the contrary, throughout the generations the Jews have displayed their readiness and ability to maintain their religious institutions without coercion and without assistance from any governmental source[24]—a dubious historical assessment which is familiar from the other writings of the memorandum's author. Nonetheless, he does acknowledge that allowing individuals the freedom to secede from small congregations, whatever their motives, could threaten the survival of such congregations. Here the author abandons his theoretical arguments and makes a practical assessment: He comes to the conclusion that even if secession is allowed by law, it will only occur in large congregations, where the minority will be large enough to establish a viable community. Secession will be very rare in small communities, because a Jew, whatever his religious position, cannot exist without a link to a Jewish community of some sort. Even if he does not use Jewish services in his lifetime, the desire to be buried among his own will prevent him from leaving the congregation.[25]

A letter from one of the leaders of the Berlin community, J. Fromm, to Hirsch, dated March 21, 1873, indicates that the memorandum was presented to government officials, including the chancellor's office, and was also distributed among members of Parliament prior to the parliamentary debate on the proposed law on March 19.[26] Close scrutiny of the protocol of this session reveals that the memorandum was in front of at least some of the members of the House; one of them mentions it as a document presented by some "Israelites," which some members of the House may have read.[27] But close examination also reveals that this memorandum was not the only factor, or even the central one, in considering the demand of the Orthodox for permission to secede from the local congregations without limiting conditions. This is important in order to determine R. Samson Raphael Hirsch's real part in the struggle for secession, as opposed to the assessment of his opponents and admirers alike, who assign him either credit or blame for everything that occurred. As does, for example, his son, Mendel, who described the events a year after his father's death: After the law concerning secession from the churches was passed in the Prussian legislature, attempts were made to apply the law to Jews as well, but to no avail. Until R. Samson Raphael Hirsch arose, and in addresses in writing and orally to central figures—"first and foremost to the delegate Lasker, who at the time was at the height of his influence and thanks to this [address by Hirsch] presented the proposal"—finally led to the granting of permission to secede.[28] Hirsch did indeed approach Lasker personally, but only at a later stage of events. We do not know if Lasker was one of those who read Hirsch's memorandum, but in any event there is no indication that those who did so knew who its true author was. There are indications to the contrary in Lasker's case, for when he explained his proposal, whose substance we shall examine immediately, and described the gap within the Jewish community between the adherents of the old form of worship and those who deviate from it, he referred to events in Berlin, and did not mention Frankfurt at all.[29]

Actually, not only the Jewish Lasker, who apparently did not take an active part in congregational life, but was acquainted with it from his youth and followed its developments,[30] but the non-Jewish legislators as well, accepted the fact that Judaism had ceased to be a religious community unified in doctrine and custom, and acknowledged that the laws of the land should be changed to accommodate the new reality. This was stated openly by the government commissar who was present at the debate,[31] and was seconded by a member of the House, von Brauchitsch, who presented himself as a member of the preparatory committee that had formulated the proposed law. According to him, "it was accepted by all my colleagues that regarding freedom of conscience, Jews must be granted an equal status with Christians."[32] The government commissar, for his part, explained why this principle had not been implemented until now. The committee considered itself bound by the accepted law that recognized only one Judaism. The committee wished to grant the individual Jew the right to leave his congregation, but according to the prevailing legal conditions, such a separation inevitably meant leaving Judaism.[33]

Unlike the committee, which could formulate proposals only within the framework of the existing law, the members of the legislature were free to attempt to change the law. Indeed, two proposals in this spirit were made prior to Lasker's proposal, one by Ludwig Windthorst, the leader of the Catholic party, the Centrum, and another by Moritz Warburg of Hamburg, the other Jewish member. Both shared the opinion that the present situation should not continue. Windthorst felt it sufficient to define the desired goal: extending permission to separate from the congregation in order to provide the opportunity to the secessionists to unite in separate religious bodies, "in accordance with the differences of outlook that are revealed among the members of the Jewish faith."[34] It can be said that Windthorst's proposal, which, aside from granting permission to secede, also legitimized formation of a separate organization, exactly fitted the aspirations of Hirsch and his circle, so that one may wonder whether an Orthodox representative had taken the opportunity to explain to the Catholic leader the exact nature of Orthodox demands.[35] However, Windthorst's proposal did not serve as the basis for debate. It was not formulated as a law, and concluded with the hope that the government would find a way to implement the reform within the framework of a new law regulating Jewish affairs. After hearing Lasker's proposal, which excelled in its precise legal language and aimed to achieve goals similar to those of Windthorst, the latter decided to withdraw his proposal from the agenda.[36]

Before we turn to Lasker's speech, let us consider Warburg's proposal and the ensuing discussion. Warburg agreed with the view of most of Prussian Jewry, that a state law enforcing congregational unity was necessary to its continued existence. At the same time, he admitted that forced unity is likely to impinge on the freedom of conscience of any person who disagrees with the form of worship practiced in the congregation. He therefore proposed freeing the dissident from contributing to the cost of maintaining the congregational ritual, without his membership in the congregation being affected in other respects.[37] This complicated solution required an explanation, both on theoretical and practical grounds, but the author of the proposal refrained from offering one, instead speaking at length about a side issue: the intention of the government to reform the laws applying to Jews but not to abolish them. Warburg claimed that the existence of this sort of law was one of the main reasons for the inferior position of Jews in society; manifestations of this inferiority continued to exist even now, despite the formal granting of equal rights to the Jews following the Emancipation. The members of the House showed signs of impatience towards the long-winded speaker; we too are interested not in his speech itself, but in the delegate von Brauchitsch's reaction to it. He first stated that Warburg had no reason to assume that the Parliament was prejudiced against the members of his faith: "I would assume that I have no need to make him aware of the great esteem in which one of the members of the House, who is of his faith, is held,"[38] and it was unnecessary to mention Lasker's name. But before we hear from Lasker himself, let us consider him as he was portrayed by his colleagues, and ask what was the source of this esteem.

A contemporary historian stated that Lasker made some contribution to every sphere of the many legislative activities called forth by the political changes of the preceding generation. He thus put his stamp on the entire legislative apparatus, and not only in the Prussian legislature, but also in the national legislature, the Reichstag.[39] He was able to do so thanks to his great talents, which he used to their full, with total devotion to his public offices, forgoing any social or personal fulfillment. The amazement of many at his great abilities was augmented by the awareness—shared by his colleagues and most of his political opponents —that he conducted his public battles according to the call of his conscience, without being affected by personal or party considerations; he worked indefatigably and without concern for the personal consequences of his actions. Let us bear in mind Lasker's method and status. His deep involvement in the process of legislation as a whole makes it entirely impossible that he needed prodding from others to take a stand on the clause that pertained to the members of his nation. Furthermore, the great esteem in which he was held by his colleagues and the public as a whole explains why his view was accepted, even though it reflected the wishes of only a small minority in the Jewish community, and was vehemently opposed by the great majority.

Lasker approached the problem not only as a legislator, but as a Jewish legislator, as he emphasized in his explanatory speech. He declared that he had at first intended to propose an amendment in the law under discussion which pertained to all of the religions in the state, without necessitating special mention of the Jewish issue. The general law determined, as stated, that a Christian is permitted to leave his church, which is a national body, but not his local religious community alone. Lasker apparently felt that this limitation should be abolished and that in line with the liberal spirit he upheld, the law should state that every local religious community should be founded and maintained on the basis of voluntary membership; this should apply to the Christian and Jewish communities alike.[40] However, he did not propose this because he feared that such a far-reaching reform would arouse much opposition, and felt it unfair to endanger the chances of passing a law favored by most of the population because of the interests of a small minority, to which he belonged. At the same time, Lasker wished to prevent discrimination against this minority. He therefore proposed the following formulation as an appendix to the law pertaining to

Christians: "In all parts of the kingdom, Jews will be allowed to leave the religious community [*Religions-Gemeinschaft*] on grounds of belief [*aus konfessionellen Gründen*] without thereby leaving Judaism."[41]

In his speech, Lasker began by describing the difference between the legal status of Jews and Christians according to the committee's proposal. A Catholic or Protestant must only declare before a judge that he is leaving his church, and he is released of all obligations connected with it. The state no longer had any interest in the religious affiliation of the author of such a declaration. A Jew, however, could not merely declare that he was leaving the congregation to which he belonged, but must leave his religion as well. Was this not coercion of conscience at its worst?[42]

Von Brauchitsch's speech had preceded Lasker's, but as a member of the preparatory committee he wished to defend its proposal: his and the committee's fear was that without requiring the Jew who leaves his congregation also to leave Judaism, the number of those who secede would multiply, until the very existence of the congregations would be in danger. The limitation proposed was thus intended for the good of Judaism.[43] To this Lasker responded that if this is a privilege granted to Judaism, it is a *privilegium odiosum*, for the good of the public is gained at the price of coercion of the individual.[44] It is clear that there are individuals among the Jews, no less than among the Christians, whose conscience compels them to leave their religious community. Lasker then described the situation as it existed in Berlin: Thousands of Jews were unable to use the official synagogue of the congregation, whose rituals they considered to embody illegitimate deviations; they maintained their own prayer services. In contrast, another group existed in Berlin that moved left from the middle position, to the extent of moving the day of rest and worship from the Sabbath to Sunday.[45] Let us note that the pious mentioned by Lasker are not the members of Hildesheimer's *Adath Israel*, which had only recently been established, and of whose existence Lasker may not even have been aware. His description reflects the reality of the mid-1860s, when the leadership of the congregation appointed Reform rabbis and enacted reforms in the synagogue, steps that motivated the observers of tradition to see to their own needs independently of the official framework.[46] After his theoretical statement that Jews have the same rights to freedom of conscience as Christians, Lasker discussed the practical results of granting permission to secede. He quoted his deceased colleague, Raphael Kosch, who had also been a member of Parliament, and had passed away a few months earlier. Kosch felt that removing governmental patronage of the congregations would lead to tragedy (and this proves that the question had occupied the members of Parliament earlier), but Lasker claimed that "the test of true religious feeling is in voluntary subjugation." If the Jewish congregation will collapse in the absence of governmental coercion, it is better that it do so, and that its members find other ways to satisfy their religious needs.[47]

With the end of Lasker's speech, the Minister of Religious Affairs, Dr. A. Falk, announced that the government was in basic agreement with the views expressed by Lasker—that in regulating Jewish affairs, attention must be paid to the changes that had occurred within the Jewish community in the last decades. As did the commissar, he ascribed the delay in proposing an appropriate law to dilatoriness in making the necessary legal preparations.[48] As a result of this declaration, and with Windthorst's announcement that he withdrew his proposal, the House approved Lasker's proposal.[49] This approval constituted a sort of recommendation to the government that it present the text of the proposal to the Parliament after examining it, to have it voted into law. In his letter from Berlin to R. Samson Raphael Hirsch, which we touched upon above, J. Fromm mentions Minister Falk's declaration. The writer was encouraged by the minister's statement to believe that the goal that they strove for—freedom to secede —was closer to realization than they had dared to think.[50]

Close scrutiny of events at this critical stage enables us to determine with considerable certainty the relative weights of the objective factors, and the parts played by the various participants in the shift in favor of the Orthodox. The memoranda that the pious in the congregations had presented to the government were not answered, but made an impression on those concerned. Moreover, the religious differences that had developed within the Jewish community could not escape the eyes of the observer, whether he was motivated by pure curiosity or official interest. Therefore, whoever recognized the right of the Christian to leave his church in the name of freedom of conscience could not deny this right to the Jew, who was considered a citizen like all others after the Emancipation Law of 1871. R. Samson Raphael Hirsch's memorandum, which reiterated this principle, perhaps influenced those legislators who had not previously considered the issue. For a man like Lasker, both an active and vigorous legislator and a Jew who kept Jewish issues close to his heart, the memorandum was superfluous.

On May 14, two months after the debate in Parliament, its members voted on the law of secession from the churches. It was approved by a majority, and along with it the addendum stating that secession from Jewish congregations is allowed only to someone who declares that he is leaving Judaism. Those who were concerned for the unity of the congregations would have had reason to be satisfied, were it not for the Parliament's recommendation to the government to change this clause according to Lasker's formulation. This remained unresolved, and became a subject of heated debate.

Individuals and institutions took part in this debate: Opposing views were presented in newspaper articles, in pamphlets, and especially in memoranda, which proponents of both views presented to the Parliamentary committee, whose job was to hear public reactions to the proposed amendment. Personal approaches were also made to the members of the House who were to decide the fate of the law. Special weight was of course attributed to Lasker's view, as he was the author of the proposal, and thus all turned to him, in writing and orally—opponents of the amendment to convince him to retract, and its supporters in order to strengthen his hand.[51] The institutions that acted in this way were the isolated congregations, at their head the large congregation in Berlin. Prussian Jewry had no unifying organization sponsored by the government, as in Baden, nor a voluntary body initiated by the congregations themselves. However, at this stage, after the unification of Germany by Bismarck in 1871, Jewish public figures decided to establish such an organization, a *Gemeindebund*, although outside of Prussia, in Leipzig (Saxony). The leaders of the organization felt that they had the right and responsibility to act on behalf of Prussian Jewry and they took an unequivocal stance against Lasker. A no less aggressive stance was expressed by the largest Jewish newspaper, not only in Germany but in the entire Jewish world, the *Allgemeine Zeitung des Judenthums*, edited by Ludwig Philippson. The Orthodox supporters of the law also relied on the press in order to state their case. The *Israelit* was a weekly with standing and reputation, and its editor, Markus Lehmann, was entirely devoted to Orthodox Jewry. In 1869, with Hildesheimer's arrival in Berlin, the *Jüdische Presse* began to appear, at his inspiration, although he was not the editor. And the major figure on the Orthodox side, R. Samson Raphael Hirsch, also orchestrated the campaign. It became known of course that he had composed the memorandum that had been in the hands of the members of the legislature during the debate in March 1873, and, as usual, knowledge of the authorship of the arguments enhanced their importance. When the opposition found a defender in Herman Makower, a well-known jurist and one of the leaders of the Berlin congregation,[52] Hirsch seized the opportunity to restate his arguments in a sharp polemic against his rival.

In his book, Makower first surveyed at length the conditions of the Jewish communities in all the Christian lands, including England and the United States. The two latter examples led him to conclude that mandatory membership in a congregation, as practiced in Europe, was not a necessary condition for their existence,[53] a view close to Hirsch's. But Makower hedged by saying that all depended on the general atmosphere prevailing in the land: In places where the state limits its activities to the minimum necessary to maintain law and order, and the population is used to addressing its needs through voluntary associations, the Jewish congregation can also act as an association of this sort. But in lands where all the needs are filled by organization from above, it is doubtful whether the Jewish community can be the exception. It was no coincidence, according to him, that the requirement to belong to a congregation had existed until now in all German lands without exception.[54] If a new demand now arose in the name of freedom of conscience, it should be addressed without forgoing obligatory membership. His proposed solution, similar to Warburg's during the debate in Parliament, was that those who disliked the form of worship in the congregation would be exempt from the expenses of maintaining it, and would at the same time be permitted to fulfill their religious needs as they wished.[55] This partial secession would be allowed only in places where the secessionists could maintain themselves as a subcommunity within the congregation, a limitation meant to prevent the departure of individuals from small congregations, since this would be likely to endanger their existence.[56] As an experienced jurist, Makower formulated an entire set of statutes at the end of his book, which he felt could serve as a basis for enacting a new law.

Makower's book appeared at the end of the summer of 1873;[57] R. Samson Raphael Hirsch's reaction, which also took the form of an entire book, was published at the beginning of the next year.[58] The tone of the book differed from that of its predecessor, which had been quiet and reasoned, in the polemical tone it took from beginning to end. This raises two questions. First, what was so terrible in Makower's proposals? His idea of exempting the Orthodox from contributing to the maintenance of Reform services had been Hirsch's aspiration during his first decade in Frankfurt, as we remember from the first part of this book. Second, in the memorandum he wrote a year earlier, Hirsch predicted that the secession of the Orthodox minority, if permitted, would not be carried out except in the large congregations, and the only difference between him and Makower on this issue was that the latter wished to anchor this limitation in law. The answer to the first question is that the concession offered to appease Orthodox public opinion by granting limited independence within the framework of the congregation, which was now advocated by many of their opponents, came too late. This was a typical instance of a missed historical opportunity—the failure to concede to the opponent at the right time. A situation that the Orthodox were ready to accept in the 1850s, which was even realized in Breslau for example, later became unacceptable because of the changing times. One of these changes was the weight given to the idea of freedom of conscience. The Hungarian Orthodox had conducted their campaign under this banner, with Hirsch's active assistance. Hirsch used this argument at this juncture as well: The term "Das Prinzip der Gewissenfreiheit," that is, the principle of freedom of conscience, is the name of his book. And this answers our second question: He expected that secession would be limited mainly to the large congregations, and he reiterated this statement in his polemical work as well,[59] but on principle he had to reject the right of legislators to deny any Orthodox Jew the opportunity of secession, if his conscience did not allow him to participate in the worship of the congregation to which he belonged. Indeed, his major grounds for attacking Makower was that although the latter acknowledged freedom of conscience, he did not give it absolute validity, and in the case of a clash with public and other interests, he preferred the latter to the former.[60]

This exhausts the theoretical content of the argument. The fifty pages of

Hirsch's book contain much propaganda, intended to influence public opinion and in particular the opinion of the legislators, who were to decide the fate of the amendment. Indeed, Hirsch writes as if the positive reaction of Minister Falk and the members of the House to Lasker's proposal were actual ratification of the proposal, to the point of mocking Makower for discussing the issue as if it were still an open question.[61] It is difficult to ascribe this to Hirsch's misunderstanding of the situation. More likely it was a tactic intended to convince readers that the die had already been cast in favor of the Orthodox. In any case, Hirsch's book is a lengthy repetition of the arguments included in the anonymous memorandum and his statements on other occasions about the authentic Jewish congregation that had always existed without coercion, about the leaders of Reform who were the first to rely on the governmental arm to subdue the pious, and other arguments of a similar nature. Hirsch even added a patriotic German note by claiming that the entire method of intervention by the state in congregational affairs did not grow on German soil: "its cradle is to be sought on French ground [*gallischem Boden*], which loves centralization,"[62] *gallisch* being a mocking appellation. But to be fair, it must be said that Makower's quiet and objective tone is unique. The polemic over the issue of secession was conducted with noticeable lack of restraint by both sides, because of their great emotional investment in the issue.

The theoretical arguments were reiterated by disputants on both sides, and there is no point in dwelling upon the fine differences between them. The activity of Ludwig Philippson, the editor of *Allgemeine Zeitung des Judenthums*, should be noted, not only because of his involvement in the debate at every stage and because of his keen analytic ability, but especially because his position seems to be based, at least covertly, on emotions and ideas that not many held. As one who closely observed public life—as a rabbi, as a partner in every Jewish cultural, religious, and organizational project, and primarily as the editor of an important newspaper for over thirty years—Philippson knew the nature of the congregations, their strengths and weaknesses alike. He was aware of the tensions in congregational life—including both disputes about principles and quarrels over trivialities. This experience led him to believe that if the legal obligation to belong to a congregation were removed, internal tensions within the congregations would lead to their disintegration.[63] However, Philippson did not accept the argument of Hirsch, Lasker, and others, that if the congregation exists only by virtue of the law, it is a coercive framework that has no right to exist. According to him, this reflected a limited view of the congregation as a religious institution alone, which exists by virtue of the association of members of a shared faith. This perspective was in line with the official status given to Judaism by the state after the Emancipation, which categorized it by comparison to the churches or Christian sects. However, official classification was one thing, historical and social reality another. Others too, with Makower at their head, claimed that the Jewish congregation was a social as well as a religious institution, and that these functions were likely to be impaired by unrestricted secession.[64] Philippson protested, and not only on this occasion, against the one-dimensional classification of Judaism as a religion. He searched for a phrase which would give a sense of Jewish belonging, beginning from birth, and resorted to the term "Stamm," tribe (which has a broader meaning in German than in English).[65] When viewed from this perspective, Jews everywhere should be considered an ethnic entity with an ancient tradition, one of whose basic tenets is an awareness of the necessity of organizing into a congregation in order to fulfill its needs—not only those of a religious nature, but every shared need as it arises. The congregation is therefore not in any way a creation of state law, although it is true that the law gives it needed support, especially under modern conditions, which are likely to impinge upon this bond. These conditions have also given birth to conflicts between those who adhere to the tradition in all its details and those who deviate from it, but this is not a reason to dissolve the congregational framework. Those who distance themselves from the religious nature of the congregational institutions can be satisfied by nurturing secondary institutions of their own, as per Makower's suggestion, to which Philippson gave the stamp of approval in his review of the book in his newspaper.[66]

Philippson wrote Lasker an open letter attempting to convince him to retract his proposal, for he believed that allowing unlimited secession would place Judaism in jeopardy.[67] The two individuals knew and esteemed each other, and Philippson allowed himself, by virtue of the experience of forty years in following Jewish issues, to remind his junior of his responsibility: Lasker remained the only influential Jewish member of Parliament after Kosch's death, and his influence doubled his responsibility. Philippson assured his colleague that most of the Jews of Prussia differed with him, and viewed him, Philippson, as the spokesman for their cause.[68]

Philippson analyzed the differences between the two positions as resting upon one point that was actually two. Lasker viewed the situation of the individual Jew vis-à-vis his congregation as parallel to the situation of the individual Christian vis-à-vis the religious body to which he belongs. Those who differed claimed that this view ignored the objective differences—both material and structural—between the two cases.

Materially, the Christian community from which the individual wished to secede, depended only partly on the contributions of its members. It had property, foundations, and governmental sources of funding, and therefore the secession of even a large number of its members would not endanger its future. In contrast, the Jewish congregation, despite its great obligations, had no financial resources aside from the economic power of its members. Therefore at times even the secession of a few affluent members could bring about its collapse.[69]

But the main difference between the two, wrote Philippson, is on the structural level. Christianity is structured in a series of three concentric circles. Its adherents unite in their local community; this religious community is a cell in a Church that constitutes a national organization. On an abstract level, it can be said that all those who identify with the principles of Christianity are one worldwide collective. Jews, Philippson wrote, have only two circles: the concrete local community and the abstract collective of all those who are faithful to Judaism. The law of secession for Christians does not recognize secession from the local community alone: The individual who secedes must declare that he is leaving the Church of which his community is a cell; the Catholic thus ceases to be a Catholic, and the Protestant a Protestant. This guarantees that secession does not occur for local reasons alone. The Jewish community needs the same degree of defense against arbitrary abandonment, and since Judaism has no intermediate circle between the local community and Judaism as a whole, such a defense can only be the demand that whoever leaves the community leaves Judaism. There can thus be no complete symmetry between the law as it applies to Christians and as it does Jews. Did Lasker not know the general rule: if two ask for the same thing, it is not necessarily the same thing?[70]

Lasker answered his friendly critic only out of politeness.[71] He refuted Philippson's and other arguments about the issue at hand only when he came to defend his proposal in the appeals committee on May 20, 1874. The claim of lack of symmetry between Judaism and Christianity had been raised with variations by other opponents to Lasker's proposal as well. Another objection was included in the memorandum that the *Gemeindebund* presented to the petitions committee.[72] As we recall, Lasker, in his proposal, had conditioned secession on the declaration of the individual that his request arises "aus konfessionellen Bedenken," that is, due to doubts or scruples concerning faith. The term "Konfession," from which the adjective "konfessionell" derives, originally meant a declaration of faith, but in common parlance it became a synonym for religion, and the corresponding adjective, "religious." The representatives of the *Gemeindebund* used the word in its original meaning, attempting to convince the Christian legislators that in contrast to Christianity, where fellowship in each sect is conditional upon avowing belief in its dogmas, Judaism does not have and has never had a system of formal and approved principles of faith. In order to validate this claim, they turned to the teachers of the three theological institutions, the rabbinic seminaries in Vienna and Breslau and the *Lehranstalt für die Wissenschaft des Judenthums* in Berlin. This idea of the absence of dogma in Judaism was a common one among the intelligentsia of the time, and those questioned unhesitatingly approved this thesis. The opinions of the first two institutions are not extant, and we have only the response from Berlin, which was published;[73] this is also the document to which Lasker referred in his response. It was not difficult to reject the conclusion of those who solicited these opinions, that in the absence of set dogmatic principles in Judaism there can be no differences of opinion about the obligations consequent upon accepting its burden. Those who relied on this argument not only failed to buttress their cause, but actually provided their opponents with weak points to attack.

From Lasker's statements in defense of his proposal, we learn that each faction not merely presented its opinions to the appeals committee, but several of their members had personally contacted and consulted with him.[74] Lasker explicitly mentions only one person, Dr. Hirsch, the head of the *Religionsgemeinschaft* in Frankfurt, that is, *Adath Jeschurun*, which had been battling for its full independence for a long time.[75] Hirsch is quoted as a sort of state's witness responding to the opinion of the *Lehranstalt* in Berlin, that Judaism has no dogmatic principles that could cause a rift in the community. Lasker was very respectful of the signatories to this opinion. Among them were Abraham Geiger, David Cassell, and Hymann Steinthal, and some of them, he claimed, he knew personally. Lasker declared outright that personally he was glad to know that his religion, Judaism, did not depend on a declaration of faith. But as a legislator he could not judge, nor could any other legislator, whether a divisive question of faith existed in one religion or another. As against the opinion of the scholars of Berlin, the members of various congregations had declared that their religious conscience forced them to withdraw from their local communities and to establish, together with others, separate religious communities.[76] In this context he quotes Hirsch: "Mister Dr. Hirsch, the most diligent and learned representative of the aspirations of his religion [*konfessionellen Bestrebungen*], declares that he feels himself separated on the religious level from those who constitute the rest of the community."[77]

As for the argument of a lack of symmetry between Christianity and Judaism, Lasker's conclusion is opposite to that reached by Philippson and his colleagues. If Judaism has only two circles, he argued, the local community and the community of believers in the Jewish religion, and individuals and groups declare that their conscience does not allow them to remain tied to the congregation, we cannot make their separation from the community conditional on their simultaneous departure from the Judaism that they espouse, for thus we will impose upon them a double dilemma. In order to allow them to ease their consciences by seceding from the congregation, we will force them to go against their consciences by demanding that they leave Judaism.[78] The purpose of the law is to grant the same freedom of conscience to the Jew as to the Christian. It is true that in the case of a Jew, freedom of secession is likely to impinge upon the harmony of the congregation, for it has no intermediate circle. However, even if we knew for certain that this would endanger the existence of the congregations, we could not deny the principle of freedom of conscience, and Judaism would be forced to accept the results willy-nilly.[79] Actually, the fears of a mass departure from the congregations are groundless, said Lasker, as is the fear of disintegration of the congregations. The congregations have their own powers of attraction, and they do not exist by virtue of the coercive powers of the state. Here Lasker revealed that many of the leaders of the congregations who opposed his proposal admitted to him that they saw no real danger to their congregations as a result of the proposed legislation.[80] The members of the committee supported Lasker, the petitions which sought to disqualify his proposal were rejected, and its acceptance as law in the next session of Parliament seemed guaranteed.

This at least was the assessment of its major opponent, Ludwig Philippson. He therefore abandoned his principles as a defender of a case and initiated an ad hominem attack upon Lasker, attributing to him personal motives for sponsoring the proposal. Philippson's diagnosis was that Lasker had no contact with the broad Jewish public in the state, and that he acted out of admiration for the two extremes: Orthodoxy because of his childhood memories, and extreme Reform because of the ideological position he reached in his maturity. Even worse, Philippson pried into Lasker's private and public life, saying that passing the law at the expense of his fellow Jews would be a form of compensation for Lasker's lack of personal satisfaction in both private and public life.[81] This armchair psychology contradicted the general assessment that Lasker was a man of principle who did not allow his personal inclinations to overrule his respect for the law and the values of justice, an assessment previously shared by Philippson.

Philippson's attacks, and the substantive arguments that were repeated after the decision of the appeals committee, did not prevent ratification of the amendment, which occurred as late as May 1876. During the interim, the government prepared a detailed proposal, based on Lasker's original formulation, with two significant changes. First, instead of the concept "Religionsgemeinschaft," that is, religious union, a term without specific meaning, "Religionsgemeinde," the accepted translation of "congregation," was now used. Second, instead of the "konfessionelle Bedenken" that the individual was required to give as his reason for seceding from the congregation, which gave those who objected room to argue that Judaism had no dogma that could give rise to division, the term "religiöse" was used—religious reasons—a classification that encompassed all the types of arguments used by the Orthodox against remaining in the general congregations.[82]

This did not, of course, silence the opposition. On the contrary, the mention of the congregation, from which the Jew could secede, highlighted the contrast between his rights and those of the Christian, who was not allowed to leave the local community without ceasing to be a member of the Church. Manuel Joel, one of the important scholars of the generation and a pillar of the rabbinic seminary in Breslau, noted this in a last-minute attempt to explain to the members of the House, in a detailed pamphlet, why they should not follow Lasker's arguments and ratify the law.[83] He argued that the law did not grant equal status to the Jewish individual and the Christian individual, but rather granted the Jew a privilege, at the price of the position of the Jewish religion vis-à-vis the Christian religions.[84] Lasker claimed that religion should not rely on the coercive power of the state, and that it is obliged to and able to exist by virtue of the loyalty of its adherents. This is a good principle, Joel wrote, and in the United States all religions, Judaism and Christianity alike, are treated in accordance with it. In Europe, and particularly in Prussia, however, the state helps preserve the institutions of the Christian religions, by, among other things, preventing the defection of individuals who wish to release themselves of the institutional burden. This is the defense that the Jewish community also demands for itself, as expressed in the appeals of most of the representatives of the congregations in the state. In contrast to their request, said Joel, the positions of Lasker and Hirsch are those of dissenters, and are not worthy of consideration.[85]

Ludwig Philippson also entered the fray. He had ties with the well-known historian Heinrich von Sybel, who was at the time a member of the Prussian Parliament.[86] He succeeded in persuading von Sybel of the justice of his arguments against the proposed law and apparently believed that the prestige of the great historian would serve as a counterweight to Lasker's view. Von Sybel did indeed voice the major arguments against the law, relying openly on Philippson, whom he presented as an authority on Jewish affairs.[87] In reality, instead of helping, he made the situation worse. As a stranger to the affair who merely voiced someone else's opinion, von Sybel was not able to evaluate the weight of the arguments he mouthed. Among other things, he advanced the argument that the differences between the Orthodox and their opponents concerned only external details of worship. These lacked theological significance and did not justify a division, such as the Orthodox had requested.[88] To this Lasker could easily respond that the decision as to what constitutes a sufficient reason for division can be made only by those involved, and the legislators are not permitted to set themselves up as judges in an area outside of their scope.[89] Lasker even taught his friend the historian a lesson in the history of Christianity, where, especially in England, sectarian divisions occurred because of differences in ritual that the outside observer might consider trivial.[90]

The opponents of the amendment were apparently aware that most of the members of the House supported its approval in the form sponsored by the government, but they still hoped to prevent its passage. They claimed that in light of its anticipated severe results, that is, the collapse of most of the congregations, it was necessary to refer the proposal to a parliamentary committee for a second examination.[91] In Lasker's estimation, this would not only create a temporary delay, but would also place the very approval of the law in jeopardy. These were the last days of the current session of Parliament, and removing the law from the agenda could bury it permanently. Therefore Lasker turned to the members of the House and requested that it be put to an immediate vote, rather than be doomed to disappear by neglect.[92] The House acceded to his request; the vote took place on May 22, 1876, and the proposal was approved by a majority vote. On July 28 the bill was publicized with the signature of the king and became law. We shall see how much effect that law was to have.

Chapter 23

Hirsch's Failure in His Own Community and His Ideological Legacy

After the long-awaited ratification of the law, and the contradictory assessments of its consequences, it is no surprise that contemporaries followed actual secession from congregations very closely. The *Allgemeine Zeitung des Judenthums* started a special column to report on important developments in this area.[1] The reports that reached the newspaper did not substantiate the dark prophecies of its editor, Ludwig Philippson, about a mass departure that could bring about the collapse of most of the congregations. The cases of secession that occurred here and there were generally individual acts, stemming from personal and local factors, and bore no signs of a collective movement.[2]

The secession of a consolidated group occurred only in Wiesbaden. It had a small Orthodox community of the Frankfurt type, and its members individually announced their departure from the mother congregation, to which they had previously belonged against their will. They had had special motivations, chief among them being the attitude of the Reform rabbi of the mother congregation, Samuel Süsskind, to the Orthodox members of his congregation. Süsskind was a militant reformer, a holdover from the previous generation, who had not only upheld Reform doctrine but attempted to force it upon others. Such reformers had displayed lack of understanding and tolerance towards the adherents of Orthodoxy, whether in its traditional or its modern form, à la R. Samson Raphael Hirsch. Among other things, Süsskind, as the government-appointed administrator of religious education in the congregation, attempted to prevent the children of Orthodox families from learning the primary religious texts, such as the *Hayyei Adam* (a nineteenth-century halakhic code), instead of schoolbooks with a reformist slant.[3] Süsskind even published a critique of the statutes of *Adath Jeschurun* in Frankfurt, which were ratified in early 1875. Even prior to the approval of the law of secession, he attempted to demonstrate that even the modern Orthodox, who claimed to uphold the authentic tradition, deviated from it in practice.[4] This hostile attitude of the rabbi of Wiesbaden to the Orthodox minority led to its consolidation and strengthened its resolve to leave the congregation as a group.

They were a small group, numbering fifty-three people, no more than ten percent of the community.[5] Luckily, they had a spiritual leader, R. Leo Kahn, an outstanding student of R. Esriel Hildesheimer, a person at once enthusiastic and practical, who knew how to conduct the campaign for his community and to see to the preservation of its institutions.[6] For the struggle did not end with its secession: This small community lacked even a synagogue worthy of the name, and it requested, at least temporarily, the continued use of the cemetery of the mother community. Permission did not depend upon the congregation's wishes alone. The law of secession set down rules about the rights of those who seceded with regard to the cemeteries: Their rights in the cemetery were maintained so long as no other cemetery was available. Unfortunately for the Orthodox in Wiesbaden, the municipality opened a nondenominational cemetery. R. Süsskind was unwilling to make any concessions beyond those demanded by the law, and the doors of the Jewish cemetery were closed to the Orthodox. The Orthodox were in a quandary, having lost their rights in the cemetery of the community, until at last they found a solution.[7] The details are of no interest, but the incident reveals the sad state of affairs that arose as a result of mutual alienation.

In Frankfurt, things were entirely different. Events there attracted much attention at the time as well as later on, because Hirsch's *Adath Jeschurun* seemed to be the natural candidate for exploiting the option of secession. It became clear, however, that the aggressive stance taken by the rabbi of the community was accepted by only a small number of his supporters. For most of the members of his community, the law of secession served only as a means to pressure the mother congregation to compromise with them. Moreover, it was to Orthodox rabbis specifically that Hirsch had to defend his doctrine. That doctrine, which upheld the ideal of "Torah and *derekh eretz*," requiring widespread cultural accommodation with the environment while maintaining total devotion to *halakhah*—a doctrine from which he also derived the demand to separate from a mother community that is not based on these principles[8]—was far from being favored by halakhists of the old school. Some of these were still to be found in his community, and others were halakhic authorities in other congregations. His bitter argument with R. Isaac Dov Halevi Bamberger of Würzburg, the details of which we shall learn below, reveals the tragedy of the man, who considered himself betrayed by those he believed would stand by him in his public struggle.

Our description of the unfolding of events in Frankfurt will be based on

Robert Liberles' book on the history of *Adath Jeschurun* and on his sources.[9] Approximately two months after the ratification of the law of secession, during the Sukkot festival, Hirsch and a small group of his close supporters, among them some of the administrators of his community, took the necessary legal steps to leave the mother congregation. This was meant to serve as an example to the members of the community to follow in the footsteps of their master and teacher. Hirsch did not content himself with setting a personal example. In one of his sermons in the synagogue, he declared that secession is not an issue of personal choice. As the halakhic authority appointed by the members of *Adath Jeschurun*, he decreed that separation from the mother congregation is an unequivocal religious obligation for every Orthodox Jew. The text of Hirsch's sermon has not been preserved, but Hirsch subsequently published a pamphlet called *Der Austritt aus der Gemeinde* (Secession from the Congregation),[10] which, according to the testimony of a contemporary, embodied the major substance of the sermon in a different form.[11] In the meantime, however, it became clear that only a minority were ready to accept their rabbi's directive and secede from the congregation; the majority wished only to wring from the mother congregation concessions that it had hitherto not been willing to make.

The situation was even graver with regard to the status and authority of the rabbi, for among those who refused to secede were most of the descendants of the oldest families in the city, and at their head was a personage whose scholarship and piety could compete with those of the rabbi, and who opposed the rabbi's halakhic ruling. This was an old householder by the name of R. Moses Mainz, a great Torah scholar of the old school, a modest and retiring man. He was one of the pillars of the *Adath Jeschurun* community, although he did not like all the external changes that the rabbi had initiated in the synagogue, such as the vestments worn by the functionaries and the choir.[12] However, he came into open conflict with R. Hirsch only over the question of secession, on which he gave a more lenient ruling than that of the rabbi. Those who refused to secede did indeed negotiate with the mother congregation, relying on R. Mainz's opinion, and these negotiations went through several stages. Some members of *Adath Jeschurun* wanted to remain members of two institutions of the congregation, the hospital and the cemetery, after the secession, while the administration made use of these institutions conditional upon formal membership in the congregation. On the other hand, it was ready to exempt the Orthodox from the expense of maintaining the institutions that their religious conscience prohibited them from using, such as the synagogue, and promised to give them access to the services they could use, and to allow them to supervise these. The nature and validity of this compromise were now at issue, and became a source of controversy.

Hirsch apparently knew from the start that such a suggestion would be made, and he rejected it in the pamphlet mentioned above. In this publication, the author relied on a literary device he had used several years earlier: He made an artisan the spokesman for his arguments, thereby implying that it was clear even to the simple folk that Reform and Orthodoxy are inherently incompatible and their adherents cannot exist within the same framework, in line with the ruling he had announced in the synagogue. The imaginary artisan was to rebut all the arguments against accepting this ruling. The essence of his answer was that the material or spiritual advantage that would be gained by remaining in the community, and the various sorts of harm that would be caused by secession, do not count when weighed against the absolute religious requirement to separate from Reform. This is an obligation for which a person must sacrifice his life, as stated in the commandment to love God "with all your might" (Deut. 5:5). He must even take the risk that upon his death he will not find a burial place and will be considered an "unattended corpse."[13]

The exaggeration contained in these words seems to have weakened their impact. In any case, publication of the pamphlet did not end negotiations with the administration of the congregation, and when these were concluded successfully, Hirsch felt it necessary to distribute a directive to his community—this time in a practical tone—stating that the concessions made by the administration did not affect his halakhic decision at all. On the contrary, by agreeing to put their doctrine on an equal level with Reform, the Orthodox were guilty of denying the exclusive truth of their faith.[14] This view was rejected by R. Hirsch's rival, R. Moses Mainz, who was, as stated, a person with much authority and prestige, so that an embarrassing and frustrating impasse was created, on both the personal and the public level.

In order to find a way out of the impasse, some of Hirsch's adherents decided to request a third opinion, to decide between the two. They therefore turned to R. Isaac Dov Bamberger, apparently without the knowledge of their rabbi. They had good reason to assume that the decision of the rabbi of Würzburg would be in favor of their rabbi.[15] R. Bamberger, who was then seventy years old, was the last surviving student of the halakhists of the generation that preceded the Haskalah. He himself was known as the author of practical halakhic guides for individuals and religious functionaries. It would not be to his detriment to describe him as a great man relative to his generation, a generation that had few great halakhic figures. In his halakhic responses, R. Bamberger generally ruled stringently, attempting to accommodate all the views with which his great erudition had acquainted him.[16] Needless to say, the rabbi of Würzburg recoiled from any hint of Reform. He was not totally out of contact with the surrounding culture, for he was also the head of a small *yeshivah* and a school for teachers, who were required to have some elementary secular education. But he attempted to limit the involvement of his students in general culture to the bare minimum, as he asserted in his polemic with Hirsch, to which we will soon turn. He was also careful not to allow the values of foreign learning and culture an equal place with Jewish tradition in the formation of the character and personality of his pupils. In this he differed with Hirsch's doctrine of combining Torah with *derekh eretz*.[17] But this did not necessarily entail a different approach to the question of secession. On the contrary, R. Bamberger's mental distance from the values of general culture seemed to put him at an even greater distance from Reform than R. Samson Raphael Hirsch. Hirsch's adherents thus hoped to find a supporter in the rabbi of Würzburg.

The first contact they made with R. Bamberger was in writing. It began during the negotiations with the administration of the congregation, when the latter had already agreed to exempt the Orthodox from contributing to the costs of Reform worship, but had not yet promised to finance the needs of the Orthodox themselves. R. Bamberger's response was that this concession was of no import, and the obligation to secede was still in force, in accordance with the ruling of the rabbi of *Adath Jeschurun*, R. Hirsch.[18] This letter, which was probably presented to R. Moses Mainz, did not change his opinion. Those who had turned to R. Bamberger still hoped that a face-to-face meeting between R. Bamberger and R. Mainz would be useful. They importuned him to agree to a meeting, and this time they appeared personally in Würtzburg. After much hesitation, the rabbi agreed, but warned them that the meeting with the great scholar Moses Mainz could also lead to results contrary to those they desired.[19] This is indeed what happened; instead of persuading R. Mainz to change his mind, Bamberger changed his, and now supported those who opposed secession.

What motivated him to do so? We shall later hear his explanation that in his meeting in Frankfurt he learned of the additional concession of the administration, namely its readiness to provide for the needs of the Orthodox. However, as he attested, R. Bamberger had warned his visitors in advance that the meeting with R. Mainz could lead to a change in his position, and at that time he did not know of the additional concession. It seems likely that personal contact with one he so much admired played as decisive a part as the new information. The great prestige that R. Moses Mainz enjoyed is puzzling; he left no writings behind, and did not even hold a public rabbinic office. However, at times a Torah scholar without any formal standing wins for himself great religious authority, thanks to his great scholarship and his outstanding qualities, which is apparently what happened in this case.

R. Bamberger's change of mind generated widespread interest, and a notice appeared in the local paper, *Frankfurter Börsen-und Handelszeitung*, that R. Hirsch had requested the opinion of his colleague from Würzburg. R. Bamberger felt it necessary to deny this announcement. His denial appeared in the March 20 issue, along with an announcement that he had indeed changed his mind upon his visit to Frankfurt, when it became known to him from "several people"—R. Mainz was not mentioned—that the administration had agreed to provide for the needs of the Orthodox. He made his permission to remain in the community conditional on sufficient guarantees that this promise would be kept.[20]

Hirsch was horrified to read R. Bamberger's opinion, which contradicted his explicit ruling. He also had a personal reason for his deep anger. The rabbi of Würzburg had been in Frankfurt, had consulted with his opponent, and had issued his ruling behind Hirsch's back. Accepted custom in the rabbinic world required a rabbi who comes to a strange place to pay a courtesy call at the home of the local halakhic authority. In his answer, Hirsch did not touch upon this point, but one of his enthusiastic admirers from among the leadership of *Adath Jeschurun*, Emmanuel Schwarzschild, who published a long leaflet against Bamberger, took him to task for this affront as well.[21] Hirsch himself retaliated to this offense when he characterized Bamberger's state of mind when writing his opinion as *nayyim ve-shakhiv*, a Talmudic phrase describing someone who says something illogical, leaving no possible explanation other than that he was half asleep.[22]

R. Bamberger responded to Hirsch's open letter with a similar publication, and repaid the personal insult with interest. At the beginning of his response, Bamberger declared that he would not refute the points that Hirsch had raised, in order not to embarrass him in public. This was a broad hint that he considered Hirsch an inadequately trained student, who made halakhic mistakes. It was therefore beneath R. Bamberger's dignity to debate with him in public.[23] There is no doubt that this statement was not made in the heat of anger; he apparently held this opinion of Hirsch's scholarship, as emerges from the halakhic discussion.

One of Hirsch's complaints against Bamberger was that he had contravened the Talmudic principle that prevented one authority from permitting something that his colleague had prohibited.[24] Bamberger pointed to a halakhic source that places a limitation on the aforesaid clause: It applies only if two scholars of the same stature are involved. If the second scholar is greater than his colleague, he can contradict his ruling and rule leniently.[25] R. Bamberger was considered a modest man, neither arrogant nor self-aggrandizing. He apparently believed that his greater learning was a well-known fact, and thus could be openly referred to in explaining his ruling. This patronizing tone towards his rival is evident throughout Bamberger's discussion, and reflected what Bamberger considered not only the weakness of Hirsch's arguments, but also his inferior scholarly position.

This was no doubt a difficult time in Hirsch's life. Members of the previous generation of scholars had expressed disdain for his scholarship earlier, but it is doubtful that he ever before knew of it.[26] But now the dismissive tone became a way to undermine his authority, particularly in connection with a cause to which he had devoted his life. Hirsch saw no reason to efface himself before his right-wing critics, despite his awareness of the difference between their style of study and his. Unlike the graduates of the *yeshivot*, who granted equal weight to studying all the talmudic sources, without distinguishing between those that do and those that do not contribute to an understanding of the basic ideas of *halakhah*, or lead to practical rulings—and for whom the greatest accomplishment was considered the student's novel interpretation of the sources—Hirsch concentrated specifically on clarifying the principles of the *halakhah*, and on determining the norms implicit in it. His concentration on these two aspects of the *halakhah* gave him the ability to master them totally, as he proved on the one hand in his work *Horeb*, which is a sort of abridged Shulhan Arukh, and on the other in his commentary on the Torah, which contains innumerable elucidations of the nature of the Oral Law.[27] His *Horeb* was the target of criticism and even of ridicule by his Reform adversaries, but halakhists found no flaw in it, although they refrained from using it because it was written in German, which ostensibly placed it beyond the pale. In terms of its contents and general outlook, Hirsch's book was in the same category as most of Bamberger's works that were published during his lifetime. It too was meant to guide those who observe the *halakhah* to execute its directives in all their detail. Bamberger's patronizing attitude, as if he was so far above Hirsch that they had no common ground for discussion, had no real justification. It is not surprising that Hirsch took umbrage at it.

Bamberger ended his open letter with the declaration that he had "attempted to touch only upon what was necessary and to deal with things in the most seemly manner."[28] He added the request that the addressee see the public debate, upon the pages of the press, as definitively closed, although he could of course continue to discuss the issue with his community and in his synagogue.[29] What did Bamberger think? Did he actually believe that Hirsch was subordinate to him because of his scholarly superiority, and that he could tell him what to do and what not to do? In any event, Hirsch had no intention of limiting his reaction to the private sphere. His adversary had made the matter public, and had publicly insulted him. Had he not responded, his silence would have been seen as acknowledgment of the correctness of Bamberger's position, whereas Hirsch was convinced he could refute his arguments one by one.[30]

We shall soon see what were the fundamental points of the controversy about the obligation to secede. However, Bamberger's intervention in his colleague's ruling raised preliminary questions, and Hirsch first addressed the glaring weak points in his adversary's arguments. In arguing for the right of a more senior halakhist to contradict the ruling of one inferior to him, Bamberger had cited the summary by one of the sixteenth-century commentaries on Shulhan Arukh, Y.D., Chapter 242—a chapter that deals with the rules guiding halakhists in their rulings.[31] In rebuttal, Hirsch referred back to the author's sources for his summary, and by Hirsch's explicating them, refuted Bamberger's assertion that they supported him.[32]

More serious than this revelation was Hirsch's objection to the fact that Bamberger had issued a ruling, for Hirsch claimed that Bamberger was forbidden to issue an opinion opposing him, the halakhic authority of Frankfurt. Bamberger had justified his action by claiming that the restriction preventing a scholar from issuing a ruling in his colleague's city is not law, and that the talmudic and halakhic sources state only that it is *lava orah ar'a* to do so. Bamberger translated these Aramaic words as "nicht üblich," not usual.[33] Here Hirsch caught him out in an attempt to justify himself, for the translation of the words *orah ar'a* is "etiquette." Thus the original meaning is not a statement of fact, that it is not customary, but a judgment that it is improper to enter the domain of a colleague.[34]

These topics, which concerned the authority of one scholar to rule against another, had been discussed in the halakhic literature from time immemorial, and the difference of opinion on this issue between the two adversaries can be examined by looking at the sources.[35] However, the essential disagreement between them centered on the question of whether to require secession from the congregation. This had no halakhic precedent, and their rulings on this question drew only indirectly on existing *halakhah*, by inference from other topics. We can therefore ask the question that was already raised in the Hungarian context: Should the decisions of the halakhists on these issues be considered halakhic rulings in the full sense of the word? The conclusion to be reached here is similar to that given in examining the arguments of Maharam Schick, his colleagues, and their adversaries: These were halakhic only in outward appearance.

Let us begin the discussion with Bamberger's reasons for his change of heart as a result of his visit to Frankfurt, which his critics, and first and foremost R. Samson Raphael Hirsch, attacked. He argued that the consent of the administration of the congregation to provide for Orthodox needs neutralized some of the religious flaws of Reform. Its adherents ceased henceforth to come under the heading of inciters and seditious transgressors, and as a result, the Orthodox were no longer obliged to distance themselves from them.[36] This was a legalistic construct which was easy to topple by demonstrating that the earlier halakhists, beginning with the Tannaim and Amoraim and ending with the great halakhists of recent generations like the Hatam Sofer, did not make these fine distinctions, and that deviations from the essentials of the tradition, in thought or deed, which were less serious than those of Reform, had placed their adherents outside of the congregation of faithful Jews.[37]

But an examination of Hirsch's arguments against Bamberger reveals that he himself, almost unconsciously, built a similar structure to support his position. After presenting his arguments against Bamberger's attempt to remove the Reform from the category of spiteful transgressors and apply to them the lesser category of transgressors motivated by physical or moral weakness, Hirsch declared the entire discussion superfluous. He himself had never applied the term transgressors or heretics to the Reform, nor had he claimed that one should distance oneself from them, as the earlier halakhists had recommended to their contemporaries. The separation that he demanded referred to heresy as personified in a Reform congregation.[38] He pointed to his words in his first pamphlet, where he had written: "I deliberately use these abstract concepts which refer to *the system and not to the people"* (emphasis in the original).[39] He then explained this distinction: "The heretics and sectarians with whom the halakhists prohibit contact no longer exist, thank God, in our time." For it was said that "there are no heretics among the nations" and "non-Jews outside of the Land of Israel are not considered idolaters," for they do not innovate idolatrous worship, but merely "follow the customs of their forefathers." This is applicable also to the sectarianism and heresy to which the Jews of this generation adhere in their thought and in their way of life. They too are the descendants of the second or third generation of those who invented the apostasy and who acted upon it while spreading propaganda in its favor.[40]

The halakhic rulings cited were made in the Middle Ages, in order to defend the public's failure to observe the mishnaic and talmudic prohibition against contact with the Christian population on their festivals, in commercial transactions and the like. Even in its original context, referring to Christians, the sentence "they follow the customs of their forefathers" is apologetic and has no real theological significance.[41] Applying it to the reformers of the nineteenth century, on the grounds that they too did not invent their doctrine, and this by someone who had battled them furiously all his life, was the height of paradox. This argument was meant to extricate Hirsch from the deep contradiction in which he found himself, for despite his zealousness against the adherents of Reform, "he sewed for them a *tallit* of human brotherhood."[42] So at any rate, argued one of his anonymous critics, who published an entire leaflet refuting Hirsch's first open letter, which he had addressed to R. Bamberger. The purpose of these mental acrobatics was clear—they were meant to quiet the fears of potential seceders that they might be forced to break off all contact with the members of the mother congregation upon seceding. On the contrary, "they must persevere in peaceful and brotherly contact with their contemporaries, who were raised without regard to Jewish truth and Jewish law."[43] This attempt to burn the candle at both ends led Hirsch to cite all the prohibitions found in earlier sources regarding idolaters, sectarians, and heretics. However, these sources refer to those people who are included in those categories, while Hirsch applied them to the ideological essence that, as it were, adhered to them—not to the sectarians and heretics themselves, who no longer exist, but to their spirit, which has a place of honor in the Reform community.

This internal contradiction did not escape his opponents. They were not interested in confronting him on halakhic grounds, as R. Bamberger had done, but because they felt that his view lacked roots in the tradition. Both of his anonymous critics formulated their accusations in similar terms, claiming that Hirsch had invented a new commandment or ruling, and wished to impose it upon his congregation.[44] This feeling was probably widespread among those members of his flock who refused to accept his ruling on this point, although they generally considered themselves subject to his halakhic authority. There were also material motives for their refusal, as the reporter for *Allgemeine Zeitung des Judenthums* pointed out. There were members of *Adath Jeschurun* who used some of the congregational institutions: the congregational school, the small houses of worship that existed within its sphere and which had not introduced reforms like those in the central synagogue, and the hospital.[45] An important factor in preventing a split was the cemetery. The descendants of the ancient families in the city were not willing to forgo their right to be buried near their ancestors. Hirsch's claim, as voiced by the imaginary artisan, that secession from the congregation during his lifetime superseded any concern about what would happen to him after his death, apparently did not gain him supporters in his struggle. Some of them even quoted Hirsch as saying that he would prefer to be buried in a Christian cemetery than near reformers.[46] Even if this was mere gossip, it arose from his written words. The members of the ancient families in Frankfurt did not need special reasons to oppose secession. Knowing that secession would force them to relinquish their part in the institutions that their parents had nurtured and to which they were linked by deep emotional ties, was enough to make them remain in the congregation.

R. Bamberger's intervention was not what caused many to oppose Hirsch's ruling; this opposition had been apparent from the outset, and drove Hirsch's adherents to turn to R. Bamberger in the first place. While R. Bamberger's ruling may have decided the matter for those who were undecided, the bulk of this camp no doubt existed beforehand. In the end, of the 360 members of *Adath Jeschurun*, seventy-five seceded; seventy accepted the compromise and remained partial members of the congregation, paying limited taxes and using only certain of its facilities; and the great majority, about two hundred, retained their former position and maintained their membership in both communities.[47]

For R. Samson Raphael Hirsch, these results were a personal tragedy. After he had helped the pious in Hungary to extricate themselves from the embrace of the Neologs, and had attempted with all his might to open an escape hatch for the devout in Prussia, such as the Orthodox in Wiesbaden already enjoyed, here on his home ground he had suffered a devastating defeat. He had bested his adversary in the battle of *halakhah*, but had had to resort to tactics that no doubt left a bad taste in his mouth. Now the public had accepted his adversary's opinion, and the price paid for the victory turned out to have been in vain.

Let us now clarify the approach of authorities who could have decided the conflict. Such a person was R. Esriel Hildesheimer, who had access to the media via the *Jüdische Presse*, which appeared in Berlin at his instigation and under his supervision. Hirsch clearly expected to receive Hildesheimer's moral support. The latter was an active partner in the battle for ratification of the secession law, and it was natural to expect that he would come to the aid of anyone who attempted to apply the law in practice. They certainly both remembered what had passed between them years ago, when Hildesheimer, discouraged after the rabbinic assembly in Buda in late 1868, turned to Hirsch, and the latter defended him in a detailed article in *Jeschurun*. Now Hirsch did not request assistance, but sent Hildesheimer his two pamphlets on the issue, and the addressee took the hint. In his letter to Hirsch upon receipt of the first pamphlet, Hildesheimer thanked the author for his personal attention, agreed with Hirsch's position, and consoled him for the anguish R. Bamberger's unexpected interference had caused him.[48] Upon receipt of Hirsch's second pamphlet, Hildesheimer expressed his admiration for Hirsch's well-thought-out argument, which demolished his rival, but also noted that the personal attacks he had made were likely to deepen the gap between the sides. He ignored the possibility that he himself would intervene in the controversy, but we know from his correspondence with a third party, in the interval between the publication of Hirsch's two pamphlets, that the question of whether to intervene weighed on his mind.

At the end of May, or early in June, the *Jüdische Presse* received an article by L. Stern of Würzburg, a senior pedagogue and regular contributor to the paper. The author of the article wished to defend his colleague, the head of the teachers' seminary. The board of the newspaper gave Hildesheimer the task of explaining to the writer why it refused to publish his article. In his letter to Stern, Hildesheimer explained the difficult position in which he found himself with the eruption of the Frankfurt controversy, which affected the entire Orthodox camp, and brought to mind the feud between R. Jacob Emden and R. Jonathan Eybeschütz. In theory, he sided with Hirsch and felt it his duty to defend him, but in practice, he was not free to act according to his personal views. He was the administrator of the rabbinical seminary and other public institutions whose existence depended upon widespread public support. His intervention would not help, but was likely to endanger all that he had built up since his arrival in Berlin, and this was not just his personal assessment. He had discussed the issue with the teachers of the seminary, Dr. A. Berliner, Dr. D. S. Hoffmann, and Dr. J. Barth, and all had decided that they must maintain silence.[49]

Similar considerations also apparently motivated Markus Lehmann, the editor of *Israelit*, to remain silent. Lehmann himself was an enthusiastic supporter of the secession law, and as early as late April and early May, he had written a long article in his paper in which he refuted the argument that the obligation to secede was only a neo-Orthodox invention of Hirsch. He quoted a responsum by the Hakham Zvi, in which the author instructed the minority of a Sephardic congregation to leave its congregation because some of the members were guilty of major transgressions.[50] One of the two anonymous critics mentioned above poked fun at him and asked: "Is Lehmann also among the prophets?"[51]

For Lehmann was not considered a great scholar, and his strengths were his literary talent and his devotion to the Orthodox cause. Nonetheless, *Israelit* was the most established and most militant of the Orthodox newspapers, and it was expected to address the major topic of the day. Any reference to that topic, however, would necessitate a stand in a quarrel between two respected public leaders, and Lehmann could not do this. So, throughout the months in which Hirsch and Bamberger exchanged written blows, there is no mention of this in the paper. Only in mid-July was a lead article published, lamenting the controversy in the Orthodox camp—which reminded the author, like Hildesheimer, of the Emden-Eybeschütz controversy—without stating what and who were the subjects of this controversy.[52]

Hirsch could find potential supporters in Hungary. Indeed, R. Hayyim Sofer included words of encouragement to Hirsch in his response to a letter by Hirsch on other matters: "I have heard that his honor . . . is fighting a righteous war against . . . and is forcefully and firmly upholding the division in his state, that his heart is following the path of God, and that he does not allow himself to be deterred."[53] The editor omitted the name of the adversary, but there is no doubt, as Michael Silber determined, that the reference is to R. Bamberger.[54] These words of encouragement were offered privately and in passing, and were not intended to influence the outcome of the conflict.

A letter by Maharam Schick to R. Bamberger in the summer of 1877, which was later published among his responsa, was an attempt to influence the controversy actively.[55] A copy of it was apparently given to Hirsch as well, for the writer takes an unequivocal stance against Bamberger's leniency, but finds certain flaws in Hirsch's methods of warfare. From his description of the positions of the two adversaries at the beginning of the letter, it is clear that Maharam Schick had only secondhand information about the confrontation. He turns to R. Bamberger with these words: "I have heard that his honor . . . ruled that if the Reform *Gemeinde* in Frankfurt guaranteed the pious that they do not wish to separate from them in all matters of our Holy Torah, it is possible to be together with them in one association." But this description of Bamberger's position is totally wrong, for the latter made his leniency conditional upon the readiness of the reformers to provide for the needs of the pious and not upon a declaration that they wish to remain together. His description of Hirsch's position is also inaccurate. Hirsch "exaggerated when he stated that anyone who does not separate from them is not loyal to God and the Torah." Here Maharam Schick became an advocate for those who refuse to separate, for there may be various reasons why they cannot stand up to this challenge, and even one who has failed to do "all this can be a completely righteous man." Hirsch would have totally agreed with this statement, for he did not claim that the refusal to secede emanates from lack of faith or disparagement of the commandments. Nonetheless, Maharam Schick's support of Hirsch was unequivocal, even though the similarity between them was limited to the goal alone, as emerges from an analysis of his words. Maharam Schick's conceptual world was entirely different from Hirsch's, and the difference is striking even where they rely on the same sources. A description of the covert debate between the two main battlers for Orthodox independence in the two lands will provide an appropriate conclusion for our portrayal of the division in the Jewish congregations.

Maharam Schick opens his critique of R. Bamberger's lenient ruling permitting one to remain together with the reformers under certain conditions, by citing the *Sifra* on the verse (Lev. 20:26) "And I shall separate you from among the nations to be for me": "If you are separated from them you shall be mine and if not, not . . ." (the source continues: then you belong with Nebuchadnezzar and his like). Maharam Schick continues: "Even though this verse was said about the nations, certainly also transgressors of the Sabbath in public and those who deny the commandments of God written in the Torah [are included] . . . we are warned by the Torah to be separated from them by a *qal va-homer* (deriving a more serious lesson from a less serious case), for it is permissible to accept sacrifices and contributions from a non-Jew, but it is forbidden to do so from apostates." Putting separation from apostates on the same plane as distancing oneself from non-Jews clearly reveals that Maharam Schick intended that one actually distance oneself from apostates. This is further made clear in the continuation, when the author adds that, aside from the evidence in the sources for the obligation to secede, experience also proves "that even if the great ones who join them are not ruined, the next generations become ruined like them." How different this view is from that of R. Hirsch, who contended that while one should distance oneself from heresy and apostasy, he should maintain continued contact with those people who are classified as heretics and apostates.

A basic difference also exists in the search for sources in support of the secession thesis. Maharam Schick does not differentiate between actual halakhic sources and aggadic ones, just as his method on all the previous occasions when he had cited proofs of the obligation to secede. The reliance on the *Sifra*, despite its seemingly halakhic wording—a *qal va-homer* from non-Jews to apostates—is revealed to be only aggadic as well. The statement in the *Sifra* is cited in various *midrashim* and by Maimonides in his *Code*, where the practical significance of the warning is spelled out. The midrash states: "All activities of Israelites are distinguished from the nations of the world, in their plowing and sowing and harvesting and threshing." In other words, Jews are different from the nations in all their activities, in that they observe the commandments connected with these activities.[56] Maimonides sees the separation as referring to a scrupulous adherence to the prohibition against following the customs of the nations: "He should not resemble them . . . The Israelite should, on the contrary, be distinguished from them and recognizable by the way he dresses and in his other activities, just as he is distinguished from them by his knowledge and his principles.[57] In both interpretations the *Sifra*'s statement is an admonition to adhere to the commandments given to Israel. By ignoring the interpretation of the Midrash and Maimonides, Maharam Schick creates a new positive commandment, the commandment of separation.

R. Samson Raphael Hirsch was wary of such proofs. In his sermon in the synagogue in which he wished to fire his listeners with enthusiasm for the idea of separation, he did use a homiletic device, according to a contemporary witness. He quoted the *Mekhilta* on the verse (Exodus 12:21) "Draw out and take for you a lamb," and explained: "Draw your hands back from idolatry and adhere to the commandments," giving as examples the Golden Calf and Elijah's battle with the prophets of the Baal on Mount Carmel.[58] However, in his controversy with R. Bamberger, he built his proofs according to the halakhic method: His rival could challenge his arguments, but could not reject them out of hand, with the claim that they are merely *aggadah*.

This seems to be a world turned upside-down. Maharam Schick, the great halakhist, relies on *aggadah*, while R. Samson Raphael Hirsch, who was viewed by the public as one whose major strength lay in providing the ideological groundwork of Orthodoxy, relies on halakhic sources alone. There is an explanation for this paradoxical situation. Maharam Schick addressed a public still rooted in Jewish tradition in all its aspects. It was isolated from the non-Jewish environment not only by virtue of religious uniqueness, in the narrow sense of the word, but by its language, its customs, and its popular culture. These ostensibly neutral elements, which became signs of Jewish singularity, enjoyed a quasi-religious status. A discernible existential break was created when one part of Jewish society divested itself of these outward signs of Jewishness, and rejected the obligation to observe certain commandments. The religious leadership, which wished to give organizational expression to this break, had good reason to anticipate that the public would be responsive. Therefore, it did not so much need formal proofs of the requirement to secede, as it did means to encourage the people to overcome the inhibitions and difficulties in their path; the use of aggadic sources, which play on the emotions, was the means.

R. Samson Raphael Hirsch's situation was entirely different. By his time, German Jewry had already divested itself of the cultural signs of Judaism, language, dress, custom and the like. There was no great difference in this matter between the circles that had abandoned the obligations of religion and those that adhered to it to whatever extent. If some survivors of the earlier generations attempted to preserve some of the cultural signs they had inherited from their ancestors, R. Samson Raphael Hirsch did not admit the justice of their aspirations. He accepted the judgment of history that had decreed extinction for popular Jewish culture, in all its external manifestations. He even seems to have viewed the adherence to popular culture negatively, for it blurred the line between folklore and formal halakhic requirements. According to his doctrine,

Judaism is based upon one thing alone, loyalty to the directives of the *halakhah*, *gesetzestreu* as he called it. *Halakhah* alone could thus serve him as the basis for the obligation to secede. The principle of freedom of conscience served him in his efforts to convince the outside world to permit secession. Within the Jewish community, however, his attempt to bring his followers to the awareness that their religious conscience should prohibit them from belonging to the mother congregation had to be based on the *halakhah*. But Hirsch's distinction between sectarians and apostates, as opposed to heresy and apostasy, created an unprecedented situation, for which no direct proofs could be found in the sources. On this point, Maharam Schick and his colleagues had an easier task than Hirsch, for they identified the Neologs and Reform with the heretics and apostates mentioned in the sources, and could claim that what was decreed against the former applied to the latter as well. Moreover, they did not rely exclusively on halakhic sources. They also upheld their right and obligation as Torah leaders to enact decrees according to the needs of the time (*migdar milta*), in order to strengthen the faith, as had the leaders of earlier generations. They claimed that their right to enact decrees regarding separation from the "sinners" superseded any possible proofs to the contrary, for only isolation from them could defend against their pernicious influence. Hirsch, on the other hand, did not decree isolation from the surrounding non-Jewish environment, nor social isolation from those Jews who divested themselves of the commandments. He could therefore rely only on the analogy to be drawn from the isolation of actual heretics and apostates to secession from heresy and apostasy in the abstract. But this analogy was far from being self-evident, and it should not surprise us to learn that his two anonymous critics attacked him for inventing a new commandment that was only the product of his imagination.[59] One of them even accused him of taking the name of the *halakhah* in vain by using halakhic sources improperly: "His honor's problem concerning secession perhaps has far-reaching significance as a religious-social problem, but has no halakhic-religious basis."

Hirsch had crushing replies to use against R. Bamberger, who employed the weapons of a halakhist. However, the decision in the public arena was based on the thinking of plain people, such as that which the anonymous critics voiced. The small number of members of his flock who accepted Hirsch's ruling was clear evidence that Hirsch had great success in spreading only one part of his doctrine of "Torah and *derekh eretz*": the combination of strict loyalty to a religious way of life and far-reaching openness to the surrounding modern culture. The second part of his doctrine, the concentration of its adherents in an independent Orthodox community, was not conveyed successfully to his followers.

Proof of this state of affairs came unexpectedly in the wake of the negotiations with the administration of the congregation. The congregation demanded, among other things, that the congregational institutions that were to provide for the needs of the Orthodox in the future would operate under the supervision of a Torah authority to be appointed for this task. The appointment was offered to Markus Horovitz, Esriel Hildesheimer's leading student, then rabbi of Gnesen, in the Posen district. Horovitz would only accept the appointment on condition that his post would include responsibility for the spiritual leadership of the pious who had remained in the congregation. Horovitz was born in hassidic northern Hungary, but after studying in the *yeshivot* of the area, including some time spent with R. Jeremiah Löw in Ujhely, he came to Eisenstadt. There he found a mentor in Hildesheimer and adopted his doctrines, and the two men forged close ties.[60] Horovitz accompanied his rabbi to the Congress in Budapest, and at Hildesheimer's request reported on it in *Israelit*. He also expressed his unequivocal opinion against secession.[61] When his teacher moved to Berlin, he went with him, and became one of the first graduates of the rabbinic seminary, receiving a doctorate from the University of Tübingen at the same time. After the congregational committee in Frankfurt accepted his conditions, Horovitz leaned towards accepting the appointment, but not without first consulting his rabbi. Hildesheimer advised him emphatically against accepting the post.[62] The rabbi and student were not of the same mind on the question of secession from the general congregations. This difference of opinion had already been obvious during the struggle for the ratification of the secession law in the Parliament. Hildesheimer was one of the leaders of the struggle, while Horovitz refused to take part in it.[63] He also preserved his independence about the appointment in Frankfurt, and accepted it despite his rabbi's vehement opposition. Hildesheimer had a special reason for opposing the appointment. The creation of a post for an Orthodox rabbi within the framework of the congregation could only be interpreted as an affront to Hirsch's efforts, and Hildesheimer did not wish to add to his pain. Horovitz, for his part, considered leading the observant among the congregation a religious mission, and attempted to fulfill this mission by positive means—by establishing institutions that met all the halakhic criteria, by bringing people closer to religion, and by providing religious inspiration of an intellectual nature, in accordance with his many talents. He was careful not to challenge Hirsch's status, and there is no record of any discord between them.[64] Nonetheless, Horovitz's activities cast a shadow on Hirsch's path. If Hirsch was considered the founder of secessionist Orthodoxy, Horovitz's way won the name of congregational Orthodoxy (*Gemeindeorthodoxie*). It demonstrated, at least superficially, that the existence of religious life according to halakhic criteria was not conditional upon secession from the general congregation.

Did R. Samson Raphael Hirsch have any misgivings or regrets about his unsuccessful campaign? We have no information on this question. In contrast, we do have information about his reaction to the results of the division in Hungary, in which he had been involved. In the summer of 1881, Hirsch was asked to rule about a controversy that had arisen in the congregation of Högyész, in southern Hungary, concerning the secession of the Orthodox minority from this congregation, which described itself as a Status Quo congregation. This caused Hirsch to read Maharam Schick's responsa on this issue, which had been published a year or two previously, shortly before the death of its author in 1879. To his sorrow, Hirsch found that he could not agree with the view of the leading scholar of the generation in this case. Let us examine the differences of opinion between these two personages on this test case.

The rabbi of the city, Elijah Goitein, described the course of events in Högyész, and we learn of the details from Hirsch's responsum, which alone has survived.[65] R. Goitein's congregation did not join either the Congress organization or the Orthodox organization, that is, it remained Status Quo. As such, its statutes had the provision that the Shulhan Arukh was to be the basis for congregational activities, and R. Goitein attested that these guidelines were actually adhered to—unlike other congregations bearing the same designation, in which a gap gradually developed between theory and practice[66] (which was a major reason why the term Status Quo had become a pejorative appellation among the Orthodox). Now some of the members of the congregation wished the congregation to join the Orthodox organization. When most of the members of the congregation refused, the minority sought to secede and form its own Orthodox congregation, a step permitted by the laws of the state. The question addressed to R. Hirsch was whether this was permitted according to the *halakhah*.

According to the questioner, those who wanted division relied on the responsum of Maharam Schick (*Responsa, O.H. no. 307*) addressed to R. Meir Perles about the controversy in Kassa, in which he first denounced the Status Quo. The editor of the responsa omitted the name of the community in which the events occurred, and the situation there was actually quite different from that of R. Goitein's city. For those who supported division in Högyész, Maharam Schick's statement that the Status Quo had removed themselves from the circle of the pious, and that the latter should have no contact with them, was sufficient. R. Goitein, on the other hand, pointed to two other responsa of Maharam Schick (*O.H.*, no. 34, and *Y.D.*, no. 14) from which he understood that Maharam Schick's directive was not intended for a congregation like his, in which observance of the laws of the Shulhan Arukh was guaranteed.[67] As stated, Hirsch read these responsa in order to understand the author's position on division, and found it difficult and incomprehensible, so that he was forced to differ with Maharam Schick and reject his view.

In his first responsum (*O.H.*, no. 34), Maharam Schick dealt with the case of a congregation—here too the name has been omitted by the editor—in which the minority of members wished to accept the Orthodox statutes and establish their own congregation. The rabbi of the congregation forbade this, relying on the *halakhah* that the members of a city may compel each other to supply their public, religious, and civil needs. Maharam Schick then ruled there that "*Hoshen Mishpat*, chapter 63, explains that a congregation is called a partnership," and just as business partners are permitted to dissolve the partnership under certain circumstances, so can the members of a congregation. And there is no better reason than the conflict in the aforesaid community, where the minority fulfills its religious obligation by accepting the statutes of the Orthodox organization, and the majority, led by the local rabbi, stands fast in its refusal.[68] This incident apparently occurred at the beginning of the movement for division.

One year before his death, in the summer of 1878, Maharam Schick returned to the question of division (no. 14 in *Y.D.*). This time it was "Sefardim," that is, hassidim, in the Ujhely congregation who wished to secede, and the responsum was addressed to R. Eliezer Löw, the son of R. Jeremiah Löw, who had taken his father's place as rabbi of the city. He was not acceptable to the hassidim and they went off on their own, despite the protests of the leaders of the congregation and its rabbi. The controversy spread beyond the boundaries of the congregation, and the rabbis of the district took opposing positions. Maharam Schick was asked about this issue and refused to answer, saying he had no opinion on the matter. When R. Löw himself insisted, he disclosed his view, once again resorting to the classification of the congregation as a partnership, which the minority has the right to quit for a good reason, "and according to the 'Sefardim,' they have many reasons."[69] He added that this permission to secede, which was granted by the government, is therefore "a 'law of the land' . . . [by which means] many devout Jews have founded congregations of their own and escaped from the wicked." Although this is not the case in R. Löw's congregation, where the division is only between hassidim and Ashkenazim, "in any case, the Sages did not deal with specific instances, but gave a general rule."[70] Once dissolution of the partnership upon which the congregation is based was permitted because of the conflict between the Orthodox and Neologs, it was also allowed in the controversy between Ashkenazim and hassidim.

R. Samson Raphael Hirsch saw these discussions, and was profoundly surprised. He took it for granted that Maharam Schick had arrived at his conclusions on the basis of halakhic considerations, and that the essence of his idea was the classification of the congregation as a partnership, whose members can establish or dissolve it at will. But he rejected this analysis categorically, as did the anonymous rabbi who was mentioned in Maharam Schick's first responsum (*O.H.*, no. 34). This rabbi also cited the *halakhah* that the members of a city may compel each other to provide their shared needs, and Hirsch added many proofs that the partnership of members of a congregation is imposed upon them by law, and is not the same as a business partnership, which is initially created by the free will of its members:

> And the Torah gave power to the public in a city or to the officials of the city appointed

by the public for this purpose, to enact statutes and decree decrees . . . to preserve the Torah and commandments . . . and there is good reason for this, for the individual has no power to observe the Torah and the commandments by himself . . . but only by joining a public body.[71]

This concept of the essence of the congregation is one of the cornerstones of Hirsch's doctrine. Divine revelation places the burden of the commandments not on the individual, but on the public. This is certainly no novelty, if the reference is to the nation of Israel in general, and in its own land. Hirsch however identified the public with the local congregation, a product of life in exile. I have noted elsewhere that Hirsch often quoted the verse (Deut. 33:4): "Moses commanded to us the Torah, the inheritance of the community of Jacob." He made it the motto of an article dealing with the essence of the congregation and, as emerges from his commentary on the Pentateuch, he believed, most surprisingly, that the word "community" meant the actual "congregation."[72] We are therefore not surprised to find that he used this verse in his argument against Maharam Schick: "And not to individuals did God entrust his holy Torah, but 'an inheritance for the community of Jacob' did the Lord say."[73]

Hirsch's reservations concerning Maharam Schick's demand that the pious congregation must join the national Orthodox organization by virtue of the decisions of the Hungarian rabbis, are based on this concept that the individual congregation carries the burden of the Torah. The individual congregation has a well-defined status in the *halakhah*. It must join the national organization only if it sent a representative to the organization when it was established.[74] In light of these considerations, Hirsch replied to R. Goitein that the congregation's refusal to join the national organization could not serve as an excuse for the minority to leave it, and moreover, that they were obligated to help shoulder the burden of the congregation and take part in its communal life. At the most, the congregation could consider adding to the name "Status Quo" the adjective "Orthodox," in order to avoid criticism.[75]

The question still remains, was a master of the *halakhah* like Maharam Schick not aware of these difficulties and others? *Hoshen Mishpat*, Chapter 163, does not provide proof that the members of a congregation are considered as partners; and even if this was said elsewhere, the clear meaning of this statement is that the members of the congregation have a share in the property of the congregation, and not that the congregation itself constitutes a partnership.[76] Particularly surprising is the statement that the government's sanction of division makes this a law of the land. The source noted by Maharam Schick is *Hoshen Mishpat*, chapter 3, but this source cites the ruling of the Ribash that if a king appoints a *dayyan* who is qualified, he may accept the appointment. Since appointment of judges is one of the functions of the king, the appointment of a *dayyan* is subsumed under the category of "the law of the land." Congregational division is permitted by the laws of the land, but it is certainly not a requirement. What does this situation have to do with the "law of the land"? We can say with confidence that had this been an ordinary case of civil or ritual law, Maharam Shick would not have built his ruling on such flimsy grounds. But in such cases the halakhic proofs were the only bases for ruling, while regarding the public questions at issue, only R. Samson Raphael Hirsch believed that his ruling was based on halakhic foundations. Maharam Schick and his colleagues in Hungary were well aware that in such matters their authority to enact decrees was the crucial factor. So it came about that this secondary source became the crucial one, and halakhic proofs were adduced only in order to buttress their decrees. There was therefore no need for those who cited them to concern themselves greatly with their applicability and validity.

We learn from a letter by Hirsch's son-in-law R. Solomon Breuer, at that time rabbi of Pápa in Hungary, that Hirsch showed the text of his responsum to R. Goitein to the rabbis Gottlieb Fischer and Shalom Kutna, and that these rabbis brought it to the attention of other halakhists.[77] The reactions were understandably hostile, for Hirsch's responsum constituted a defense brief for the Status Quo position, which was shunned and defamed by the entire Orthodox camp in Hungary. Hirsch was deterred, decided to file the responsum away, and even forbade the addressee to make use of it. R. Breuer was at first surprised at his father-in-law's retreat, for he thought his arguments justified and well-supported. However, after further thought he justified Hirsch's fear of controversy: "I know our allies well, my dear father-in-law; you have escaped much aggravation." There is indeed no doubt that had he published this responsum, the Orthodox establishment in Hungary would have had no mercy upon their former ally, and would have dealt with Hirsch as "a rebellious elder." Thus, the responsum was filed away, and was unknown until its recent publication by Mordechai Breuer, Hirsch's great-grandson.[78]

These two figures, Maharam Schick and R. Samson Raphael Hirsch, remained linked in the mind of the next generation as two fighters for the same goal. This is well illustrated in a scene found in one of the books written by Isaac Breuer, Hirsch's grandson and spiritual heir, who among other things fostered the idea of the independent Orthodox congregation as a miniature kingdom of Torah and *halakhah*. His book, *Der neue Kusari* (The New Kuzari), was a narrative designed to win followers to this idea.[79] It is the tale of a youth from a home devoid of Jewish content, who by his own efforts becomes aware of the essence of Judaism. In his search, the youth meets representatives of the different camps in Judaism, beginning with a Reform rabbi and ending with the secular and religious Zionists, but he is still confused and unsatisfied. He already knows that Torah and commandments give meaning to life, but the little that he has learned has made him realize that the Torah was not given to the individual Jew, but is a law intended for an entire community. Now he asks himself if such a community exists in reality. He discusses this problem with the rabbi of the congregational Orthodox community (*Gemeindeorthodoxie*), whose house is the last stop in his searches. The rabbi describes to him the advantages of the Orthodox part of the congregation over the Reform part. This explanation enrages the youth: He cannot understand how this community can remain in the same framework as the Reform community, for this contradicts the demand that the Torah rule the entire community. The youth then remembers that he has heard of a separate community in the city, which is entirely subject to the Divine law. The rabbi cannot but admit that such a community, which battles for its independence, exists. "And you, your honor the rabbi," cries the youth, "on principle you admit the justice of their battle, but you do not take part in it! Don't you feel like a traitor?" Upon hearing these words, the rabbi, who of course knows the history of the confrontation between the Orthodox and their opponents, retreats and says in a soft voice, as if speaking to himself: "Are these not the words of Maharam Schick, 'For they did not come to the help of the Lord against the mighty'"? This verse from the Song of Deborah (Judges 5:23)[80] was used by Maharam Schick in Hungary to denounce the Status Quo congregations. And so the innocent youth, even before reaching the congregation of R. Samson Raphael Hirsch, unknowingly identified with the view of the great scholar from another land, whose name he had never heard.

The Orthodox aspiration to independence was limited to two countries alone, Hungary and Germany. It spread outside of this framework with the establishment of *Agudat Israel*, two years before World War I. The founders of *Agudat Israel* wished to unite the pious throughout the world to act independently, without any link with organizations that do not uphold Orthodox principles. The idea originated among the members of *Adath Jeschurun* in Frankfurt, among them Solomon Breuer, the rabbi of the community and the son-in-law of R. Samson Raphael Hirsch, and his son Isaac, the main ideologue of secession. Remaining loyal to this principle, they wished to prevent the "congregation Orthodox" from taking part in the organization.[81] After World War I, in the wake of the Balfour Declaration, the arena of battle moved to Palestine. The general religious Jewish public organized as *Knesset Israel*, while broad circles in the Old Yishuv, who appointed R. Joseph Hayyim Sonnenfeld as their spiritual leader, strove for organizational independence with the active assistance of the ideologue Isaac Breuer, and with the inspiration of the worldwide *Agudat Israel*. Breuer wrote an entire book to explain the Ashkenazi community's demand for independence to the Mandatory government. His arguments are a summary of his ideology about the Orthodox congregation as a miniature kingdom of Torah.[82] Breuer even visited Palestine during the prolonged struggle, and cooperated with the local leader, R. Sonnenfeld. Sonnenfeld was probably not interested in following the sophisticated arguments of his partner from Frankfurt, however; the tradition of the Hungarian rabbis was sufficient for him.

Sonnenfeld had spent his youth there at the time of the Orthodox struggle, and had been closely associated with two of its leaders, the Ketav Sofer and R. Abraham Schag. He came with the latter to Palestine after the struggle ended in the victory of the Orthodox.[83]

The meeting and cooperation between the representatives of the two camps, the Hungarian and German, a meeting that nurtured the secessionist tendency, is one of historical significance. As we know, their struggle was successful. R. Sonnenfeld's community was recognized as an independent Jewish entity, and the secession of the Orthodox was thereby given an official seal of approval. Even the two major trials that the Jewish nation has undergone since then, the horrors of the Holocaust and the experience of the establishment of the State of Israel, ostensibly watershed events, were not sufficient grounds for second thoughts. The breach that was created with the secession of the Orthodox did not heal; it has likely even widened and deepened in Orthodox ideology of all types.

Are the spokesmen for and nurturers of isolationist concepts among the Orthodox in our day aware of their link to the creators of the split, and the reality that served as the background to their deeds and decisions? Those whose roots are in the past generally have a certain image of the nature of that past. The historian cannot rely on images of this sort, but is also not interested in shattering these images. A historian who approaches the past in order to influence the present has worked in vain. My description of the history of the division in the Jewish congregations is not meant to change prevalent ideologies held by the public in either direction. If, however, some of these ideologues will reexamine their perceptions in the light of what I have written here, this will be a desirable—although unanticipated—by-product of my work.

Notes

Works frequently cited have been identified by the following abbreviations:

AZJ	Allegemeine Zeitung des Judenthums
BCH	Ben Chananja
BT	Babylonian Talmud
CZ	Congress-Zeitung
H.M.	Hoshen Mishpat
IMIT	Izraelita Magyar Irodalmi Társulat
JSS	Jewish Social Studies
MZs	Magyar Zsidó
MZsL	Magyar Zsidó Lexikon
MZsSz	Magyar Zsidó Szemle
O.H.	Oreh Hayim
PT	Palestinian Talmud
Y.D.	Yore Deah

1. The First Signs of Conflict within the Community (pp. 7–19)

1. Most of these articles are now found in English translation in: *Divine Law in Human Hands: A Study in Halakhic Flexibility* (in press).
2. J. Katz, *Tradition and Crisis: Jewish Society at the End of the Middle Ages* (New York, 1993), 271. For an in-depth treatment of Mendelssohn's view, see A. Altmann, *Moses Mendelssohn, A Biographical Study* (Alabama, 1973), 518–597.
3. For the establishment of the *consistoire* and its functions, see S. Schwarzfuchs, *Napoleon, the Jews and the Sanhedrin* (London/Boston/Henley, 1979), 115–142.
4. Basic facts are given in L. Auerbach, *Das Judenthum und seine Bekenner in Preussen und in den anderen deutschen Staaten* (Berlin, 1890).
5. For the status of the *kehillah* and its functions in the *ancien regime*, see Katz, *Tradition and Crisis* (note 2), chapter 2, 9–11.
6. See my article: "The Controversy over the Temple in Hamburg and the Rabbinical Assembly in Braunschweig" (note 1).
7. This argument was advanced in an article which we shall discuss in chapter 11.
8. J. R. Berkowitz, *The Shaping of Jewish Identity in Nineteenth Century France* (Detroit, 1989), 118–126, 230–239. And see note 10.
9. See my article: "The Controversy over the *Mezizah*" (note 1).
10. For an exhaustive description of events in France, see P. Cohen Albert, *The Modernization of French Jewry: Consistory and Community in the Nineteenth Century* (Hanover, N.H., 1977), 51–55; according to the index, "Minyanim" and "Orthodoxy."
11. The broadest and most exhaustive description of Jacobson's career is still to be found in the study: J. R. Marcus, *Israel Jacobson, The Founder of the Reform Movement in Judaism* (Cincinnati, 1972). For a more recent analysis, see M. Meyer, *Re-*

sponse to Modernity. A History of the Reform Movement in Judaism (Oxford, 1988), 30–43.
12. See both Marcus and Meyer (note 11). For details of the opposition of the conservatives, see B. H. Auerbach, *Geschichte der israelitischen Gemeinde Halberstadt* (Halberstadt, 1866), 139–143, 215–226.
13. Meyer (note 11), 43–53.
14. The debates in the assembly of the estates in Würtemberg and the wording of the laws concerning Jews are summarized in I. M. Jost, *Neuere Geschichte der Israeliten in der ersten Hälfte des XIX Jahrhunderts*, vol. 1 (Breslau, n.d.), 158–192.
15. The constitution of the Authority is found in the collection A. Gunzenhauser, *Sammlung der Gesetze, Verordnungen, Verfügungen und Erlasse betreffend die Kirchenverfassung und die religiösen Einrichtungen der Israeliten in Würtemberg* (Stuttgart, 1909), 11–16.
16. Ibid., 15, paragraph 25.
17. No biography of Maier has been written; for details of his wide-ranging activities within the Reform movement, see D. Philipson, *The Reform Movement in Judaism*, 2nd ed. (Cincinnati, 1930), according to the index.
18. *Gottesdienstordnung für die Synagogen des Königreichs Würtemberg* (Stuttgart, 1838). A full English translation is found in J. J. Petuchowsky, *Prayerbook Reform in Europe* (New York, 1968), 113.
19. *AZJ* of April 7, 1845, 216–217. The prohibition against holding a private service is found in the first paragraph of the constitution (note 18).
20. Gabiah ben Psisa [L. Stern], *Wohin kommen wir. Ein Wort an die gesetzestreuen Israeliten Würtembergs* (Mainz, 1864), 18.
21. The constitution of the council was published in *AZJ*, 1839, nos. 80–81.
22. Ibid., paragraph 18 of the constitution (333).
23. Holdheim remained a controversial figure among his biographers as well, as L. Donath noted in *Geschichte der Juden in Mecklenburg* (Leipzig, 1874), 229–236. I think that there is still room to describe the man against the background of his time.
24. For an English translation of the regulations, see Petuchowsky (note 18), 117–119. They differ from those of Würtemberg in minor details alone.
25. A notice to this effect is found in the *Orient*, April 9, 1844, 106. The writer requests the opinion of experts about this reform.
26. Holdheim's response is found in the *Orient*, April 30, 1844, 187–188.
27. Holdheim's report was published in the *Orient*, June 27 to August 25, 1843. The news items cited are found on pages 222, 253.
28. Donath (note 23), 226–227.
29. The protest is found in the *Orient*, July 2, 1844; for the responsiveness of the government see the *Orient*, September 17, 1844, 211–212.
30. *Der treue Zions-Wächter* of February 2, 1847.
31. Details of this are found in Donath (note 23), 237–244; and in my article "The Struggle over Preserving the Rite of Circumcision" (note 1).
32. The article is: "Kleine Bilder aus der jüdischen Gegenwart, von J. Die Einführung einer Synagogenordnung, eine Geschichte von Vielen," *Jeschurun* 5 (1859), 648–658.
33. Ibid., 658.

34. See my article (note 31).
35. Note 30.
36. The last article is from February 21, 1846.
37. This idea was already expressed in an abstract way in the Hamburg controversy, and more vigorously in the Braunschweig polemic. See (note 6), "The Controversy over the Temple in Hamburg and the Braunschweig Assembly." R. Samson Raphael Hirsch's reaction to the decisions of the Braunschweig Assembly is typical: "For if your words will bear fruit, this time the house of Israel will be torn into two parts . . . There will be no maintenance of our shared covenant, and in tears we shall part from each other" (Z. H. Lehren, ed., *Torat ha-Qenaot* [Amsterdam, 1845], 5b). But these were random thoughts, which did not clarify the theoretical and practical aspects of the idea, as Hirsch himself did later on, as we shall see.
38. The author quotes the work of Solomon Judah Rapoport (*Shir*), who in his address to the Reform Rabbinical Assembly in Frankfurt in 1845, warned of the destructive consequences of division to the status of the congregations. See *Der treue Zions-Wächter* of February 10, 1846.
39. Ibid., in the February 17 issue.
40. Someone with the initals D. Y. critiqued his ideas on the practical level in the issues of March 10 and 17, in an article entitled "Das Schisma."
41. These words were apparently aimed at people and events which the reader of the times had no difficulty in identifying: "Hast Du es gehört mein würdiger Landesrabbiner H. zu E. und Du mein Trauter E. in S., hast Du es vernommen, jenes schreckerregende Gesetz?"; see *Der treue Zions-Wächter* of January, 1849.

2. Breslau-Style Compromise, Frankfurt-Style Conflicts (pp. 20–28)

1. Jost (chapter 1, note 14), vol. 3, 169.
2. M. Brann, "Die schlesische Judenheit vor und nach dem Edikt vom 11. März 1812," *Jahres-Bericht des jüdisch-theologischen Seminars Fränkel'scher Stiftung für das Jahr 1912* (Breslau, 1913), 25–27.
3. For a short summary of the Tiktin-Geiger controversy, see ibid., 28–32. A description from Geiger's perspective appears in the biography written by his son: L. Geiger, *Abraham Geiger's Leben in Breslau* (Breslau, 1889), 107–114. The primary sources for the controversy are *Bericht des Ober-Vorsteher-Collegis an die Mitglieder der hiesigen Israeliten-Gemeinde über die gegenwärtig vorliegende Rabbinats-Angelegenheit* (Breslau, 1842); S. A. Tiktin, *Darstellung des Sachverhältnisses in seiner hiesigen Rabbinats-Angelegenheit* (Breslau, 1842); the response to Tiktin was published in the second report of the congregational administration, Breslau 1842.
4. The opinions were published in Tiktin (note 3), 23–31.
5. *Rabbinische Gutachten über die Verträglichkeit der freien Forschung mit dem Rabbineramt* (Breslau, 1842–1843).
6. *Schreiben der grossen Mehrzahl der Mitglieder der Breslauer israelitischen Gemeinde* (Breslau, 1846).
7. Jost (note 1), 182.

8. The last stage of this controversy was described and documented in M. A. Meyer, "Rabbi Gedaliah Tiktin and the Orthodox Segment of the Breslau Community 1845–1854," *Michael*, 2 (1973), 92–107.
9. For the founding of the Philanthropin see R. Liberles, *Religious Conflict in Social Context: The Resurgence of Orthodox Judaism in Frankfurt am Main* (Westport/London, 1985), 24–26 and the sources cited there. The school was founded primarily to meet the needs of poor children, but within a short time turned into a general educational institution. About the Freemason lodge, see J. Katz, *Jews and Freemasons in Europe 1723–1939* (Cambridge, Mass., 1970), 54–72.
10. Katz, *Jews and Freemasons*, 91–95.
11. For the struggle of the *beit din* to preserve circumcision, see my article (chapter 1, note 31).
12. The quarrel over the two synagogues is described in Liberles (note 9), 32–35. Liberles should be corrected on one point. One of the synagogues was called the "Frauensynagoge," and he therefore assumed that it was a synagogue for women only (see page 241, note 33), which is not possible, for a wall separated the two buildings; the women could therefore not join the male prayer, and there was certainly no such thing as a separate women's prayer. In my opinion, these were actually two separate synagogues, and so it seems in all of the negotiations over their future, but a women's section existed in only one of them, and therefore it had the aforesaid name.
13. *Actenstücke die hiesige israelitische Religions-Gemeinde betreffend* (Frankfurt, 1839), 31, and see pp. 32–33.
14. Ibid., 5–7.
15. About Fuld see A. Fuld, *Beth Aaron* (Frankfurt am Main, 1890), introduction, written by Mordechai Halevi (Markus) Horovitz, i–vii.
16. For the affluent status of the founders of Hirsch's congregation, see Liberles (note 9), 95–99, and see note 21, for a contemporary witness.
17. The memorandum was published in *Nachlath Z'wi* 7 (1937), 237.
18. Liberles (note 9), 94–98. The original debunker of the legend—whom Liberles acknowledges, while adding his own contribution—is Simi Japhet. See S. Japhet, "The Secession Movement of S. R. Hirsch," *Historia Judaica* 10 (1948), 118.
19. For Stein's reformist tendencies, see Liberles (note 9), 87–88.
20. For the choice of Sachs, and his eventual refusal, see ibid., 110–11.
21. *Israelit, Samson Raphael Hirsch—Jubiläums-Nummer*, 1908, 36.
22. I do not recall where I saw this question formulated; in any case it deserves to be posed.
23. The request is made in an 1858 memorandum to the Senate, which was presented in the name of the community's administration: *An Hohen Senat der freien Stadt Frankfurt. Gehorsamste Vorstellung von Seiten des Vorstandes der Israelitischen Religionsgesellschaft* (Frankurt, 1858).
24. [S. R. Hirsch], *Die Religion im Bunde mit dem Fortschritt von einem Schwarzen* (Frankfurt am Main, 1854).
25. Mendel Hirsch's statements are included in a series of articles in *Israelit*, 1897, which were later published as a book. See M. Hirsch, *Samson Raphael Hirsch und die israelitische Religionsgesellschaft zu Frankfurt am Main* (Mainz, 1897), 83–88. Li-

berles (note 9), 180, assumed correctly that Hirsch identified with the content of the memorandum, but was not aware of the proof that he himself had composed it.
26. He opens with: "Mehr war damals nicht zu erreichen."
27. *Jeschurun* 1 (1855), 43–44.
28. *An Hohen Senat der freien Stadt Frankfurt . . . das Verhältnis der Mitglieder der Religionsgesellschaft zur israelitischen Gemeinde betreffend* (Frankfurt, 1858), 4.
29. *An Hohen Senat der freien Stadt Frankfurt . . . gehorsamste Vorstellung und Bitte von Seiten des Vorstandes der Israelitischen Religonsgesellschaft dahier, das Verhältniss ihrer Mitglieder zu der hiesigen Israelitischen Gemeinde . . . betreffend* (Frankfurt, 1858), 6–7.

3. Quiet Cultural Adaptation (pp. 31–39)

1. I see no need to give sources for the data concerning Hungarian history, except where it is relevant to Hungarian Jewry. I will similarly forgo providing references for the basic facts about the history of Hungarian Jewry. The Hebrew reader will find these in the *Pinqas ha-Kehillot, Hungaria* (Jerusalem, 1976), introduction by N. Katzburg. In Hungarian, see Zs. Grossmann, *A magyar zsidók a XIX század közepén* (Budapest, 1917).
2. Michael K. Silber, *Roots of the Schism in Hungarian Jewry* (in Hebrew) (Ph.D. diss., The Hebrew University, Jerusalem, 1985).
3. Leopold Löw published the Hatam Sofer's memorandum of October 25, 1832, in which he requested that Jewish community officials and their rabbis be authorized to enlist the assistance of the local authorities in order to enforce the observance of religious laws, in L. Löw, *Zur Neueren Geschichte der Juden in Ungarn* (Budapest, 1874), 153–155.
4. Kossuth's view is examined at length in Silber (note 2), 150–158.
5. Y. Ben-David, "The Beginnings of Modern Jewish Society in Hungary during the First Half of the Nineteenth Century" (in Hebrew), *Zion* 17 (1952), 101–128.
6. The text of the governmental order of October 25, 1852, to disband the Reform society and to close its synagogue was published by Löw (note 3), 186–187. The order is also cited in *AZJ*, December 6, 1852, 597. According to the reporter, the order was given at the request of the leadership of the Jewish community. See chapter 5, note 6, concerning Löw's authorship of this article.
7. Nationalist Hungarian historiography depicted the period of neo-absolutist rule as one of suppression. Modern research has reached a more balanced appreciation of the period, and as a result, its major impact on the life of Hungarian Jews is being clarified. See P. J. Hidas, *The Metamorphosis of a Social Class in Hungary during the Reign of Young Franz Joseph* (New York, 1977).
8. The number of schools and their situation is discussed in detail in Silber (note 2), 214–215.
9. The statements here and below are based on Löw (note 3), 214–225.
10. P. J. Adler, "The Introduction of Public Schooling for the Jews of Hungary (1849–1869)," *JSS*, 26 (1974), 124, n. 14.

11. Simon Bacher wrote in *AZJ*, May 19, 1856, 282–284, that in northern Hungary, the Jews were the only ones who knew German. The officials of Austrian extraction who served in these districts could find no one except Jews to teach their children.
12. For the statistics see Silber (note 2), 114–115.
13. *MZsL*, 58, 536, 629.
14. See M. Eliav, "Rabbi Esriel Hildesheimer and his Influence on Hungarian Jewry" (in Hebrew), *Zion* 27 (1962), 61. For Hildesheimer's remark, see I. Hildesheimer, *Erster Bericht der Lehranstalt für Rabbinats-Kandidaten zu Eisenstadt* (Wien, 1858), 26. Elsewhere (see chapter 11, note 11) Hildesheimer relates in passing how he succeeded in setting up a financial basis for the school. He assembled the parents of the students, asked them to write down how much they paid their Jewish teachers or tutors, and proved that the total sum would be sufficient to establish the school.
15. Silber (note 2), 220, estimates that the ratio of the number of children studying in the schools in the two parts of the country was one to ten.

4. The Emergence and Characteristics of the Neolog Movement (pp. 40–47)

1. Löw (chapter 3, note 3), 217.
2. Ibid., 223–224.
3. Ibid., 274–275. He wrote this in the early 1870s, after the Congress. The constitution ratified at the Congress adopted many elements of Löw's proposal, in particular those relating to the establishment of a central national organization. In the interim, however, Löw himself had gone even farther, maintaining that the conditions of freedom of religion, ostensibly guaranteed by Hungary's achievement of independence in the wake of the compromise with Austria, should imply that each community was free to take care of its own needs. This is the basis for Löw's self-justifying remark concerning political conditions in 1851. He also took into account the religious tendency of the times, which both the government and the general Jewish public supported.
4. Ibid., 252.
5. Löw published his opinions concerning various questions put to him by the government or the communities in the periodical *Ben Chananja*, which he edited, and his son reprinted them in his father's *Gesammelte Schriften*, vols. 1–5 (Szeged, 1899–1900), iii, 218–279, 283–304.
6. Schwab, like Löw, was from Moravia. He studied with Mordechai Banet in Nickolsburg, as well as with the Hatam Sofer of Pressburg. Schwab later corresponded with the Hatam Sofer concerning a halakhic issue, and the latter bestowed upon him the encomium, "the great and wondrous light, his honor . . . Loeb Schwab" (Hatam Sofer, *Responsa, E.H.*, no. 11). The Ketav Sofer, in his letter to R. Jacob Ettlinger of Friday, portion *Va'erah*, 1845, wished to include Schwab's signature on the letter of protest against the Reform Rabbinical Assembly in Braunschweig, even though he described Schwab as a "hypocrite." See Solomon Sofer, *Iggrot Soferim* (Vienna, 1869), Part 3: *Letters of the Ketav Sofer*, 7.
7. L. Schwab, *Gutachten an den Israelitischen Gemeinde—Vorstand zu Pesth, in Betreff der daselbst sich gebildeten, sogenannten Central-Reform-Genossenschaft* (Pest, 1848), 10–14.

8. Ibid., 14.
9. For examples of requests for leniencies in the wake of the new conditions, see my book, *Shabbes Goy, A Study in Halakhic Flexibility* (Philadelphia, 1984), 185–225.
10. *AZJ*, April 11, 1862, 648.
11. For the notice about Dunaföldvár, see *AZJ*, January 24, 1859, 68. I have misplaced the reference to Szarvas.
12. In 1864, the communities in the northern districts petitioned the consul in the capital city to repeal the program to found a rabbinical seminary. The request to transfer the national market days from Sabbaths and Jewish holidays to other days was added, as if by the way, to one of these petitions. See *BCH*, November 23, 1864, 957. For the discussions in the Congress, see chapters 12–15.
13. In *Israelit* of March 6, 1867, 153–155, Hildesheimer urged the public to join the Sabbath Observers Society, whose purpose was to help those whose livelihood suffered as a result of Sabbath observance. He promised to enlist the first two hundred members in the society himself, and to contribute to it. In *BCH*, August 15, 1867, 502–503, a supposedly Orthodox rabbi reacted scornfully to the circular that Hildesheimer had dispatched on this topic.
14. M. K. Silber, "The Entrance of Jews into Hungarian Society in Vormärz: the Case of the 'Casinos'," *Assimilation and Community, The Jews in Nineteenth-Century Europe*, eds. J. Frankel and S. J. Zipperstein (Cambridge, 1992), 284–323.
15. *BCH*, 1858, 176. For a similar notice about Szombathely, see B. Bernstein, *A zsidók története Vasmegyében 1687–1905* (n.p., n.d.), 100–101.
16. For statistics about the phenomenon of conversion, see B. Kempeler, *Magyarországi zsidó és zsidó eredetü családok*, vols. 1–3 (Budapest, 1937–1939).
17. L. Festinger, *A Theory of Cognitive Dissonance* (New York, 1957).
18. M. A. Meyer, *Response to Modernity, A History of the Reform Movement in Judaism* (New York and Oxford, 1988). D. Philipson, *The Reform Movement in Judaism* (New York, 1907), preceded Meyer's book, and is still worthy of study. Philipson describes the historical background of the debate about Sabbath observance in the Third Reform Rabbinical Assembly in Breslau in 1846, that is, the difficulties that the Jews encountered as a result of the changes in Jewish occupations, and the rabbis' attempts to find a guideline to distinguish between permitted and forbidden (195–196). For an example of the gap between the rabbis' approach and that of the householders, of which the rabbis were aware, see J. Katz, "The Orthodox Defense of the Second Day of the Festivals," *Divine Law in Human Hands* (in press). The members of the *beit din* who opposed the foundation of the Hamburg Temple in 1818 perceived a link between this event and the presence in the community of non-observers, whom no one could restrain. See my article, "The Controversy over the Temple in Hamburg," ibid.
19. For his struggle, see *BCH*, 1859, 30, 298. For details, see A. Kecskeméti, *A csongrádmegyei zsidók története* (Makó, 1929), 48–54. According to this source, the rabbi fought against the institution of a choir, but acquiesced in the relocation of the *bimah*, and in placing the marriage canopy within the synagogue (53). For Bonyhád, see the biography of the author by his grandson contained in I. M. Perles, *Bayit Ne'eman* (Máramarossziget, 1907), 33–43.
20. See chapter 6, note 39.

21. J. D. Margolis, *Har Tabor* (Pressburg, 1861), 29a. This is a small book in which the author defends his major work, *Meholat ha-Mahanayim* (Pressburg, 1859), against its critics.
22. Cited by N. Katzburg, "The Rabbinical Decision of Michalovce in 1865," *Studies in the History of Jewish Society in the Middle Ages and in the Modern Period* (in Hebrew), eds. E. Etkes and Y. Salmon (Jerusalem, 1980), 278, note 14. Among those who yielded unwillingly to changes was the rabbi of Szombathely, Loeb Koenigsberg, as described by Bernstein (note 15), 94–96, 109. See above concerning the rabbi of Makó, R. Solomon Ullmann, who also compromised to some extent.

5. The Reaction of the Pious, "Oberland"-Style (pp. 48–55)

1. The first one to point out this policy of the Hatam Sofer was Moshe Samet, in his dissertation of 1967. The relevant part of his dissertation was published in his article "Halanat Metim," *Asupot: Annual for Jewish Studies of Yad Harav Nissim* (in Hebrew) 3 (1989), 413–475. On p. 459, Samet cites the Hatam Sofer's programmatic statement in a letter to R. Zvi Hirsch Chajes: "It is good to raise the level of the prohibition." The issue discussed in the letter is that of leaving the dead unburied overnight, which is ostensibly prohibited only by a negative commandment. The Hatam Sofer finds grounds for asserting that "it is both a positive and negative commandment." Concerning the second day of the festivals, see my article (chapter 4, note 18). The Hatam Sofer's decision about *qitniyot* is discussed in my article: "Towards a Biography of the Hatam Sofer," in *From East and West, Jews in a Changing Europe, 1750–1870*, eds. F. Malino and D. Sorkin, (Oxford, 1990), 251–254.
2. *Even ha-Ezer*, 11.
3. See chapter 8, note 8.
4. The testament has been published many times. See Y. Hacohen Schwartz, *Zikhron Moshe* (Grosswardein, 1938), 42–44.
5. See Meyer, *Response* (chapter 4, note 18), 174–177.
6. The article mentioned here (dated August 11, 1852) is one of eight that appeared in *AZJ*, the first dated September 20, 1852, and the last, May 30, 1853. They supposedly originated in Pressburg, but were called "Ungarische Briefe." The articles have almost nothing about Pressburg, but are full of information about events throughout the country as a whole. Anyone familiar with Leopold Löw's works will recognize his style. Several of the articles have the by-line, "L." Conclusive proof of his authorship is found in the seventh article, of February 21, 1853, where the author reports on the controversy surrounding the divorce which R. Zipser gave in Székesfehérvár (see below). The reporter notes with surprise that R. Zvi Hirsch Fassel of Nagykanizsa, who was counted among the progressive rabbis (he succeeded Löw as rabbi of one of the first congregations to enact reforms), joined the critics of the divorce. In the collection of Löw's correspondence (*Gesammelte Schriften*, vol. 5 [Szeged, 1900], 741) there is a letter from Fassel to Löw (dated April 15 of the same year as the article), in which Fassel explains his position on the issue and justifies his opposition in the face of Löw's criticism. It is evident that this is his second letter on the topic, and that the correspondence began with Löw's article.

7. Meir Eisenstädter, *Responsa Imrei Esh*, vol. 2 (Ungvar, 1894), no. 25.
8. This following Katzburg (chapter 4, note 22).
9. *AZJ* is full of notices from Hungary, particularly with respect to educational matters. Most of the reporters were teachers who originated from Bohemia and Moravia. *Der treue Zions-Wächter*, like its parallel Hebrew version *Shomer Zion ha-Ne'eman*, is also full of such articles. Several rabbis from Hungary, among them Maharam Schick, contributed to the rabbinic section. The latter also quotes the German organ at times (see *Responsa Maharam Schick, Y.D.*, no. 244). R. Abraham Glasner, about whom we shall hear below, made a vow in 1848, while still in his father-in-law's house in Pressburg, to devote his time to the study of Torah alone and not to read newspapers, but added: "except for the *Zions-Wächter*." See chapter 7, note 6.
10. *AZJ*, May 30, 1853, 281. For the identification of the author, see note 6. The candidate was Moritz Duschak, and according to Löw, Hirsch found flaws in his orthodoxy.
11. J. Wohlgemuth, "Etwas über die Termini, orthodoxes und gesetzestreues Judentum," in *Festschrift zum siebzigsten Geburtstag David Hoffmann's*, ed. S. Epstein (Berlin, 1914), drew attention to the novelty of the term. He claims, p. 448, that Hirsch coined the term, or at least disseminated it. Mordechai Breuer called this reference to my attention.
12. In 1839, Leopold Löw, who followed the rise of the new Orthodoxy with critical eyes, noted (Elias) Grünebaum and (Solomon) Plessner as anticipating Hirsch in their tendency to buttress the details of religious directives with symbolic interpretation ("Eine künstlich ausgesponnene Symbolik muss ihnen alles beschönigen helfen"). See his introduction to Aaron Chorin's *Kind des hohen Alters* (Wien, 1839), 2.
13. This is his approach throughout *Meholat ha-Mahanayim* (chapter 4, note 21). See my article about the second day of the festivals (chapter 4, note 18), 94–100.
14. The history of the Jewish community in this period was described by: J. Steinherz, "A székesfehérvári zsidók története (1840–1892)," *MZsSz* 10 (1893), 548–558, 622–627; 11 (1894), 102–109, 177–190, 539–546, 623–637.
15. The reforms are cited in ibid., in the first part of the article.
16. For Zipser's biography, see I. Reich, *Beth-El, Ehrentempel verdienter ungarischer Israeliten*, vol. 2 (Pest, 1868), 265–297, and following him, Steinherz (note 14), 553–554.
17. The Würtemberg reforms (see chapter 1, note 18) could have served as precedents for several of Zipser's reforms.
18. Steinherz (note 14), 1894, 104. At that time Fischer himself was the head of the congregation, and together with several colleagues, attempted to rescind the reforms, but to no avail. Most of the congregation did not heed him.
19. The course of the controversy is depicted in ibid., 105–106.
20. One of the rabbis involved was R. Isaac Moses Perles, rabbi of Bonyhád, mentioned chapter 4, note 19. His role, and that of the other rabbis, is described in his biography (40–41).
21. Meir Zipser, *Mei ha-Shiloah* (Ofen, 1853).
22. According to Löw (note 6), Zipser also had his supporters, led by Schwab, Löw's father-in-law. Löw later dealt with the question of the legality of such a *beit din* in an opinion written at the request of the lieutenant governor in Buda. He described the

background of the issue, and concluded that, while the involvement of brothers in arranging a divorce is valid according to the letter of the law, where it is customary to appoint a *beit din* to arrange a divorce, this should be permitted only in cases of emergency. See *BCH*, 1859, 241–245.
23. Gottlieb Fischer, *Delatayim u-Bariah le-Mei ha-Shiloah* (Wien, 1855); the letters of approbation, 2a–3b.
24. Ibid., 2b. Fischer complained about Zipser for daring to question a decision of the Noda' bi-Yehudah: "I was filled with the wrath of God at seeing . . . the words of arrogance and scorn that this author wrote against our rabbi, the rabbi of all the members of the Diaspora, the *gaon* Noda' bi-Yehudah, may his memory be blessed, may his righteousness protect us, my eyes filled with tears." Zipser was subsequently vindicated from an unexpected source. Some time after Gottlieb Fischer's attack upon him, the responsa of the Hatam Sofer on *Even ha-Ezer* appeared in print, and it became clear that the Hatam Sofer rejected the Noda' bi-Yehudah's opinion, that a divorce requires a *beit din* of three. He claimed that the Noda' bi-Yehudah's basic proof involved a misunderstanding of Rashi's commentary on the first *mishnah* in Sanhedrin, exactly as Zipser had said. However, what the outstanding halakhist of the generation was permitted to say about the outstanding halakhist of the previous generation, could not be uttered by a rank-and-file rabbi, especially one who was suspected of breaching the norms of accepted adjudication. Zipser erred not in understanding the sources, but in evaluating his place in the rabbinic hierarchy. See M. Zipser, "Zur Streitfrage, ob bei einer Ehescheidung ein Beth-din von nöthen," *BCH*, 1865, 913–915. The Hatam Sofer's harsh words against the Noda' bi-Yehudah are found in the second part of *E.H.*, no. 130.
25. In the introduction to his book (note 23, 6a–b) Fischer cited Zipser's statement from the pamphlet *Zulässigkeit und Dringlichkeit der Synagogen-Reformen* (Wien, 1845), 72, and protested against it. He also noted Zipser's reference to the Reform Rabbinical Assemblies' being able to solve the problems of the times. This remark also disqualified him for his post.
26. The details are found in Steinherz (note 14) 1894, 540–543.
27. For the text of the letters from the leadership to the rabbis, see *BCH*, 1860, 285–288. Hirsch Fassel's response is found on pp. 353–357, 389–392. Pp. 401–405 contain Guggenheimer's petition to the city authorities concerning the desired prayer times on Sabbath morning and the authorities' application to Leopold Löw on this issue. His response is found on pp. 433–445.
28. *Jeschurun* 6 (1859–1860), 638–659.
29. See note 27.
30. Steinherz (note 14, 1894), 540–541.
31. A summary of the statements of the conservatives appears there in the continuation; for the full text of their responsa, see *Jeschurun* 8 (1862), 38–47. All quotations are from this source.
32. Ibid., 40.
33. Ibid., 41.
34. Ibid., 43–44. The term is found occasionally in general pedagogical literature. Hirsch used the term to express the idea that general education is necessary to the civic life of the Jews. Hirsch's unique vocabulary is worthy of study; see note 11.

35. Steinherz (note 14), 1894, 546–548.
36. *Jeschurun* 9 (1863), 280–282.
37. Steinherz (note 14), 1894, 631–633.

6. Hassidim and the Zealous in the Unterland (pp. 56–69)

1. For an exhaustive treatment of the Jewish settlement in the Unterland, see Silber (chapter 3, note 2), 172–187. Silber returned to this topic in his article: "The Emergence of Ultra-Orthodoxy: The Invention of a Tradition," *The Uses of Tradition: Jewish Continuity in the Modern Era*, ed. J. Wertheimer (New York/Jerusalem, 1992), 23–84, esp. 41–42. Many of the personalities and issues discussed here, particularly in this section, are treated also in Silber's article. Silber's article and the present book were written in close collaboration. Their different emphases stem for the most part from different goals—the depiction of the progress of events and development of processes on the one hand, and the quest for a solution to a specific problem on the other.
2. A. J. Brawer, *Studies in Galician Jewry in the Eighteenth Century* (in Hebrew) (Jerusalem, 1965), particularly section 2, 141–194.
3. The religious-cultural situation in the districts under discussion is described in Y. Y. Cohen's wide-ranging articles: "Torah Life in Hungary at the Time of the Rise of Hassidism (1630–1780)," (in Hebrew) *Moriah* 14 (1986), 142–184; "The Penetration of Hassidism into Hungary," *The Jews of Hungary, Historical Studies* (in Hebrew), ed. A. Gonda and Y. Cohen (Tel Aviv, 1980), 57–91.
4. Later hassidic tradition attributes to R. Yitzchak Isaac Taub (1751–1821), of the Nagykálló congregation, the first hassidic setttlement in Hungary. See for example: Y. Y. Gruenwald, *Pe'erei Hakhmei Medinatenu, Shem ha-Gedolim* (Sziget, 1910), 91. But it seems that his enthusiastic religiosity and his charismatic personality were a function of his individual personality, with no relation to the hassidic movement in Poland in his time. See Katzburg (chapter 3, note 1), 33; and in particular N. Ben-Menahem, "Rabbi Yitzchak Isaac Taub of Kalov," *Israel Elfenbein Jubilee Volume* (in Hebrew) (Jerusalem, 1963), 30–32. In a letter to his congregation, R. Taub requested that they supplement his meager salary, which was not sufficient for his household needs, and the congregation acceded to his request. This proves that the rabbi did not have a circle of hassidim who supported him financially, as was accepted among the *Admorim* of his time.
5. For primary biographical information, see P. Z. Schwartz, *Shem ha-Gedolim me-Eretz Hagar* (Paks, 1914), part 2, 9b–10a.
6. *Pinqas ha-Qehillot, Hungariah* (Jerusalem, 1976), 513–514.
7. For the Teitelbaum dynasty, see Y. Alfasi, *Sefer ha-Admorim* (Tel Aviv, 1961), 67–68.
8. For primary biographical information, see Schwartz (note 5), part 1, 52a. Below we shall learn from his actions of his personality and intellectual horizons.
9. Ibid., part 2, no. 90, 32b.
10. See chapter 3, note 9; chapter 4, note 1.
11. For information about him, see Schwartz (note 5), part 2, 3a.

12. The history of the Sofer family is described and documented in the work of Y. Z. Sofer, *Toldot Sofrim* (London, 1963). The history of the founding father: ibid., 65–99.
13. See his testament, ibid., 103, note.
14. Evidence of his independence is the fact that he left Pressburg to study with other rabbis, contrary to his father's wishes (ibid., 91). The temptation to study a useful profession came, according to the description of the author, his son, from one of "the most wealthy men of Pressburg," but the fact that he attributed his rescue to his rabbi indicates that he himself wrestled with this temptation (ibid., 92).
15. Ibid., 106–115.
16. Ibid., 115–122.
17. The facts are found in Y. Y. Cohen, *Sages of Transylvania (1630–1944)* (in Hebrew) (Jerusalem, 1989), 142–143. Cohen's summary is based on two complete biographies, one written by the rabbi's student, R. Heller, *Sefer Beit Hillel* (Munkács, 1890); the second by his grandson, H. Y. Lichtenstein, *Toldot ve-Zihronot* (Szatmár, 1931). The grandson was his grandfather's student, and his statements constitute firsthand testimony. The first work was republished with notes by Y. Weinberger, *Beit Hillel ha-Shalem* (Tirnau, 1941).
18. About Friedman, see Cohen (note 17), 189–190.
19. *AZJ*, April 10, 1854, 284–285.
20. See "Veshet," *Talmudic Encyclopedia*, 11, 610. In Hatam Sofer, *Responsa, Y.D.*, no. 46, the author discusses a specific case: "A goose that was slaughtered and the gullet examined, as is customary."
21. A letter of thanks to his congregation, Wednesday, *Parshat Pinehas*, 1854. Printed in his book *Responsa Beit Hillel* (Szatmár, 1928) no. 124.
22. Weinberger (note 17), 34–35. R. Hillel requested and received a letter of approbation from R. Hayyim of Sanz for his book *Maskil el Dal*; ibid., 41–42. He also approved the *pesaq beit din*, see chapter 8, note 17.
23. The non-Jew would thus become a legal owner. Katz, *Shabbes Goy* (chapter 4, note 9), 171–175.
24. *Responsa Beit Hillel* (note 21), nos. 6, 7.
25. The quote is found in the work of H. Z. Winkler, *Huqei Hayyim* (Munkács, 1897), 13b.
26. *Responsa Beit Hillel* (note 21), no. 3.
27. R. Lichtenstein was very precise in his language. He did not call the new type of transgressors *reqanim*—idle—for the primary association called forth by the term is the Talmudic adage: "Even the idle among you are full of good deeds like a pomegranate" (BT Berakhot 57a), and he did not wish to allude to any redeeming factor in the new type of sinner.
28. There is no biography of Maharam Schick worthy of the name. For a description along traditional hagiographical lines, see the introduction of his grandson, Elijah Schick, to the *Derashot Maharam Schick* (Cluz, 1937), 5b–22b. Many anecdotes and descriptions of his personality and behavior were collected by H. Y. T. Braun, *Darkhei Moshe he-Hadash* (Grosswardein, 1944), but most of them are secondary, reflecting the image of the hero two generations later. A real eyewitness was his student R. Zalman Spitzer, who studied with him in Szent György (Georgen) (ibid., 49–

51) and eulogized him after his death. R. Spitzer corroborates Maharam Schick's reputation for great diligence and unceasing study. R. Zalman Spitzer, who was the son-in-law of the Hatam Sofer, faithfully depicted the differences between the two personalities: the Hatam Sofer, whose modesty nonetheless carried an awareness of his greatness, and Maharam Schick, whose modesty prevented him from appreciating his own stature.

29. *Responsa Maharam Schick, O.H.*, no. 305. I discussed this issue in my work, *Divine Law in Human Hands* (chapter 4, note 18).
30. *AZJ*, January 18, 1858, 51–52. According to the writer, the number of householders increased tenfold during a brief period.
31. One of the duties of R. Meir Austerlitz, who was appointed rabbi in Eperjes in 1860, was teaching religion to children who studied in the gymnasium. See W. Austerlitz, *Leben und Wirken von weiland Rabbi Dr. Austerlitz* (n.p., n.d.), 21.
32. *MZsL*, 377.
33. [Hayyim David Lippe], *Sechs Briefe zur Beleuchtung der religiösen Wirren in Ober-Ungarn* (Kaschau, 1866). The work is written in German, and the notes in Hebrew.
34. Ibid., 4–5, 17–18, 21.
35. The author speaks of the area in general, but at times mentions these two cities specifically.
36. For a report about the discussion, see *BCH*, 1860, 52. For a description of the outcome, see the statement of the congregational administration, cited in the following note.
37. The most important source for the progress of events is the opinion of the rabbi, called *Divrei Shalom ve-Emet*, which was published in order to explain his position. It was published as an appendix to *BCH*, March 9, 1864, together with a description of events by the congregational administration.
38. *BCH*, 1863, 363.
39. *Divrei Shalom ve-Emet* (note 37).
40. This emerges from the rabbi's description, ibid. See the responsum mentioned in note 42, according to which the rabbi was considered by the zealots to be a completely righteous man.
41. For a detailed report of the dedication, see *BCH*, September 21, 1863, 698–699.
42. From a responsum of the tenth of Av, 1862, *Responsa Beit Hillel*, no. 47.
43. In a letter to the brother of R. Hayyim Sofer, R. Sussman Sofer, dated 1860, R. Lichtenstein reminisced about "an old love for his father, may his memory be blessed"; *Responsa Beit Hillel*, no. 3.
44. Appendix to *BCH*, February 10, 1864.
45. See the administration's description mentioned above, note 37. About his appearance before the city governor, see R. Judah Aszod's response of 4 Shevat 1864 to a letter of R. Sofer. See *Toldot Sofrim* (note 12), *Kan Sofer*, 11–12.
46. See note 37.
47. See note 45. In his letter, R. Judah Aszod supports the prohibition against the Miskolc synagogue. For a similar letter from R. Wolf Hirsch of Tapolcsány, see *BCH*, March 16, 1864, 228.
48. Ibid., March 9, 1864, 205.
49. The following description of the progress of events relies on the notices in the news-

papers: *BCH*, March 9, 1864, 205, and March 23, 251–252; *AZJ*, April 5, 1864, 227. The meeting in Ujhely was also discussed in a letter by R. Jeremiah Löw to R. Hayyim Sofer of 1864 (no month or day given). See *Toldot Sofrim* (note 12), 10. It emerges from the letter that R. Löw was the one who issued the invitations to the assembly at Nyiregyháza.

50. There are two detailed descriptions of the assembly at Nyiregyháza in *BCH*, one dated March 23, 1864, 251–252, and the other in an appendix to the April 6, 1864, issue. R. Jeremiah Löw's cooperation with the zealots aroused great astonishment, as emerges in the official complaint to the authorities made by the officials of Miskolc against the zealots. They cite R. Löw as well, with accompanying expressions of amazement. The members of his congregation, on the other hand, denied that he was in league with the zealots. See *BCH*, May 18, 1864, 412–413.

51. Akiva Joseph Schlesinger writes (*Lev ha-Ivri* [Ungvár, 1865], 38a, in the note): "And for our sins, one of the Zadokite rabbis joined with them, who until now had appeared to be one of the Perushim. Although they knew him from before to be a hypocrite, they did not want to exclude him, so that he would have no cause for complaint . . . and because of this Zadokite they had many delays and obstacles . . . until they overcame him with the force of holiness." Eliav (chapter 3, note 14), 70, note 44, assumed that the venue was the convention in Vienna prior to the delegation's appearance before the king, and that the reference was to R. Esriel Hildesheimer. However, Schlesinger speaks explicitly of "an assembly larger than the first [Ujhely] in the city of Nyiregyháza," and Hildesheimer did not attend this convocation. One of the participants did indeed support Hildesheimer's view, as mentioned in the first report, where the seminary was ostensibly approved, on condition that it be run by those loyal to tradition. This person may have been Meir Perles.

52. See Eliav (chapter 3, note 14), 67–70. Hildesheimer had one public supporter, R. Solomon Kutna, who succeeded him as rabbi when he left Eisenstadt.

53. The reception given the rabbinic delegation by the king, and its influence, were subjects of wonder. See the description in *Toldot Sofrim* (note 12), 46–49, and the sources cited by Jakobovitz (chapter 8, note 1), 68–69.

54. *BCH*, November 18, 1863, 846.

55. This opinion was published as an appendix to *BCH*, May 11, 1864. Echoes of the unpleasant experience were preserved in the family tradition. See Weinberger (note 17), 40–41.

56. In the opinion, *BCH*, May 11, 1864.

57. An exhaustive biography of Akiva Joseph Schlesinger is being written by Michael Silber. I have been greatly assisted by the information he provided about the man, and I restrict myself here to data pertinent to the subject under discussion.

58. The two documents were published in the introduction to *Lev ha-Ivri*, ed. M. A. Schlesinger (Jerusalem, 1988), 6–7.

59. *Ketav Yosher Divrei Emet* (Pressburg, 1865). For the motivation behind this broadside, see chapter 7.

60. See *Lev ha-Ivri* (note 51), 7b, 35a.

61. The view prevalent in current scholarship, according to which Schlesinger's battle was entirely against Esriel Hildesheimer, is unacceptable. See *Lev ha-Ivri*, 37b: "Some years ago, when the members of their *yeshivah* returned, they brought with

them a light unto Israel . . . but from the time when they were allowed to eat contaminated food, secular learning, and to mingle with strangers . . . from that time some of the rabbis pretend that they do not know how to return home."

7. Pressburg as the Target of Zealot Arrows (pp. 70–76)

1. This document has been published many times. See, for instance, H. Hacohen Schwartz, *Zikhron le-Moshe* (Grosswardein, 1938), 42–44.
2. For a description of the fall of the ghetto walls in Pressburg, in both physical and spiritual terms, see S. Mayer, *Ein jüdischer Kaufmann 1831 bis 1911* (Leipzig, 1911), 85–104.
3. For Mayer's studies at the Catholic gymnasium and the Evangelical lyceum, see ibid., 100–104. For statistics about Jewish pupils in secondary schools, see *BCH*, 1863, 232. Thirty-four gymnasium pupils from the Pressburg district are mentioned.
4. *AZJ*, December 16, 1850, 696. The foundation of such a school was something of a novelty, for until now the Catholics and Protestants frequented separate educational institutions. See Mayer's description (note 3).
5. R. Kestenberg-Gladstein, *Neuere Geschichte der Juden in den böhmischen Ländern* (Tübingen, 1969), 71–72.
6. Y. Joseph Cohen copied these astonishing words from R. Glasner's notebook of novellae, which is preserved in manuscript, and is found in the library of the Rav Kook Institute in Jerusalem. See Cohen, *Sages of Transylvania* (in Hebrew) (chapter 6, note 17), 36–37.
7. According to a notice in the *AZJ*, May 17, 1862, 289, worshipers gathered on the Sabbath and festivals in the assembly hall of the school in order to celebrate the day "in geordneter und weihevoller Weise."
8. Eliav already noted the warm relationship between these two personalities (chapter 3, note 14), 63–65. The Ketav Sofer's letter to Hildesheimer of Friday, portion *Shelah*, 1861, was published recently, and it clearly reveals the Ketav Sofer's desire to have R. Hildesheimer serve together with him in the rabbinate. See M. Hildesheimer, "Hungarian Rabbis and the Michalowitz Conference," *Qiryat Sefer* 63 (1990–1991), 947–948. Read on for the reason why this plan was aborted.
9. About R. Feisch Fischmann, see Cohen (chapter 6, note 17), 181–182.
10. About R. Glasner, see ibid., 38–40.
11. *Responsa Beit Hillel* (chapter 6, note 21), no. 34.
12. See chapter 6, note 59.
13. *Responsa Beit Hillel*, no. 30.
14. Ibid. R. Lichtenstein's opposition to R. Fischmann's appointment as preacher in Pressburg is mentioned frequently in the scholarly literature. P. Fischer noted his protest against the appointment of R. Glasner as rabbi of Kolozsvár, "Zur Würdigung der Wirksamkeit Dr. E. Hildesheimers in Ungarn," *Jeschurun* 15 (1928), 337.
15. *Responsa Beit Hillel*, no. 35, and all that follows in the text.
16. Ibid., no. 34.
17. *Lev ha-Ivri*, part I, appeared in Ungvár in the last third of 1864.
18. "I greatly regret not having merited to serve the holy rabbi, may his memory be blessed, for hearing is not comparable to seeing"; *Lev ha-Ivri*, 10b, in the note.

19. Ibid., 32a.
20. A long critical review was published in *BCH*, January 25, 1865, 72–75. The writer did not attempt to identify the author of the book. In ibid., 425, R. Lichtenstein is mentioned as the author of *El ha-Adarim*.

8. The Fruits of Zealousness (pp. 77–85)

1. A photograph of the two letters appears on the frontispiece of the New York, 1963 edition of R. Lichtenstein's book, *Maskil el Dal*, vol. 4 (Ungvár, 1867-Lemberg 1871). B. Z. Jacobowitz copied them from there, in *Zikhron Yemot Olam*, vol. 1 (Bnei Brak, 1986), photograph no. 10 in the collection of photographs at the end of the book. This author describes the history of the split in Hungary from the perspective of the zealots, who considered the secession and all the resulting stringencies a positive phenomenon. The book is full of repetitions and rhetoric, but it is replete with information, and the author's expertise in the sources is impressive.
2. *Responsa Beit Hillel* (chapter 6, note 21), no. 3, and see chapter 6, note 26.
3. Eliezer Sussman Sofer was later rabbi of Paks. A brief biography is found in S. D. Sofer, *Mazkeret Paks* vol. 2 (Jerusalem, 1966). For his struggle with the leftists of the Kiskúnhalas congregation see 14–24.
4. For R. Eisenstädter's statement, see *Kerem Shlomo* 12, no. 114 (*Shevat*, 1989), 21–22. For R. Panet's response, see *Derek Yivhar, Responsa* (Munkacs, 1893), no. 1. Hildesheimer referred to these sources (chapter 7, note 8), 941–942. Maharam Schick's response was published in the collection of responsa of the Hatam Sofer edited by J. Stern, *Ligutei Hatam Sofer* (London, 1965), 73–75.
5. Maharam Schick's responsum is divided into paragraphs, numbered alphabetically. The details of the laws pertaining to the *Chorschul* are found in paragraphs 4–10.
6. Ibid., 3.
7. Ibid., at length, 11.
8. I have noted this method of the Hatam Sofer on various occasions. See chapter 5, note 1.
9. In his protest against calling a synagogue a place of idol worship (paragraph 3), Maharam Schick suggested that it was possibly a tactic employed to prevent the public's being swept after the Reformers. According to him, however, "To try to uphold the bulwarks by means of a lie is futile, for a lie cannot stand."
10. M. Hildesheimer, "Responses of the Maharam Schick (The Book, Its Compilation and Edition)," *Tzfunot* 6 (1990), 92–94.
11. In the article mentioned above (chapter 7, note 8), 942, Meir Hildesheimer assumed that the desired number of fifty signatures had been collected, and this made the conference possible. But this asumption does not fit the chronology of events.
12. See chapter 4, note 22. M. Hildesheimer has added important information in the two articles mentioned above, notes 10 and 11.
13. For the publication of the decision (Ungvár, 1866) and its subsequent dissemination, see Katzburg (chapter 4, note 22), 276–277.
14. His testimony is found in *Lev ha-Ivri*, vol. II (Lvov, 1868), which contains an entire chapter about the "judicial decision." Both parts were reprinted; we quote from the Jerusalem, 1988, edition. About the bans see 170–171.

15. Schlesinger came to live in the Land of Israel in 1870. For his statement, see his *Beit Yosef he-Hadash* (Jerusalem, 1875). Katzburg (note 13), 277, cites his words.
16. Hildesheimer (chapter 7, note 8) compared the two versions in detail, and found no substantive differences.
17. *Lev ha-Ivri* (note 14), 169–170. Two hassidic rebbes from Galicia added their endorsement ex post facto: R. Hayyim of Sanz and R. Yitzchak Isaac of Zhidachow.
18. Jacobowitz (note 1), vol. 1, 84–107, lists all the important signatories to the Michalowitz ruling and their works, but see note 21.
19. Heller (chapter 6, note 17), 13a.
20. *Responsa Maharam Schick, O.H.*, no. 70.
21. See Jacobowitz (note 1), vol. 1, 81–83. Maharam Schick's grandson (chapter 6, note 28), 15a–17a, already tried to explain away the failure of the great rabbis to sign, but could only say of his grandfather that he upheld the prohibitions ex post facto.
22. Katzburg (chapter 4, note 22), 282, also dealt with the question and did not find a satisfactory answer.
23. Hildesheimer (note 10), 92–94.
24. Maharam Schick relies on the statements of Rashbah and Maimonides, who sought to emphasize the difference between prohibitions arising from the law, and those that were added as hedges around the original prohibitions.
25. Ibid., in the continuation. According to a source in manuscript, which Y. Y. Gruenwald saw (*le-Pelagot Yisrael be-Ungaria* [Deva, 1929], 65b), Maharam Schick reiterated his endorsement of the prohibition to his bewildered student, Wolf Sofer, on another occasion.
26. *BCH*, 1866, 587.
27. *Sechs Briefe* (chapter 6, note 3), 36–37.
28. Ibid., 38–40. In the notes, written in Hebrew, the author criticized the Michalowitz ruling on the halakhic level, from the perspective of a maskilic Torah scholar.
29. *Lev ha-Ivri* (note 14), vol. II, 167.
30. *Responsa Maharam Schick, O.H.*, no. 71.
31. A. D. Deutsch, *Responsa Goren David* (Paks, 1885), no. 7.
32. S. Brach, *Avot al Banim* (Saini, 1926), introduction.
33. Hildesheimer published his critique of the ruling in *Israelit*, 1866, in a series of five articles. These were included in his collected works (with a change in title). See I. Hildesheimer, *Gesammelte Aufsätze*, ed. M. Hildesheimer (Frankfurt am Main, 1923), 1–23, from which we quote. For the agreement between three of his colleagues to publish an opinion against the ruling, see 23.
34. Ibid., 24–26.
35. Ibid., 25.
36. Ibid., 26.
37. He deals with this at length in the body of the article, ibid., 12–18.
38. He reiterated this belief at this juncture as well, ibid., 2–3.
39. Katzburg (chapter 4, note 22), 278–279.
40. An example of the angry reaction to this term is voiced by Lippe (chapter 6, note 33), Hebrew part, 6: "Is there a greater desecration of God's name than to call the synagogues of Israel, in which several Torah scrolls are found, by the name of idol worship?"

9. Emancipation and the Idea of a Nationwide Jewish Organization (pp. 89–95)

1. See A. Zeller, *A magyar egyházpolitika 1847–1894*, vol. 1 (Budapest, 1894), 260.
2. For the sequence of events, see L. Venetianer, "Az emancipáció története," *IMIT* (1918), 32–52, as well as the article by M. Mezei, "Visszaemlékezés az emáncipació idejére," ibid., 11–32. Both articles were written in honor of the jubilee of the enactment of the Emancipation Law.
3. J. Eötvös, *A zsidók emancipátiója* (Budapest, 1840). The book was translated into German and Italian.
4. Venetianer (note 2), 334.
5. See Mezei's article (note 2). He took an active part in the struggle for equal rights.
6. See note 19, for the responses of the communities to the memorandum of the leaders of the Pest community, which will be discussed below. These were written in the summer of 1867, and repeatedly voiced reservations about continuing to struggle for emancipation.
7. Zeller (note 1), 220–221.
8. Ibid. The idea of making enfranchisement of local Jews conditional upon prevention or restriction of immigration from neighboring countries occurred to many, in all the European countries. This was due to the fear that the improvement in the status of Jews in one place would draw Jews from other lands, where they lacked such rights. See J. Katz, *Out of the Ghetto* (Cambridge, Mass., 1973), 214.
9. According to Mezei (note 2), he and his colleagues among the intelligentsia battled for this.
10. Zeller (note 1), 221.
11. For Eötvös's religiosity, see Ambrus Oltványi's long introduction to Eötvös's letters: J. Eötvös, *Levelek* (Budapest, 1976), 47–48.
12. For the ties between these two personalities, see ibid., 48–51; and Eötvös's letters to Montalembert, according to the list of addressees, ibid., 824.
13. For Montalembert's theories, see his biography: J. C. Finlay, *The Liberal Who Failed* (Washington and Cleveland, 1968), especially chapter 5.
14. Eötvös's thought was clarified by his biographer: P. Böly, *Joseph Eötvös and the Modernization of Hungary* (Philadelphia, 1972), chapter 8.
15. Zeller (note 1), 108. For further details, see Böly (note 14).
16. For his speech in Parliament on this topic, see J. Eötvös, *Beszédek* (Budapest, 1886), 56 ff.
17. For Eötvös's battle with his church, see Böly (note 14), 121–124.
18. P. Tencer, *Album, első füzet—1869, Januar 24* (Budapest, 1869), 12.
19. The memorandum was published in a collection of documents which the leaders of the Congress presented to Parliament after its conclusion, as its response to an appeal against it made by the Orthodox. The abridged title of the book is *Izraelita Congressus Emlékirata* (Pest, 1870), that is, a memorandum about the Jewish Congress. The book is divided into three parts: The first part depicts the course of events from the time the idea of the Congress was raised until the debate in Parliament about the appeal of the Orthodox against its decisions. The second part contains the supporting documents. The third part collects the opinion of rabbis from other countries

about the nature of the Congress's decisions, from the religious point of view. Each part is numbered independently. We will cite it as follows: Memo A, B, C. The section discussed here is in Memo B, 1–2. A German translation of this was published in *BCH*, May 1, 1867, 292–295.
20. Thus in a counter-memorandum by the Orthodox to Eötvös, ibid., Memo B, 26. This view took root among the Orthodox. See *Responsa Maharam Schick, Y.D.*, no. 333.
21. Memo B (note 19), 1–2.
22. Ibid., 2.
23. Ibid.
24. Leopold Löw (*BCH*, May 1, 1867, 296–298) sharply criticized the memorandum for its subjectivity.
25. About Dr. Hirschler, see Tencer (note 18), 7–12.
26. The accompanying letter was published only in *BCH*, May 1, 1867, 294–296.
27. So, for example, the reservations expressed by the community of Debrecen—Memo B (note 19), 5; Nyiregyháza—Memo B, 16; and others.
28. Ibid., 20.
29. Ibid., 9.
30. Ibid., 12–14.
31. Ibid., 7.

10. The *Shomrei Ha-Dat* Society and the Assembly of Notables (pp. 96–107)

1. *BCH*, May 1, 1867, 297–298.
2. Details about him are found in *MZsL*, 260.
3. *BCH*, May 1, 1867, 298.
4. M. Eliav, ed., *Rabbiner Esriel Hildesheimer, Briefe* (Jerusalem, 1965), 49–50.
5. Löw did not know what had been decided at the meeting (see note 1). The counter-memorandum included among the documents of Memo B (chapter 9, note 19), 26–29, alludes to its being the fruit of that meeting.
6. All of this is found in the memorandum, ibid.
7. Ibid., 25.
8. The number 120 is mentioned at the beginning of the memorandum and at its conclusion.
9. We know the date of submission from Löw's critical article in *BCH*, September 15, 1867, 585. A notice appeared in *Neuzeit*, August 2, 1867, 363, about a group of rabbis gathering in the capital in order to take action against the memorandum of the Pest leaders. Nothing of the sort appears anywhere else. The statement that the rabbis had no money to return home also attests to its being a fabrication.
10. All the documents pertaining to the founding of the *Shomrei ha-Dat* society are included in their book of statutes; the name of the society appears there in three languages: Hungarian, Hebrew, and German. See *A "Hitör" Magyar Zsidó Egylet Alapszabályai, Shomrei ha-Dat, Statuten für den ungarisch-jüdischen Verein, Glaubenswächter* (Pest, 1868).
11. The appeal in Hungarian is found on page 5; in German, on page 17. For the content of the appeal, see below in the text.

12. Meir Trebitsch was included in the book *Shem ha-Gedolim me-Eretz Hagar*, vol. 2, by Pinehas Zelig Schwartz (Paks, 1914), 3a, although the book is devoted to the biographies of rabbis. Schwartz makes reference to a note in Samuel Ehrenfeld's work, *Hatan Sofer* (Ungvár, 1874), 94, where the author, Trebitsch's relative by marriage, argues with him over a halakhic issue. He is mentioned there as a student of the Hatam Sofer, a learned householder, who at the time of the correspondence lived in Buda. Ehrenfeld was the son of the Hatam Sofer's daughter, and Trebitsch was connected with the family of the rabbis of Pressburg.
13. Statutes (note 10), 16.
14. Ibid., the statutes in Hungarian, 8–16, in German, 20–29.
15. The third chapter of the statutes is devoted to the religious council—in Hungarian, 10, in German, 22.
16. Ibid., 29. We shall later speculate about the timing of this certification.
17. Thus L. Venetianer in his *A zsidóság szervezete az európai álamokban* (Budapest, 1901), 503. Katzburg referred to this source in his bibliographical article (N. Katzburg, "The Jewish Congress of Hungry in 1868, List of Sources," *Areshet* 4 [1960] [in Hebrew], 322–367). In his article in English, "The Jewish Congress of Hungary 1868–1869," *Hungarian Jewish Studies*, vol. 2, ed. R. L. Braham (New York, 1969), 12, Katzburg expressed his reservations about this conjecture.
18. *Israelit*, March 18, 1868, 198.
19. Ibid., February 28, 1868, 146. The Neolog leaders explained that the large number of delegates from its camp was a function of the disproportionate number of its sympathizers in the large communities. Memo A (chapter 9, note 19), 11–13.
20. According to the notice in *Israelit*, March 11, 1868, 136–137, traditionalists whom the Neologs wanted to draw to their side were invited to this meeting.
21. The delegates to the assembly met with the minister a day before the assembly began, for a first acquaintance, and at that opportunity the minister made his statement of principle. The following day, at the official opening, he defined the assembly's tasks. The correspondent of *Neuzeit* reported his words, as an eyewitness, on February 21, 1868. The *AZJ*, March 10, 1868, 203–205, based its report on that of the correspondent for *Pester Lloyd*, as did *Israelit*, March 4, 1868, 161–162.
22. *Neuzeit* (note 21), 86–87.
23. *AZJ* (note 21), 205.
24. *AZJ* (note 21); Kraus's name is mentioned in the next issue, 228. He published his speech in the pamphlet *Transaction zur Ausgleichung der sich gegenüberstehenden Parteien im ungarishcen Vaterland*. I have not seen this publication, and rely on the references in the press.
25. *Neuzeit* (note 21), 86; *AZJ* (note 21).
26. Venetianer (note 17), 505–506, quotes a letter written by Dr. Hirschler to Leopold Löw of March 6, 1868, that is, less than a week after the close of the assembly. It justifies the concessions to the Orthodox, which in the end did not even prevent them from presenting their reservations about the decisions of the assembly. See also note 34, for the bitterness expressed at the inconsistency of the Orthodox.
27. Memo B (chapter 9, note 19), 29.
28. The presence of the rabbis is mentioned in *Neuzeit* (note 21), 85, 87; in *AZJ* (note 21), 228; and in *Israelit*, March 18, 1868, 198–199.

29. Memo A, (chapter 9, note 19), 12–13.
30. See note 28.
31. Memo B, (chapter 9, note 19), 29–30.
32. *Entwurf des Wahlstatuts für den israelitischen Kongress* (Pest, 1868). The essentials were published in *AZJ*, March 17, 1868, 224–231, and will be cited from this publication.
33. *AZJ* (note 21), 224.
34. Thus in Dr. Hirschler's letter, cited above, note 26. After several months, the Neolog leaders sent a secret exculpatory letter to some rabbis of Leopold Löw's type, in which they accused the Orthodox delegation of having disavowed their own initiative. See L. Löw, *Der jüdische Kongress in Ungarn, historisch beleuchtet* (Pest, 1871), 277–278. Their claim reached the press as well. See *AZJ*, June 16, 1868, 497. Hirschler made the accusation openly after the Congress, in describing the course of events. See Memo A (chapter 9, note 19), 7.
35. This was expressed by Maharam Schick in his description of the course of events leading up to the Congress—*Responsa Maharam Schick, O.H.*, no. 309, the second paragraph. According to the testimony of his son, the rabbi of Pressburg, the Ketav Sofer requested that his congregation not choose him as a delegate to the Congress, although he followed the discussions closely, staying nearby in the capital for the entire time it was in session, and being party to consultations during this time. See Abraham Samuel Benjamin Sofer, *Commentary of the Ketav Sofer on the Pentateuch* (in Hebrew) (Vienna, 1884) introduction by his son Solomon, xxiv.
36. The text of the minister's response was published in the press: *Neuzeit*, March 18, 1868, 124; *AZJ*, April 7, 1868, 288, following *Pester Lloyd*.
37. The text of the certification is found in the book of statutes of the *Shomrei ha-Dat* society (note 10), 28.
38. Ibid., 5; the German version, 17.
39. The letter of recommendation of the rabbis is to be found at the beginning of the booklet, ibid., 3–4 in Hebrew, 5–7 in Hungarian, and 18–19 in German.
40. Ibid., 3.
41. *Festschrift für Jacob Rosenheim anlässlich der Vollendung seines 60. Lebensjahres dargebracht von Seinen Freunden* (Frankfurt am Main, 1932), 159.
42. See *AZJ*, June 16, 1868, 496; *Neuzeit*, April 24, 203, and October 9, 483.
43. During my visit to the Municipal and University Library in Frankfurt in December 1992, I found a package of twelve stenciled circular letters of the *Shomrei ha-Dat* society, in Yiddish, or actually in German in Hebrew letters. Some of them were dated and some not, but all belong to the years 1868–1869. The pages in the package are not arranged chronologically, and I numbered the photographs which I obtained. Number 8 is the first in chronological terms. It is not yet addressed to the committees of the *Shomrei ha-Dat* society, but to specific addresses, and presents the statutes of *Shomrei ha-Dat*. Below I will cite these circular letters according to the number I assigned them.
44. A microfilm of the newspaper is found in the Jewish National and University Library in Jerusalem. Many issues of the first year are missing, and it is therefore difficult to determine the exact date of the change of editors.
45. *BCH*, 1858, 42–43.

46. Zs. Kraus, *Die grosse Synode, ihr Ursprung und ihre Wirkung nebst einem Anhang, Eine Barmizwarede* (Pest, 1859).
47. The poem with its Hungarian translation by Farkas, and its Hebrew translation by M. Ehrenteil, was published as an appendix to *Magyar Zsidó*, no. 19. A copy of it is found in the Jewish National and University Library in Jerusalem.
48. *BCH*, 1858, 97–98.
49. Both poems are found ibid., 289–292, 535–536.
50. I. Reich, *Beth-El, Ehrentempel verdienter ungarischer Israeliten*, vol. 2 (Pest, 1865), 461–478. The poem "Rose of Jericho" was reprinted on the last two pages. The citations are from the second edition, 1868.
51. Kraus was the fourth-generation descendant of Hanoch Henech Schick, patriarch of the clan, as was Maharam Schick, whose great-grandfather was the cousin of R. Abraham Schick. See Solomon Zvi Schick, *From Moses to Moses* (in Hebrew) (Munkács, 1909), 20a–23a.
52. See note 24.
53. See note 55.
54. *Ha-Magid*, September 23, 1868, 248.
55. *Israelit*, March 18, 1868, 199. According to the notice there of May 26, 1868, 438, Farkas resigned as editor of the newspaper because he refused to support the split.

11. Tensions and Fluctuations in the Orthodox Camp (pp. 108–121)

1. "Beleuchtung der die Gemeinden und Schulorganisationen betreffenden Vorlagen der ungarisch israelitschen Konferenzmajorität von einem Mitgliede des Schomre-Hadath Vereins," *Jeschurun* 14 (April-June 1868), 226–249. In his article "The Emergence of Ultra-Orthodoxy: The Invention of a Tradition," *The Uses of Tradition: Jewish Continuity in the Modern Era*, ed. J. Wertheimer (New York/Jerusalem, 1992), 46, n. 41, Michael Silber quoted the article in *Israelit* and suggested Kraus as a possible author, but with a question mark. This doubt is confirmed by the fact that Kraus, although his views are close to those expressed in the article, could not have written in quite that style.
2. In response to my query, Mordechai Breuer informed me that he had also reached the conclusion that the article was written by Hirsch himself.
3. See note 5.
4. The proposals were published in two pamphlets. They also appeared as an appendix to Esriel Hildesheimer's book, mentioned in note 11. Their main points are included in the article that appeared in installments in *AZJ*, March 17, 1868, 223–228, and on March 24, 1868, 246–249, and will be cited from there.
5. *Jeschurun* (note 1), 231–232.
6. *Jeschurun* 14, October-December, 1868, 27.
7. *Jeschurun* (note 1), 236–238.
8. Ibid., 246.
9. Ibid., 240.
10. Katzburg, in his bibliographical article (chapter 10, note 17), 44.
11. I. Hildesheimer, *Zum Congresse, Beurteilung der drei von der Majorität der in*

Pest versammelten Conferenz dem Kultus-Minister unterbreiteten Statute, Wahl, Gemeinde-und Schul-Statut (Prag, 1868). The signed introduction is dated 15 Sivan, which matches the date of Hirsch's article. Each man wrote without having seen the other's work.
12. Ibid., introduction.
13. Ibid., 26–31.
14. Ibid., 4–7.
15. Ibid., 17–19.
16. Ibid., 102.
17. Found in R. Jeremiah Löw's letter to R. Hayyim Sofer, see Y. Y. Sofer, *Toldot Soferim* (London, 1963), the letters (*Qan Sofer*), 10.
18. Hildesheimer (note 11), 59–64.
19. *AZJ*, May 19, 1868, 418. See also the editor's note in the margins of the first notice of the decision, March 17, 295–296.
20. The text of the memorandum is found in *AZJ*, July 17, 1868, 574–575, and in *Neuzeit*, July 3, 321–322.
21. J. Nobel, *Hildesheimer und Kutna, Zwei Rabbiner Eisenstadts* (Székesfehérvár, 1908).
22. According to the remarks of the editors of both journals mentioned in note 20.
23. A notice from the office of the minister about election procedures, which includes the rabbis among those with full voting rights, is found in *Neuzeit*, September 25, 1868, 458–459, and in *AZJ*, September 22, 1868, 776–777.
24. The details are in the two newspapers, ibid.
25. The secret circular letter was published in *Neuzeit*, May 29, 1868, 263–264. The correspondent of the *AZJ*, June 16, 1868, 495, considered leaving the editorship in the hands of the former editor an inefficient procedure. He was an educated man, but lacked roots in the Jewish world.
26. *Neuzeit*, October 16, 1868, 497–498.
27. Ibid., November 13, 1868, 548.
28. B. Z. Jacobowitz, *Zekhor Yemot Olam*, vol. 1 (Bnei Brak, 1986), the photographs at the end of the book, no. 17 (the frontispiece of the statutes of the *Shomrei ha-Dat* society in Yiddish) and no. 24 (a pamphlet entitled *Divrei Shalom ve-Emet* [Words of Peace and Truth] addressed to "our brethren the Sefardim"). For a summary of the pamphlet, see p. 154. I have not seen the pamphlets themselves.
29. See chapter 6.
30. Z. W. Joseph, *Darkhei ha-Yashar veha-Tov* (Munkacs, 1910), 38b–40a. The author is the grandson of the rabbi. Only the first letter is dated, but there is no doubt that the second, also addressed to Pressburg, is of a similar date. Michael Silber drew my attention to this source.
31. Ibid., 40a.
32. The notice is found in *Israelit*, August 5, 1868, 604; *AZJ*, September 29, 1868, 797–799.
33. About Hirsch see Reich (chapter 10, note 50), vol. 3 (1882), 30–50.
34. The German title page of Hirsch's book is M. Hirsch, *Gutachtlicher Bericht vom religiösen Standpunkt . . . über die in der Kaschauer isr. Kultusgemeinde ausgebrochenen Parteiungen* (Pest, 1868). Both the title and the text of the book are also written

in Hungarian, and the two versions are printed on facing pages. The Hebrew sources are given at the end of the book. The discussion about the validity of the ruling is found on pages 24–27, and the reference to Hildesheimer on the last page.

35. Memo B (chapter 9, note 19), 32–35.
36. In the paragraph that mentions Hirsch's negation of the validity of the ruling, in opposition to the position of the extremist minority in Kassa, the memorandum notes in parentheses: "Without stating whether it [the ruling] is correct or not"; ibid., 33.
37. See Eliav, *Hildesheimer* (chapter 10, note 4), 56–59. The two letters in manuscript are found in Hildesheimer's archives. I obtained them through the generosity of Meir Hildesheimer, and am grateful to him for this valuable source. I shall henceforth cite them as: Letter A and Letter B.
38. Stated in Letter B (note 37) and alluded to in Hildesheimer's letter.
39. To substantiate this theological argument he refers to an essay in one of R. Moses Hayyim Luzzatto's books, which I could not identify.
40. Eliav (note 37), 57.
41. About this quarrel see B. Bernstein, *A zsidók története Vasmegyében 1687–1904* (Budapest, 1915), 97–122.
42. Eliav (note 37), 57–58.
43. Letter B (note 37).
44. Ibid. The reference to Maimonides is apparently to his *Commentary on the Mishnah*, in the introduction to Sanhedrin, chapter 10 ("He Who Has a Share in the World to Come"), where Maimonides discusses how to educate the minor by promises of physical rewards. Nonetheless, the term "trickery" is not used there.
45. As Kraus states in the pamphlet *Rundschreiben an meine Glaubensgenossen in der Stadt und auf dem Lande*, quoted in *Neuzeit*, April 24, 1868, 203.
46. *Neuzeit*, November 6, 1868, 533, and November 27, 1868, 571. Both articles are hostile to Hildesheimer, but nonetheless faithfully report his statements and promises.
47. Circular letter no. 7 (chapter 10, note 43). This letter is undated, but it states that the rules for the election procedures had not yet been published.
48. Circular letter no. 5 (chapter 10, note 43), of August 1868.
49. Circulars no. 2, 12 (chapter 10, note 43), the first dated November 2, 1868, and the second *Parshat Noah*, 1868. These warnings were reiterated in the introduction to the Yiddish translation of the official rules for the elections, which the *Shomrei ha-Dat* disseminated in the north. Two copies of these are found in the Jewish National and University Library.
50. These letters attest to the fact that such incidents actually occurred. Adolf Munk tells of similar attempts in his autobiography, *Önéletrajz* (Nagykanizsa, 1942), 172–173.
51. In circular letter no. 6, dated Tuesday, *Parshat Mikez*, 1868, which was disseminated after the rabbis' meeting and the conference of activists, which we shall hear about below, the members of the administration praise themselves for the achievements made by the society in such a short time. The correspondent for *AZJ* published similar words of praise, not unmixed with envy, already on July 9, 1868, 479. And finally Leopold Löw, businesslike as usual, noted the achievements of the society: *Die jüdischen Wirren in Ungarn* (Pest, 1868), 94.

12. The Conference of Rabbis in Buda in Advance of the Congress (pp. 122–133)

1. Simon Bacher printed R. Schag's letter of invitation in *Ha-Magid*, 1868, 315–316. Katzburg summarizes its essential points in his bibliography (chapter 10, note 17), 95. I have one of the original mimeographed letters, from the Frankfurt library (chapter 10, note 43).
2. The allusion is to BT Horayot 3b.
3. For details about him see: *Shem ha-Gedolim me-Eretz Hagar* (chapter 10, note 12), *Ma'arekhet Gedolim*, 6b.
4. Circular letter no. 11 (chapter 10, note 43), *Parshat Nizavim*, 1868.
5. The publication of this statement in *Ha-Magid*, 1868, 323, was accompanied by strong criticism of the author's inconsistency.
6. Noted at the end of the statement.
7. For the text of the invitation, see *Ha-Magid*, 1868, 353–354. A circular letter from Pressburg was published in *Ivri Anokhi* 5 (1868), 67–68 (see Katzburg's bibliography [chapter 10, note 17], no. 156), encouraging the rabbis to make haste and come to the conference, but this was not an official invitation.
8. Circular letter no. 1 (chapter 10, note 43).
9. The connection to the fair is mentioned in the circular letter, ibid. Unlike the invitation addressed to the rabbis, the invitation to the householders was not individual. The organizers succeeded in obtaining a fifty-percent reduction in train and ship fares for anyone who stated in advance that the purpose of his voyage was participation in the convocation.
10. Mentioned in Hildesheimer's speech before the rabbinic conference; see his article (note 11), 933.
11. We have descriptions of the first days of the conference by two participants: Esriel Hildesheimer in *Israelit*, appendix to the fiftieth issue of 1868, 933–937; and H. Pollak, who used the title of district rabbi (it is not clear from which district) in *Neuzeit*, December 11, 1868, 591.
12. Hildesheimer (note 11), 933.
13. Ibid., 933–934.
14. Pollack (note 11), 591.
15. Ibid.
16. Hildesheimer (note 11), 934 ff.
17. Ibid., 935.
18. A note appears on p. 935, at the end of the first part: "Ofen am 12 Kisslev 5629"— the date of the third day of the conference. This means that Hildesheimer kept a sort of journal of daily events and sent it immediately to the newspaper.
19. This according to Pollak (note 11). According to him, Hildesheimer also supported this proposal, but this issue is not mentioned in the latter's report. Each author apparently concentrated on those issues in which he took an active interest, and their statements complement each other.
20. The description of the scene following is according to Hildesheimer (note 11), 936–937.

21. Hildesheimer mentions three colleagues who left the conference together with him: the rabbi of Kaposvár, R. Shalom Kutna; the rabbi of Csongrád, R. Joseph Nobel, his nephew; and the rabbi of Szobatko (apparently Szabadka), R. Moses Kutna, his brother. He did not list the names of his colleagues who were of the same opinion as him but who apparently did not leave the conference, in order to avoid embarrassing them. The names of the two senior people who left are given in another report in *Israelit* (note 11), 928–929, signed by M. H., Marcus Horowitz. According to him, R. Jeremiah Löw was also among those who left, but he was not certain if his was a final exit.
22. So testifies Hildesheimer, but only in his letter to R. Samson Raphael Hirsch, mentioned in note 23.
23. Eliav (chapter 10, note 4), 61.
24. "Die jüdischen Hoffnungen in Ungarn," *Jeschurun* 14, October–December 1868, 18–29.
25. For the citation of this announcement, see note 28.
26. The text of the decision is found in a pamphlet by S. Ganzfried, *Sefer Galuy* (Ofen, 1869), 2: "Even if they give it another name [that is, the seminary], that is if they wish to prepare a professor or teacher at the *yeshivot* to teach the pupils sciences and knowledge, let this idea sink without a trace, and not be mentioned in our country." I have found no mention of this pamphlet of S. Ganzfried anywhere, and received a copy of it through the generosity of Meir Hovav.
27. Hildesheimer already reported this rumor in his letter to Hirsch (note 23), 62, and called it "ein Curiosum." *Ha-Magid*, December 23, 1868, 395, publishes a similar version of the story.
28. In *Magyar Zsidó*, January 5, 1869, 5, the story is cited as public knowledge, and the correction from Pressburg is brought in the name of the Ketav Sofer in the January 20 issue, 30.
29. A notice of this appeared in *AZJ*, December 22, 1868, 1036–1037. There the number of participants is estimated at about forty. A statement on behalf of the convocation, signed by the two people mentioned in the text (alongside Löb Brill, a member of the *beit din* in Pest), was published in *Neuzeit*, December 11, 1868, 592–593. I obtained a photograph of the original issue through the generosity of Abraham Schischa of London. The Hebrew heading of this statement is: "With God's Help! Every Gathering Which is for the Sake of Heaven is Destined to Endure."
30. Pollak (note 11); Hildesheimer, in his letter to Hirsch (note 23).
31. Circular letter no. 10 (chapter 10, note 43), dated Monday, *Parshat Vayeze*, 1868.
32. Circular letter no. 3, ibid. The dates are given according to various systems.
33. *Jahresbericht des Schomre-Hadath-Vereines*, signed Pest, December 1, 1868; this was the day when the report was presented. It was of course composed before this date. The words of self-glorification and self-justification are found on page 3.
34. This surprising fact was noted in the December 6 issue of *Magyar Zsidó*, alongside the text of the memorandum.
35. Ibid. The Hungarian version of the memorandum, which was published only in the next issue of the newspaper, on December 15, added to the term for legal recognition the adjective "vallási," that is, religious recognition. This is no doubt an intentional softening, as if the reservations were based on religious considerations alone. But

this change contradicts the entire spirit of the memorandum; there is no doubt that the German version was the one that was debated in the plenum, signed by the president of the conference, and presented to the minister.
36. *AZJ* (note 29), ibid.
37. This was R. Sofer's testimony in his letter to the community of Sziget, concerning the controversy over the community's joining the Orthodox national organization. See *Milhemet Mizvah* (Sziget, 1886), 108a. This letter is cited by Maharam Schick's traditional biographers: *Introduction to the Sermons of Maharam Schick* (in Hebrew) (Cluj, 1937), 17b; *Maharam Schick on Tractate Avot* (in Hebrew) (Sziget, 1929), introduction. Following them, Jacobowitz (chapter 11, note 28), 173, cites these words, but he was unable to explain their significance in the context of events.
38. In circular letter no. 6 (chapter 10, note 43), of Tuesday, *Parshat Miqez*, 1868, which includes a short report on the two conferences that had just ended, the authors give the number two hundred and fifty for the rabbinic conference. No number is given for the lay convocation. See *Magyar Zsidó*, December 6, 1868, 424.
39. See note 9.
40. See note 38.
41. Ibid.

13. The Composition of the Congress and Its Chances of Success (pp. 137–148)

1. For a general description of the Congress, see Zs. Grossmann, *A magyar zsidók a XIX század közepén* (Budapest, 1917); N. Katzburg, "The Jewish Congress of Hungary 1868–1869," *Hungarian Jewish Studies*, vol. 2, ed. R. L. Braham (New York, 1969), 1–33; T. Domján, "Der Kongress der ungarischen Israeliten 1868–1869," *Ungarn-Jahrbuch*, vol. 1 (Mainz, 1969), 139–161. This last article adds nothing to the preceding ones, and is not sufficiently accurate. The Hungarian source for the proceedings is the protocols of the Congress: *Izraelita Congressus* (Budapest, 1869). The book is not consecutively paginated, so each session will be cited according to its number, date, and separate pagination. Eötvös's speech—Session 1, December 14, 1868, 1–2. An abridged German translation is found in *AZJ*, December 29, 1868, 1048–1049. A complete translation was published in the first issue of *Congress Zeitung*, December 15, 1868, 5–6.
2. I. Hildesheimer, *Ausführlicher Rechenschafts-Bericht der . . . zu einer Partei gegliederten Mitglieder des ungarischen israelitischen Congresses* (Prag, 1869), 11. See also *Israelit*, December, 1868, 981. For the author, see note 7.
3. Hildesheimer (note 2), 8.
4. Ibid., 8–9.
5. *AZJ* (note 1), 1047–1048.
6. Hildesheimer (note 2), 13.
7. The reporter was Marcus Horovitz, as his son, who heard it firsthand, tells us in the introduction to the pamphlet M. Horovitz, *Von Liszka nach Berlin* (Frankfurt am Main, 1914). Horovitz was studying in the Eisenstadt *yeshivah* at the time and accompanied his teacher to the Congress. His source of information is his teacher; he gives a detailed report of the activities of the committee in which Hildesheimer sat,

but we get only fragmentary and delayed information about the other committees. This is apparently the reason that Horovitz only initialed the article, unlike those articles he wrote on his own initiative. See chapter 12, note 21.
8. *Israelit* (note 2), 982.
9. Hildesheimer (note 2), 6–7.
10. Ibid., 11.
11. Solomon Sofer, in the introduction to his father's book, Abraham Samuel Benjamin Sofer, *Commentary on the Pentateuch* (Vienna, 1883), xxiv. For a testimony *en passant* in R. Nathan Miller's eulogy of the Ketav Sofer, see *Zekhor le-Avraham* (Jerusalem, 1972), 274–275. For a secondhand testimony see, ibid., 339–340.
12. Y. Weinberger, *Beit Hillel ha-Shalem* (Tirnau, 1941), 48.
13. This information was given to me by Michael Silber, who is researching the biography of Schlesinger. According to his sources, the two guests from Galicia did not receive permission to reside in the capital. They therefore stayed in a nearby town, and travelled back and forth throughout the Congress.
14. Protocols (note 1), Session 15, February 3, 1869, 3.
15. *Israelit* (note 2) reports on this in an objective manner, while Hildesheimer (note 2) adopts a bitter tone. His complaint on this matter is also found in the secessionist Orthodox group's memorandum to Minister Eötvös (chapter 15, note 3), 8.
16. The description is based on the two sources mentioned in note 2: *Israelit*, 983; Hildesheimer, 12–13. The descriptions of the personalities are according to F. Liebig, *Photographien aus dem ungarisch israelitischen Congresse* (Wien, 1869). N. Katzburg, (chapter 10, note 17, 222–367, no. 190), identifies the author as Ignaz Friedlieber, the son of Albert Friedlieber, the representative of Ujhely. However, he was a student at the time in Prague, as explained in his booklet (ibid., no. 55). This Liebig was a seasoned writer, well versed in the details of Jewish life.
17. See note 24.
18. Hildesheimer in *Israelit*, January 13, 1869, 25–27.
19. Zipser's statement, ibid., 27–29; Steinhardt's statement, ibid., 30–31.
20. Ibid., 27
21. Ibid., 29.
22. Ibid., 31.
23. N. Katzburg, "The Struggle of Hungarian Jewry for Religious Equality in the 1890s" (in Hebrew), *Zion* 22 (1957), 119–158.
24. Protocols (note 1), Session 11, January 15, 1869, 1–2.
25. *Israelit* (note 18), 32.
26. Liebig (note 16), 54, tells of one of the delegates, Deutsch by name, who invited members of both camps to his home in an attempt to mediate between them. Hildesheimer (note 2), 8, also reports attempts at mediation, but with the benefit of hindsight, in view of their lack of success, they appeared to him to have been fruitless from the outset. There was also another kind of attempt to end the disagreements. R. Solomon Ganzfried, in a pamphlet called *Sefer Galuy* (with German translation) (see chapter 12, note 26), suggests the following in the name of kindred souls of both camps: Since there is no way to arrive at an agreement, especially on the question of the seminary, let each party choose representatives who would seek a way for the camps to pursue their divergent paths peacefully.

27. *AZJ*, February 9, 1869, 111; *CZ*, January 2, 1869.
28. See chapter 11, note 10.
29. S. Kraus, *Worte des Frieden, gerichtet an die verehrten Mitglieder des ungarisch israelitischen Landes-Kongresses* (Pest, 1868), 9–12, 33–36.
30. *Magyar Zsidó*, January 17, 1869, 25–27; January 24, 37.
31. Leon de Modena Redivivus [Leopold Löw], *Die jüdischen Wirren in Ungarn, Beitrag zur Zeitgeschichte, vor dem Kongresse* (Pest, 1868), 9–12, 33–36.
32. See Katzburg (note 16), no. 71. He lists R. Abraham Hochmuth's pamphlet against Löw without having seen it; I too was unable to obtain a copy. Kraus (note 29), 7, also explicitly rejects Löw's arguments, although he should have considered Löw an ally, as an advocate of Kraus's original position in favor of separation, although Löw had his own reasons for this policy. We know of Hochmuth's opinion of Löw from his book, which was published only after the Congress: A. Hochmuth, *Leopold Löw, als Theologe, Historiker und Publizist* (Leipzig, 1871).
33. See note 11. The son claims that his father categorically rejected any compromise. It is understandable that this claim should be made, once the decision had already been made in favor of the split.
34. Protocols (note 1), Session 2, December 16, 1868, 6. Grün's declaration is found in *Israelit*, December 3, 1868, 983.
35. About Grün see Liebig (note 16), 17–18.
36. The presentation of the document is mentioned in the protocols (note 1), December 18, 1868, 3. The text of the announcement is found in *Israelit*, January 6, 1869, 10. Grün was the one who presented the document, as emerges from his statements in the protocols (note 1), Session 6, December 22, 1868, 3. The names of the other signatories are not given.
37. Hildesheimer (note 2), 16–17.
38. Protocols (note 1), Session 6, December 22, 1868, 3.
39. Ibid.
40. Protocols (note 1), Session 6, December 22, 1868, 3.
41. Hildesheimer (note 2), 18.
42. Protocols (note 1), Session 7, December 23, 1868, 13.
43. Protocols (note 1), Session 8, December 28, 1868, 9–10.
44. *Israelit*, January 6, 1869, 12.
45. Protocols, ibid., 10.

14. The Inevitable Clash (pp. 149–158)

1. *AZJ*, January 12, 1869, 28.
2. Hildesheimer (chapter 13, note 2), 17.
3. The appointment of the committees is discussed in the protocols (chapter 13, note 1), Sessions 7–10, December 23–30, 1868.
4. For the full list of those chosen, see ibid., Session 10, 5–6. The list was also published in *Israelit*, January 13, 1869, 25.
5. See chapter 11, note 4. The text of the majority proposal is found in the protocols (chapter 13, note 1), Session 19, February 8, 1869, 2–10, in both languages of the Congress.

6. The platform of the Orthodox was reprinted in *MZsSz* 14 (1897), 182–190.
7. Ibid., paragraphs 1, 3, 4.
8. Ibid., paragraph 16.
9. Ibid.
10. Ibid., paragraphs 27–39.
11. Published as an independent pamphlet, Pest, 1869, but also included in the protocols (chapter 13, note 1), Session 15, February 3, 1869, 2–4.
12. Published as a pamphlet, see note 13.
13. It is sufficient to read the reasons given for his proposals: E. Eisler, *Elaborat eines Fundamentalstatutes für die israelitischen Gemeinden Ungarns und Siebenbürgens* (Pest, 1869).
14. *Das traditionelle Judenthum*, March 23, 1871. See chapter 18.
15. Protocols (chapter 13, note 1), Session 14, January 28, 1869, 4.
16. Ibid., Session 15, February 3, 1869, 4.
17. See chapter 10, note 25.
18. According to information given by the *Israelit* reporter, January 20, 1869, 47, Dr. Hirschler proposed to the Progressive club his version of the paragraph about the statutes of the congregational organization, according to which even a Reform minority, like Holdheim's, would be allowed to exist within the framework of the congregation. The members of the club rejected the proposal. Leopold Löw argued publicly in favor of complete freedom for each community to choose the religious character it wished. See his book (chapter 13, note 31), 16.
19. I have described this development in several of the articles included in my book *Divine Law in Human Hands: A Study in Halakhic Flexibility* (forthcoming).
20. Protocols (chapter 13, note 1), Session 16, February 3, 1869, 3.
21. Ibid., including all that follows.
22. Hildesheimer (chapter 13, note 2), 33.
23. See chapter 15, note 12. He apparently continued to uphold this view in the following sessions as well.
24. Steinhardt's speech is to be found in the protocols (chapter 13, note 1), Session 16, February 3, 1869, 15–18. For the declaration of his positivist attitude, see the last page.
25. Ibid., 17. The story about the pious fool is cited by the Tosafot, BT Sotah 21b, s.v.: *heikhi dami*. The Babylonian Talmud there describes the pious fool as one who refrains from saving a woman from drowning for fear that he will look at her.
26. Protocols (note 24), 17. In more detail in *Israelit*, February 24, 1869, 138. According to this report, the number of those who walked out was about fifty.
27. Hollander's speech—protocols (chapter 13, note 1), Session 17, February 5, 1869, 12–16.
28. The notice is cited in *AZJ*, February 2, 1869, 87, from *Litographische Pester Correspondent*.
29. *MZs*, January 24, 1869, 38; January 31, 1869, 49–50; February 14, 1869, 74.
30. Some of the allusions apparently referred to events that occurred within the non-Jewish community, but one thing explicitly related to the rabbi of Pressburg, the Ketav Sofer: "Noch sonderbarer schien es mir, dass gerade jener hochwürdige Herr, der jetzt auf dem hochberühmten Rabbinerstuhle seines Vaters thront, sich mit diesen

Persönlichkeiten in Rapport setzte, mit Persönlichkeiten, die man erst kürzlich mit einem Titel beehrt hat, dessen Nennung Sie mir wohl erlassen werden." See protocols (note 27), 14. Did he mean that the Ketav Sofer wished to add Hildesheimer, a native of Germany, to the rabbinate (perhaps the multiple noun "Persönlichkeiten" is meant to conceal the allusion to the esteemed person who was present at the time)? Perhaps a search through the contemporary press could solve this riddle.

31. *Israelit*, February 24, 1869, 137.
32. For the text of the declaration and the list of signatories, see protocols (chapter 13, note 2), Session 17, February 5, 1869, 9–10.
33. Ibid., 10.
34. For the list of members, see Hildesheimer (chapter 13, note 2), on the reverse side of the frontispiece.
35. Protocols (chapter 13, note 1), Session 18, February 5, 1869, 27–28.

15. A Rump Congress and a Divided Orthodoxy (pp. 159–168)

1. *Israelit* (chapter 14, note 31), 137–138.
2. *Israelit*, February 17, 1869, 118.
3. *Verwahrung der am Schulchan Aruch festhaltenden Partei des isr. Congresses* (Pest, 1869).
4. Ibid., 12.
5. Ibid., 14–15.
6. Ibid., 14.
7. See chapter 16.
8. See chapter 12 and chapter 18. Liebig (chapter 13, note 13), 16, overheard the following assessment in the Orthodox club: "If as president of the club he shed light on the topics under discussion, he never clarified his own view sufficiently."
9. Liebig (chapter 13, note 16), 48, described R. Sofer's appearance: "When he gets agitated, his eyes glisten, his face gets red as fire, his sidelocks swing back and forth until everyone is afraid to look at him." His son's description is similar. According to him, after the Progressives "said openly that they have no interest in the Shulhan Arukh, and when they later began to discuss [issues] at the Congress, and the chairman did not want to give him permission to speak, he (may he rest in peace) jumped on the table and called in a loud voice with fiery fervor: 'Who is on God's side, [come] to me! And everyone whose heart is touched by the love of God let him leave the Congress and not sit in the same room as the Reformers!'" See: Y. Z. Sofer, *Toldot Sofrim* (London, 1963), 124.
10. Maharam Schick, *Commentary on Tractate Avot* (Sziget, 1869), introduction, biography of the author, no pagination.
11. Maharam Schick, *Responsa, O.H.*, no. 309. This is his well-known description of the course of events that brought about the split.
12. *Israelit*, February 24, 1869, 138.
13. According to the reporter of the *AZJ*, March 18, 1869, 204, the minister set the end of February as the final date. The haste with which the Congress was ended, a week earlier, indicates that this was indeed the deadline.

14. *Israelit*, January 20, 1869, 47. For the formal vote, see protocols (chapter 13, note 1), Session 31, February 20, 1869, 14.
15. Protocols, ibid., 9–12.
16. Memorandum (note 3), 12. The reporter of the *AZJ*, March 18, 1869, 204, denounced the hypocrisy of this argument.
17. Ibid.
18. The reporter of the *AZJ*, February 6, 1872, 106, who served as the head teacher in the Ujhely school, related that the *Admor* of Liszka consulted him about the possibility of founding such a "simultaneous school" in his city. See chapter 18, note 32.
19. See note 15.
20. Discussed at length in Sessions 7–10, December 24–30, 1868. A short summary is found in *Israelit*, January 13, 1869, 7.
21. This argument is included in the protest presented by Pappenheim and signed by himself and several of his colleagues, upon the appointment of the committees. See *Israelit*, ibid.
22. *Israelit*, January 20, 1869, 46–47.
23. *Israelit*, February 10, 1869, 102–103.
24. The response of Samuel Kohn, the great adherent of the seminary idea, is cited in the *AZJ*, March 18, 1869, 205. In the debate in the committee, Abraham Hochmut pointed to the Eisenstadt *yeshivah* as a counter-example. He is cited in *Congress Zeitung*, January 20, 1869, 60.
25. Protocols (chapter 13, note 1), Session 33, February 23, 1869; the decision is on p. 2. For the president of the Congress's assessment that the foundation of the seminary is an act "that a large part of educated Jewry has yearned for many years . . . and that the land and the nation have awaited," see p. 13.

16. The Battle over Ratification of the Statutes (pp. 169–182)

1. Published in *Neuzeit*, March 19, 1869, 139; and then in *AZJ*, April 20, 1869, 314.
2. See chapter 9, notes 9–10.
3. Chapter 15, note 3.
4. *AZJ*, March 16, 1869, 207.
5. Hildesheimer (chapter 13, note 2), 11.
6. Ibid., 5.
7. I quote the article according to *Jeschurun* 15 (1869), where it was reprinted, as I explain below.
8. Ibid., 140–144.
9. Ibid., 145–146.
10. Ibid., 146–147.
11. Ibid., 152–153.
12. Ibid., 153–154.
13. Kraus's remark appears only in *Magyar Zsidó*, March 7, 1869.
14. See note 7.
15. *Jeschurun* (note 7), 137.
16. *Rabbinische Gutachten über die Statuten des Ung-Isr. Kongresses* (Pest, 1869).

17. Ibid., 12–18.
18. Ibid., 18.
19. See chapter 6, note 53.
20. *Israelit*, May 5, 1869, 350.
21. Menahem Mendel Glick, *Zikhron Elazar* (Miskolc, 1937), 71b.
22. *AZJ*, May 18, 1869, 395.
23. Glick (note 21), 716, emphasis mine.
24. So they state in the proclamation reproduced in *Neuzeit*, October 8, 1869, 500.
25. Glick (note 21), 71b–72a.
26. A good deal of slanderous gossip about this circulated. See the lead article of *Neuzeit*, October 29, 1869, 520.
27. Published in *Neuzeit*, April 9, 1869, 174. For the circular letter, see pp. 173–174.
28. *Ivri Anokhi*, April 23, 1869, 230, carries an announcement setting the date of the meeting for April 14.
29. Other names are mentioned in the ultra-Orthodox literature. The real composition of the delegation is given in *Israelit* (note 20), by someone who wished to refute Markus Horovitz's accusation (ibid., 396) that the delegation consisted exclusively of Hassidim. The respondent was no doubt closely associated with the organizers. The description below is based on *Magyar Zsidó*, April 29, 1869, 154; *Neuzeit*, May 7, 1869, 223; and *Izraelita Közlöny*, May 14, 1869, 185.
30. A biography of Reich has never been written. Biographical information is found in the various newspaper articles that appeared after his death, at the end of April 1896: *Egyenlöség*, May 1; *Neuzeit*, May 8; *Allgemeine jüdische Zeitung*, April 29. The testimonial in *Egyenlöség* was written by the editor, Miksa Szabolcsi, his old rival and critic, who praised him after his death as a charming, just, and forceful personality.
31. See Y. Y Grünwald, *Qorot ha-Torah veha-Emunah be-Hungaria* (Budapest, 1921), 77; S. B. D. Sofer, *Mazkeret Paks*, vol. 2 (Jerusalem, 1966), 39; and later B. Z. Jacobowitz, *Zekhor Yemot 'Olam*, vol. 1 (Bnai Brak, 1986), 285. None of them checked the origin of the story.
32. *AZJ*, May 18, 1869, 395.
33. *Die Sanktionirten Statuten und Beschlüsse des ... Landes-Kongresses der Israeliten in Ungarn und Siebenbürgen, Amtliche Ausgabe* (Pest, 1869). The book was published in German and Hungarian, on facing pages. A Hebrew translation was prepared by S. Bachrach, *Taqqanot ha-Na'asot mi-Shelihei ha-Qehillot be-Asseifat ha-Va'ad ha-Gadol "Congress"* ... (Ofen, 1869).
34. J. Eötvös, *Levelek* (Budapest, 1976), 605.
35. So states the proclamation of the *Shomrei ha-Dat* society, issued shortly before the New Year, which fell on September 6. See note 44.
36. This emerges from the course of subsequent events.
37. Y. Z. Sofer, *Toldot Soferim*, letters (*Qan Sofer*) (London, 1963), letter 29, 27.
38. Hayyim Sofer, *Mahaneh Hayyim*, II (Ungvár, 1872), no. 5, 8. The date appears at the end of the responsum, p. 14.
39. Sofer (note 37), letter 30. And see note 38. The long responsum, consisting exclusively of exhortation, preaches rejection under any circumstances.
40. See chapter 6, note 45, about his clash with the authorities during the battle over the new synagogue in Miskolc. A scandal erupted in his city, Munkács, upon his return

from the Congress, concerning the public desecration of the Sabbath by two physicians, and he once again came into conflict with the authorities. See Sofer (note 37), 125, the source cited there.
41. See *Magyar Zsidó*, June 9, 1869, 194–196.
42. See below.
43. See below in the text.
44. The letter was printed in *Neuzeit*, October 15, 1869, 499. The date of its circulation was the end of August or beginning of September. It ends with blessings for the New Year, which fell that year on September 6.
45. Ibid., 499–500.
46. For information about the conflict in Pressburg, where the heads of the community refused to hold elections for the representatives of the district organization and the commissar was aided by the members of the opposition, see *Neuzeit*, October 15, 1869, 498–499.
47. The proclamation is included in a responsum by R. Hayyim Sofer (note 38), 6. For the number of signatories, whose names were not given, see ibid., 8. Katzburg attributed authorship of the proclamation to R. Sofer, but the latter only copied it and often used it in his responsa. See N. Katzburg, "The Jewish Congress of Hungry in 1868, List of Sources" (in Hebrew), *Areshet* 4 (1960), 322–367, no. 240.
48. Ibid., as with all the quotations in the following paragraph.
49. See note 21. The phrase *laqahat mo'ed* that appears in both sources is a Germanism, "sich Zeit nehmen."
50. I received this pamphlet through the generosity of Michael Silber.
51. A remark by "the *Gaon, Av Beit Din* of Sziget," is cited in paragraph sixteen.
52. Circular letter (note 44), 500–501.
53. *Gutachten* . . . (note 16). The introduction notes carefully that this is a selection of the opinions that were received. In his proclamation, Maharam Schick indeed lists the cities from which responses were received that were not published.
54. Ibid., 6.
55. More of this below.
56. Ibid., 8–18.
57. And see above in the text near note 16.
58. Ibid., 20–30.
59. Ibid., 3–4.
60. Ibid., 4.
61. The order was published by L. Löw, *Der jüdische Kongress in Ungarn, historisch beleuchtet* (Pest, 1871), 293.
62. The link between these arguments was clearly understood by the reporter for *AZJ*, March 1, 1870, 172.

17. The Parliamentary Decision (pp. 183–190)

1. The turning of the tide of public opinion excited much interest at the time. See for example *Israelit*, March 2, 1869. This change is documented in a pamphlet published by the *Shomrei ha-Dat* society: *Journalstimmen über den ungar. Israeli-*

tischen Landes-Kongress und die von denselben gefassten Beschlüssen und Statuten (Pest, 1870).
2. Opponents of the Orthodox attributed the press's surprising support for the Orthodox to the influence of Ede Horn, formerly Ignác Einhorn, the rabbi of the Reform congregation in Pest at the time of the revolution, who, with his return from "exile," had become the editor of *Neue freie Lloyd*, the organ of the radical opposition. According to this version, the *Shomrei ha-Dat* supported the opposition candidates in exchange for their help for Orthodox causes. See *AZJ*, March 1, 1870, 172; April 5, 1870, 262. Horn's support of the Orthodox is a fact, and his articles are included in the pamphlet cited in the previous note. Nonetheless, his support would make sense even if there were no formal agreement with the Orthodox. In any event, their victory did not come about thanks to the opposition, but because the pillars of the ruling party accepted their protest.
3. A. Zeller, *A magyar egyházpolitika 1847–1894*, vol. 1 (Budapest, 1894), 478–483.
4. Ibid., 609–611.
5. Wahrmann's words are reported, ibid., 639–646.
6. Ibid., 643.
7. Ibid.
8. See chapter 16, note 1.
9. Zeller (note 3), 985, and see below.
10. See chapter 9, note 19, Memo A, 4.
11. Zeller (note 3), 681.
12. For Jókai's speech, see ibid., 663–668.
13. Ibid., 665.
14. Ibid., 665–666.
15. Ibid., 665.
16. Throughout the speech.
17. Ibid., 665–666.
18. Ibid., 666.
19. *Neuzeit*, February 25, 1870, 94.
20. For Németh's speech, see Zeller (note 3), 675 ff.; the part that concerns us is on pp. 680–682.
21. Ibid., 643.
22. Ibid., 681–682.
23. Ibid., 682. Németh's attack was malicious, but not totally unsubstantiated. Jewish behavior in the struggle between the Hungarians and the Austrians, in all its stages, did not follow the patriotic Hungarian pattern that the Jewish leadership, both Orthodox and Neolog, claimed to have followed after the Hungarian victory. The subject is now accessible for examination by unbiased historians, but it is outside of our purview.
24. Ibid., 985–986.
25. Ibid., 986.
26. The *Shomrei ha-Dat* announcement was published in *Israelit*, August 10, 1870, 605. *Magyar Zsidó*, April 7, 1870, has a notice from Pressburg that in his sermon on the Sabbath preceding Passover the Ketav Sofer celebrated the victory of the Orthodox as a miracle of Purim. The formula is reiterated by ultra-Orthodox preachers and his-

torians. See Y. Y. Grünwald, *Leplagot Yisrael be-Ungaria* (Deva, 1929), 81; and recently Jacobowitz (chapter 16, note 31), vol. 1, 308, not as a mere figure of speech, but on the basis of proofs that the miracle was meant to happen precisely on that day.
27. The directive is found in Löw (chapter 16, note 61), 295–296.
28. Zeller (note 3), 545–553.
29. See chapter 9, note 19. The memorandum is divided into three sections, which will be cited as A, B, and C.
30. Memo C, ibid.
31. *Israelit*, May 19, 1870, 358, reports on consultations that preceded the formulation of the petition, and attributes the intention to abolish the decision of March 18 to one of the participants. The authors of the memorandum rejected the idea.
32. The accompanying letter was published in German translation in *AZJ*, December 30, 1870, 1002–1004.
33. Ibid., 1003. This is a direct quotation from the Orthodox petition.
34. Ibid. These words are reminiscent of the argument presented by the Hamburg *beit din* to the Senate that the founders of the Reform Temple are members of a new sect, which does not have the same status as the Jews. See what I wrote in *Divine Law in Human Hands* (forthcoming).
35. Memo A (note 29), 42–43; *AZJ* (note 32), 1003.
36. Ibid.
37. *AZJ*, ibid., 1003.
38. Ibid; see also Memo A (note 29), 39.
39. Memo A (note 29), 45–46.
40. Ibid.
41. The text of the recommendation is found in Zeller (note 3), 937. For an analysis of it see the beginning of chapter 18.
42. N. Katzburg, "The Struggle of Hungarian Jewry for Religious Equality in the 1890s" (in Hebrew), *Zion* 22 (1957), 119–148.

18. The Orthodox Organization and Its Founders (pp. 191–203)

1. The text of the request is not extant. We learn of its contents from the minister's response; see the following note.
2. The response is found in *AZJ*, September 20, 1870, 747–748.
3. Sofer (chapter 16, note 37) letter no. 39, 34–36. Hayyim Sofer's response is dated April 18.
4. Ibid., 31.
5. Ibid.
6. See below.
7. The announcement is found in *Israelit*, August 1870, 605–606. It was preceded by another announcement, apparently of similar content, which I have not seen.
8. The announcement stated that membership in the planned organization would depend on the will of the congregations, and I. R., that is, Ignác Reich reiterated this promise in an article in *Magyar Zsidó*, August 4, 1870, a week before the opening of the assembly.

9. The list of the congregations was published serially in *Magyar Zsidó*, July 20–August 25, 1870.
10. *Israelit*, September 7, 1870, 673–676.
11. Ibid, 675. This was already stated during the assembly. Many of the delegates came late, and the number of letters of appointment eventually reached 350.
12. Maharam Schick, *Responsa, Y.D.*, no. 336.
13. My description is based on the reports in *Magyar Zsidó* (note 9) and in *Israelit*, September 7, 1870, 673–676.
14. *Israelit*, ibid., 673.
15. Ibid., 675.
16. This important document was published by D. Sofer, *Mazkeret Paks*, vol. 3 (Jerusalem, 1973), 109–110. It was copied from there by Jacobowitz (chapter 16, note 31), 323–324.
17. Jacobowitz, (chapter 16, note 31), 328.
18. They are Zvi Mannheimer, Menahem Katz, Yoel Ungar, Simon Judah Fonfeder, and Aron Fried. See note 9.
19. Solomon Zvi Schick, *Mi-Moshe ad Moshe*, the genealogy of the Schick family (Munkács, 1903), 22a.
20. The decisions of the assembly were published in *Israelit*, September 14, 1870, 689–691.
21. Ibid., 690–691; the explanation appears on 674.
22. According to *AZJ*, September 20, 1870, 748, this decision, which appears liberal, received much praise from the press.
23. See note 21.
24. *Israelit* (note 20), ibid.
25. Ibid., 691.
26. Ibid., 676, contrary to what was stated in the decisions, 692.
27. The invitation/announcement (note 7) stated that it was published with the consent of "all the great scholars of our time."
28. Sofer (chapter 16, note 37), letter no. 40, 36; we thus learn that R. Hayyim Sofer remained steadfast in his refusal, mentioned in note 3.
29. See chapter 16, note 21.
30. Hayyim Sofer sent his book, *Sha'arei Hayyim* (Ungvár, 1869), which had just appeared, to R. Jeremiah Löw. In this book the author listed all the legal stringencies that should govern behavior towards religious transgressors: their illness is not considered sufficient reason to desecrate the Sabbath, they are not to be buried in a Jewish cemetery, and so on. R. Löw told him that he had not stated anything new, but it was not wise "to bring it to the attention of everyone at this time" without explanation, for publication would be detrimental rather than beneficial. To Sofer's question to whom among the members of his congregation he should send the book, the rabbi of Ujhely responded that opinions had changed since the Congress.
31. For the letter, see *Mazkeret Paks* (note 16), 106–107. Further on, the letter mentions the idea, which had apparently come up in discussion at the assembly, to require the congregations to write in their protocols that they would not accept a rabbi who had graduated from the seminary, thereby undermining its existence. R. Deutsch opposed this proposal, claiming that it would not work, and that the congregations would not

abide by it. He asserted that the only option was to publish a total ban on the seminary, a proposal that was apparently discussed during the assembly, but rejected as ineffectual without the signature of the rabbi of Ujhely. No ban was declared at that time.

32. *AZJ*, July 16, 1872, 572. Rosenheimer was accepted by rabbinic circles. The *Admor* of Liszka consulted him on the subject of the interdenominational school in his city, which the hassidim preferred to the Jewish school (*AZJ*, February 6, 1872, 106), and the report bears the stamp of authenticity. See chapter 15, note 18.
33. See note 28.
34. J. Grünfeld, "Geschichte der orth. israelitischen Kultusgemeinde," *Die Juden und die Judengemeinde, Bratislava in Vergangenheit und Gegenwart*, ed. H. Gold (Brünn, 1932), 109, 117.
35. *Das traditionelle Judenthum*, February 23, 1871, 173–174.
36. The following description is based on Eisler's article and on the official document that was published in *AZJ*, October 3, 1871, 807–808; in *Neuzeit*, October 6, 1871, 475–477, with critical comments.
37. I. Berger, *Offener Brief an Ehrwürden Herrn Jeremias Löw Oberrabbiner in S-A-Ujhely* (Wien, 1872), 21.
38. *Jüdische Presse*, 1871, 418.
39. Also in *Neuzeit* (note 36).
40. *Das traditionelle Judenthum*, March 9, 1871, 191.
41. Ibid., 206.
42. The county prefect responded to the request of the Orthodox congregation, as stated explicitly at the beginning of the document, note 36.
43. The letter of resignation was published in *Neuzeit*, February 28, 1872, 89.
44. We do not have the text of the memorandum.
45. *Neuzeit*, February 10, 1871, 64–66; February 17, 1871, 75–76; February 24, 1871, 85.
46. So wrote R. Hayyim Sofer in his letter to the *Shomrei ha-Dat* a month after the March 18, 1870 (*Shushan Purim*), decision: "God saw the tears of the righteous, their fasts and cries, and rescued them because of the merits of their forefathers, and they should not believe that their wisdom was responsible, only their self-sacrifice went up before the Lord." See Sofer (chapter 16, note 37), 35. Michael Silber told me that Akiva Joseph Schlesinger noted that Eötvös's demise was an act of Divine deliverance for the Orthodox.
47. *Das traditionelle Judenthum*, February 10, 1871, 161.
48. Ibid., March 6, 1871, 194.
49. Zeller (chapter 17, note 3), 934.
50. The Neologs made a desperate attempt to forestall this development. Hirschler presented a memorandum to the new minister on April 26, in which he protested retroactively against granting to the Orthodox assembly a status comparable to that of the Congress. The latter had been chosen according to all details of parliamentary procedure, while there had been no supervision over the election of the participants in the former. Moreover, at the time, Minister Eötvös had categorized the assembly as merely a private gathering. But all this was to no avail. The step taken by Pauler was typical of legislative procedure in Hungary, which provoked much criticism and

ridicule. The Parliament discussed the issue at length, and at the end left the decision to the executive branch. A similar procedure is described later in connection with the founding of the seminary, this time in the Neologs' favor. Hirschler's memorandum was published in *MZsSz*, 8 (1891), 771–773.
51. *Das traditionelle Judenthum*, November 23, 1871, 456. This was exhaustively reported in the next issue, of November 30, 1871, 457–459, and there the connection to the miracle of Chanukah is made.
52. *AZJ*, January 2, 1872, 6.

19. The Fate of the Uncommitted (pp. 204–214)

1. *Shevet Ahim*, March 28, 1872.
2. S. Kohn, *Was haben die jüngsten Vorgänge innerhalb der ungarischen Judenheit zu bedeuten* (Pest, 1870), 6.
3. Published in an open letter (Sziget, 1886), 2–3; reprinted together with *Sefer Milhemet Mitzvah* (Sziget, 1888). Jacobowitz (chapter 16, note 31) reprinted it in his book, 368–374, without the signatures, and determined its date (ibid., note 15) according to its publication in *Shevet Ahim*.
4. The signatory for Pressburg was Simhah Bunim ben Abraham Samuel Benjamin, the Shevet Sofer. The Ketav Sofer had died two months before, on December 30, 1871.
5. For documentation, see the works mentioned in note 3, and *Ohev Mishpat* (Lvov, 1888).
6. For biographical information, see P. Z. Schwartz, *Shem ha-Gedolim me-Eretz Hagar* (Paks, 1914), 12a–b.
7. The letter to R. Hayyim of Sanz mentioned below was written, according to his testimony, "in the name of the executive committee." See *Milhemet Mitzvah* (note 3), 59.
8. See chapter 18, note 31.
9. The letter is quoted in the open letter (note 3). It lacks a date, but mentions that the statutes were "upheld by the kaiser," so it must have been written after December 1871.
10. See note 7. The rabbi of Sanz's letter to R. Panet is found in *Milhemet Mitzvah* (note 3), 59. The writer notes explicitly that he is acting at the behest of R. Deutsch.
11. See Y. Y. Cohen, *Sages of Transylvania (1630–1944)* (in Hebrew) (Jerusalem, 1989), 36.
12. R. Deutsch's letter is printed in *Milhemet Mitzvah* (note 3), 58a–59a.
13. Ibid, 58b: "how should we institute the regulations, when the previous generations did not do so."
14. Ibid., 51a.
15. This expression is not used in the letter, but there is no doubt that the different external appearance of the Oberland Jews created a sense of estrangement from them.
16. See note 13.
17. See *Toldot Soferim* (chapter 16, note 37), 126, for the reason he left Munkács: evil men had embittered his life and the rabbi of Sanz came to his defense.
18. Z. Wolf, *Darkei ha-Yashar veha-Tov* (Munkács, 1910), 28b and 39b.

19. *Milhemet Mitzvah* (note 3), 58b.
20. Ibid., 59a. In contrast to the others, R. Deutsch relied on "the law of the land," that is the doctrine of the school of Minister Eötvös, which he still considered valid. According to this doctrine, each religion was required to organize according to its laws and principles and to uphold order and discipline within its community by itself. Now that the Jewish community has been divided into two, each group must organize in this manner, and there is no place to stand aside and refuse to join either one.
21. Ibid.
22. Also in Ujhely, Sziget, and elsewhere.
23. For basic information about R. Perles and his congregation, see Cohen (note 11), 197–198. For his character and personality see below, in the text.
24. R. Perles's name appears among the signatures on the manifesto previously mentioned; see note 3.
25. See chapter 11.
26. *AZJ*, May 14, 1872, 997.
27. Ibid. The reporter copies the content of the secessionist manifesto concerning the motives for the split. They blame the Orthodox for arbitrary behavior and impure motives. The role of the rabbi in the quarrel is not mentioned, but is proved by subsequent events, as we shall see.
28. About his father and genealogy, see J. J. Grünwald, "The Grandchildren of the Ramah and their Influence in Hungary" (in Hebrew), *Sinai* 28 (1951), 79–87.
29. See note 26.
30. The two were R. Simon Juda Fonfeder of Tokaj and R. Zvi Hirsch Weiss of Szobráne. Both are among the signatories mentioned in note 3.
31. For his biography see Schwartz (note 6), 26a–b.
32. *Milhemet Mitzvah* (note 3), n.p.
33. Published in *Shevet Ahim* 2, no. 10, *Parshat Vayaqhel*, 1872. I have seen only a photograph of this page in Jacobowitz (chapter 16, note 31), photograph 55.
34. The rabbi of Sebeskelemes, a village near Kassa, was chosen temporarily, until a permanent rabbi could be found for the city. This indicates that the intention was to replace R. Katz, who had a six-year contract. See *Shevet Ahim*, ibid.
35. The statements of those who upheld the secessionists were published in a circular of their own, but is not extant. We learn of their content from the responses of their opponents.
36. *AZJ*, May 14, 1872, 397; *Das traditionelle Judenthum*, April 18, 1872, 126; *Shevet Ahim*, April 6, 1872.
37. See *Milhemet Mitzvah* (note 3), n.p.
38. Maharam Schick, *Responsa, O.H.*, no. 307.
39. Jacobowitz (chapter 16, note 31), 364 ff., was aware of the difficulty. He attempted to solve it by assuming that the Status Quoers acted as a group against the Orthodox during the legislative discussions on the right of the Orthodox not to join the Congress organization, an assumption that has no basis in fact.
40. All this is found in the responsum noted in note 38.
41. This question was exhaustively treated in the course of a controversy in Sziget about the community's enrollment in the Orthodox organization. The author of *Ohev Mishpat* (Lemberg, 1887), n.p., Section A, offers many proofs that a congregation that

was not represented at the assembly is not obligated to accept the ruling of those assembled even concerning contemporary religious problems. The author of *Ein Mishpat*, a work that is included in *Milhemet Mitzvah* (note 3), disagrees with him.
42. The books are *Pnei Abraham* (Lvov, 1878); and *Igra de-Hespeda* (Munkács, 1896). Some strange things are found in the letters of approbation for the first book. The book was apparently written many years before it was published. The author had obtained letters of approbation for the book in the 1860s, and errors crept into the dates and perhaps also the places.
43. The responsum is at the end of *Igra de-Hespeda*, ibid.
44. *Shevet Ahim*, March 9, 1872; *Das traditionelle Judenthum*, May 9, 1872, 132.
45. See his letter of July 23, 1868, mentioned above, chapter 11, note 39.
46. *Offenes Sendschreiben der Status-quo-Gemeinde su Klausenburg in Angelegenheit der gegen sie veröffentlichten Isser's* (in Yiddish) (Klausenburg, 1882), 15.
47. Y. Y. Cohen, in his book on the sages of Transylvania (note 11), 198, cites R. Perles's statement of 1889 (letter 14): "Those who take honor in the shame of others . . . I have nothing to do with them, I do not desire (their company), and thank God, my time is dedicated to the cause of Heaven . . . and I know for sure that soon they will be completely exposed, and the nation will know who are those that trample on the heads of the holy [nation], and no more need be said."

20. Theoretical and Practical Limits of the Schism (pp. 217–224)

1. For the Orthodox struggle against parliamentary ratification of the establishment of the seminary, see A. Zeller, *A magyar egyházpolitika 1840–1894*, vol. 2 (Budapest, 1894), 503–508. A German translation of the essentials is found in *AZJ*, July 28, 1874, 520–525. A critical analysis of the debates appeared in the previous issue, of July 21, 503–508. Echoes of the struggle that preceded its opening are discernible in the inaugural speech by Samuel Kohn, who took an active part in establishing the institution. See *A budapesti országos rabbiképzöintézet értesitöje az 1886–1887 iki tanévröl* (Budapest, 1888), 10.
2. The report issued by the institution a decade after its foundation notes explicitly that most of the students come after having studied in *yeshivot*. See Kohn (note 1), 60, 62.
3. In an academic lecture given ten years earlier, in 1862, Trefort had admonished Hungarian Jews for their preference for German over Hungarian. Leopold Löw protested. See *BCH*, 5 (1862), 425–430.
4. Zeller (note 1), 244–368.
5. He was widely criticized for this. See Zeller (note 1), 974–1109.
6. A description of these events is found in N. Katzburg, "The Struggle of Hungarian Jewry for Religious Equality in the 1890s" (in Hebrew) *Zion* 22 (1957), 119–148.
7. We learn of Koppel Reich's part from a recently published article: J. Kis, "Reich Koppel, egy rabbi a Felsöházból," *Múlt és Jövö* 4, 2 (1993), 91–92.
8. R. Zalman Spitzer, who served in Vienna but was counted among the Hungarian rabbis, and R. Solomon Schick, rabbi of Karcag, explicitly expressed this view. See M. Ehrentheil, *Reception und Orthodoxie* (Budapest, 1892), 22, 30–31, 69–70. Ehrentheil himself, the editor of the Orthodox newspaper *Allgemeine jüdische Zeitung*,

represented the view of the Orthodox intelligentsia, and his book levels devastating criticism at Ignác Reich.
9. This is what happened in Pressburg. When the Ketav Sofer died in 1871, his son Simhah Bunim (later the Shevet Sofer) took his place. In reaction, a modernistic minority of the congregation, which had hitherto been accommodated within the framework of the congregation, seceded. See D. Gross, "Die Israelitische Religionsgemeinde," *Die Juden und die Judengemeinde Bratislava in Vergangenheit und Gegenwart*, ed. H. Gold (Brünn, 1932), 134–138.
10. An exhaustive treatment of the topic has recently been published. See G. Haraszti, "Két világ határán, Tradició és modernitás. A rumbach utcai zsinagóga és hivei" *Múlt és Jövö* vol. 4, no. 2 (1993), 15–27.
11. *MZsL*, 156.

21. The Painful Process and Its Aftermath (pp. 225–233)

1. Maharam Schick, *Responsa, O.H.*, no. 177.
2. J. Schweitzer, *A Tolna megyei zsidók története* (Budapest, 1982), 191–192.
3. See Gross (chapter 20, note 9), 137–138.
4. D. Schön, ed., *A tegnap városa, A nagyváradi zsidóság emlékkönyve* (Tel Aviv, 1984), 68–71.
5. Solomon Zvi Schick, *Mi-Moshe ad Moshe* (Munkács, 1903), 62b–65a. Ehrentheil (chapter 20, note 8), 58, estimated that in 1892, in most of the congregations that had split, the burial society remained united.
6. Maharam Schick, *Responsa, O.H.*, no. 305.
7. Hayyim Sofer, *Sha'arei Hayyim* (Ungvár, 1869).
8. This emerges from the opening of Maharam Schick's responsum, *O.H.*, no. 304, which will be discussed below.
9. Ibid.
10. For a detailed description of what occurred between the Hatam Sofer and the rabbi of Trieste, see my book *Halakhah in Straits, Obstacles to the Emergence of Orthodoxy* (in Hebrew) (Jerusalem, 1992), 46–48.
11. Hatam Sofer, *Responsa* (Maharam Schick mistakenly gives the reference as part V), part VI, no. 89.
12. B. Z. Jacobowitz, *Zekhor Yemot Olam*, vol. 2 (Jerusalem, 1966), 16, claims that this passage from the Hatam Sofer served as support for Maharam Schick's advocacy of a division, although he does not refer to it explicitly.
13. Hatam Sofer (note 11), at the end of the passage.
14. See note 8. In delineating the two personalities, we should note a responsum by Maharam Schick, *Y.D.*, no. 238, that also takes issue with Hayyim Sofer. Sofer (note 7) suggested that attempts should be made to persuade the government to grant the *beit din* permission to circumcise a child against his father's wish, as stated in the Shulhan Arukh. This would mean that a Neolog who wanted to circumcise his son would be refused, while someone who did not want to have his son circumcised would be overridden. Maharam Schick responded that "even if the government would give permission, it is impossible to provoke such an evil man," and supported his view at length.

15. Ibid., no. 304, at the end of the responsum.
16. The expression "we should not arrange matches with them" does not mean the same thing as "their daughters are forbidden to us."
17. B. Eckfeld, *Peat ha-Sadeh*, vol. 2 (Munkács, 1907), no. 6.
18. Schick (note 5), 64b: "The sons of the devout take the daughters of the reformers as wives." And similarly in his *Responsa Rashban, O.H.*, no. 105.
19. Ehrentheil (chapter 20, note 8), 58.
20. R. Abraham Isaac Glück was asked about the law concerning one who desecrates the Sabbath in public: Is it permissible to sell him the wine of a non-Jew, for he will certainly drink it (*Yad Yitzchak*, vol. 2 [Varal, 1902], no. 95)? Is he considered a non-Jew regarding *eruv hazerot* (creating a common space to allow carrying items from one place to another on the Sabbath), when he and a devout Jew live in the same courtyard (ibid., vol. 1, no. 195)? R. Eliezer Deutsch (*Pri ha-Sadeh*, vol. 1 [Paks, 1906], no. 61) discusses the status of wine produced by Jewish residents of a city who are all considered desecrators of the Sabbath, but he does not refer to them as Neologs. R. Deutsch also deals with the case of someone who receives profits from a business in which one of the partners is not a Sabbath observer (ibid., vol. 3, no. 97). Schick, *Responsa Rashban, O.H.* by Mordechai Winkler (note 18), no. 67, strives to find a reason why "we in our time say the Grace after Meals together with transgressors and Sabbath desecrators, and we include them in a *minyan*." About a *kohen* who says the priestly blessing in the synagogue, see ibid., no. 4.
21. J. Katz, *Shabbes Goy, A Study in Halakhic Flexibility* (Philadelphia, 1984).
22. For the ruling about an observant Jew who lives in the same courtyard as a non-observant Jew with regard to the *eruv*, see A. I. Glück, *Yad Yitzchak*, vol. 1, no. 195. The same question is discussed in *Responsa Levush Mordechai, O.H.* (Tolcsva, 1912), no. 70. In ibid., no. 43, the author discusses the case of three brothers who are partners in a business, one of whom is Sabbath observant while the other two are not: What is the status of the profits made on the Sabbath? In *Responsa Meishiv Devarim, O.H.*, no 22, by Gershon Litsch Rosenbaum (Munkács, 1900), the author deals with a stock company in which most of the Jewish stockholders do not sell their *hametz* (leavened bread) on Passover. Many further examples can be given.
23. See my book, *Divine Law in Human Hands* (note 10), "The Controversy over the Mezizah."
24. Maharam Schick replied in the fall of 1875, two years before the seminary opened, to someone who had protested the position taken by the Orthodox rabbis in forbidding the seminary. The editors of his responsa omitted the name of the addressee, but it seems that here, as in the controversy in Kassa, it was R. Meir Perles. Maharam Schick reminded him that he had also attended the meeting of rabbis in 1864 at Nyiregyháza, which decided to oppose the establishment of a seminary. R. Perles was indeed there, and he was the most likely of the participants to adopt an attitude of compromise towards the seminary. Maharam Schick listed all the decisions and activities undertaken by his colleagues in order to thwart the establishment of the seminary, and refuted his adversary's claim that the prohibition does not include those who were not represented at the meetings that decided on the prohibition. Two weeks later, Maharam Schick once again summarized his reasons for rejecting the seminary, this time without addressing anyone specifically: "I was asked what prohi-

bition is to be found in a seminary, for it is good to have Torah learning with a livelihood . . . and this is my answer." The main point of his argument is that only exclusive concentration on Torah study will ensure both mastery of the *halakhah* as needed by an adjudicator, and preservation of faith without heretical thoughts. The responsa appear in separate places. The first is in *O.H.*, no. 308, the second in *Y.D.*, no. 335. The latter was apparently directed at other questioners, when the issue of the seminary became a subject of public debate.

25. My father studied at the *yeshivah* of R. Moses Aryeh Roth in Pápa in the late 1890s. Akiva Sofer was one of the outstanding political figures of the congregation at the time. According to my father, anyone who wished to be accepted to the *yeshivah* had to sign a vow that he would not study at the seminary. I also read about this practice in one of the contemporary books of responsa, but the exact reference escapes me. The name of Akiva Sofer appears in the contemporary press. He was a candidate for delegate to the Congress, but was not chosen. He was part of the delegation sent by the congregation to R. Moses Zvi Fuchs, whom the congregation of Pápa wished to appoint as rabbi; see the introduction to the rabbi's book, *Yad Ramah* (Orádea, 1940).

26. This was of course the import of the ruling of the *beit din* presided over by R. David Silberstein in Kassa, which Maharam Schick supported unconditionally. See chapter 19, notes 33 and 38.

27. The status of the *shohet* in a Status Quo congregation was discussed in connection with events in Marosvásárhely. A minority seceded from the Status Quo community there and formed an Orthodox congregation. In 1879, the minority chose as rabbi R. Jacob Koppel Lichtenstein, the brother of R. Hillel Lichtenstein. Members of his congregation certainly did not eat the slaughter of a Status Quo butcher; the battle was over the clientele from the surrounding communities. R. Lichtenstein forbade the Status Quo slaughter, and his prohibition was upheld by the rabbi of Sziget, R. Yekutiel Judah Teitelbaum, who himself was unable to bring his congregation to join the Orthodox organization. It too was formally a Status Quo community. An opinion was distributed in support of the prohibition, signed by the great rabbis, among them some already deceased (such as the Ketav Sofer, who had died in 1871). It is evident from the content that it is a forgery. The controversy in Marosvásárhely continued in later years as well. A rumor spread that R. Menahem Mendel Panet, rabbi of Dés, had given permission to a butcher to accept a position in a Status Quo community, and his son Moses, his successor, felt called upon to deny this rumor in 1885. The three documents mentioned above were published in *Mikhtav Galuy* (Sziget, 1888), 3–4. About the community and its rabbi, see Y. Y. Cohen, *Sages of Transylvania (1630–1944)* (in Hebrew) (Jerusalem, 1989), 147, 273. Jacobowitz (note 12), part I, 385–387, did not detect the forgery, and dated the prohibition of the Status Quo to 1871 on the basis of the letter, attributing it to the events in Marosvásárhely, which ostensibly preceded the incident in Kassa. This chronology is completely mistaken.

28. Eckfeld (note 17), no. 7.

29. Menahem Mendel Panet, *Responsa Sha'arei Zedek, O.H.*, no. 17–18.

30. A letter by R. Joel Ungar, rabbi of Paks, attests to such a situation, in which R. Shalom Ullmann of the congregation of Vác, found himself. Because he was unable to convince his congregation to join the Orthodox organization, R. Ullmann was forced

to accept the classification of his congregation as Status Quo. As a result, some rabbis were to be found "who find a flaw . . . in the righteous . . . Rabbi Shalom . . . and classify him as an evil person, God forbid." See Meir Stein, *Even ha-Meir* (Munkács, 1907), 100–101.
31. Maharam Schick displayed understanding of the difficulties of religious functionaries in earning a livelihood as a result of the split, and was lenient regarding the precentors, refraining from disqualifying them because they served in "illegitimate" synagogues, but he did not display the same leniency towards *shohetim*. See Maharam Schick, *Responsa, Y.D.*, no. 19.
32. In the large congregations, *dayyanim* were employed to give rulings on halakhic technicalities. They dealt with *kashrut* problems, arranged divorces, and the like. These were generally great scholars who lacked the ability or aspirations to be spiritual leaders. Neolog communities also had such types, and there was no lack of candidates for these jobs. See the story told in Maharam Schick's *Responsa, Y.D.*, no. 236, of a community which had split and "the *dayyanim* remained with the Congress organization." A similar case occurred in Bonyhád, where the rabbi of the Orthodox congregation, R. Moses Polák, reported on the opinion of a *dayyan* in the Neolog community concerning a shared *eruv* for the two congregations. See Maharam Schick, *Responsa, O.H.*, no. 115. In the congregation mentioned in a responsum of R. Hayyim Sofer, *Mahaneh Hayyim*, vol. 2 (Jerusalem, 1967), no. 3, the *Shomrei ha-Dat* community separated from the mother congregation, which was part of the Congress organization, but was not yet able to build its own *mikvah*. They relied on the old *dayyanim*, who had remained in the mother congregation, to ensure that the *mikvah* of the Neolog congregation was permissible.
33. Abraham Isaac Glück, *Responsa Yad Yitzchak*, vol. 3 (Szatmár, 1909), no. 28.
34. About R. Hayyim Sofer see chapter 18, note 46. Maharam Schick, in his letter to R. Meir Perles (note 24) about the Status Quo, wrote: "And why do they not appreciate all the hard work of the heads of the *Shomrei ha-Dat*, and God performed wonders for us by making them the instruments of a great salvation for Israel." He referred to the Tapolcsán congregation in the same vein, *Responsa, Y.D.*, no. 333.
35. For the numerical ratio between the congregations and their members see *Pinqas ha-Qehillot, Hungariah* (Jerusalem, 1976), introduction by N. Katzburg, 89.
36. *Yad Ramah* (end of note 25) no. 104.
37. *Magyar Rabbik* 3 (1907), 82.
38. See Simon Szidon, *Shevet Shim'on* (Wien, 1888), introduction; and similarly in R. Joel Ungar's letter (note 30) justifying R. Shalom Ullmann's behavior in the congregation of Vác.
39. Maharam Schick, *Responsa, Y.D.*, no. 333.
40. An author in *Magyar Rabbik* 2 (1906), 11–12, who signs as "a rabbi who graduated the *yeshivot*," and who undoubtedly served in a Status Quo congregation, described the state of the Status Quoers from a critical perspective. Its rabbis, who uphold the synthesis of Torah and *derekh eretz*, do nothing to realize this ideal by establishing a suitable seminary or *yeshivah*. They are too weak to stand up for their ideas against the factions to their left and right. The Status Quo congregations conduct themselves according to the Shulhan Arukh, and their members are pious, but their future is doubtful. Because of the weakness of the leadership, the tendency to annex them-

selves to the Orthodox is spreading, as evidenced by recent events in such congregations as Kaposvár and Stomfa. Other congregations intend to follow suit. The Status Quo congregation has a strong position only where the Orthodox have seceded, and those who tend to Neologism are afraid that the more conservative among them will join the Orthodox.

22. Eduard Lasker, the Prophet of Freedom of Conscience (pp. 237–256)

1. Hirsch listed these congregations in his opinion on the Karlsruhe controversy. See Hirsch (note 6), 129.
2. *Die israelitische Synagogengemeinde (Adass Jisroel) zu Berlin* (Berlin, 1904), 9–13.
3. Hirsch (note 6), 129.
4. See A. Lewin, *Geschichte der Badischen Juden seit der Regierung Karl Friedrichs (1738–1909)* (Karlsruhe, 1909), chapter 14.
5. Ibid., 385–390. This is the source for the description in this passage.
6. "Die Trennungsfrage in Carlsruhe," *Jeschurun* 25 (1870), 114–131.
7. Ibid., 128.
8. Ibid.
9. See J. Katz, *Halakhah in Straits* (in Hebrew), "Obstacles on the Path of Orthodox Coalescence" (Jerusalem, 1992), 36–37.
10. Hirsch (note 6), 128.
11. Ibid., 131.
12. This emerges from the exchange of letters between Hildesheimer and Hirsch, whose content will be discussed below.
13. Hirsch's letter is found in M. Eliav, ed., *Rabbiner Esriel Hildesheimer, Briefe* (Jerusalem, 1965), 101.
14. Hildesheimer's response has been preserved in manuscript in the Sänger Collection at Bar-Ilan University, German MSS., no. 206. My thanks to Mordechai Breuer, who brought it to my attention and copied it for me.
15. This reconstruction of events relies on the report of the discussion over the Jewish issue in the Parliament, the description of which will come below.
16. This was the line of thought espoused by those who opposed secession, as formulated by the head of the Berlin community, H. Makower (see note 52), 3. An identical assessment is found in *AZJ*, January 29, 1873, 70.
17. *Denkschrift über die Judenfrage in dem Gesetz betreffend den Austritt aus der Kirche* (Berlin, 1873). The memorandum was reprinted in Hirsch's collected works: *Gesammelte Schriften*, vol. 4 (Frankfurt am Main, 1902–1912), 239–252. I quote from the original edition.
18. Ibid., 8.
19. Ibid., 3–4.
20. Ibid., 5.
21. Ibid., 6.
22. Ibid., 8.
23. Ibid., 12.
24. Ibid., 9.

25. Ibid., 10.
26. Sänger Collection (note 14), ms no. 189. Fromm viewed it as a great achievement that the memorandum was received with thanks by two of the offices.
27. *Haus der Abgeordneten, Stenographische Berichte*, March 19, 1873, 1754, the speech by von Brauchitsch.
28. M. Hirsch, *Samson Raphael Hirsch und die Israelitische Religionsgesellschaft zu Frankfurt a.M.* (Mainz, 1897), 90. The book is an anthology of articles that were previously published in *Israelit* of the same year. H. Schwab, *The History of Orthodox Jewry in Germany* (London, 1950), 67, repeats this evaluation. Liberles (chapter 23, note 2) is of the same mind. He dismisses Lasker's role in fifteen lines (ibid., 207–208). He did not bother to read the protocols of the Parliament.
29. Protocols (note 27), 1755–1756.
30. The Jews of Germany followed Lasker's meteoric career with admiration and pride. Tobias Cohn, the rabbi of Potsdam, wrote a lengthy biography of Lasker, *Jahrbuch für die Geschichte der Juden* 6 (1869): 3–141. According to Cohn, Lasker was well versed in Jewish affairs from his childhood, and followed modern developments in this area from his youth.
31. Protocols (note 27), 1753.
32. Ibid.
33. Ibid.
34. Ibid., 1750.
35. J. Toury noted that some of the Orthodox, headed by Markus Lehmann, the editor of *Israelit*, were the only ones among the Jews who did not take part in the general attack on Windthorst's Catholic party. See J. Toury, *Die politischen Orientierungen der Juden in Deutschland* (Tübingen, 1966), 246.
36. Protocols (note 27), 1757.
37. For Warburg's speech, see ibid., 1753 ff.
38. Ibid., 1753; Lasker's proposal is on the same page.
39. R. W. Dill, *Der Parlamentarier Eduard Lasker und die parlamentarische Stilentwicklung der Jahre, 1867–1884*, Ph.D. diss. (Ehrlangen, 1956), Vorwort.
40. This, in my opinion, is the meaning of the somewhat obscure sentence: "Von Hause . . . aus hatte ich die Absicht, einen Antrag einzubringen, der in dieses Gesetz schon eingepflanzt werden soll . . . mit einem weitergehenden Erfolg . . . Es hat mir nicht angemessen geschienen, indem ich die Rechte eines kleinen Bruchtheils des Volkes vertrete, so wichtige Gesetze . . . zu gefährden"; Protocols (note 27), 1756.
41. Ibid., 1755.
42. Ibid.
43. Ibid., 1754.
44. Ibid., 1756.
45. Ibid., 1755–1756.
46. *Adass Jisroel* (note 2), 9–12.
47. Protocols (note 27), 1756.
48. Ibid., 1757.
49. Ibid., 1757–1758.
50. See note 26.
51. We will hear more of this with regard to the committee discussions.

52. H. Makower, *Über die Gemeinde-Verhältnisse der Juden in Preussen* (Berlin, 1873).
53. Ibid., 18–24.
54. Ibid., 25.
55. Ibid., 31.
56. Ibid., 25–26.
57. A review of the book, positive, of course, appeared in *AZJ*, October 21, 1873, 494–496.
58. S. R. Hirsch, *Das Princip der Gewissensfreiheit und die Schrift des Herrn Rechtsanwalts und Notars Makower* . . . (Frankfurt am Main, 1874).
59. Ibid., 31. The passage was printed in bold face, no doubt in order to emphasize the claim that freedom of secession would destroy the congregations.
60. Ibid., 7, and see 32–34, a description of the individual who is driven into isolation under pressure of his conscience.
61. Ibid., 8–9.
62. Ibid., 21–22.
63. Philippson published a series of articles in *AZJ*, beginning July 10, 1873, in which he expressed his candid concern for the continued existence of the congregations in the developing circumstances.
64. Makower (note 52), 25–26. The Berlin community collected data on the Jewish institutions and their obligations throughout the state, in order to emphasize the great responsibility they bore and the danger to their existence. See ibid., and 105–106.
65. The term appears in this context in *AZJ*, July 1, 1873, 430.
66. *AZJ*, October 21, 1873, 693.
67. *AZJ*, November 25, 1873, 781–783.
68. Ibid., 781.
69. Ibid., 782.
70. Ibid.
71. *AZJ*, January 20, 1874, 53.
72. For the role of the *Gemeindebund* in this affair, see B. Jacobsohn, *Der Deutsch-Israelitische Gemeindebund* (Leipzig, 1879), 20–25.
73. *AZJ*, June 23, 1874, 437–438.
74. His statements are contained in the protocols of the Parliament (note 27), of the year 1874, 1844–1846. The personal meeting is mentioned several times in the speech.
75. Ibid., 1845.
76. Ibid., 1844.
77. Ibid., 1845.
78. Ibid.
79. Ibid.
80. Ibid., 1846.
81. *AZJ*, 1874, in a series of four articles, July 9 (394) to July 30 (449 ff.)
82. The text of the law was published in *AZJ*, July 11, 1876, 443–444. It was reprinted many times, for example: I. Freund, *Die Rechtsstellung der Synagogengemeinden in Preussen und die Reichsverfassung* (Berlin, 1925), 38–40, and will be quoted from this source.
83. M. Joel, *Lasker's Resolution den Austritt aus der Synagogen-Gemeinde betreffend* (Breslau, 1875).

84. Ibid., 4–7.
85. Ibid., 8–9. Joel mentions Hirsch and Lasker as the initiators of the proposal in his introduction, 3.
86. V. Dotterweich, *Heinrich von Sybel, Geschichtswissenschaft in politischer Absicht (1817–1866)* (Göttingen, 1978), 328.
87. Protocols (note 27), May 22, 1876, 1601–1604. Philippson's name appears on the last page.
88. Ibid., 1602–1603.
89. Ibid., 1605.
90. Ibid., in the continuation.
91. This was the conclusion drawn by von Sybel at the end of his speech.
92. The conclusion of Lasker's speech, ibid., 1609.

23. Hirsch's Failure in His Own Community and His Ideological Legacy (pp. 257–278)

1. The *AZJ* began the column "Die Folgen des Austrittgesetzes" in issue no. 7, November 7, 1876, 173, and continued it in almost every issue.
2. The details are found in R. Liberles, *Religious Conflict in Social Context: The Resurgence of Orthodox Judaism in Frankfurt am Main, 1838–1877* (Westport/London, 1985), 211.
3. The details are found in L. Kahn, *Zur Geschichte der altisraelitischen Kultusgemeinde zu Wiesbaden* (n.p., n.d.). The book was published after 1895, twenty-five years after the foundation of the congregation by its rabbi. The essential information is substantiated via official documents. The attempt to forbid the Orthodox rabbi to use the *Hayyei Adam* in religious classes is found on p. 5.
4. I have not seen this publication of Süsskind; its content can be surmised from two anonymous pamphlets written against him by members of *Adath Jeschurun* in Frankfurt: *Die Angriffe des Herrn Rabbiner Süsskind in Wiesbaden gegen die Statuten der Israel. Religiongesellschaft zu Frankfurt A.M. Beleuchtet von S.* (Frankfurt am Main, 1876; [Hirsch Isaak]), *Heimleuchtung des Herrn Rabbiner Süsskind, Von Einem, Paganus* (Frankfurt am Main, 1876).
5. The numbers are given by Kahn (note 3), 6. The numerical proportion is based on the statistical data found in *Pinqas ha-Kehillot, Germania*, vol. 3 (Jerusalem, 1992), 476.
6. These qualities are reflected in his actions, as described in his book (note 3). See for example the description on p. 12 of how he acquired the means to build the synagogue.
7. Ibid., 6–8.
8. I discussed the link between these two doctrines in my article, "R. Samson Raphael Hirsch, the Right- and Left-Winger," *Halakhah in Straits* (in Hebrew) (Jerusalem, 1992), 230–231.
9. Liberles (note 2), 210–226.
10. S. R. Hirsch, *Der Austritt aus der Gemeinde* (Frankfurt am Main, 1876). I have a copy of the second edition, of 1904, and will quote from there. This pamphlet, like all of the pamphlets in the Hirsch-Bamberger controversy, was reprinted in Hirsch's *Gesammelte Schriften*, IV (chapter 22, note 17).

11. *Offene Antwort auf den offenen Brief des Herrn Rabbiner S. R. Hirsch an Herrn Rabbiner S. B. Bamberger von X* (Frankfurt am Main, 1877), 13.
12. This characterization of Moses Mainz relies on the description by Isaac Heinemann: "Supplementary Remarks on the Secession from the Frankfurt Jewish Community under Samson Raphael Hirsch," *Historia Judaica* 10 (1948), 194. Heinemann was born in Frankfurt, and his father, from whom he heard the story, was involved in the secessionist controversy. We shall hear below of R. Bamberger's great admiration for Mainz.
13. Hirsch (note 10). About the obligation for self-sacrifice, see p. 14. The reference to burial is found on p. 16.
14. *Beleuchtung der Zusatzbestimmungen zu dem Regulativ der Israelitischen Gemeinde* (Frankfurt am Main, 1877). This was printed together with an accompanying letter to the administration of *Adath Jeschurun*. The two documents were included in Hirsch's collected works, vol. IV (note 10), 311–315.
15. R. Bamberger's biography was written by his son: N. Bamberger, *Rabbiner Seligman Bär Bamberger. Dessen Leben und Wirken* (Würtzburg, 1897). See also S. Bamberger, *Zekher Ya"d, The Biography of the Great Rabbi Isaac David Halevi Bamberger* . . . (in Hebrew) (Qiryat Motzkin, 1941).
16. I gave examples of his halakhic method in my book, *Shabbes Goy, A Study in Halakhic Flexibility* (Philadelphia, 1984), 145–155. Solomon Adler, the editor of R. Bamberger's responsa, *Responsa Yad Halevi* (Jerusalem, 1955), quoted in his introduction declarations scattered throughout the responsa about the necessity of being stringent.
17. About the difference between their views, see my article (note 8), 14–16.
18. Bamberger himself printed the text of his letter of February 1, 1877, in his response to Hirsch (note 23), 14–15.
19. Bamberger's description, note 23, 18–19.
20. For the text of the announcement in the newspaper, see note 23, p. 16.
21. E. Schwarzschild, *Ein offenes Wort an S. Ehwürden Herrn Distrikts-Rabbiner Seligmann Bär Bamberger zu Würzburg* (Frankfurt am Main, 1877), 28–29.
22. S. R. Hirsch, *Offener Brief an S. Ehrwürden Herrn Distrikts-Rabbiner S. B. Bamberger in Würzburg* (Frankfurt am Main, 1877), 18–19.
23. *Offene Antwort des Distrikts-Rabbiners Seligmann Bär Bamberger zu Würzburg auf den an ihn gerichteten Offenen Brief Sr. Ehrwürden des Herrn S. R. Hirsch* (Würzburg, 1877), 3.
24. Hirsch (note 22), 3, 20.
25. Bamberger (note 23), 8–10.
26. See my article (note 8), 25.
27. Dr. Michael Posen told me that he heard from his father, who was a *dayyan* in *Adath Jeschurun* during Hirsch's time, that it was as if Hirsch kept halakhic material "in a box," that is, it was in his memory ready for use at any time.
28. Bamberger (note 23), 27.
29. Ibid.
30. Hirsch's last long responsum was *Die offense Antwort Sr. Ehrwürden des Herrn Distrikts-Rabbiners S. B. Bamberger zu Würzburg . . . Gewürdigt von Samson Raphael Hirsch*. I have not seen this pamphlet, and I cite it according to his *Gesammelte Schriften* (note 10), 344–407.

31. Bamberger (note 23), 8–10.
32. Hirsch (note 22), 352–356.
33. Bamberger (note 23), 11.
34. Hirsch (note 22), 361–364.
35. There was a third subject of this nature. Bamberger claimed that Hirsch's ruling was not valid because it was not disseminated, that is, it was not accepted without immediate objection, for R. Moses Mainz had differed with him. Hirsch claimed that this was not the meaning of the word "disseminated." See Bamberger (note 23), 10; Hirsch (note 22), 358–362.
36. Bamberger (note 23), 16–18.
37. These arguments are the main content of Hirsch's last response (note 30), 368 ff. The famous ruling of the Hatam Sofer, *Responsa*, part VI, no. 89, is mentioned there, 409.
38. Ibid., 372.
39. Hirsch (note 22), 7.
40. Ibid., 10.
41. I dealt with this at length in my book, *Exclusiveness and Tolerance* (Oxford, 1961), chapters 3–5.
42. The anonymous pamphlet (note 11), 12. The critic mocks Hirsch's reliance on the application of the phrase "they follow the customs of their forefathers," to contemporary reformers.
43. Hirsch (note 22), 10.
44. The anonymous pamphlet (note 11), 4. The second pamphlet is *Betrachtungen einer Mücke Entgegnung auf den Offenen Brief des Herrn Rabbiner Samson Raphael Hirsch* (Frankfurt am Main, 1877), 5.
45. *AZJ*, February 27, 1877, 135–136.
46. The second pamphlet (note 44), 8.
47. Liberles (note 2), 215.
48. See Hildesheimer's two letters to Hirsch, of April 20 and June 26, 1877, in Eliav (chapter 22, note 13), 116.
49. Ibid., 117–119.
50. *Israelit*, April 25, 1877, 385–387; May 2, 1877, 409–411; the responsum is in *Responsa Hakham Zvi*, no. 38.
51. The second pamphlet (note 44), 11.
52. *Israelit*, July 11, 1877, 647–648.
53. Y. Y. Sofer, *Toldot Soferim*, the letters (*Qan Sofer*) (London, 1963), 55.
54. In an article in manuscript.
55. *Responsa Maharam Schick, O.H.*, no. 306.
56. *Midrash Bamidbar Rabbah*, 10, 11.
57. Maimonides, *Code*, trans. M. Hyamson (Jerusalem, 1962), Laws of Idolatry, 11, 1.
58. Anonymous pamphlet (note 11), 12–13.
59. Ibid., 5; the second pamphlet (note 44), including the following quotation.
60. Joseph Unna gave a summary of Horovitz's biography in an appendix to a new edition of Horovitz's book: M. Horovitz, *Frankfurter Rabbinen* (Jerusalem, 1969), 339–370.
61. See chapter 13, note 7. The articles in *Israelit*, April 7, 1869, 260–261; May 19,

1869, 396–397; and July 23, 1869, 498–500, were written after Hildesheimer had left the Congress. The last is signed M. H. and has an accompanying note from the editor stating that the author is unknown, but comes highly recommended. The reference is of course to Hildesheimer's recommendation. This testimonial was necessary, for the articles were highly critical of the policies of the Orthodox.

62. For Hildesheimer's letter advising against the appointment, which was written after personal contact between himself and Horovitz, see Eliav (chapter 22, note 13), 121–122.
63. Noted by Unna (note 60), 343. The source of this information is Horovitz himself, as his son Jacob wrote in the September 1932 issue, 4, of the *Gemeindeblatt* of the congregation, published in honor of the jubilee year of Horovitz's synagogue.
64. I have learned from Mordechai Breuer of a family story, that when Horovitz came to Frankfurt he wished to visit Hirsch, but was not received by him. This story accords with what is known of the two personalities and their stances.
65. Hirsch's responsum was published by M. Breuer, *Hama'ayan* (1989), no. 2, 22–24. We shall hear below of the reason for the delay in publication.
66. Ibid., 22.
67. All this is found in ibid.
68. *Responsa Maharam Schick, O.H.*, nos. 34–35.
69. A description is found in *Responsa Maharam Schick, Y.D.*, no. 14.
70. Ibid.
71. Breuer (note 65), 24.
72. See my article (note 8), 28–29.
73. Breuer (note 65), 24.
74. Ibid., 15.
75. Ibid., at the end of the responsum, 28–29. Hirsch also examined the statutes of the Orthodox organization in Hungary and found flaws in them, such as that they did not prevent those who were not observant from holding positions of leadership in the congregations, in violation of the laws of the Shulhan Arukh.
76. In *Responsa Maharam Schick, Y.D.*, no. 14, a responsum that deals with the secession of the hassidim in Ujhely, he writes: "It is stated in some of the responsa that the public are like partners and were not sold or indentured to one another, but came into association in order to make it easier to meet the needs of the public." Where are these responsa? In the *Talmudic Encyclopedia*, vol. 3, 374–379, s.v. *benei ha-'ir*, there is no mention of this view.
77. The letter is preserved in Hirsch's archive, in Bar-Ilan University. I saw the document through the generosity of Mordechai Breuer.
78. See Breuer (note 65). In the introduction to the text of the letter, Breuer writes that he disobeyed Hirsch's request not to publish the responsum partly because it had already been published in the journal *Moriah* in corrupt form.
79. I. Breuer, *Der neue Kusari, Ein Weg zum Judentum* (Frankfurt am Main, 1934).
80. Ibid., 112.
81. J. Rosenheim, *Zikhronot* (Bnei Brak, 1979), 111–112. This describes the convention in the city of Homburg near Frankfurt in August, 1909, in which preparations were made for the establishment of the *Agudah*. A representative of the Orthodox establishment in Hungary was also present and he supported the tendency to limit mem-

bership to seceders alone. In practice, the rabbis of Hungary refrained from joining *Agudat Israel*. I remember the first article I ever published, in the Hungarian Orthodox newspaper *Zsidó Ujság* (October, 1927), in which I protested against the fact that Hungarian Jews considered themselves "the choicest of the chosen people."

82. I. Breuer, *Das Jüdische Nationalheim* (Frankfurt am Main, 1925). The book was translated a year later into English, certainly in order to achieve its purpose as a document addressed to the Mandatory government.

83. For much material about R. Sonnenfeld and this struggle, see the three volumes of M. M. Gerlitz's biography of Joseph Hayyim Sonnenfeld, *Mara de-Ar'a Yisrael* . . . (Jerusalem, 1974).

Index of Names and Places

Abaujszántó, 46
Abeles, Samuel, 98, 103
Adler, Nathan, 203
Admor of Liszka. *See* Friedman, Zvi Hirsch
Alsace, 11
Altona, 17, 49
Arad, 32, 34, 38, 44, 155, 171
Aszód, Judah, 49, 83
Aussee, 53
Austria, 8, 31, 33, 56, 92, 139, 170, 238

Bacher, Simon, 107
Baden, 8, 14, 238, 248
Baja, 50
Balassagyarmat, 83, 175
Bamberger, Isaac Dov Halevi, 181, 258, 261–266
Barth, J. 267
Batthyány, Count, 186
Bavaria, 14
Berlin, 9, 12, 16, 18, 26, 171, 237, 239–243, 246, 247, 248, 252, 253
Berliner, A., 267
Bettelheim, Kalman, 74
Bettelheim, P., 95
Billitzer, Isaac, 213
Bismarck, 239, 248
Bohemia, 34, 37, 57, 174
Bonyhád, 46, 225
Brauchitsch, von, 243, 245, 246
Braunschweig, 17, 45, 62, 226
Breslau, 9, 19, 20, 21, 117, 165, 249, 252
Breuer, Isaac, 277
Breuer, Solomon, 276, 277
Buda, 32, 95, 122–133, 138, 148, 155, 157, 162, 267
Budapest, 35, 187, 221, 229, 272

Carlsbad, 176
Cassell, David, 253
Chorin, Aaron, 34, 142, 155
Cracow, 229
Csát, 81

Darmstadt, 237
Deák, Francis, 90, 91, 187
Dés, 81, 114
Deutsch, Aaron David, 83, 123, 176, 194, 206, 207, 212
Deutschkreutz, 175, 193
Dunaföldvár, 44, 143

Eckfeld, Barukh, 228
Ehrenfeld, David, vi, 71
Ehrenfeld, Samuel (Hatan Sofer), 74
Ehrentheil, M., 228
Einhorn, David, 16
Einhorn, Ignác, 35, 42
Eisenstadt, 32, 112, 130, 198
Eisenstädter, Judah Leib, 78
Eisenstädter, Meir (Maharam Ash), 36, 40, 49, 58, 162
Eisenstädter, Menahem, 58, 78–79, 82, 104, 115, 116, 155, 176, 177
Eisler, Emmanuel (Manó), 149, 151, 193, 196, 198, 199, 200
Emden, Jacob, 267
England, 113, 248
Eötvös, Joseph, 89–95, 98–101, 103, 107, 112, 118, 130, 132, 137, 138, 141, 147, 148, 151, 159, 163, 164, 169, 170, 176, 177, 181, 183, 184, 185, 191, 201, 202, 217, 218, 223
Eperjes, 58, 63, 82
Ettlinger, Jacob, 17, 49, 181
Eybeschütz, Jonathan, 268
Ezra the Scribe, 226

Falk, A., 247, 250
Farkas, Albert, 96, 105, 118, 123, 132, 191
Fenyvessy, Adolph, 113
Fischer, Gottlieb, 52, 53, 125, 276
Fischer, Leo von, 196
Fischer, Leo, 99
Fischmann, Ezekiel Moses, 46, 64, 65, 72, 117
Fischmann, Feish, 64, 72–75

Fleissig, Jacob, 199, 201
France, 8, 10, 33, 91, 100, 111, 181
Frankfurt, 9, 18–28, 50, 107, 237, 241, 253, 257, 261, 264, 267, 272, 277
Frankfurt-an-der-Oder, 15
Franz Joseph, Kaiser, 66, 164, 170, 173, 175
Frieden, Pinehas Loeb, 52
Friedman, Abraham, 60
Friedman, Zvi Hirsch (*Admor* of Liszka), 57, 115, 116, 124, 125, 129, 194, 205, 206
Friedrich Wilhelm III, 12, 20
From, J., 243, 247
Fuld, Aaron, 24

Galánta, 59
Galgóc, 151, 199, 201, 224
Galicia, 31, 34, 38, 56, 57, 61, 62, 140
Geiger, Abraham, 21, 22, 253
Geisenheimer, Sigismund, 23
Georgen (Szent György), 62
Germany, 8, 10, 11, 12, 18, 21, 25, 33, 37, 38, 45, 48, 49, 128, 137, 180, 221, 226, 238, 248, 277
Ginzler, Samuel Shmelke, 206
Glasner, Abraham, 71, 72, 73
Glück, Abraham, 230
Gnesen, 272
Goitein, Elijah, 273, 275
Göncz, 95
Grün, Israel, 100, 146, 147, 158, 161
Guggenheimer, Joseph, 53, 174, 175, 181
Gyömöre, 59
Győr, 59, 106

Hacohen, Elijah, 61
Hajdunánas, 131
Hakham Zvi, 267
Halberstadt, 12, 38
Halberstamm, Hayyim (the *Admor* of Sanz), 61, 206
Halvi, Abraham Eliezer, 227
Hamburg, 9, 18, 23, 244
Hatam Sofer, 34, 36, 42, 48, 49, 58–62, 65, 70–79, 82, 84, 123, 206, 227, 264
Herend, 99
Hildesheimer, Esriel, 38, 44, 54, 66, 72, 96, 103, 110–112, 117–119, 125–129, 138–141, 142, 147–149, 155, 158, 159, 162, 164, 165, 171, 223, 237, 239–241, 246, 248, 258, 266, 272
Hildesheimer, Meir, 78
Hirsch, Marcus (Mordechai), 64, 117, 118, 129, 176
Hirsch, Mendel, 27, 28
Hirsch, Samson Raphael, 10, 16, 26–28, 49, 50, 54, 55, 106–110, 128, 146, 151, 156, 157, 172–174, 181, 199, 203, 237–243, 246–250, 253, 257–277
Hirschler, Ignaz, 94, 100, 113, 138, 139, 147–149, 157, 159, 188
Hochmut, Abraham, 149
Hoffmann, D. S., 267
Högyesz, 273
Holdheim, Samuel, 15–18
Holländer, Leo, 63, 141, 149, 155, 156, 157
Horovitz, Markus, 176, 272
Horschetzky, Moritz, 106
House of Hapsburg, 31, 35
Hunfalu, 95
Huszt, 52

Irány, Daniel, 184
Isidore, Lazare, 181
Italy, 31, 34

Jacobson, Israel, 9, 12
Jeiteles, Leo, 106
Jerome, brother of Napoleon, 11
Joel, Manuel, 254, 255
Jókai, Mór, 186, 187
Jolesz, Leibisch, 82, 213
Joschafat, Gershom, 26
Joseph II, Kaiser, 31
Jost, Marcus, 20, 22

Kahn, Leo, 258
Kaposvár, 112
Karcag, 194
Karlsruhe, 237–239
Kassa, 58, 63, 82, 95, 117, 208, 210, 212, 213, 224, 273
Katz, Abraham. *See* Seelenfreund, Abraham Katz
Katz, Menahem, 175, 194
Kecskemét, 64

Ketav Sofer. *See* Sofer, Abraham Samuel Benjamin
Kiskúnhalas, 77
Klein, Mordechai Leib, 82
Kobersdorf, 122, 205
Kohn, Samuel, 129, 149
Kollin, 174
Kolozvát, 60, 61, 73, 74, 96, 213
Komárom, 52
Körösladány, 100, 106
Kosch, Raphael, 246
Kossuth, Lajos, 35
Kraus, Sigmund, 100, 105–107, 110, 117–120, 130, 133, 140, 143, 144, 149, 151, 156, 158, 161, 172, 178, 193, 195, 196, 213
Kutna, Shalom, 112, 125, 276

Landau, Ezekiel, 52
Landsberg, Isaac Aaron, 66, 127
Lasker, Eduard, 237–256
Lehmann, Markus, 50, 248, 267
Leipzig, 248
Lichtenstein, Hillel, 59–61, 64–68, 72–83, 116, 129, 140, 153, 211, 231
Liebig, Friedrich, 162
Lippe, Hayyim David, 63, 82
Lipschitz, Isaac Nathan, 46
Liptószentmiklós, 38, 82
Liszka, 57
Lolmea, 140
Löw, R. Benjamin Wolf, 59
Löw, Eliezer, 274
Löw, Jeremiah, 57–59, 66, 79, 104, 115, 116, 118, 124, 126, 140, 146, 159, 161, 174, 175, 179, 196, 206, 207, 272, 274
Löw, Leopold, 40–42, 49, 50, 96, 105, 146

Maharam Ash. *See* Eisenstädter, Meir
Maharam Schick (Moses Schick), 48, 62, 68, 78, 79, 81–84, 131–133, 140, 162, 174, 175, 177–180, 192–197, 206, 210–214, 225–228, 231, 264, 268–271, 273–277
Maier, Joseph, 14
Mainz, 27, 50, 83, 237
Mainz, Moses, 259–261
Makó, 46, 67, 95

Makower, Herman, 248–251
Mandelbaum, Benjamin Z'ev, 210
Mannheimer, Hayyim Hirsch, 229
Mannheimer, Isaac Noah, 49
Márámáros, 57, 206
Margitta, 59, 61
Margoliot, Israel David, 46, 51
Maria Theresa, 31, 32
Mattesdorf, 36
Mauther, Johann, 200
Mecklenburg-Schwerin, 12, 14, 15
Mendelssohn, Moses, 7, 45, 239
Michalowitz, 77–84, 104, 114, 126, 129, 156, 211
Miskolc, 46, 58, 63–68, 82, 95, 116, 143
Mittelmann, Lipo, 142, 143
Montalembert, Charles, 91
Montefiore, Moses, 203
Moravia, 26, 34, 37, 51–53, 198, 206
Munkács, 56, 125, 196, 198, 205

Nagykanizsa, 38
Nagykároly, 66, 127, 208
Nagyvárad, 35, 44, 60, 61, 66, 127, 226
Napoleon, 8, 11, 100, 137
Németh, Albert, 186
Neumann, Wilhelm, 145
Nikolsburg, 26, 49, 51, 68
Nyireyháza, 66, 81
Nyitra, 198

Pádpa, 32, 53
Padua, 117
Panet, Hayyim Bezalael, 78
Panet, Menahem Mendel, 81, 114, 205, 206
Pappenheim, Kalman, 95, 99, 141, 143, 146, 149
Pappenheim, Wolf, 104
Paris, 8, 137, 145, 165
Pauler, Tivador, 202, 205, 209, 218
Pécs, 35
Perles, Meir, 66, 81, 127, 208, 210, 212, 213, 227, 273
Perls, R. Isaac Moses, 46
Pest, 32, 40, 42, 96, 101, 124, 129, 132, 137, 141, 145, 146, 171, 191, 196, 221
Philippson, Ludwig, 248, 250–252, 254, 255, 257

Index of Names and Places

Poland, 56, 57, 212
Pollak, H. 125, 126, 129
Popper, Joseph, 149, 151
Popper, Leopold, 139, 141, 144
Posen, 15, 22, 272
Prague, 23, 52
Pressburg, 32, 34, 49, 58, 59, 68, 70–76, 95, 141, 198, 205, 226, 232
Prossnnitz, 51
Prussia, 8, 12, 20, 34, 238, 239, 243, 248, 255
Putnok, 81

Reich, Ignaz, 106, 107
Reich, Isaac (Ignác), 161, 175, 178, 193, 196, 219
Reich, Koppel, 219
Rohonc, 114
Rosenheimer, J., 197
Rothschild, Anschel Meyer, 25
Rothschild, House of, 25
Rothschild, Meyer Carl, 25
Rothschild, Willy von, 203

Sabolc, 230
Sachs, Michael, 26
Sanz, 61, 208
Sátoraljaujhely. *See* Ujhely
Schag, Abraham, 122, 123, 140, 141, 205, 222, 278
Schick, Abraham, 106
Schick, Moses. *See* Maharam Schick
Schick, Solomon Zvi, 194, 226, 228
Schlesinger, Akiva Joseph, 68, 72, 75, 76, 80, 82, 140
Schwab, Loeb, 42, 43, 48, 51
Schwarzchild, Emmanuel, 262
Schwerin, 16, 17
Sebeskelemes, 82, 213
Seelenfreund, Abraham Katz, 209, 212
Silberstein, David, 209, 210, 212, 213
Silesia, 22
Sofer, Abraham Samuel Benjamin (Ketav Sofer), 54, 62, 65, 66, 70–74, 104, 116, 124, 125, 128, 133, 146, 162, 175, 194–196, 198, 226, 278
Sofer, Akivah, 229
Sofer, Eliezer Zusman, 62, 77

Sofer, Hayyim, 59, 62, 64–68, 127, 131, 140, 146, 155, 162, 177, 192, 196, 207, 226–228, 231, 268
Sofer, Mordechai Ephraim Fischel, 59, 131
Sofer, Simhah Bunim, 232
Sofer, Simon, 229
Sofer, Wolf, 81
Sonnenfeld, Joseph Hayyim, 277, 278
Stein, Leopold, 25
Steinhardt, Jacob, 142, 143, 149, 155, 156, 171
Steinthal, Hymann, 253
Stern, L., 267
Stern, Ludwig, 14
Strasser, Eleazar, 72
Stuttgart, 13
Süsskind, Samuel, 257, 258
Sybel, Heinrich von, 255
Szarvas, 44
Szatmár, 210
Szeged, 40, 44
Székesfehérvár, 40, 51–53, 142
Szentpéter, 59, 65
Szerdahely, 83
Sziget, 57, 81, 205, 209
Szikszó, 59, 61, 64, 65, 67, 68
Szobránc, 78
Szombathely, 118

Tapoksány, 198
Tasnád, 78
Teitelbaum, Moses, 57
Teitelbaum, Yekutiel Judah, 81, 205
Temesvár, 32, 44, 161, 226
Tennenbaum, Jacob, 81
Tennenbaum, Shraga, 81
Tiktin, Gedaliah, 22
Tiktin, Solomon, 21, 22
Transylvania, 58, 60, 96, 147
Trebitsch, Meir, 98, 103, 118, 132, 133, 178, 192, 193, 196
Trefort, August, 218
Trier, Solomon Abraham, 23–25
Trieste, 227
Tübingen, 272

Ujhely (Sátoraljaujhely), 57, 66, 124, 198, 208, 274

Ullmann, Solomon, 46, 67
Ungar, Joel, 213
Ungvár, 36, 49, 56, 124, 130
United States, 7, 170, 184, 248

Vác, 122
Vágujhely, 198
Vázsonyi, Vilmos, 219
Venetianer, L., 99
Verbó, 59
Vienna, 31, 32, 49, 66, 96, 176, 187, 252
Visó, 206

Wahrmann, Israel, 141, 184–187, 189

Wahrmann, Mór, 141
Warburg, Moritz, 244, 245
Weisbaden, 21, 237, 257, 266
Weiss, Kalman, 148
Wenkheim, 106
Westphalia, 12
Windthorst, Ludwig, 244, 247
Württemberg, 8, 12–15, 111

Zalaszentgrót, 81
Zipser, Meir, 40, 51–54, 114, 142, 149, 171, 176
Zirndorf, H., 106

Index of Subjects

"Accepted" or "acknowledged" religion, 90, 143, 169, 188, 190; "Law of the land," 128, 274, 275; "Purim miracle," 183, 187; "Rose of Jericho," 105
Adath Israel, 237, 239, 241, 246
Adath Jeschurun, 27, 28, 203, 237, 238, 253, 257–259, 266, 277
Admorim, 56, 57, 61, 115, 116, 124, 125, 195, 205, 206
Agudat Israel, 277
Ashkenazim, 116, 206, 274
Assembly of Notables, 96, 99–101, 104, 107, 108, 111, 113, 138, 140, 144, 145, 150, 221
Autonomy of the congregations, 160, 171, 172, 237, 238

Balfour Declaration, 277
Ban, excommunication, 62, 80, 207, 229
Bimah, 42, 63, 77, 83
Burial society, 225, 226

Cemetery, 26, 150, 225, 258, 259, 266
Chief rabbi, 15, 16, 17, 60
Chorschul, 63, 67, 84, 259
Circumcision, 9, 11, 35
Conference of Rabbis in Buda, 122–133, 138, 148, 155, 162, 222, 267
Congregational Orthodoxy, 221, 272, 276, 277
Congress, the, chapters 9–15, 89–165
Consistoire, 8, 11, 12, 100, 145

Decisions of the Congress, 176, 177, 178, 179, 180, 182, 183

Education fund, 37, 93, 96, 97, 164, 184, 186, 218
Emancipation, 89–95, 99, 114, 137, 184, 190, 219, 247, 250
Executive committee, 196, 204, 205, 213, 214

Freedom of conscience, 109, 117, 142, 144, 154, 160, 172, 179, 205, 237, 241, 243, 246, 248, 253
Freedom of religion, 171, 172, 183, 184, 187, 188
Freemasons, 23

Halakhah, 24, 43, 45–47, 50, 51, 55, 62, 83, 153, 172, 214, 223, 258, 260, 262, 263, 264, 265, 266
Hamburg Temple, 9, 18
Hassidim, Hassidism, 56–61, 115, 116, 118, 125, 205–207, 274
Hazzan, 63, 230
Heder, 36, 37, 54, 164, 195
Heretics, apostates, 264, 265, 269, 271

Judicial decision. See Michalowitz ruling

Kashrut, 24, 43, 119, 239

Landtag (Prussian Parliament), 240, 243
Liberalism, 12, 92, 139, 170, 184, 245
Lieutenant governor, 32, 54

Mandatory education, 8, 115, 163, 164
Marriage canopy, 42, 46, 77
Marriage with Neologs, 228, 230
Mezizah, 11, 229
Michalowitz ruling (judicial decision), 77, 80, 81, 83, 114, 117, 126, 153, 156
Migdar milta, 67, 82, 84, 271
Mikvah, 26, 150, 162
Modernization, 33, 34, 36, 43, 47, 51, 58

Neolog, Neologs, 40–43, 45, 46, 102, 113, 118, 120, 208, 209, 210, 214, 223, 225, 226, 229, 230–232
Nondenominational school, 163, 195

Oberland, 38, 48, 58–60, 66, 83, 84
Organ in synagogue, 221
Orthodox club, 140, 146, 155, 161

Orthodox organization, 189, 191, 197, 202, 204, 220, 221, 273–275

Paletine, 32
Parliament, 90, 94, 95, 108, 169, 170, 183–188
Precentor, 14, 41, 108
Private prayer service, 14, 15, 52
Progressive club, 139
Progressives, 63, 67, 84, 138–142, 144, 149, 150, 153, 156, 162, 165, 183

Qitniyot, 12, 48

Rabbinic delegation, 66, 175, 176
Rabbinic ordination, 15, 49, 195
Rabbinic-Mosaic faith, 150, 153, 154, 180
Rabbinical seminary, 65, 66, 97, 115, 117, 126–129, 155, 163–165, 218, 219, 223, 230, 267
Reform, reformers, 9, 10, 12, 14, 15, 17, 32, 34, 40, 41, 45, 46, 50, 51, 57, 62, 76, 156, 181, 250, 257, 260, 265
Religious council, 98, 104, 116, 124, 125, 132, 178, 196, 223
Revolution of 1848, 18, 25, 28, 33, 42, 95, 156, 170
Ritual butchers, 13, 15, 18, 24, 60, 65, 82, 144, 209, 220, 230

Sabbateans, 226
Sabbath (observance and desecration), 42–44, 63, 119, 142, 143, 180, 206, 207, 229, 238, 246
Secession, separation, schism, split, division, 17, 18, 54, 107, 109, 181, 200, 201, 217, 220, 224, 225, 226, 230, 231, 238, 240–242, 244, 246, 247, 250, 252, 259, 264, 266, 267, 271, 272, 273, 277, 278
Secular studies, 24, 36, 71, 155, 165
Sephardim, 116, 274
Shomrei ha-dat, 96, 97, 101, 103, 107, 108, 113–124, 129, 130, 132, 133, 137, 146, 161, 173–183, 185, 191, 193, 194, 196, 204, 222, 223
Shulhan Arukh, 54, 61, 64, 104, 125, 150, 152–154, 156, 158, 179, 180, 186, 195, 225, 232, 263
Sinaitic law, 15
Status-Quo, 198, 204, 209–214, 224, 227, 229, 231–233, 273, 275, 276

Unterland, 38, 55–58, 63, 81, 84, 126

Weekly market, 43, 44, 142
Writ of divorce, 52, 228

Yeshivah, yeshivot, 36, 41, 51, 65, 66, 69, 70, 71, 106, 117, 128, 165, 218, 223, 229, 230, 260, 272
Yiddish, 21, 22, 48, 69, 99, 115
Yiddish-German, 37, 48, 69, 78

Zealots, 56, 66, 76, 95, 114, 116, 117, 156

University Press of New England publishes books under its own imprint and is the publisher for Brandeis University Press, Dartmouth College, Middlebury College Press, University of New Hampshire, Tufts University, and Wesleyan University Press.

Library of Congress Cataloging-in-Publication Data

Katz, Jacob, 1904–
 [Ḳera' she-lo nit'aḥah. English]
 A house divided : orthodoxy and schism in nineteenth-century Central European Jewry / Jacob Katz ; translated by Ziporah Brody.
   p. cm. — (The Tauber Institute for the Study of European Jewry series ; 27)
 Includes bibliographical references and index.
 ISBN 0–87451–796–6 (cl)
  1. Orthodox Judaism—Relations—Nontraditional Jews. 2. Orthodox Judaism—Hungary—History—19th century. 3. Orthodox Judaism—German—History—19th century. I. Title. II. Series.
 BM376.H8K3813 1998
 296.8'32'094309034—dc21   97-36812

www.ingramcontent.com/pod-product-compliance
Lightning Source LLC
Chambersburg PA
CBHW030302080526
44584CB00012B/409